THE GREAT ENCYCLOPEDIA OF
MUSHROOMS

Acknowledgements
The author and the editorial team would like to express their warmest thanks to René-Jacques
Bouteville for his help and cooperation.

For the original edition: © LOSANGE – 63400 Chamalières – France
Original title: *Grand guide encyclopédique des champignons*

© 2005 for the English edition:
KÖNEMANN*, an imprint of Tandem Verlag GmbH, Königswinter

Translation from French and adaptation: Chanterelle Translations, London (Josephine Bacon)

Project Coordination: Bettina Kaufmann and Nadja Bremse

*KÖNEMANN is a registered trademark of Tandem Verlag GmbH

Printed in Germany

ISBN of this edition: 3-8331-1239-5
ISBN of the German edition: 3-8331-1087-2

10 9 8 7 6 5 4 3 2 1
X IX VIII VII VI V IV III II I

THE GREAT ENCYCLOPEDIA OF
MUSHROOMS

Jean-Louis Lamaison

Jean-Marie Polese

KÖNEMANN

Key to pictograms and abbreviations

 Excellent: a mushroom which is generally considered to be particularly good eating.

 Edible: a mushroom whose eating qualities are not so well known but which deserves to be tasted.

 Poisonous: a mushroom known to have caused poisoning of varying degrees of severity. Some mushrooms are poisonous raw but perfectly edible when cooked.

 Deadly: a mushroom which has caused at least one death.

If there is no pictogram this means that the mushroom is not edible, even though it is not poisonous.

Cl : class - O : order - F : family - H : height - W : width - Ø : diameter

Notice to readers

The greatest care has been taken in choosing the illustrations, describing the species and working out the keys to recognition in this book. However, we would remind readers that it is advisable to avoid eating any kind of wild mushroom if there is the slightest doubt as to its edibility. It is a good idea for the novice to have the wild mushrooms they have picked checked by an expert.

CONTENTS

1 - Boletales

- The fertile part (gills or tubes), in adult specimens, is very easy to separate from the cap by scratching it with a fingernail.
- These are species with tubes and a central stem (boletes); although a few have gills which are strongly decurrent.

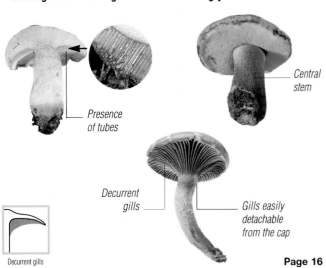

Presence of tubes

Central stem

Decurrent gills

Gills easily detachable from the cap

Decurrent gills

Page 16

2 - Russulales

- Mushrooms with friable flesh with a chalky consistency, not fibrous as in the other groups of mushrooms.

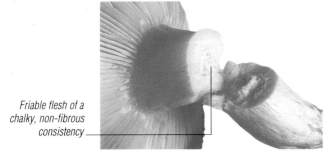

Friable flesh of a chalky, non-fibrous consistency

Page 38

3 - Tricholomatales

- Flesh has a fibrous texture.
- Gills attached to the stem (not free), decurrent, sinuate, or adnate.
- Gills white or pale-colored.
- Absence of volva and ring (except in *Oudemansiella*, *Armillaria*, and *Tricholoma cingulatum*).
- Cap and stem not separable.

White or pale-colored gills

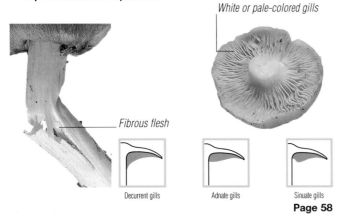

Fibrous flesh

Decurrent gills   Adnate gills   Sinuate gills

Page 58

4 - Pluteales

- Flesh has fibrous texture.
- Pinkish gills in the adult mushroom.
- Absence of a ring.

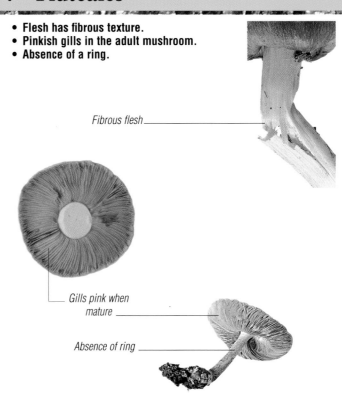

Fibrous flesh

Gills pink when mature

Absence of ring

Page 112

5 - Cortinariales

- Flesh has fibrous texture.
- Stem and cap cannot be separated.
- Gills attached to stem (not free), but not decurrent.
- Color of gills at maturity: rusty, brown, purple-brown, blackish.

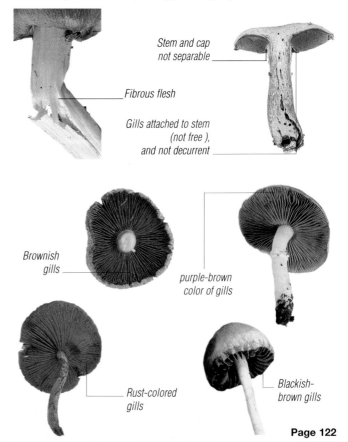

Stem and cap not separable

Fibrous flesh

Gills attached to stem (not free), and not decurrent

Brownish gills

purple-brown color of gills

Rust-colored gills

Blackish-brown gills

Page 122

PRINCIPAL CHARACTERISTICS OF MUSHROOMS

6 - Agaricales

- Fibrous texture of flesh.
- Cap and stem more or less separable.
- The white gills stay white or turn black upon maturing (sometimes passing through a pink stage, as in the case of the genus Agaricus).

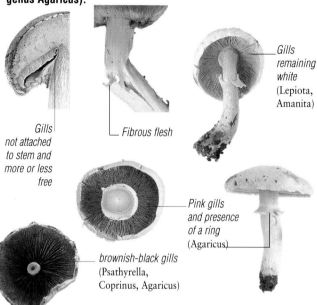

Gills remaining white (Lepiota, Amanita)

Fibrous flesh

Gills not attached to stem and more or less free

Pink gills and presence of a ring (Agaricus)

brownish-black gills (Psathyrella, Coprinus, Agaricus)

Page 152

7 - Gasteromycetes

- Fungi which, prior to their development, are spherical in the immature state before they develop fully and are partially buried in the soil.
- In the course of their development, the shape may remain round or develop into very diverse forms. These fungi have neither tubes or gills.

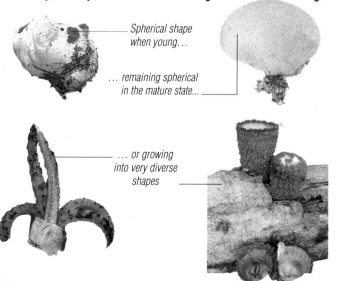

Spherical shape when young…

… remaining spherical in the mature state…

… or growing into very diverse shapes

Page 188

8 - Aphyllophorales Phragmobasidiomycetes

- Funnel-shaped fungi with smooth fertile surfaces or surfaces covered in widely spaced decurrent folds resembling crude gills beneath the cap.
- Bushy, non-viscous fungi.
- Fungi forming a crust on wood (or on the ground).
- Fungi with spines instead of gills under the cap.
- Fungi with pores under the cap which grow exclusively on wood.
- Gelatinous- or rubber-textured fungi growing on wood.

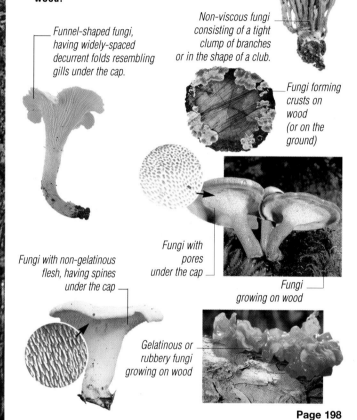

Funnel-shaped fungi, having widely-spaced decurrent folds resembling gills under the cap.

Non-viscous fungi consisting of a tight clump of branches or in the shape of a club.

Fungi forming crusts on wood (or on the ground)

Fungi with non-gelatinous flesh, having spines under the cap

Fungi with pores under the cap

Fungi growing on wood

Gelatinous or rubbery fungi growing on wood

Page 198

9 - Ascomycetes

- The main characteristic of the this group is purely microscopic. Like the Gasteromycetes, they may take widely diverse forms, but, with the exception of the truffles, they never start with a spherical shape in the immature stage. They may be shaped like a cup, a sponge, a hare's ear, stag's horns, etc.

Looking like black excrescences in the earth

Button-shaped growths on dead branches

Sponge-like

Cup-shaped

Shaped like stag's horns

Page 222

Glossary

Adnate: *where the gills or tubes are attached to the stem along all or most of their length.*

Adnexed: *where the gills or tubes are only narrowly joined to the stem.*

Anastomosed: *refers to folds and sometimes gills which are forked and joined by veins. The gills of the Paxillus family are anastomosed.*

Apothecium: *receptacle, usually cup-shaped. Example: the pezizas.*

Appendiculate: *said of the margin of the cap when it overhangs the gills and is scalloped.*

Appressed, adpressed: *closely flattened down, as in the case of scales of fibrils pressed down against the cap or stem.*

Brittle: *used to describe the flesh of the Russulas and Lactarius species, which are chalky and crumbly.*

Bulb: *swelling at the base of the stem. The stem of the Parasol Mushroom ends in a bulb.*

Campanulate: *bell-shaped, used to describe a cap or pileus, as in Liberty Caps.*

Cerebriform: *looking like a brain, consisting on a series of convolutions, as, for instance, in the cap of Gyromitra esculenta.*

Cespitose: *growing in clumps, where the stem of each specimen is attached to its neighbor, as in the case of the Pholiotas.*

Concolorous: *of uniform color, when the cap, stem, and sometimes gills are the same color.*

Convexo-expanded: *used to describe a cap whose margin is bent over the gills.*

Convexo-plane: *used to describe a cap which is convex when young but which flattens as it expands with age*

Cortina: *thin veil covering the edge of the cap and joined to the stem in young specimens of some species.As the mushroom grows, the veil tears, leaving a few fragments attached to the cap. Example : the Cortinarius family.*

Cuticle : *thin skin covering the cap. The cuticle may be dry or viscous (slimy), smooth, fibrillose, or scaly.*

Decurrent: *describes gills, tubes or spines which run down the stem or stipe. The gills of the Clitocybe family are decurrent.*

Deliquescent: *dissolving into liquid. Most species of Coprinus deliquesce as they mature; the cap liquifies into an inky liquid.*

Detached: *said of gills which are not attached to the stem.*

Dimidiate: *describes fungi without a stem which are attached at one side to the substrate, as in many polypores.*

Emarginate: *used to describe gills which have a notch at the point of attachment to the stem.*

Endoperidium: *an internal membrane or sac encasing the fruiting bodies of certain fungi, especially Puffballs and other Gasteromycetes.*

Excoriated: *said of a surface broken up into scales, as in the Excoriated Lepiota.*

What is a Mushroom?

Extraordinary Living Things

Although they have no leaves, stalks, or roots and are unable to extract carbon dioxide from the air because their cells do not contain chlorophyll, mushrooms, known scientifically as fungi, were once classified as plants, alongside algae, mosses, and ferns, that is to say along with the cryptogams or plants without flowers. However, scientists reconsidered when they realized how very special these living things are and reclassified fungi into a separate kingdom, on a par with the plant and animal kingdoms.

Fungi are divided into two groups, relating to their size, the Micromycetes, which are microscopic and which are an extremely interesting group but which are not dealt with in this book and the Macromycetes or Macrofungi, the mushrooms, which include all those which are avidly collected by enthusiasts in the woods and fields.

How they reproduce

There are several thousand species of mushroom and they adopt a wide variety of shapes. the best-known Amanita, Fly Agaric, with its umbrella-shaped cap, looks nothing like a Morel, whose cap is pitted like a sponge, nor a Fairy Club, some of which look more like a cauliflower. Yet all these species are showing the same part of their anatomy—the fruiting body, also called the sporophore. This is the part that carries the fertile area of the mushroom, the hymenium. In Agarics, the hymenium covers the gills, in Boletes, it is inside the tubes and in Morels it is in the crevices or cavities, and so on. Upon maturity, the hymenium releases the spores in their thousands and if the temperature and humidity are right, the spore will germinate and produce a complex network of underground threads, known as the mycelium. The mycelial filaments, known as hyphae (singular: hypha), ensure the continuity of the species because when two mycelia fuse, they produce a new sporophore or fruiting body which produces spores and thus completes the life cycle of the fungus.

Simplified diagram illustrating the reproductive cycle of the mushroom.

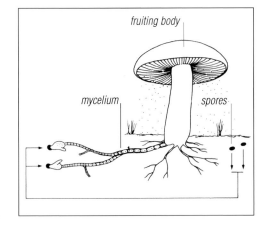

In the kitchen

It is one small step from mycology to mycogastronomy, and leading mycologists (wild mushroom experts), such as P. Ramain, R. Fauvel, and R. Heim have taken it long before us. This has given universal pleasure, because their recipes have adorned many cookbooks, past and present.

In addition to the attention lavished on the culinary properties of mushrooms by the great names in mycology, edible fungi have given pleasure to many amateur enthusiasts. There are countless recipes, ranging from the simple to the highly sophisticated.

Preparation and cooking

Although it is relatively simple to prepare wild mushrooms, certain rules need to be observed in order to eat them at their best. First and foremost, as soon as you return from a picking expedition, the mushrooms must be carefully examined one by one. The mushrooms are then sorted, unless this has already been done out in the field, eliminating those which are not suitable for eating and discarding any parts that are inedible. The mushrooms are then cleaned, preferably

This is a very generalized picture. The reproductive organs of fungi vary considerably, depending on their classification. The largest group is the Basidiomycetes, or club-fungi, which contains all the gill fungi, as well as Boletes, Chanterelles, and several other families. The second largest group is the Ascomycetes, or sac-fungi, which includes the Morels and Cup fungi. The Basidiomycetes have four spores attached to the end of the basidium, a club-shaped excrescence on the hymenium. The Ascomycetes have eight spores contained inside a single cell called the ascus.

How Fungi Live

Even though it may not be immediately obvious, fungi contribute to maintaining the biological balance of nature, by using their many enzymes to break down much of the organic matter in the soil or at least this is true of the saprophytic species.

Saprophytes may grow in the soil, like the Field Mushroom or Shaggy Ink Cap, or on dead branches, fallen tree trunks, or cut wood. Sulfur Tuft, The Umbellate Polypore, and the Dry Rot Fungus belong to this last category.

Parasitic fungi, on the other hand, develop at the expense of living trees. One of the greatest plagues of forestry is The Honey Fungus. Some fungi which are normally saprophytic, such as The Poplar Agrocybe or the Birch Polypore, may attack damaged trees.

Symbiotic fungi, however, are extremely valuable in forestry. Their mycelial filaments intertwine with the roots of young trees forming a thick web called mycorrhyza, which literally means fungus roots. This association benefits both partners because the fungus makes it easier for the tree to assimilate the minerals in the soil that it needs for growth which the tree produces organic matter which promotes growth of the fungus. Most forest-dwelling mushrooms form mycorrhiza.

Means of Identification

Valid Criteria

Learning to recognize wild mushrooms is a serious matter, since the most delicious specimens may grow alongside the most highly poisonous varieties. It is no good relying on old wives' tales or rules of thumb which are supposedly infallible, but in fact have absolutely no scientific basis.

The only valid means of identification are microscopic, organoleptic, and macroscopic are the scientific, botanical criteria.

just by scraping or by washing very quickly in cold water, to rid them of dirt, vegetable matter and especially sand. Prolonged soaking should be avoided as it can seriously spoil the flavor and aroma of fresh mushrooms. If a mushroom has a slimy cap, the cuticle should be peeled, as should any fibrous stems which are inedible.

Some fungi can be eaten raw. These include the Field Mushroom and Caesar's Mushroom, (the latter only grows in Mediterranean climates). Most wild mushrooms need to be cooked, however, and in the case of some fungi, such as the Grisette, the Blusher or Morels, it is compulsory. As a general rule,

the cooking method should preserve all of the flavor and texture of the mushroom. Certain mushrooms, such as the Field Mushroom, the Bleeding Milk Cap, and others, just need to be lightly sautéed in butter or oil in an omelet pan or skillet.

In the age of the microwave oven, mushrooms can now be blanched or pre-cooked before they are used in a dish. This also means they can be cooked in a little liquid and without fat. The reader will find this book contains all the species that are worth eating, so that he or she can enjoy the results of foraging and harvesting these wild foods.

Glossary

Exoperidium: *Skin or membrane covering the fruiting body of certain fungi, especially Gasteromycetes, such as the Puffballs.*
Fasciculate: *growing in tight clumps consisting of many specimens. Example: Sulfur Tuft.*
Fibrillose: *covered in fine hairs or filaments. Describes the cuticle of certain fungi and used exclusively for an external feature.*
Fibrous: *of a fibrous consistency. Some fungi have an internally fibrous consistency, especially the stem or stipe.*
Fimicolous: *describes fungi which grow on dung or heavily manured soil.*
Fold: *a structure looking like a vein bulging out of the skin, which bears the hymenium in the Chanterelles. Unlike gills, these folds are thick, irregular and to some extent anastomosed.*
Free: *used to describe gills which touch the stem but are not attached to it. Amanitas have free gills.*
Fruiting body: *synonym for sporophore.*
Fugaceous: *ephemeral; often used to describe a ring or cortina which disappeares with age.*
Fungal: *relating to fungi.*
Fungus: *pl. fungi. The name used to describe all the species in this kingdom, the largest in the natural world, which includes the mushroom. The word mushroom is usually used to describe the larger fungi which resemble the cultivated mushroom, having a cap and stem.*
Furfuraceous: *covered in bran-like or scurf-like particles.*
Gelatinous: *having a jelly-like consistency, such as the Jew's Ear.*
Gill: *blade arranged in series on the underside of the cap of certain fungi. The gills bear the hymenium.*
Glabrous: *smooth, devoid of hairs or fibrils.*
Gleba: *mass of spore-bearing tissue in fungi such as Puff Balls, Earth Balls, and Truffles.*
Globulose: *describes fungi that are almost spherical, such as the Earth Balls. .*
Glutinous: *slimy, covered with a slimy film, as in the case of Gomphidius glutinosus.*
Greasy: *used to describe thick gills with a fatty consistency, as in The Charcoal Burner.*
Hemolysin: *substance which destroys red blood cells in humans. the Helvellas, the Blusher, and several other fungi contain hemolysins*
Humicolous: *describes mushrooms that grow on humus or leaf-mold.*
Hygrophanous: *used to describe a mushroom which changes its appearance and color depending on the degree of humidity in the atmosphere, as in the case of the Two-toned or Changing Pholiota.*
Hymenium: *the fertile part of the fruiting body. Depending on the species, the hymenium may be on the gills, tubes, spines, etc.*

Glossary

Hypogeous: *describes mushrooms whose fruiting body is subterranean, as in the truffles*

Irregular: *used to describe gills interspersed with smaller gills of various sizes.*

Lignicolous: *growing on wood. Examples are the Honey Fungus and the Polypores.*

Maculate: *spotted or speckled, as in the Spotted Tough-shank.*

Margin: *edge of the cap.*

Marginate: *used to describe a bulb with a clearly marked edge or ledge. Smoothly rounded bulbs are said to be emarginate.*

Mucilaginous: *having the consistency of mucilage, viscous.*

Mycelium: *network of underground filaments, or hyphae, which are the actual vegetative part of the fungus. The mycelium ensures that the species survives from year to year. When hyphae fuse, they produce a fruiting body or carpophore.*

Mycology: *the branch of natural history devoted to the study of fungi, including mushrooms.*

Mycorrhiza: *a symbiotic association between the mycelium of a fungus and the roots of higher plants, usually trees. Boletes frequently form mycorrhizal associations with trees.*

Ostiole: *small orifice through which the spores of certain species, such as the Puff Balls can escape into the air.*

Partial veil: *envelope which protects the hymenium of certain young mushrooms. It may persist in the form of a ring, as in the Agarics.*

Pedicelate: *having a tiny stalk or pedicel, as in the Scarlet Elf Cup.*

Peridium: *membrane enveloping mushrooms such as the Puff Balls, Earth Balls and Truffles. The peridium consists of two layers the exoperidium and the endoperidium.*

Pileus: *another name for the cap.*

Pore: *the opening or orifice of a tube. The tubes of boletes and polypores end in pores through which the spores are ejected.*

Pruinose: *having a powdery covering over the cuticle. The Clouded Agaric (Clitocybe nebularis) has a pruinose cuticle.*

Pubescent: *covered in fine hair.*

Pulverulent: *powdery, turning to powder. Used to describe consistency of the flesh, as in Puff Balls when they mature.*

Ramule: *little branch or twig. The Fairy Clubs often have ramules or branchlets.*

Receptacle: *fruiting body or sporophore.*

Recurved: *also called convexo-expanded. (q.v.).*

Reticulate: *like a net; a network of slightly protruding filaments which cover the stem of certain Boletes.*

Rhizomorph: *a root-like extension of the mycelium which extends into the host. For example, Megacollybia platyphylla has rhizomorphs growing from the base of the stem.*

Microscopic features

These properties are essential for the correct classification of specimens. The criteria used are the shape, color, and size of the spores. These characteristics are studied in laboratories by scientists, but lay people may only be able to use macroscopic features, taste and smell, which can be checked out in the field. However, these ought to be sufficient to be able to recognize the principal edible and poisonous varieties of wild mushroom.

Organoleptic features

These call into play four of the five senses: sight, smell, taste, and touch. In fact, the mushroom gatherer should always carefully check the color and odor, and sometimes even the taste and consistency of a specimen.

Take the first of these yardsticks, color. This is typically white in the Snow-white Wax Cap, red-yellow in the Annatto-colored Cortinarius, and red-brown in the Foxy Russula.

However, the color of a mushroom, especially the cap may vary considerably within a species or in individual specimens. Color changes also depend on age and surroundings (humidity, type of soil or substrate, etc.) The color may also not be clearly defined and may consist of patches of color or several colors superimposed on each other. Hygrophanous fungi change color dramatically when the weather changes from wet to dry and vice versa. Color is nevertheless an important identifier.

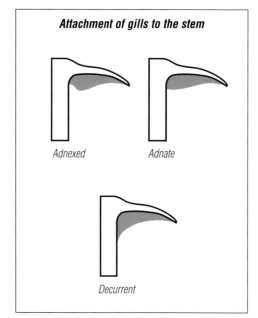

Attachment of gills to the stem

Adnexed

Adnate

Decurrent

MAIN FEATURES USED TO IDENTIFY MUSHROOMS

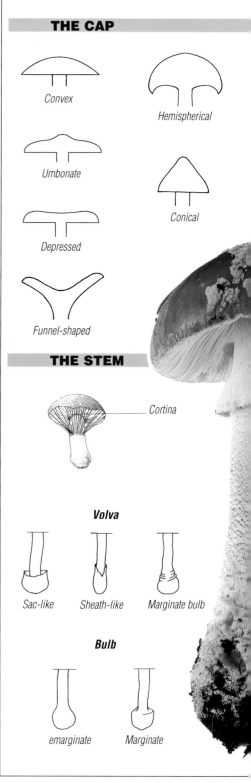

THE CAP

Convex

Hemispherical

Umbonate

Conical

Depressed

Funnel-shaped

THE STEM

Cortina

Volva

Sac-like

Sheath-like

Marginate bulb

Bulb

emarginate

Marginate

The identification of fungi is often difficult due to the fact that there is such a large number of species. The initial guide consists of identifying simple morphological characteristics, as listed here. The keys to identification shown here are based on these criteria.

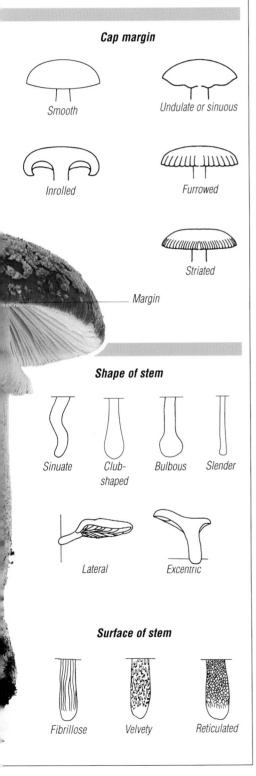

Cap margin

Smooth

Undulate or sinuous

Inrolled

Furrowed

Striated

Margin

Shape of stem

Sinuate

Club-shaped

Bulbous

Slender

Lateral

Excentric

Surface of stem

Fibrillose

Velvety

Reticulated

As for smell, a gaseous smell is noticeable in several species of Tricholoma, particularly the Sulfur Tricholoma. Other mushrooms smell of wheat flour, especially St. George's Mushroom and Miller, both of which are deliciously edible, though the same smell is present in the Livid Entoloma, which is highly poisonous.

As for texture, Jew's Ear has a gelatinous consistency, the Cep and the Chocolate or Bronze Cep, soft in the Destroying Angel, elastic in the stem of the Fairy Ring Champignon, and hard in the Lacquered Bracket.

Macroscopic characteristics

These are consist of easily identifiable characteristics such as shape, any decoration of the stem (such as a ring or volva), the texture of the cap (scaly, fibrillose, etc.), and of the hymenium, the spore-bearing surface of the fruiting-body. Some mushrooms are extremely easy to identify. These include the Parasol Mushroom, the Conical Wax Cap, the Oyster Mushroom, and the Horn of Plenty. The volva and ring, typical of many Amanitas, including the Death Cap, make it easy to distinguish them from species of Tricholoma with which they might otherwise be confused. The hymenium of fungi also constitutes an essential feature for identification, and this is one of the principal ways of classifying fungi into families.

Importance and Limitation of Keys to Identification

The keys to identification used throughout this book have been simplified as far as possible, and refer mainly to macroscopic characteristics. Organoleptic features are mentioned, but microscopic features are not discussed. We have tried to help the reader to identify a mushroom as quickly as possible. However, we must point out that if an error in identification may not have serious consequences if the book is used merely for the study of mushrooms, the results could be serious if the key is used to identify species of mushrooms for the purpose of consumption.

For this reason, we always advise anyone embarking on the collection of wild mushrooms with a view to eating them to first submit the contents of the collecting basket to the scrutiny of a knowledgeable person.

Poisonous mushrooms

There are about one hundred poisonous mushrooms but they vary in their degree of toxicity.
A dozen or so mushrooms have been discovered thus far which are highly poisonous—though rarely fatal—especially to the very young or the very weak. They cause serious poisoning, the initial effects of which are displayed quite soon after they have been eaten. Anyone eating such a mushroom should seek hospital treatment. Other dangerous species, which are generally less toxic, should also be avoided. Some members of the Hebeloma and Entoloma families, such as Poison Pie (*Hebeloma crustiliniforme*), may cause gastro-enteritis.
Sulfur Tuft (*Hypholoma fascisculare)* has also been responsible for serious poisoning.

A Poisonous mushrooms of the fields

Ivory or Sweating Mushroom
Clitocybe dealbata

Silky Entoloma
Entoloma sericeum

The Star-spored Entoloma
Entoloma conferendum

Liberty Caps
Psilocybe semilanceata

Mountain Psilocybe
Psilocybe montana

Brown Hay Cap
Panaeolus foenisecii

B Poisonous mushrooms of mixed woods

Red-staining Inocybe
Inocybe patouillardii

Panther Cap
Amanita pantherina

Semisanguine Cortinarius
Cortinarius semisanguineus

Blood-red Cortinarius
Cortinarius sanguineus

Cinnamon Cortinarius
Cortinarius cinnamomeus

Ocher-and-red Cortinarius
Cortinarius bolaris

Fly Agaric
Amanita muscaria

Speckled Tricholoma
Tricholoma pardinum

Sulfur Tricholoma
Tricholoma sulphureum

Pure Mycena
Mycena pura

Star-spored Entoloma
Entoloma conferendum

Ocelot Entoloma
Entoloma cetratum

Jonquil Amanita
Amanita junquillea

Warty Amanita
Amanita echinocephala

Brick Cap
Hypholoma sublateritium

Sulfur Tuft
Hypholoma fasciculare

Poison Pie
Hebeloma crustuliniforme

Veridigris Russula
Russula æruginea

The Devil's Bolete, The Sickener, and The Woolly Milk-Cap, are species which may have a violently emetic effect, especially if eaten raw. Individuals may be intolerant of certain mushrooms which others find edible. The Honey Fungus, The Clouded Agaric, the Grainy Bolete and the Yellow-staining Mushroom all fall into this category.

Certain species may be quite simply indigestible.

Even cultivated mushrooms may contain concentrations of pesticides which may render them toxic.

Below is a selection of the commonest poisonous mushrooms.

Two-tone Hebeloma
Hebeloma mesophaeum

Conical Wax Cap
Hygrocybe conica

Yellow-staining mushroom
Agaricus xanthoderma

Dung Fungus
Panaeolus semiovatus

Hoop Petticoat Fungus
Panaeolus sphinctrinus

Earthball
Scleroderma verrucosum

Spruce Parasol
Lepiota ventriosospora

Cat Parasol
Lepiota felina

Crested Lepiota
Lepiota cristata

Torn-capped Inocybe
Inocybe lacera

Common White Inocybe
Inocybe geophylla

Deceiving Inocybe
Inocybe fraudans

Fastigiate Inocybe
Inocybe rimosa

Earthball
Scleroderma verrucosum

Common earthball
Scleroderma citrinum

Penetrating Agaric
Gymnopilus penetrans

Beautiful Coral Fungus
Ramaria formosa

Pale Coral Fungus
Ramaria pallida

Hairy-stemmed Psilocybe
Psilocybe crobula

Mushrooms have conquered almost every type of environment and produce fruiting bodies at almost any time of the year. However, many have a restricted habitat and only appear for a limited time.

Mushrooms of the fields grow in grassland, such as meadows and lawns in gardens and parks, grass verges, etc.

Mushrooms of mixed woods can be found in both deciduous and coniferous woods. They also live in woods in which both these types of trees grow.

Mushrooms of deciduous woods, deciduous trees being those which normally shed their leaves in winter (broadleaved trees), have a symbiotic with these trees alone. A wood or thicket may also contain conifers, but fungi which only grow under deciduous trees will never be found under conifers.

C Poisonous mushrooms of deciduous woods

Jack O'Lantern
Omphalotus olearius

Deceiving Funnel Cap
Omphalotus illudens

Leaf-mold Agaric
Clitocybe phyllophila

Star-spored Inocybe
Inocybe asterospora

Green-capped Inocybe
Inocybe corydalina

Mauve-stemmed Inocybe
Inocybe griseolilacina

Fiery Agaric
Gymnopilus spectabilis

The Sickener
Russula emetica

Fragile Russula
Russula fragilis

Nitrous Entoloma
Entoloma nidorosum

Pink-and-Gray Entoloma
Entoloma rhodopolium

Peppery Hebeloma
Hebeloma sinapizans

Deadly Mushrooms

History is littered with deaths caused, intentionally or otherwise, by mushrooms. As far as is currently known there are fifteen or so deadly species, but the list has grown longer with time; among the most recent to be included is The Close Amanita (*Amanita proxima*). Such ignorance may be surprising, but it is often only when there is an accident that a species is revealed to be poisonous.

A The Deadly Amanitas

The Death Cap
Amanita phalloides

Spring Amanita
Amanita verna

The Destroying Angel
Amanita virosa

Close Amanita
Amanita proxima

Livid Entoloma
Entoloma lividum

Shield-shaped Parasol
Lepiota clypeolaria

Phoenician Cortinarius
Cortinarius phœniceus

Red-banded Cortinarius
Cortinarius armillatus

Devil's Bolete
Boletus satanas

Yellow Milk Cap
Lactarius chrysorrheus

Whitish Bolete
Boletus radicans

Pink Mycena
Mycena rosea

Two-toned Mycena
Mycena pelianthina

Woolly Milk Cap
Lactarius torminosus

The Scaly Mushroom
Agaricus præclaresquamosus

The delay before the first symptoms appear varies considerable, depending on the type of poison in question,
but it is generally long, being a minimum of six hours for the Death Cap but up to six days for deadly species of Cortinarius.
Most of the toxic elements are known; they attack the liver, kidneys, nervous system, and the blood.

B Other Poisonous Mushrooms

Red-brown Parasol
Lepiota bruneoincarnata

Lilac-brown Parasol
Lepiota bruneolilacina

Brown Parasol
Lepiota helveola

Annatto-colored Cortinarius
Cortinarius orellanus

Suspect Cortinarius
Cortinarius speciosissimus

Marginate Galera
Galerina marginata

Autumn Galera
Galerina autumnalis

Turban Fungus or False Morel
Gyromitra esculenta

The Brown Roll Rim
Paxillus involutus

Violet Elf Cup
Sarcosphaera coronaria

15

- **Dry cap, hollow stem.**

Dry cap

Hollow
stem

GYROPORUS **Page 18**

- **Species connected solely with conifers.**
- **Slimy or very slimy cap.**

Slimy or very
slimy cap

SUILLUS
Page 19

- **Elongated stem covered in rough gray or reddish tufts.**

Elongated
stem

Stem covered in
rough gray or
reddish tufts

1/1

1/1

LECCINUM **Page 22**

- **Dry or velvety cap, wide pores, stem not very
thick or tall and straight.**

Cap dry or
velvety

Wide
pores

1/1

Stem not very thick or tall and
straight

CHALCIPORUS AND XEROCOMUS **Page 24**

FEATURES OF THE BOLETALES

- The fertile area (gills or tubes) in mature specimens is very easy to separate from the cap by scratching it with a fingernail.
- These species have with tubes and a central stem (boletes); however, a few of them have strongly decurrent gills, although they still belong to this family.

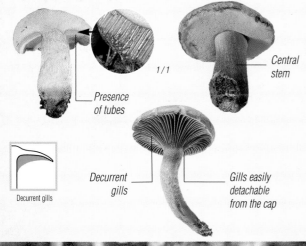

Presence of tubes

1/1

Central stem

Decurrent gills

Gills easily detachable from the cap

Decurrent gills

▶ ▶ ▶ 1 - Mushrooms with tubes: boletes

- White pores turning pink when touched.
- Marked reticulation on stem.

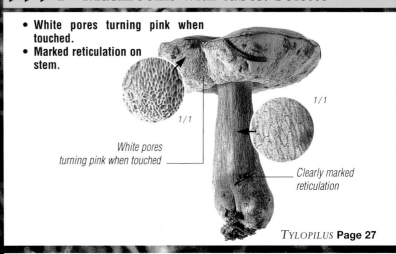

1/1

White pores turning pink when touched

1/1

Clearly marked reticulation

TYLOPILUS **Page 27**

- Very fleshy non-slimy cap, very large central stem, covered with red reticulation or spots, very small pores

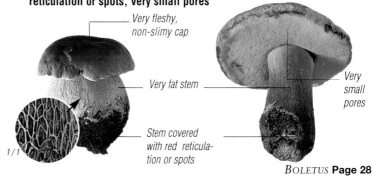

Very fleshy, non-slimy cap

Very fat stem

Very small pores

Stem covered with red reticulation or spots

1/1

BOLETUS **Page 28**

2 - Mushrooms with gills

- Slimy cap with widely spaced gills which blacken upon maturity.

1/1

Viscous cap

Widely spaced gills which blacken upon maturity

GOMPHIDIUS **Page 34**

- Non-slimy cap with tightly packed, orange or reddish-brown gills.

Non-slimy cap

1/1

Tightly-packed orange or reddish-brown gills

PAXILLUS, HYGROPHOROPSIS, OMPHALOTUS **Page 35**

The Chestnut Bolete

Gyroporus castaneus

Alternative Latin name: *Boletus castaneus*.

Classification: Cl. Homobasidiomycetes - O. Boletales - F. Boletaceae.

- H: 2¾-4 in (7-10 cm)
- Ø: 1¼-3¼ in (3-8 cm)
- Pale yellow spores

White pores

Irregular stem of the same color as the cap

Chestnut-colored, firm cap

■ How to recognize it

This is a rather small Bolete, recognizable by the beautiful, uniform color of its **cap** which ranges from chestnut to brownish-fawn. The flesh is fairly thin but very firm, and the shape is flat to convex. The surface is dry and irregular, with a velvety texture.

The white **tubes** are almost free along the stem and are very short. The **pores**, are so tiny that they are almost invisible in young specimens. They are white in color, in sharp contrast with the typical brown of the rest of the mushroom. They turn lemon-yellow when old and become splashed with patches of rusty brown where damaged. The chestnut-brown **stem** is unusually slender for a bolete. It is very firm but soon becomes hollow.

The **flesh**, which is white, unchanging and friable, has slightly fungal odor and a faint fragrance of hazelnuts.

■ Where and when to find it

The Chestnut Bolete is uncommon but widespread. Single specimens can be encountered but it is usually found growing in small groups, on siliceous soil, in the undergrowth or beside woodland paths. It is particularly fond of dense deciduous forests but also appears in well-lit plantations of conifers, from summer through fall.

■ Edibility and culinary interest

The Chestnut Bolete is widely eaten. Some specimens are said to taste slightly bitter, but it is perfectly safe to eat. The firm consistency and nutty flavor, as well as its Cep-like smell, which is often quite strong, especially when it grows at high altitude, make it a deliciously edible mushroom.

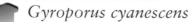

Related species

THE BLUEING BOLETE
Gyroporus cyanescens

The Blueing Bolete is much paler in color, ranging from beige to pale ocher, and larger than the Chestnut Bolete. The flesh turns bright blue (indigo) when broken. It is also very good to eat despite the tough stem which soon becomes hollow as the mushroom ages.

- H: 3-6 in (8-15 cm)
- Ø: 2-5 in (6-12 cm)
- Pale yellow spores

The Bovine Bolete
Suillus bovinus

Latin name: *Boletus bovinus.*

Classification : Cl. Homobasidiomycetes - O. Boletales - F. Boletaceae.

- H: 2-3 in (4-8 cm)
- Ø: 2-4 in (5-10 cm)
- Olive-brown spores

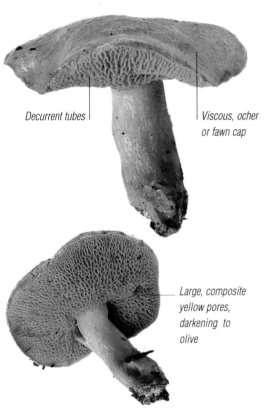

Decurrent tubes

Viscous, ocher or fawn cap

Large, composite yellow pores, darkening to olive

How to recognize it

The Bovine Bolete belongs to the genus *Suillus*, boletes with slimy caps. The Bovine Bolete is quite small compared to related species.

The **cap** is convex and not very fleshy for a bolete, but soon expands and flattens, and may even be depressed or have an irregular surface. The cuticle is glabrous and shiny, due to the surface slime; it is generally fawn in color, but may vary from ocher to pinkish-brown. The margin is paler, almost whitish and is slightly upturned at first, but wavy in older specimens. Some of the **tubes** are short and clearly decurrent, and open into rather unusual **pores**, since they are very wide and angular (they may attain a width of ½ in (2 mm)), interspersed with smaller pores. At first the pores are olive-brown, but they darken to brown when the spores mature.

The **stem**, is often curved, cylindrical, and rather slender and short. The surface is smooth and concolorous with the cap. The base is often covered with a fluffy pinkish mycelium.

The **flesh** is quite firm in young specimens but softens and even takes on an elastic consistency with age. It is pale yellow tending to turn pink on contact with the air. It is insipid and almost odorless.

Where and when to find it

The Bovine Bolete is quite common in damp places in southern pine forests, both at altitude and beside the sea. In some years it is particularly widespread in forests along the coasts, such as those of the Landes in France. The growing season lasts from summer through to winter in mild climates.

Features and edibility

Medieval knights, who were particularly fond of the Saddle-shaped Tricholoma (*Tricholoma equestre*), despised this species and left it to the cattle-drovers, hence its name. The bovine bolete is not particularly good to eat, even when young. As it ages, the soft yet elastic consistency of the flesh makes it virtually inedible, especially as it quickly becomes worm-eaten. Like Slippery Jack and the Granular Bolete, the Bovine Bolete forms mycorrhiza with pine trees, which helps them develop and grow. This association does much to help the saplings overcome competition with such ground cover as the common heather (*Calluna vulgaris*).

Related species

THE VARIEGATED BOLETE
Boletus variegatus

The Variegated Bolete is very similar to the Bovine Bolete. The cap is convex and fleshy, and fairly dark ocher in color. It is covered with characteristic speckles. The pores are small and angular, yellow at first then greenish-brown, and they turn slightly blue when touched. The stem is concolorous or paler and is quite long and sturdy. The flesh is pale yellow and turns slightly blue when exposed to the air. This bolete is also common under pine trees in the mushroom season. It smells slightly of chlorine and has a rather disagreeable flavor, making it unpalatable. It is even said to cause stomach upsets.

- H: 4-6 in (10-15 cm)
- Ø: 2-6 in (5-15 cm)
- Olive-brown spores

Slippery Jack
Suillus luteus

English synonyms: The Yellow Bolete, The Pine Bolete.
Alternative Latin name : *Boletus luteus*.

Classification : Cl. Homobasidiomycetes -
O. Boletales - F. Boletaceae.

- H: 2¾-5 in (7-13 cm)
- Ø: 2-4½ in (5-12 cm)
- Ocher-brown spores

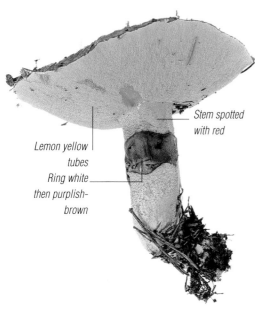

Lemon yellow
tubes
Ring white
then purplish-
brown

Stem spotted
with red

Viscous brown
cap

■ How to recognize it

Slippery Jack, the Yellow Bolete, or the Pine Bolete is quite a large species, distinguished by the ring on the stem. The **cap** is thick and fleshy and quite large. At first it is rounded and convex and only flattens when the fungus is fully mature. The cuticle is shiny and very slimy. It is typically dark brown but occasionally yellow specimens are found. It is streaked with a slightly darker shade. The margin retains fragments or shreds of the white veil which may be fugacious and which covers the hymenium for a long time.

The **tubes** are golden, then chamois leather-colored, and the small **pores** are bright yellow and rounded, darkening with age. The **stem** is cylindrical, straight or curved. It is thick and sturdy and of a firm consistency. The white lower part darkens to brown with age. The ring is large and membranous and white in young specimens, turning purplish-brown with age. The top of the stem is covered in reddish-brown dots, and these turn to pale yellow just above the ring.

The **flesh**, which is white to yellowish, soon loses its firmness in the cap, but not in the stem, which soon becomes fibrous.

■ Where and when to find it

Slippery Jack grows in clumps in grass under conifers, especially pines. It is quite common especially on high ground, throughout the temperate northern hemisphere. It appears in the fall, sometimes late, but may occur in spring.

■ Features and edibility

Once the slimy cuticle, which separates easily from the cap, is peeled away, Slippery Jack is

Young Slippery Jack.

good to eat. It is quite common and is large in size, so that large amounts can be picked. However, only the younger specimens are worth eating because the flesh of this mushroom is firm when young but soon softens. Slippery Jack is often dried or pickled and sold in Europe under the name of Pine Bolete (or even Cep). Even though it grows under pine trees it cannot be compared for flavor with the genuine Pine Bolete (*Boletus pinophilus*) which is highly prized. Like other boletes, Slippery Jack grows in a mycorrhyzal association with trees, in this case pine trees. This symbiotic association not only fosters the growth of the tree but also that of the mushroom.

Tests have been performed which show that it would be possible to cultivate Slippery Jack under pine trees for sale commercially.

Related species

THE GRANULAR BOLETE
Suillus granulatus

The Granular Bolete is similar in color to Slippery Jack but has no veil or ring. It exudes tiny milky drops, hence its alternative name of Weeping Bolete.
- H: 3¼-6 in (8-15 cm)
- Ø: 2-4½ in (5-12 cm)
- Ocher-brown spores

Droplets oozing from the pores

Absence of a ring

THE ELEGANT BOLETE
Suillus grevillei

THE LARCH BOLETE
Suillus viscidus

The Larch Bolete or Viscous Bolete is another species which attaches itself to a single species of tree, in this case the larch. The pale, brownish cap bears shreds of an evanescent veil on the margin. The wide pores turn grayish brown or olive-colored. The stem may turn reddish below the ring. The flesh is too soft for this bolete to make good eating.
- H: 2¼-6 in (7-15 cm)
- Ø: 2-4 in (5-10 cm)
- Tobacco-brown spores

THE PLACID BOLETE
Suillus placidus

The Placid Bolete is quite a rare species which only grows under Weymouth pine in hilly or mountainous regions. The very viscous cap is white at first, then tinged with pale violet at the margin. In young specimens the pores exude drops as do those of the other species of *Suillus*.
- H: 3¼-6 in (8-15 cm)
- Ø: 2-4 in (5-10 cm)
- Yellow brown spores

The Elegant Bolete is also rather common but is found exclusively under larches, especially in the mountains. It really deserves the name of "Yellow (Larch) Bolete," because the whole fungus is bright yellow. It is taller than Slippery Jack and can be distinguished from it through two features of the stem. These are the white ring which remains immaculate even when the fungus is fully grown and the surface of the stem above it which has a faint reticulation, though this is not always obvious. It can be eaten if the slimy cuticle is removed but is not particularly tasty.
- H: 2¼-6 in (6-15 cm)
- Ø: 5-10 cm
- Ocher-brown spores

The Orange Bolete

Leccinum aurantiacum

Classification : Cl. Homobasidiomycetes - O. Boletales - F. Boletaceae.

- H: 4½-9 in (12-23 cm)
- Ø: 3½-8 in (8-20 cm)
- Ocher-brown spores

Fairly bright orange cap

Orange-brown tufts

▌How to recognize it

The **cap** is straight and spherical at first and is barely wider than the stem. It later becomes convex, then flat, and can grow quite wide. It is typically reddish-orange in color and the cuticle is dry and velvety. It overlaps the margin, especially in young specimens.

The **tubes** are long and slender, free, whitish and open into concolorous **pores** which turn gray with age.

The **stem** is sturdy and firm and even tough and generally swells toward the base. The whitish surface is covered with orange-to-brown tufts which make it look rough-textured.

The **flesh** is white, pinkish then turning grayish and turns blue or green at the base of the stem. It is firm at first, especially in the stem, but softens with age.

▌Where and when to find it

The sturdy Orange Bolete generally fruits in summer through fall, and can be found under various types of deciduous tree, including hornbeam, birch, and poplar.

▌Features and edibility

The caps of young specimens make a good meal if the flesh is still firm. The stems are too tough and should be discarded. However, the species has a slight taste of carbolic and turns an unappetizing black color when cooked and so it does not rank among the great delicacies.

Related species

Other boletes in this group have orange or brick-cap caps

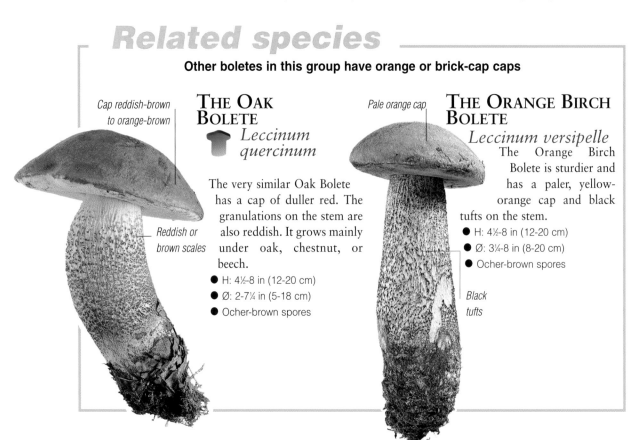

Cap reddish-brown to orange-brown

THE OAK BOLETE

Leccinum quercinum

The very similar Oak Bolete has a cap of duller red. The granulations on the stem are also reddish. It grows mainly under oak, chestnut, or beech.

- H: 4½-8 in (12-20 cm)
- Ø: 2-7¼ in (5-18 cm)
- Ocher-brown spores

Reddish or brown scales

Pale orange cap

THE ORANGE BIRCH BOLETE

Leccinum versipelle

The Orange Birch Bolete is sturdier and has a paler, yellow-orange cap and black tufts on the stem.

- H: 4½-8 in (12-20 cm)
- Ø: 3¼-8 in (8-20 cm)
- Ocher-brown spores

Black tufts

The Hornbeam Bolete
Leccinum carpinum

Alternative Latin name : *Leccinum griseum*.

Classification : Cl. Homobasidiomycetes - O. Boletales - F. Boletaceae.

- H: 4-8 in (10-20 cm)
- Ø: 2-4 in (5-10 cm)
- Tobacco-brown spores

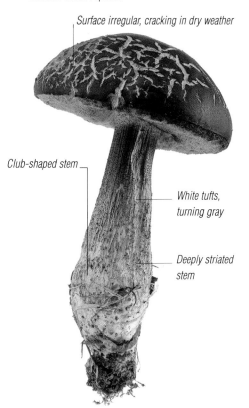

Surface irregular, cracking in dry weather

Club-shaped stem

White tufts, turning gray

Deeply striated stem

▌How to recognize it

The **cap** of the Hornbeam Bolete is hemispherical and thick at first, but soon flattens. The cuticle is fawn to brown and irregular. It cracks in dry weather, though it is slightly viscous in humid conditions.

The **tubes** are long and slender, firm at first then becoming spongy upon maturity. The **pores** are white, turning gray with age.

The **stem** is club-shaped. The whitish surface is covered in tufts which are pale at first then darker, and make it look rough-textured.

The white **flesh** turns pink then darkens, changing from violet to black when broken. The consistency under the cap is rather soft but becomes much firmer in the stem, which eventually turns spongy.

▌Where and when to find it

This bolete commonly grows under hornbeams and can be found from late summer onward.

▌Features and edibility

The Hornbeam Bolete is edible as long as only the caps of young specimens are eaten. The stem, tubes, and cuticle should be discarded from older mushrooms, which will mean that little is left. Furthermore, the flesh softens and turns very black during cooking.

Related species

There are several species of rough-stemmed bolete which are hard to distinguish from each other and were once known collectively as Boletus scaber. There are also several sub-species, which adds to the complication.

Chocolate or yellow-brown cap

THE BROWN BIRCH BOLETE
Leccinum scabrum
The Brown Birch Bolete differs from the Hornbeam Bolete in that the cap is not lumpy and the stem is thicker. It grows mainly under birch trees in very acid soil. It also makes poor eating.

- H: 4-10 in (10-25 cm)
- Ø: 2-6 in (5-15 cm)
- Tobacco-brown spores

THE GRAY BIRCH BOLETE
Leccinum variicolor
The Gray Birch Bolete also grows under birches but is less common. The cap is gray-black with lighter patches of paler color.

Velvety cap typically gray-brown, marbled with paler areas.

Gray granulations often less accentuated than on the photo.

- H: 4-13 in (10-18 cm)
- Ø: 2-4½ in (5-12 cm)
- Ocher-brown spores

The Peppery Bolete
Chalciporus piperatus

Latin name : *Boletus piperatus.*

Classification : Cl. Homobasidiomycetes - O. Boletales - F. Boletaceae.

- H: 2-3½ in (5-9 cm) ● Ø: ¾-2½ in (2-6 cm)
- Rust-brown spores

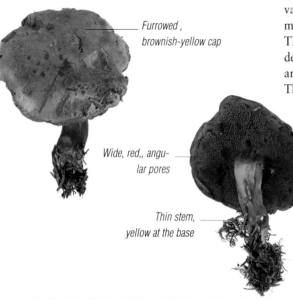

Furrowed , brownish-yellow cap

Wide, red,, angular pores

Thin stem, yellow at the base

▐ How to recognize it

The Peppery Bolete is recognizable by its small size and beautiful copper color. The **cap** is very small for a bolete but it is thick and fleshy. It is convex at first, then flattening out as the mushroom matures. The cuticle appears to be dry but becomes slightly sticky in wet weather. It varies in color from a coppery gold to cinnamon brown.

The **tubes** are orange-brown and slightly decurrent on the stem, opening into wide, angular **pores** which look almost like a lattice. The pores are fawn to orange at first, later turning rusty as the spores mature.

The slender and generally curving **stem** is concolorous with the cap, except at the base, where it is brightly colored, thanks to the presence of the mycelium which ranges from lemon to chrome yellow in color.

The **flesh** of the Peppery Bolete is brightly colored and strongly flavored. It is pinkish just under the cuticle, bright yellow where it joins the stem, and pale yellow elsewhere. The flesh has a typically peppery flavor.

▐ Where and when to find it

This mushroom is quite common in coniferous woods, growing mainly under pines, but it also lives in woods in which conifers are mixed with birch. It appears in summer and fall.

▐ Features and edibility

The Peppery Bolete has such an acrid flavor that it is inedible. When dried and powdered, it could be used as an acceptable condiment.

The Red-cracking Bolete
Xerocomus chrysenteron

Latin name : *Boletus chrysenteron.*

Classification : Cl. Homobasidiomycetes - O. Boletales - F. Boletaceae.

- H: 2-4 in (5-10 cm) ● Ø: 2-4 in (5-10 cm)
- Olive-brown spores

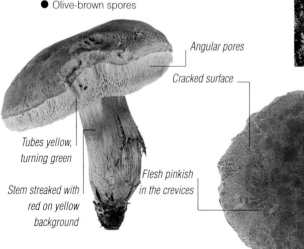

Angular pores

Cracked surface

Tubes yellow, turning green

Stem streaked with red on yellow background

Flesh pinkish in the crevices

▐ How to recognize it

The Red-cracking Bolete is of average size. The **cap** is not particularly fleshy. It is convex and varies in color from brown to olive. The surface is dry and velvety in young specimens, but cracks open with age, revealing a characteristic dark crimson coloring beneath the cuticle.

The **tubes** are yellow, turning dull green with age. They are the same color as the **pores** which are rather small, angular and of varying sizes. The pores extend beyond the cap.

The **stem** is quite slender, but tough and solid. It is covered in long red streaks or patches, the background color being yellow.

Red-cracking Bolete

The **flesh** of the Red-cracking Bolete is yellowish, sometimes turning blue. There is a thin layer of red under the cuticle, which is revealed when the cap cracks. It is softer in the cap, and is almost odorless and insipid.

▐ Where and when to find it

The Red-cracking Bolete is a very common mushroom and grows in deciduous and coniferous woods in summer and fall.

▐ Features and edibility

This bolete does not make good eating as it is not very fleshy and it soon softens and becomes mushy. It has little flavor.

Related species

THE PARASITIC BOLETE
Xerocomus parasiticus

The Parasitic Bolete is a small bolete which parasitizes earthball fungi, growing at the base.

- H: 1¼-2¾ in (3-7 cm)
- Ø: 1¼-2¾ in (3-7 cm)
- Olive-brown spores

Two boletes parasitizing an earthball. They grow in clumps at the base.

THE RED-CAP BOLETE
Xerocomus rubellus

The Red-cap Bolete also reveals yellow flesh through cracks in the cap. The cap is dull red or pinkish, sometimes tinged with ocher or brown.

- H: 2-4 in (5-10 cm)
- Ø: 2-4 in (5-10 cm)
- Olive-brown spores

Cap often pinkish red

Stem swollen at base

Stem also pinkish-red

BLACKENING BOLETE
Xerocomus pulverulentus

The Blackening Bolete becomes blue-black as soon as any of its parts are touched. The yellow flesh also turns blue immediately it is exposed to the air.

- H: 3¼-5 in (8-13 cm)
- Ø: 2-4 in (5-10 cm)
- Olive-brown spores

Stem yellow at the top, reddish-brown at the base

Cap viscous in young specimen

THE YELLOW-CRACKED BOLETE
Xerocomus subtomentosus

The Yellow-cracked Bolete sometimes grows alongside the Red-cracked bolete which it strongly resembles, but the flesh showing through the cracks or any damage reveals the flesh to be yellow, not red.

- H: 23/4-6 in (7-15 cm)
- Ø: 5-12 cm
- Olive-brown spores

THE PLUM-FLESHED BOLETE
Xerocomus pruinatus

The Plum-fleshed Bolete, like the Red-cracking Bolete, reveals a pinkish flesh in the cracks of the cap, but the dark red or dark brown cap is covered in a whitish bloom like a plum.

- H: 2-4 in (5-10 cm)
- Ø: 2-4 in (5-10 cm)
- Olive-brown spores

Flesh shows pink under cap

Dark cap covered with a white bloom

The Bay-brown Bolete
Xerocomus badius

English Synonyms: Bay-capped Bolete, False Cep.
Latin name : *Boletus badius.*

Classification : Cl. Homobasidiomycetes - O. Boletales - F. Boletaceae.

- H: 3¼-6 in (8-15 cm)
- Ø: 2-6 in (5-15 cm)
- Olive-brown spores

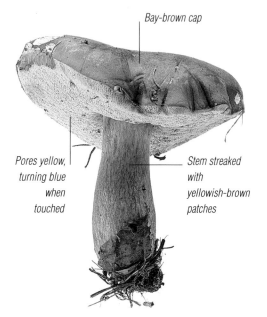

Bay-brown cap

Pores yellow, turning blue when touched

Stem streaked with yellowish-brown patches

■ How to recognize it

This bolete is of average size and derives its name from the **cap** which is the shiny brown color of a bay horse.

The cap is convex at first and not very fleshy, but soon flattens. The cuticle is velvety in dry weather but is smooth and slightly sticky when the atmosphere is damp.

The **tubes** are quite long but are sometimes shorter just around the stem, leaving a slight hollow. The **pores**, are quite small and angular, and are cream to white at first, then lemon yellow, becoming olive-colored when the mushroom is past its prime. They turn blue or green when touched, leaving a colored imprint.

The pale-brown **stem** varies in length and in shape from cylindrical to bulbous or slender. It is reticulated with long yellow or brown fibrils, which make it look woody. It is firm at first, toughening with age.

The **flesh** stays firm for a long time but eventually softens under the cap. It is yellowish, tinged with brown under the cuticle and in the stem. It turns blue or green when in contact with the air, especially in damp weather.

■ Where and when to find it

The Bay-brown Bolete grows under conifers, as well as under deciduous trees. Although it grows in the soil, it can be found in among decayed stumps. It is one of the few bolete which does not form mycorrhizas with the roots of the tree under which it grows. It is found in temperate zones throughout the northern hemisphere, and fruits at the height of the mushroom growing season in late fall.

■ Features and edibility

It is worth getting to know the Bay-brown Bolete which is sometimes found in abundance late in the season, and which does not seem to mind unfavorable weather conditions too much. The flesh is sweet and the odor is fruity, so it makes good eating, as long as the tough stem is first discarded.

Some gourmets prefer it to the Cep which some people find indigestible. However, the flesh is not very thick and this is not in its favor. The way it turns bright blue when washed and cooked may be found unattractive.

As regards this last point, it should be remembered that this reaction has nothing to do with toxicity. It is merely due to the oxidation of the boletol, a harmless substance found in a great many boletes.

The stem may be straight as in this photograph or very fat and bulbous .

	Bay-brown Bolete *Xerocomus badius*	Yellow-cracked Bolete *Xerocomus subtomentosus*
Cap	bay-brown, slightly sticky	yellow-brown, dry
Pores	quite narrow	wide
Stem	yellow and brown	brownish-yellow
Blue-staining	strong	little or none
Features	very good to eat	not good to eat

The Bitter Bolete
Tylopilus felleus

Latin name : *Boletus felleus*.

Classification : Cl. Homobasidiomycetes - O. Boletales - F. Boletaceae.

- H: 4-7¼ in (10-18 cm)
- Ø: 2-6 in (5-15 cm)
- Dirty pink spores

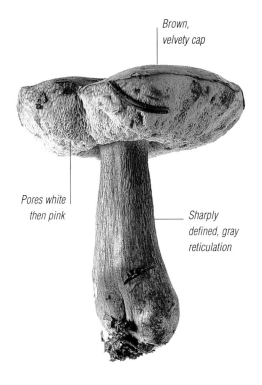

Brown, velvety cap

Pores white then pink

Sharply defined, gray reticulation

▮ How to recognize it

The **cap** is of medium height and is convex at first then flattened, quite thick and soft in texture. The surface is dry and tomentose, almost velvety, is brownish in color and may vary from fawn to yellowish. The margin is inrolled at first but flattens out completely with age.

The **tubes** start out as whitish but redden typically as the spores mature. The **pores** are quite large and concolorous with the cap, coarse and they turn carmine when rubbed both in young and mature specimens.

The **stem** is generally swollen at the base. It may be the same color as the cap or paler. It is typically covered in coarse reticulation of a darker color, which is reminiscent of fishnet stockings.

The **flesh** is soft and whitish to cream, tending to turn slightly pink in contact with the air. As the Latin name implies, this bolete tastes as bitter as gall and also has a faintly disagreeable odor.

▮ Where and when to find it

The Bitter Bolete is fairly uncommon. It grows in well-lit woods in siliceous soil, from summer to fall. It is not evenly distributed and may be found in abundance in some localities.

▮ Features and edibility

Although it is harmless, the Bitter Bolete is rendered inedible by the extreme bitterness of the flesh which is actually enhanced when cooked. The species is said to have anti-cancerous properties, though no false hopes should be entertained on that score. The alleged active principal is a mucilage whose structure has been established. This chemical is said to have properties which stimulate the immune system and thus put up a defense against infection. The initial research was conducted in Poland and is being pursued in conjunction with a Japanese pharmaceutical laboratory. Even if the research does not produce spectacular results, it will have been an interesting experiment in many ways and may well add another form of treatment to the fight against cancer.

Lookalikes

How can the Bitter Bolete and similar boletes that are either inedible or make less good eating be distinguished from that great delicacy, the Cep? When young, the stem of the Bitter Bolete, which looks as if it is encased in a fishnet stocking, is a good indication. The pores of this bolete are quite coarse and stained with pink, which later turns salmon-colored. However, the best test is to taste a tiny piece of flesh before cooking it because the bitterness is the surest sign of all.

The **Summer Bolete** *(Boletus aestivalis), (p. 29) also has reticulation on the stem, but the pores turn yellow, then green, without a trace of pink.*

The **Cep** *(Boletus edulis) (p. 28) has very fine white reticulation that is barely visible but always there, on the upper part of the stem.*

 Lookalikes:
Summer Bolete *(Boletus aestivalis)* (p. 29)
The Cep *(Boletus edulis)* (p. 28)

	Bitter Bolete *Tylopilus felleus*	Summer Bolete *Boletus aestivalis*	Cep *Boletus edulis*
Cap	brownish	ocher or reddish	beige to brown, velvety
Pores	wide, white, then pink to brownish	fine, white, yellow yellow, then olive color	fine, white, yellow, then olive color
Stem	filled, pale-colored	brownish	thick and filled, pale
Reticulation	coarse, brown	raised, white to brownish	fine, white at the top
Flesh	soft	firm but soon softening	firm then soft
Flavor	very bitter	sweet	sweet
Features	inedible	good to eat	excellent eating

The Cep
Boletus edulis

English synonym: The Penny Bun Mushroom

Classification : Cl. Homobasidiomycetes -
O. Boletales - F. Boletaceae.

- H: 4-10 in (10-25 cm)
- Ø: 2-10 in (5-25 cm)
- Olive-brown spores

White edge

Pores white then yellow and finally green

Tubes yellow in the mature specimen

Cap very fleshy, beige to reddish-brown

Bulbous stem

Fine white reticulation

How to recognize it

Imposing and sometimes huge, the Cep is one of the best-known mushrooms. The **cap** is hemispherical in young specimens and not much wider than the stem giving it its typical "champagne cork" appearance. It later expands, but remains thick, fleshy, and rounded. The cap is smooth or slightly rough-textured and becomes sticky when wet. The color of the cuticle varies from beige to reddish-brown; it may even be whitish. The margin is edged with a thin white border.

The **tubes** are long and thin, white in young specimens, turning yellow on maturity and eventually becoming olive-colored. The **pores** change color in the same way.

The **stem** is massive, swollen and firm, but later straightens out. It is white with some brown patches and has a very fine white reticulation which is characteristic of this species. The **flesh** is white but reddish-brown under the cuticle. It is thick and firm with a delicate odor, but softens in an old specimens.

Where and when to find it

At low altitudes, it prefers deciduous woods, especially oak and chestnut, while at higher altitudes it shelters under conifers, mainly pines and spruces. It tends to fruit spectacularly and in large numbers after heavy rain in late summer and in the fall.

Features and edibility

The Cep must be the best-known edible mushroom, even more famous than the Chanterelle. Many consider it to be also the finest eating, of all, the very yardstick by which other mushrooms are judged. For one thing, it is very large and there is great excitement in warm, wet years, as it is likely to be found growing in huge quantities. The Cep is sold fresh in the markets in summer and fall, and can be found dried and canned throughout the year in gourmet stores. However, the flesh softens considerably with age and the mushroom soon becomes worm-eaten in the natural state. That is why wild Ceps must be sorted meticulously and only whole, healthy specimens which still have their delicious aroma should be eaten. Although some people like to eat firm, young specimens, others prefer the mushroom when it is mature and the flavor is fully developed.

Some people actually believe there are two separate species, the firm Cep and the soft Cep. It is true that, apart from its consistency, the mushroom looks very different when it is older. When the tubes turn green with age, some consider them a great delicacy, though others find them slimy and indigestible.

In Hungary, the Cep was reputed to have anticancerous properties. Research was undertaken in the United States to check out this claim, but the initial results were unsatisfactory and the work was not pursued.

▼ Lookalike:
The Bitter Bolete *(Tylopilus felleus)* (p. 27)

	Cep *Boletus edulis*	Bitter Bolete *Tylopilus felleus*
Cap	beige to brownish	brownish
Pores	fine, white, yellow, then olive-brown	wide, white, then pink to brownish
Stem	white, then more or less brown	white to brownish
Reticulation	fine, white at the top of the stem	coarse, brown
Flesh	white, reddish-brown under the cuticle	white
Flavor	sweet	very bitter
Features	excellent eating	inedible

Lookalike

The **Bitter Bolete** (Tylopilus felleus) *(p. 27), is so bitter that a single specimen is enough to ruin any dish. The stem has a coarse ring and white pores which turn pink when touched or upon maturity. Unfortunately, the Bitter Bolete is almost identical to the Cep or Penny Bun Mushroom, especially when young. It could thus be picked in mistake for a Cep, especially as it has the same habitat, namely deciduous and coniferous woods.*

Related species

Boletes with a tall, thick stem covered in reticulation and flesh which does not turn color include species other than the Cep which make good eating.

THE SUMMER BOLETE
Boletus aestivalis

The Summer or Reticulated Bolete most closely resembles the Cep and the hardest to distinguish from it. That is because it only has a few features that are different from the Cep although these are very recognizable, the absence of dark red coloration under the cuticle being the most obvious and reliable.

The cap is never sticky or slimy even when wet and the color is more uniform and paler than in the Cep. It is ocher, reddish, or yellow-brown, even at the margin which has no strip of white. The ocher stem is covered all over with a well-defined reticulation.

This is an early species, as the name implies, appearing in May, but disappearing by the end of September. It prefers open spaces, forest clearings, and the edges of deciduous woods. Although the flesh softens more quickly than that of the Cep and often becomes worm-eaten, it is pleasantly sweet to the taste and makes excellent eating.
- H: 3¼-8 in (8 - 20 cm)
- Ø: 2-6 in (5-15 cm)
- Olive-brown spores

Cap of uniform color sometimes cracked

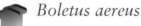

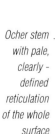

Ocher stem with pale, clearly - defined reticulation of the whole surface

NEGRO-HEAD BOLETE OR TANNED CEP
Boletus aereus

This Bolete grows in the south where it prefers dryish areas, only among broad-leaved trees. It can be recognized by its typically sepia-colored cap, which is almost black when young, but lightens in stages as it matures. The flesh of the cap is sometimes exposed through having been eaten by animals (especially slugs). The stem is ocher to rust-colored. It is swollen, but may taper at the top.
- H: 4-6 in (10-15 cm)
- Ø: 2-8 in (5-20 cm)
- Olive-brown spores

THE PINE BOLETE
Boletus pinophilus

The pine bolete has a pinkish-red cap, which varies from the color of pomegranates to the color of mahogany. When young it is slightly umbonate and has a bloom. The fat stem is ocher or reddish. It grows in the south and on high ground, and despite its name is does not grow only among pines, but can also be found in mixed woods and growing under chestnut trees.

- H: 4-8 in (10-20 cm)
- Ø: 2-8 in (5-20 cm)
- Olive-brown spores

The Spotted-stem Bolete

Boletus erythropus

Classification : Cl. Homobasidiomycetes -
O. Boletales - F. Boletaceae.

- H: 3¼-8 in (8-20 cm)
- Ø: 2¾-8 in (7-20 cm)
- Olive-brown spores

Velvety brown cap

Red pores

Stem finely spotted
with red on a
yellow background

The yellow flesh turns
bright blue when
exposed to the air

Lookalikes:
The Devil's Bolete (*Boletus satanas*) p. 31
The Red-stemmed Bolete (*Boletus calopus*) p. 33

▮ How to recognize it

The Spotted-stem Bolete looks something like a red-tinted Cep.

The **cap** of this handsome mushroom is hemispherical then convex, later flattening out. It is thick and fleshy and has a very firm, almost tough, consistency. The cuticle is velvety, dry and matt and is colored fawn to brown, sometimes tinted red.

The **tubes**, which are free on the stem are yellow and end in very small, bright red **pores** which are often orange near the margin. They turn blue when touched.

The **stem** is very sturdy and its flesh is firm, like the cap. The surface is not covered with reticulations but is spotted with red against a yellow background and this ornamentation is often so thick that the stem looks to be uniformly red. The mushroom thus richly deserves its name! The yellow **flesh** is thick and very firm. It instantly turns an intense Prussian blue as soon as it is cut, broken, or damaged.

▮ Where and when to find it

The Spotted-stem Bolete lives under several broad-leaved trees, especially oaks, and under conifers. It often grows in small clumps in grass verges on siliceous soil. It can be found throughout the temperate zones of the northern hemisphere at all altitudes. It first appears in May and continues fruiting until the fall.

▮ Features and edibility

The Spotted-stem Bolete is good to eat and some consider it as good as the Cep. It has the advantage of having firm flesh which is rarely infested by insect larvae.The intense blueing of the flesh when cut or damaged does not affect its quality and does not make it toxic. However, this feature has often deterred the uninitiated from eating it.

The Spotted-stem Bolete deserves to be tasted. However, it must be eaten cooked because it has some emetic properties if eaten raw. It is delicious in sauces, mixed with other boletes if necessary, and tastes delicious despite the blackening of the flesh when cooked.

Lookalikes

The **Devil's Bolete** (Boletus satanas) *(p. 31) has a beige or whitish cap and the stem has a fine red reticulation.*

The **Scarlet-stemmed Bolete** (Boletus calopus) *(p.33) has a cap which ranges in color from gray to pale brown. The pores are yellow and there is a faint network on the red-and-yellow stem. It is bitter-tasting and thus inedible.*

	Spotted-stem Bolete *Boletus erythropus*	Devil's Bolete *Boletus satanas*	Scarlet-stemmed Bolete *Boletus calopus*
Cap	dark, fawn to brown	pale, dirty white	pale gray or pale brown
Pores	red	yellow, then red	yellow
Stem	swollen, spotted with red	convex, fine red network	swollen, white network
Blue-staining	intense	not very intense	not very intense
Habitat	siliceous soil	calcareous soil	siliceous soil
Features	very good to eat	poisonous (especially raw)	inedible

Of the large-stemmed boletes, the Lurid Bolete is one of those with red pores and blueing flesh.

THE LURID BOLETE

Boletus luridus

The Lurid Bolete grows in woods on calcareous soil, and can be distinguished from other bolete by the red or orange flesh under its tubes. The stem is covered with red reticulation on a yellow background. It is good to eat despite intense blueing of the flesh when cut or broken.

- H: 4-7¼ in (10-18 cm)
- Ø: 3¼-8 in (8-20 cm)
- Olive-brown spores

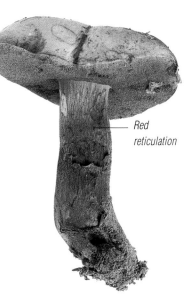

Red reticulation

THE ORANGE-PORED BOLETE
Boletus queletii

The Orange-pored Bolete takes on a variety of forms but the cap is never truly brown. The stem is never reticulated and is always reddish-brown at the base. It is considered to be less tasty than the Spotted-stem Bolete.

- H: 4½ -7¼ in (12-18 cm)
- Ø: 3¼ - 6 in in (8-15 cm)
- Olive-brown spores

The Devil's Bolete

Boletus satanas

English synonym: Satan's Bolete

Classification : Cl. Homobasidiomycetes - O. Boletales - F. Boletaceae.

- H: 4-8 in (10-20 cm)
- Ø: 4-10 in (10-25 cm)
- Olive-brown spores

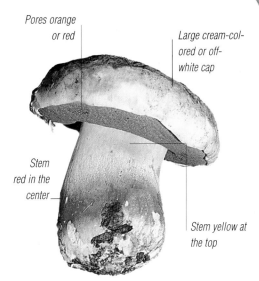

Pores orange or red

Large cream-colored or off-white cap

Stem red in the center

Stem yellow at the top

cuticle is generally dry, matt, and velvety, very pale, and varying in color to whitish and grayish and even pale brown. It is typically the color of milky coffee, shaded with green in older specimens.

The yellow **tubes**, have **pores** which start out the same color as the cap but soon turn red or orange. The **stem** is short thick, and bulbous, brightly colored in blood-red at the base and gold at the top, overlaid with a fine network of composite scales.

▌ How to recognize it

The Devil's Bolete is enormous and often deformed in shape. Under the livid mask of the cap it is a mass of bright colors.

The **cap** is handsome, very thick and fleshy, rounded at first, then flattening slightly, when the surface becomes irregular. The

The **flesh** is thick and compact, but softens as the mushroom ages. It is white or cream-colored and turns blue when touched though not very intensely, contrary to certain received ideas.

Devil's Bolete

▌Where and when to find it

The Devil's Bolete grows on chalky soil under deciduous trees in fairly southern regions, where it may be abundant locally in plantations, at the edge of woods or in clearings. Its distribution is irregular and it is absent from many regions. The Devil's Bolete recently featured on a British stamp as an endangered species in the United Kingdom. It grows during the fall mushroom season.

▌Toxicity

Although the Devil's Bolete is often attacked by insect larvae and slugs, adding to its deformed shape, it is very poisonous, especially in the raw state. However, it is not deadly poisonous, despite its unpleasant odor and flavor, and its lurid appearance. When eaten it will cause gastro-enteritis of varying degrees of severity.

Lookalikes

The Devil's Bolete, like its poisonous relatives, should not be confused with certain other boletes, with red and yellow pores and stem which are very good to eat :

*The **Spotted-stem Bolete** (Boletus erythropus) (p. 30) appears in woods on siliceous soil. It is distinguished from the Devil's Bolete by its brown cap and particularly by the lack of reticulation on the stem, where it has red spots instead. It turns bright blue when broken.*

*The **Scarlet-stem Bolete** (Boletus calopus) (p. 33) has yellow pores and grows in siliceous areas or on acid soil.*

*The **Lurid Bolete** (Boletus luridus) (p. 31), which is found on chalky soil, has a brown to pinkish cap. The thin red reticulation just under the tubes, is a unique feature. It turns bright blue when cut or damaged.*

▼ **Lookalikes:**
The Spotted-stem Bolete *(Boletus erythropus)* (p. 30)
The Scarlet-stem Bolete *(Boletus calopus)* (p. 33)
The Lurid Bolete *(Boletus luridus)* (p. 31)

Related species

Several species, most of them poisonous are related to Satan's Bolete but are more uncommon. They are typified by the reddening of the cap and the bright color of the pores.

THE REDDISH-PURPLE BOLETE
Boletus rhodopurpureus

The Reddish-purple Bolete is also a southern species. One easy way to distinguish it from the Devil's Bolete is the way in which the flesh changes color immediately from yellow to dark blue when cut or damaged. The pores also turn deep blue when pressed with the finger. This mushroom, unlike the others in this group, is probably edible but the risk of confusion with poisonous ones is too great to take the chance.

- ● H: 4-8 in (10-20 cm)
- ● Ø: 4½-7¼ in (12-18 cm)
- ● Olive-brown spores

⚠ THE WOLF BOLETE
Boletus lupinus

The Wolf Bolete, like the Reddish-Purple Bolete, has golden-colored flesh which turns deep blue when cut. The pink color of the cap is brighter and the thick stem has no reticulation except at the top.

- ● H: 2½-6 in (7-15 cm)
- ● Ø: 3¼-6 IN (8-15 cm)
- ● Olive-brown spores

Pink coloration

Not network on stem

THE ROYAL BOLETE
Boletus regius

The Royal Bolete has a berry red or rose red cap; the rest of the mushroom is lemon yellow. The stem is also finely reticulated in yellow. The flesh turns bright blue when broken. It grows in southern latitudes and is good to eat but rare.

- ● H: 3¼-7¼ in (8-18 cm)
- ● Ø: 21/4-8 in (6-20 cm)
- ● Olive-brown spores

	⚠ The Devil's Bolete *Boletus satanas*	⚠ Spotted-stem Bolete *Boletus erythropus*	Scarlet-stem Bolete *Boletus calopus*
Cap	off-white to beige	darker, fawn to brown	pale gray to brown
Pores	yellow, then red	red	yellow
Stem	swollen, fine red network	swollen, red spots	swollen, white network
Blue-staining	not very intense	intense	not very intense
Habitat	calcareous soil	siliceous soil	siliceous soil
Features	toxic (especially raw)	very good to eat (cooked)	inedible

The Scarlet-stemmed Bolete
Boletus calopus

Classification : Cl. Homobasidiomycetes - O. Boletales - F. Boletaceae.

● H:4-6 in (10-15 cm) ● Ø: 2¼-6 in (6-15 cm) ● Olive-brown spores

Pale coffee-colored Cap

Yellow pores, straining green when touched

Stem yellow at the top, red below

Reticulation clearly defined

Flesh turning blue

Lookalikes:
The Spotted-stem Bolete *(Boletus erythropus)* (p. 30)
Fechtner's Bolete *(Boletus fechtneri)*

The **flesh** is pale yellow, turning white with age, and turns blue on contact with the air. Although it would appear to be edible due to its firm flesh, the taste is too bitter.

▮ Where and when to find it

The Scarlet-stemmed Bolete grows in coniferous woods in siliceous soil. It can also be found in deciduous woods, however, but only occasionally. It commonly grows in groups of several individuals from summer through fall.

▮ Features and edibility

The Scarlet-stemmed Bolete is inedible due to the bitterness of its flesh which increases when cooked. It could be blanched, in which case the acridity of the flesh would reduce, but it is also indigestible, so that some writers have marked it down as suspect.

Despite all this, the Whitish Bolete and the Scarlet-stemmed Bolete which are closely related have both been eaten.

Nevertheless, it is advisable to avoid them due to the risks of poisoning which are serious when these mushrooms are raw. The symptoms are similar to those observed for the Devil's Bolete.

▮ How to recognize it

The **cap** of this bolete is of average size, hemispherical to convex, and quite fleshy. The cuticle is finely tomentose, dry and matt. It is whitish or grayish, gradually becoming flecked with brown.

The **tubes** are yellow, then olivaceous, opening into small, rounded **pores**. They are pale yellow, becoming splashed with green when touched or when the spores mature.

The **stem** is thick at first, becoming straighter but swollen, always sturdy and tough in consistency. It is brightly colored, being red below and yellow toward the cap. It is covered with a raised white network which reddens toward the base, adds to the beauty of this mushroom.

Lookalikes

The Scarlet-stemmed Bolete and the Whitish Bolete should not be confused with the Spotted-stem Bolete and the following boletes of the sub-genus appendiculatus *which are good to eat.*

The **Spotted-stem Bolete** (Boletus erythropus) *(p. 30) has a pale-brown to dark-brown cap, red pores and a stem spotted with red, but it has no reticulation.*

Fechtner's Bolete (Boletus fechtneri)*, is quite a rare member of the* appendiculatus *sub-genus whose stem has a reddish-pink zone in the middle. The smell is faint.*

Related species

THE WHITISH BOLETE
Boletus radicans

The Whitish Bolete is a fat mushroom which looks a little like the Cep. The cap is whitish, convex and the margin strongly inrolled. The cap turns gray and then brown. The tubes are short and the thin pores are pale yellow which soon turns greenish. The stem is filled and yellow. It has a fine reticulation in the same yellowish-white color on the surface. In the *eupachypus* variety the network is reddish. The flesh turns blue and the flavor is bitter, so the mushroom is inedible. Serious stomach upsets have been attributed to the red-stemmed variety. This poisonous bolete is rather uncommon.

● H: 4-8 in (10-20 cm)
● Ø: 4-8 in (10-20 cm)
● Olive-brown spores

The Glutinous Gomphidius

Gomphidius glutinosus

Classification : Cl. Homobasidiomycetes - O. Boletales - F. Gomphidiaceae.

- H: 2¼-5 in (6-12 cm) ● Ø: 2-4 in (5-10 cm)
- Blackish spores

Slimy cap

Veil in young specimen

Inrolled margin

Decurrent gills, very easily separable from the cap

Stem yellow at the base

▼ **Lookalike:**
The Yellow-gilled Wax Cap *(Hygrophorus hypothejus)* (p. 67)

▍How to recognize it

The Glutinous Gomphidius looks like a species of wax cap due to its viscosity, coloration, and the shape of its gills. The **cap** is fleshy and hemispherical, then flattened, and becomes depressed in older specimens. The cuticle is gray or brown, shaded with violet, and covered in a thick layer of mucous. When old, it stains black.

The **gills** are thick and widely spaced. They are decurrent, whitish at first and covered with a slimy veil which turns black when mature.

The **stem** is full and firm, white at the top and bright yellow at the base, and is also very viscous. A ring zone which may or not be well marked can be seen toward the top. It is marked by the remnants of the veil, blackened by spores.

The **flesh**, is thick and rather soft, white but yellowing in the base of the stem.

▍Where and when to find it

The Glutinous Gomphidius is a common sight in coniferous woods. It is to be found growing beside forest paths under spruces from summer through fall.

▍Features and edibility

Beneath its easily removable coating of slime, the Glutinous Gomphidius is, in fact, good to eat. The base of the stem should be discarded.

Lookalike

*The **Yellow-gilled Wax Cap** (Hygrophorus hypothejus) (p. 67) looks very similar due to its slimy brown cap and stem shading from yellow through white which shows a clear ring zone. However, its gills are yellow and inseparable from the cap. It has the same habitat but it is not good to eat.*

Related species

THE SLIMY GOMPHIDIUS
Chroogomphus rutilus

This mushroom is a common sight in pinewoods in the fall, and derives its scientific name from its nail-like shape — *gomphos* means "nail" in Greek. Despite its name, it is not as slimy as other Gomphidius species, but is not very tasty.

- H: 2½-6 in (7-15 cm)
- Ø: 2-4 in (5-10 cm)
- Blackish spores

Coppery or reddish umbonate cap

THE PINK GOMPHIDIUS
Gomphidius roseus

The Pink Gomphidius is less common. It is found under pine trees, where it frequently grows alongside the Bovine Bolete *(Suillus bovinus)*. It can be clearly distinguished from the Glutinous Gomphidius by its cap which varies from pink to red, turning russet with age, and the white stem, which tends to blacken. It is not good to eat.

- H: 1½-2½ in (4-7 cm)
- Ø: ¾-2¼ in (2-6 cm)
- Blackish spores

The Brown Roll-rim

Paxillus involutus

Classification : Cl. Homobasidiomycetes - O. Boletales - F. Paxillaceae.

● H: 2¼-4½ in (6-12 cm) ● Ø: 2-6 in (5-15 cm)
● Brown spores

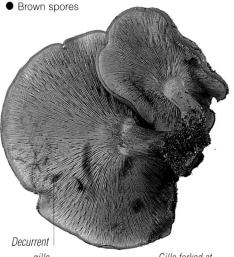

Decurrent gills

Margin inrolled and slightly fur-rowed.

Gills forked at the base

▌ How to recognize it

The Brown Roll-rim, which is of average size, has the appearance of a milk cap but it has no milk.

The **cap** is thick and soon flattens, becoming depressed and irregularly lobed. The cuticle is dry, becoming slightly sticky when wet and varies from fawn to reddish-brown, turning paler in dry weather. The margin is the most typical feature. At first it in very inrolled, hence the name, and has regularly spaced furrows along the margin.

The **gills** are cream-colored at first then turning rusty brown, and staining reddish-brown when touched. They are typical of Roll-rims in that they are strongly decurrent, and are forked where they meet the stem. They are also easily separable from the cap, a characteristic which relates the Paxillaceae to the Boletales.

The **stem**, is sturdy, full and firm at first. It is the same color as the cap or paler.

The **flesh** is thick and soft, especially in older specimens. It is yellowish, tending to reddish brown in contact with the air.

▌ Where and when to find it

The Brown Roll-rim is among the commonest species. It fruits under broad-leaved trees and conifers, from oak woods to beech woods and to mountain fir trees. It prefers damp grassy places. It is common throughout Europe and in the U.S., where it grows under birch. It often appears in large numbers and fruiting may last from spring through fall.

▌ Toxicity

The Brown Roll-rim was long considered perfectly edible. Its very abundance ensured that it was consumed in large quantities, especially in central Europe, until at the end of World War II an Austrian mycologist died after ingesting a few raw specimens.

The upsets it causes are mainly when the mushrooms are eaten raw, and are similar to other types of poisoning associated with certain boletes, which are never fatal, however. They can be compared with those caused by the False Morel (*Gyromitra esculenta*), a fungus which is poisonous and even fatal when eaten raw, but even when cooked may affect certain individuals who are susceptible due to a congenital enzymatic deficiency. Although the type of illness caused is similar, the symptoms produced by eating the Brown Roll-rim are different. A stomach upset with the usual symptoms is soon followed by cardio-vascular disturbances. Hemolytic anemia, caused by the destruction of the red cells, may cause a fatal collapse. Despite all the warnings, the Brown Roll-rim still seems to be eaten here and there, and does not seem to do much damage. However, it is of limited culinary interest so there is no point in risking death for it. Accidents have been reported as being due to insufficient cooking of the mushrooms, if they are broiled, for instance, but even well-cooked mushrooms have produced unpleasant symptoms. The Brown Roll-rim must thus be considered to be a highly poisonous mushroom and so it should never be eaten.

Related species

THE BLACK-STEMMED ROLL-RIM
Paxillus atrotomentosus

This mushroom is larger than the Brown Roll-rim and less common. It has a thicker cap, which is sometimes large and ranges from yellowish-brown to brown. The gills are cream and forked at the base. The stem is typical, short and fat, lateral and covered with a dark brown to black velour which is typical of the species.

The Black-stemmed Roll-rim grows on decaying conifer stumps. It is too bitter to eat.

● H: 2¼-7¼ in (6-18 cm)
● Ø: 4-10 in (10-25 cm)
● Brown spores

The False Chanterelle

Hygrophoropsis aurantiaca

Alternative Latin name : *Clitocybe aurantiaca*.

Classification : Cl. Homobasidiomycetes - O. Boletales - F. Paxillaceae

● H: 1¼-3¼ in (3-8 cm) ● Ø: 1¼-3¼ in (3-8 cm)
● White spores

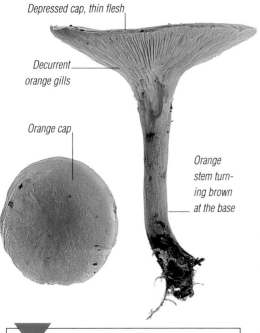

Depressed cap, thin flesh

Decurrent orange gills

Orange cap

Orange stem turning brown at the base

▼ Lookalike:
The Chanterelle
(Cantharellus cibarius) (p. 202)

■ How to recognize it

This small, bright-orange species is notable for its soft flesh.

The **cap** is convex at first with an inrolled margin. It later flattens, then becomes funnel-shaped. The cuticle is ochraceious-yellow to orange and is slightly tomentose.

The **gills** are thick and tightly-packed, quite thin and very decurrent. They are forked at the margin. They are a beautiful orange in color.

The **stem** is quite slender, elastic and relativly tenacious. It varies in color from pale orange to brown and even black, especially at the base and with age.

The **flesh** is soft and spongy, yellowish and turns brownish in the cap and stem.

■ Where and when to find it

The False Chanterelle grows in small clumps in coniferous woods, especially pine woods but can also be found under broad-leaved trees, from July through October.

■ Features and edibility

This mushroom has been falsely accused of causing some poisonings accompanied by halucinations. In fact, the False Chanterelle is perfectly edible but there are conflicting ideas as to how good it tastes. At any event, its thin flesh does have the wonderful aroma and flavor of the true Chanterelle.

Lookalike

*The **Chanterelle** (Cantharellus cibarius) (p. 202) differs from the False Chanterelle mainly in its firm, thicker white flesh and uniform color, which is a more luminous yellow.*

Jack O'Lantern

Omphalotus olearius

English synonym: Olive-tree Pleurotus
Alternative Latin name : *Clitocybe olearia*.

Classification : Cl. Homobasidiomycetes - O. Boletales - F. Paxillaceae.

● H: 2¾-6 in (7-15 cm)
● Ø: 2¼-4½ in (6-12 cm)
● White spores

Decurrent gills

Fluted stem

■ How to recognize it

Jack O'Lanterin is quite a large mushroom of the Clitocybe genus which is orange in color. The **cap** is quite thick in the center and becomes funnel-shaped while retaining its sinuous, inrolled margin. The cuticle which is normally orange may vary from pale yellow to brown or even coppery-red. It is satiny and streaked with radiating fibrils, but cracks with age, especially in dry weather.

The **gills** are thin and tightly-packed, very decurrent, and are always orange-yellow in color. They are luminous in the dark, showing up as blue-green.

The **stem** is very variable. It may be sturdy or pointed and slender. The color may be brown, yellow, or pale orange. It is very fibrous, and even tenacious and is clearly marked with vertical fluting which is an extension of the decurrent gills.

The **flesh** has a fibrous but elastic consistency and is yellow in color, tending toward saffron.

Yellow-orange underside

Jack O'Lantern

The first symptoms appear early, one or two hours after eating. There are very violent stomach pains accompanied by uncontrollable vomiting and profuse diarrhea, signs of severe gastro-enteritis. The patient then becomes very weak and breaks out in cold sweats, there is vertigo and some nervous disorders. Although these effects require hospitalization, fortunately they are short-lived.

Lookalikes

Jack O'Lantern takes on very diverse forms and so needs to be clearly recognized. It is very attractive with a superficial resemblance to a large Chanterelle and grows in thick clumps. Although it looks inviting, the mushroom-eater should always avoid it. Not only does it look like the Chanterelle it occasionally appears to be growing in the ground, when it forms smaller tufts or grows in isolation on tree roots. .

*The **Chanterelle** (Cantharellus cibarius) (p. 202) has white, firm, compact flesh. The flesh of Jack O'Lantern, on the other hand, is yellow and very fibrous.and the stem, which has clear furrows along its length is tough.*

*The **False Chanterelle** (Hygrophoropsis aurantiaca) (p. 36) has thick, forked gills and soft flesh. It is not luminescent.*

> **Lookalikes:**
> The Chanterelle *(Cantharellus cibarius)* (p. 202)
> The False Chanterelle *(Hygrophoropsis aurantiaca)* (p. 36)

◼ Where and when to find it

Jack O'Lantern normally grows in clumps on tree stumps in the Mediterranean region. Despite its name, it grows on both olive and oak. It can also parasitize tree roots and then appears to be growing atypically in the ground, in tufts or in isolation.

It is unequally distributed and is rare in the temperate zones of the northern hemisphere but more frequent in southern Europe. It appears from July through October and is often found later in warm regions.

◼ Toxicity

Jack O'Lantern may look very handsome in its orange coat, and closely resembles the Chanterelle, but it is dangerously poisonous. There is a closely related species known as The Deceiving Funnel Cap (*Omphalotus illudens*) in English-speaking countries, though in North America is it also known as Jack O'Lantern. Despite being poisonous is has a pleasant smell. Both types of Jack O'Lantern should never be eaten, or even tasted thought they are fairly common in their natural habitats.

Related species

THE DECEIVING FUNNEL CAP
⚠ *Omphalotus illudens*

Jack O'Lantern (*Omphalotus olearius*), which grows on olive trees and has as darker cap and a shorter stem is hard to distinguish from the Deceiving Funnel Cap (*Omphalotus illudens*), which grows further north on oak trees and whose stem is slender and pointed. There may, in fact, be several closely related forms of the same mushroom.

Jack O'Lantern is currently classified in the family of Paxillaceae, related to the boletes.

- ● H: 2½-6 in (7-15 cm)
- ● Ø: 2¼-4½ in (6-12 cm)
- ● White spores

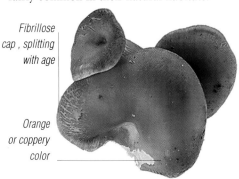

Fibrillose cap , splitting with age

Orange or coppery color

	⚠ Jack O'Lantern *Omphalotus olearius*	Chanterelle *Cantharellus cibarius*	False Chanterelle *Hygrophoropsis aurantiaca*
Cap	yellow, orange to brown	egg yellow	yellow to orange
Hymenium	thin, tightly-packed, fluorescent gills	gill-like folds, widely spaced no fluorescence	thick, forked gills no fluorescence
Stem	thick or slender, fibrous, unchanging	unequal, not fibrous,unchanging	slender, elastic, blackening
Flesh	yellow, tenacious	white compact	yellowish,soft
Habitat	wood (not always obvious)	earth, deciduous and conferous	earth, deciduous and conferous
Features	poisonous	great delicacy	quite good eating

FEATURES OF THE RUSSULALES

- Mushrooms whose flesh has a friable, chalky consistency, not fibrous as in the other groups of fungi.

Flesh friable like chalk, not fibrous

1 - Russula

- No milk oozes from the flesh when it is broken.
- Gills forked or of equal length.
- Straight, cylindrical stem (thicker than ¼ in (1 cm) in diameter.)

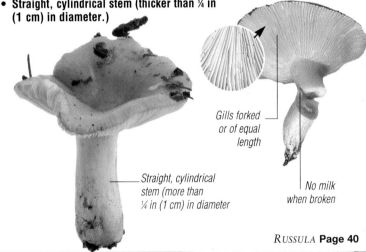

Gills forked or of equal length

Straight, cylindrical stem (more than ¼ in (1 cm) in diameter

No milk when broken

RUSSULA **Page 40**

2 - Milk cap

- Gills tapering or decurrent, not forked.
- White, watery, or colored milk (latex) oozes out when broken.

Gills tapering or decurrent, not forked

White, watery, or colored milk (latex) oozes out when broken

LACTARIUS **Page 48**

The Blackening Russula
Russula nigricans

Classification : Homobasidiomycetes -
O. Russulales - F. Russulaceae

- H: 1¾-4 in (4-10 cm)
- Ø: 2-7¼ in (5-18 cm)
- White spores

Cap marbled with grayish-black

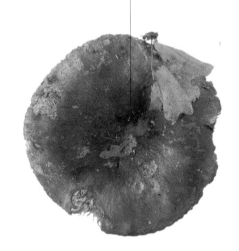

Very widely spaced gills, thick and friable

■ How to recognize it

The **cap**, is convex at first, but soon becomes depressed in the center, though it retains its inrolled margin for a long time. When it first emerges from the ground it is white, but soon becomes marbled with gray.

The **gills** are thick and widely-spaced. Gills of varying lengths are interspersed with each other, a feature which is uncommon in russulas. They are fragile, and break easily if pressed between finger and thumb. They are at first white or cream, later turning red and blackening at the touch.

The **stem** is short and thick, and is also white.

The **flesh** is firm and thick, reddening and blackening when cut. There is little or no odor but any smell will be slightly fruity.

■ Where and when to find it

The Blackening Russula grows in any type of soil and is common in late summer through fall in deciduous or coniferous woods where it propagates in groups. This russula is able to dry out without rotting and may thus persist for several weeks. Mushrooms of the genus *Nyctalis* may then develop on these decayed and dried out russulas, which will have turned completely black.

Related species

THE MANY-GILLED RUSSULA
Russula densifolia

This white-capped species is smaller than the Blackening Russula and has the same characteristic of reddening before blackening when the flesh is cut. It would be hard to distinguish it from a young Blackening Russula, if the gills were not so thin and tightly-packed. The acrid taste makes the species inedible .

- H: 2-4 in (5-10 cm)
- Ø: 1¼-4 in (3-10 cm)
- Whitish spores

THE MILK-WHITE RUSSULA
Russula delica

This Russula looks very much like a milk cap, which is why in French it is known as the Milk-free Russula. It is not very good eating. The cap reddens with age and the gills have an unusual bluish reflection.

- H: 1½-4 in (4-10 cm)
- Ø: 2-6 in (5-15 cm)
- Cream-colored spores

The Common Yellow Russula
Russula ochroleuca

Classification : Cl. Homobasidiomycetes -
O. Russulales - F. Russulaceae.

- H: 2¼-4 in (6-10 cm)
- Ø: 1½-4 in (4-10 cm)
- White spores

Cap yellow to ocher

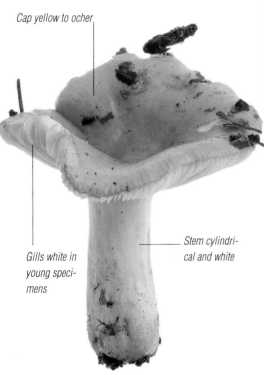

Gills white in young specimens

Stem cylindrical and white

▮ How to recognize it

The **cap** is convex at first, then flattens, becoming undulating or even slightly depressed. The cuticle is smooth and shiny, easily separable over most of the cap. At first it is a pale daffodil yellow, later turning ocher or olive with age.

The tightly-packed **gills** are sinuate or convex, adhering to the stem. They are white at first, finally turning pale yellow.

The **stem** is roughly cylindrical, thickening at the base, full then spongy, rough or striated. It is white at first, gradually turning gray.

The **flesh** is white, but yellow under the cuticle, and friable. There is little or no odor, and the flavor has varying degrees of acridity.

▮ Where and when to find it

The Common Yellow Russula is one of the commonest russulas, growing in acid or sandy soils. It grows under conifers or broad-leaved trees where it appears in large groups from late summer through fall. Having said this, its preferred habitat seems to be pinewoods growing in sandy soil.

Related species

Two other species of Russula are common but inedible and have an ocher-colored cap.

THE BITTER RUSSULA
Russula fellea

The cap, gills, and stem are uniformly ochraceous yellow. This russula emits a very strong odor of applesauce when fresh, but the taste is acrid, hence the name.

- H: 1½-2¾ in (4-7 cm)
- Ø: 1½-4 in (4-10 cm)
- Whitish spores

THE STINKING RUSSULA
Russula foetens

The cap is large and slimy, the color of honey or straw, and the margin has long furrows. The white gills ooze droplets which leave a russet-colored stain on them.

The white stem is also splashed with red. It is hollow but divided into compartments. The odor is strong and fetid and the flesh tastes acrid.

- H: 2¾-6 in (7-15 cm)
- Ø: 3¾-6 in (8-5 cm)
- Cream spores

The Beech Russula
Russula fageticola

Classification : Cl. Homobasidiomycetes -
O. Russulales - F. Russulaceae.

- H: 2¼-4 in (6-10 cm)
- Ø: 1¼-4 in (4-10 cm)
- White spores

White stem

▮ How to recognize it

The bright scarlet **cap**, which is concave at first with an inrolled margin, tends to depress in the center. The cuticle is detachable over about one third of the surface and is almost velvety.
The **gills** are tightly-packed, curved then straight, and they have a bluish or greenish reflection at first. The white **stem** is firm, of equal width or thickening at the base.

The **flesh** is tough, white, but pinker under the cuticle, and smells faintly of coconut or honey. The flavor is very acrid.

▮ Where and when to find it

The Beech Russula is a common sight in fall growing in acid soils mainly in beechwoods, though it is occasionally found under oak. Its acridity makes it inedible.

Related species

There are several closely-related species of Russula whose cap is bright red and whose flavor is acrid and it is hard to distinguish between them. The best-known is The Sickener (Russula emetica) although it occurs much less frequently than the other members of the group.

THE BLACK AND PURPLE RUSSULA
Russula krombholzii

Bright red surface more or less velvety,

Apart from its snow-white spores, this Russula is notable for its deep purple cap which is almost black in the center, and splashed with ocher. The margin is not striated and the short white stem turns gray with age. It has a faint odor of apples and it is less acrid than related species.

- H: 1¾-2½ in (4-7 cm)
- Ø: 2-4½ in (5-12 cm)
- White spores

Cap very dark in the center

THE SICKENER
⚠️ *Russula emetica*

This Russula is relatively rare because it grows in the mountains in very wet or marshy places, in the shade of conifers, especially spruce. The cap is vermillion and the margin is slightly furrowed. the gills and stem are pure white.

● H: 2-4 in (5-10 cm) ● Ø: 1¼-3¼ in (3-8 cm) ● White spores

THE FRAGILE RUSSULA
⚠️ *Russula fragilis*

This Russula, also known as the Tooth-gilled Russula has a cap that can vary in color from lilac through purple or reddish, with a darker center. It shows greenish-ocher patches when old. The margin is clearly furrowed and the gills are toothed at the edges, as can be seen through a magnifying glass. The very friable flesh has a distinctive odor. This Russula may be toxic but it any case it has an acrid flavor which makes it inedible.

● H: 1½-2¾ in (4-7 cm) ● Ø: ¾-2½ in (2-6 cm) ● White spores

The Entire Russula
Russula integra

Classification : Cl. Homobasidiomycetes - O. Russulales - F. Russulaceae.

● H: 2-4½ in (5-12 cm) ● Ø: 2-4½ in (5-12 cm)
● Yellow spores

Thick white gills turning bright yellow

Very white stem

Shiny cap varying in color

▌How to recognize it

The **cap**, which is almost globose at first, soon becomes flattened or depressed. The cuticle is shiny, varying in color, but generally brown, tinged with violet, purple, yellow, or green.
The **gills** are thick and widely-spaced, friable, white at first eventually turning bright yellow.
The **stem** is thick and white but it stains yellow or russet with age.
The white **flesh** is very firm with a mild flavor.

▌Where and when to find it

The Entire Russula often grows in large groups. It is to be found in spruce or fir forests in the mountains. It does not seem to prefer a particular soil type. In its habitat, it is very common in summer and early fall.

▌Features and edibility

This Russula is good to eat with a crunchy texture and nutty flavor, and it is all the better for rarely growing in isolation. It is particularly prized in northern Europe.

The Charcoal Burner

Russula cyanoxantha

Classification : Cl. Homobasidiomycetes -
O. Russulales - F. Russulaceae.

- H: 2-4¼ in (5-11 cm)
- Ø: 2-6 in (5-15 cm)
- Whitish spores

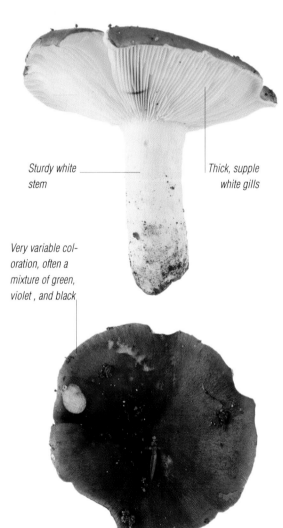

Sturdy white stem

Thick, supple white gills

Very variable coloration, often a mixture of green, violet , and black

▼ **Lookalike:**
The Death Cap *(Amanita phalloides)*
(p. 176)

▌ How to recognize it

The **cap** is large and convex to flat, firm and fleshy at first. The color of the cuticle ranges from violet to greenish, tinged with shades of blue and yellow. It develops large dark patches that are almost black, hence the name of Charcoal Burner. The cap is covered with fine radiating fibrils and may have a few russet spots. The margin is regular, appearing smooth or slightly wrinkled as the mushroom develops.

The white **gills** are very typical, thick and forked at the base, very supple, neither fragile nor friable to the touch. Their consistency is almost greasy a texture known as "lardate".

The **stem** is sturdy, firm at first, becoming hollow later, and quickly turning spongy. The white surface is faintly wrinkled.

The firm **flesh** tends to soften with age. It is white, but tinged with pink under the cuticle. It has a faintly nutty flavor and odor.

▌ Where and when to find it

The Charcoal Burner is abundant under broad-leaved trees, and sometimes under conifers, whatever the soil type. It can be found in large clumps, especially under oak, beech, and birch. This Russula is very common in the temperate zone of the northern hemisphere. It may appear as early as June but is most likely to be found in the fall.

▌ Features and edibility

The Charcoal Burner has very firm flesh, which is both crunchy and melting, with a nutty flavor. It can thus be said to be good to eat. Furthermore, it is a species which appears abundantly in some locations, so that anyone gathering it for the pot can be sure of plenty of good specimens for culinary purposes. As is the case with many species, it is best eaten young,

	Charcoal Burner and Green-Cracking Russula *Russula cyanoxantha and R. virescens*	Death Cap *Amanita phalloides*
Cap	green, gray-green, violet, variable color	white to yellow-green, yellow to brown, thick or thin
Gills	whitish	white
Stem	short, thick, not fibrous, friable, white	long, fibrous,white and slightly striped
Ring	absent	full to wide
Volva	absent	sac-like, fairly large
Flesh	friable	soft to fibrous
Habitat	deciduous or coniferous woods	deciduous or mixed woods, sometimes pines
Features	good to eat	fatal

when the mushrooms are still firm and in good condition. Older specimens become spongy and soft, and are often wormy or eaten by slugs.

Lookalike

The Death Cap (Amanita phalloides) *(p. 176)*, has both a volva and a ring on its stem, and might just be confused with the Charcoal Burner, though this is unlikely. However, vigilance is needed, especially if the stem is cut off at cap level and is not available for inspection.. If this happens, the coloration of the cap and the "lardate" consistency of the gills are a good indication that this is a Charcoal Burner.

Related species

PELTEREAU'S RUSSULA

Russula cyanoxantha var. *peltereaui*

This variety is sturdier and firmer, with slightly decurrent gills. It differs from the Charcoal Burner in its consistently green coloration – which may be washed with violet.

- H: 2-4½ in (5-12 cm)
- Ø: 2-6 in (5-15 cm)
- White spores

THE EDIBLE RUSSULA

Russula vesca

The cap of this Russula does not contain a trace of green, and tends toward reddish-brown or purple-brown. The margin is furrowed and can easily be retracted, revealing the white, forked, elastic gills, which are not lardate and are quite fragile. The white stem is sometimes washed with pink. The flesh has an agreeably nutty flavor. This mushroom is commonly found under broad-leaved trees and conifers. It appears very early in the season, often in

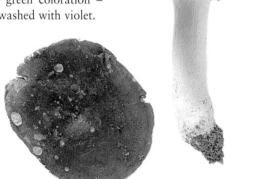

May and lasts through summer. It is good to eat.

- H: 2-4 in (5-10 cm)
- Ø: 2-4 in (5-10 cm)
- White spores

Pink or pale orange cap

GREEN-CRACKING RUSSULA

Russula virescens

The gray-green color of the cap of this fungus is very characteristic. It grows in the grass in deciduous woods, and according to the experts, it has the finest flavor of any Russula.

- H: 2-4 in (5-10 cm)
- Ø: 3¼-4½ in (8-12 cm)
- Whitish spores

THE FOXY RUSSULA

Russula mustelina

This Russula is frequently found at high altitudes, especially under spruce. The cap is reddish-brown or sepia. The gills are white then ochraceous and lardate in texture.

- H: 2½-4½ in (6-12 cm)
- Ø: 4-6 in (10-15 cm)
- Creamy spores

THE VERDIGRIS RUSSULA

⚠ *Russula aeruginea*

This Russula occurs frequently under birch or in mixed woods. The cuticle is washed with yellow-green and the gills are yellowish-white and very friable. It is suspect and is believed to cause stomach upsets.

- H: 2-3½ in (5-9 cm)
- Ø: 3¼-6 in (8-15 cm)
- Cream spores

The Beautiful Russula
Russula lepida

Alternative Latin name : *Russula rosacea.*

Classification : Cl. Homobasidiomycetes - O. Russulales - F. Russulaceae.

- H: 1½-4 in (4-10 cm)
- Ø: 1½-4½ in (4-12 cm)
- Whitish to cream pores

Surface matt and velvety, pinkish-red color

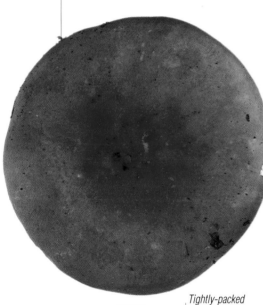

Tightly-packed white gills

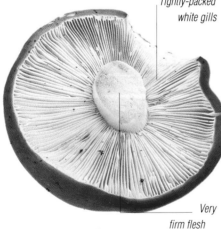

Very firm flesh

Stem white tinged with pink

■ How to recognize it

As with the other Russulas, the **cap** is convex at first, then flat and slightly depressed. The cuticle which is not separable from the flesh is velvety, bright or dull red, which may become faded and turn pink in places.

The tightly-packed **gills** are white, then cream.

The **stem** is often thicker at the base. It is white, washed with pink.

The **flesh** is extremely tough and compact. It is white, graying slightly when broken, but pink under the cuticle. The odor and flavor are distinctly minty, which makes the species barely edible. This species contains so many color variations that several varieties are recognized.

■ Where and when to find it

The Beautiful Russula is common in summer and fall, growing mainly in the leaf litter under beeches, but it can also be found under other broad-leaved trees.

Related species

TURCO'S RUSSULA
Russula turci

The cap is pinkish violet or amethyst in color with a darker circle in the center. It smells of iodine. Turco's Russula is edible, though not good; the stem should be discarded. It is common, growing exclusively under conifers.

- H: 1½-3¼ in (4-8 cm)
- Ø: 1½-4 in (4-10 cm)
- Yellow spores

The Tapering Russula
Russula sanguinea

Classification : Cl. Homobasidiomycetes -
O. Russulales - F. Russulaceae.

- H: 1¾-4 in (4-10 cm)
- Ø: 1¾-4 in (4-10 cm)
- Pale ocher spores

Tightly-packed, slightly decurrent gills

Stem often slightly tapering

...d cap, ...ing to cream

Stem tinted with the same color as the cap

▌ How to recognize it

The fleshy **cap** is convex at first then flattened but without becoming depressed. The thin margin remain inrolled for a long time. The carmine cuticle pales and may become discolored with white patches. The texture is finely granular, dry, but turning slightly sticky in the rain. The cap tends to split when old.

The **gills** are tightly-packed, rather decurrent, and colored cream to pale ocher.

The **stem** is cylindrical or slightly tapering. It is full, firm, slightly tinted with the same coloring as the cap, but turning gray when mature. It has a slight bloom and is lightly streaked.

The **flesh** is firm, white, red under the cuticle, and very thick. However, the acrid, bitter flavor makes this mushroom quite inedible.

▌ Where and when to find it

The Tapering Russula is common in summer and fall growing under conifers, but it also grows under mountain pines right up to the limit of the tree line.

Related species

THE SARDONYX RUSSULA
Russula drimeia

The Sardonyx Russula is frequent in pinewoods in sandy soil. The cap and stem range in color from lilac to dark red. The gills are bright lemon yellow. Although the odor is fruity, the flesh is very strong and acrid and for this reason it is not edible.

- H: 2-4½ in (5-12 cm)
- Ø: 1½-4 in (4-10 cm)
- Pale ocher spores

Bright yellow gills

Lilac to dark-red cap

The Blond Milk Cap
Lactarius helvus

Classification : Cl. Homobasidiomycetes -
O. Russulales - F. Russulaceae.

- H: 3½ -4½ in (8-12 cm)
- Ø: 2-6 in (5-15 cm)
- Cream-colored spores

Brownish-yellow color

Finely granulose surface

Reddish-orange stem

◼ How to recognize it

The fleshy **cap** is convex then sunken in cross-section. The cuticle is brownish-yellow, dull red, finely granulose and fluffy.

The decurrent **gills** are cream-colored in the young mushroom but darken to ocher with age. The **stem** is more or less equal or swollen at the base. It is reddish-orange, downy, or even velvety toward the bottom.

The **flesh** is pale and darker at the edge, reddening when exposed to the air. The pale milk is not abundant but has a mild flavor. It is the odor of the Blond Milk Cap which is its most striking feature. It has been compared to roast-ed chicory, though others consider it to smell like celery, and still others of bouillon cubes. The species is not edible, and may, in fact, be slightly poisonous.

◼ Where and when to find it

The Blond Milk Cap is frequent on high ground in late summer and early fall. It prefers damp ground beneath birch and spruce, thick with undergrowth such as blueberries, ferns, and heather, which indicates that the soil is ericaceous or acidic. It can also be found growing in sphagnum moss.

Related species

Other species of Milk Cap are also very common on acid soils under birch trees or confers.

RED MILK CAP
Lactarius rufus

The fibrillose, reddish-brown cup has a little umbo in the center of the depression. The cream gills redden with age, and the stem is almost the same color as the cap. When raw, it is unbearably acrid and burns the mouth in a few seconds. It is common in coniferous woods, growing in acid or siliceous soil.

- H: 2½-4½ in (6-12 cm)
- Ø: 1¼-4 in (3-10 cm)
- Spores white or pink

COCONUT-SCENTED MILK CAP
Lactarius glycyosmus

This milk cap is not very fleshy and is smaller than the other two species in this group. Like them, it is inedible. The cap is beige or greyish with a pinkish tint. The white milk is not abundant and is mild or slightly peppery. Its most typical feature is the strong smell of coconut. It is particularly common in damp beechwoods.

- H: 1¼-2½ in (3-7 cm)
- Ø: ¾-2 in (2-5 cm)
- Pale yellow spores

The Oak Milk Cap
Lactarius quietus

Classification : Cl. Homobasidiomycetes - O. Russulales - F. Russulaceae.

- H: 1½-4 in (4-10 cm)
- Ø: 1½ -4 in (4-10 cm)
- Pinkish cream spores

Russet cap

Creamy-colored milk

▮ How to recognize it

The **cap** is convex at first with an inrolled, regular margin which subsequently becomes lightly depressed and undulating. The cuticle seems to be covered with a frosty glaze; it is russet, splashed with darker patches which sometimes take the form of zones or rings.

The **gills**, are an average distance apart and slightly decurrent. They are paler than the cap but stain rusty brown when damaged.

The **stem** is the same color as the cap, but darker at the base

The **flesh** contains a creamy white, fairly copious milk which hardly changes color. The flavor is mild or slightly bitter. It smells unpleasantly of woodlice.

The species is not edible.

▮ Where and when to find it

The Oak Milk Cap does not much mind the soil type, although it seems to show some preference for acid soil. It is much more selective, however, in the type of trees with which it chooses to associate, since it only grows under oaks. It is commonly to be found in oakwoods in summer or fall.

Related species

THE YELLOW MILK CAP
⚠ *Lactarius chrysorrheus*

When exposed to the air, the milk of the Yellow Milk Cap changes in a few seconds from white to sulfur yellow. The milk is extremely acrid and the zoning of the cap which presents patches or concentric circles which are alternately light and dark are two other features which make the species recognizable.

- H: 2-4 in (5-10 cm)
- Ø: 1½ -4 in (4-8 cm)
- White spores

The Oak Milk Cap

THE BEECH MILK CAP
Lactarius subdulcis

The white milk of this species is mild at first but with a bitter aftertaste. The cap is ocher to brown in color. It grows in clumps mainly under beeches.

- H: 1¼-2¾ in (3-7 cm)
- Ø: 1¼-2½ in (3-6 cm)
- Cream spores

THE TAWNY MILK CAP
Lactarius aurantiofulvus

The cap and stem of this species are brightly colored in a uniform orange or fawn-orange. The abundant white milk does not change color but is mild at first, then bitter. It is edible but not worth eating.

- H: 2½-3¼ in (6-8 cm) ● Ø: 1¼-2½ in (3-6 cm) ● Cream spores

THE DECEPTIVE MILK CAP
Lactarius decipiens

This milk cap is indeed deceptive, since the color of the cap can vary widely, making it resemble another species, especially *Lactarius subdulcis*. The cap is usually pinkish, but it is the scent of geranium that reveals its identity. The milk turns bright yellow when removed (on the corner of a tissue, for example).

- H: 1½-3¼ in (4-8 cm)
- Ø: 1½-2¾ in (3-7 cm)
- Cream spores

The Leaden Milk Cap
Lactarius plumbeus

English synonym: The Ugly Milk Cap
Latin synonyms : *Lactarius necator, Lactarius turpis.*

Classification : Cl. Homobasidiomycetes - O. Russulales - F. Russulaceae.

- H: 2-4 cm (5-10 cm)
- Ø: 2-8 cm (5-20 cm)
- Pale cream spores

Cap graying in patches

▮ How to recognize it

The Leaden Milk Cap is firm and concave, dipping into a shallow depression, with a margin which remains inrolled for a long time. It is covered in hairs in young specimens. The slimy cuticle is dark gray-brown or olive-brown.
The **gills** are tightly packed and very slightly decurrent. The creamy color turns brown at the edges of the gills and when damaged.
The short, thick **stem** is paler than the cap.
The firm, white, compact **flesh** exudes abundant milk when broken. The milk is very acrid, white at first then turning grayish-white when drying on the gills.

The Leaden Milk Cap is not considered edible and its very ugliness would appear to be a deterrent to its edibility.

▮ Where and when to find it

The Leaden Milk Cap grows at all altitudes and is frequent in summer and fall under broad-leaved trees and conifers, though it seems to show a preference for birch growing in acid soil.

Related species

In these species, the white milk changes to grayish-green when dry, especially on the gills which become spotted with brownish-gray patches.

THE COMMON MILK CAP
Lactarius trivialis

This large species which favors damp woods of birch and conifers has a thick stem which becomes hollow and saturated with water. The cap is lilac-gray, shading to violet. It is edible, greatly in some places, less so in others.
- H: 2½-7 in (6-18 cm) ● Ø: 2½-8 in (6-20 cm) ● Pale yellow spores

SLIMY MILK CAP
Lactarius blennius

The grayish-brown cap of the Slimy Milk Cap varies in color and has small round or oval blotches of darker colors which may be arranged concentrically on the margin. It is inedible.
- H: 1½-4½ in (4-12 cm)
- Ø: 1½-4½ in (4-12 cm)
- Spores cream to pale yellow

Cap splashed with small patches of darker color

GRAY MILK CAP
Lactarius vietus

This inedible milk cap, has gray milk and a pinkish-gray cap. The gills also have a tendency to turn gray with age. It prefers saturated and marshy ground, growing mainly near pines and birch trees.
- H: 2-4 in (5-10 cm)
- Ø: 1¾-3¼ in (4-8 cm)
- Spores white to cream

The Peppery Milk Cap
Lactarius piperatus

Classification : Cl. Homobasidiomycetes -
O. Russulales - F. Russulaceae.

- H: 3½-6 in (8-15 cm)
- Ø: 2½-4½ in (6-12 cm)
- White spores

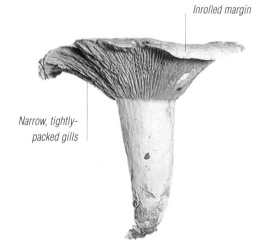

Inrolled margin

Narrow, tightly-
packed gills

▌How to recognize it

The Peppery Milk Cap is an all-white mush-room of medium size with a typically funnel-shaped cap and short, attenuating stem.
The fleshy **cap** only becomes depressed at a late stage. It is firm, even tough, and covered with a dry cuticle which splits when the weather is dry. The margin remains inrolled for a long time.
The **gills** are thin, narrow, and tightly packed, and are typically decurrent and very forked. They are white, tending to yellow with age.
The **stem** is relatively short, cylindrical, and tough, and attenuated at the base.
The **flesh** is thick, firm, and friable. When broken it exudes a whitish milk which does not change color and has a peppery flavor.

▌Where and when to find it

The Peppery Milk Cap grows in large groups usually under deciduous trees, and sometimes under conifers. It can be found throughout the temperate zone of the northern hemisphere. It fruits in summer and fall, during the high season for mushrooms.

▌Features and edibility

Despite its peppery flavor, this mushroom is gathered for food in central Europe, especially Poland and Russia. It becomes much less acrid when cooked or when dried. It is either dried under a broiler or pickled in vinegar. The crunch flesh is thus rendered acceptable.

Related species

There are many species of firm-fleshed white milk cap (*Lactarius*), which are simply known as "large white milk caps".

THE PARCHMENT MILK CAP
Lactarius pergamenus

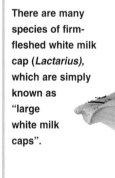

Much rarer than the Peppery Milk Cap but just as poor eating, the cap of this mushroom is rougher in texture, the gills are not decurrent and the milk is white at first, but turns slightly green as the mushroom matures.

- H: 3¼-7 in (8-18 cm)
- Ø: 2½-6 in (6-15 cm)
- White spores

THE VELVET MILK CAP
Lactarius vellereus

This common milk cap with its acrid flesh and white coloration is often con-fused with the Peppery Milk Cap. It is larger than the latter and the cap is clearly depressed with an inrolled margin. The velvety texture is also typical. The gills are thick and widely spaced. The stem is very short and thick, the flesh is tough and the sparse milk is peppery.

- H: 4-8 in (10-20 cm)
- Ø: 4-10 in (10-25 cm)
- White spores

THE PINK-GILLED MILK CAP
Lactarius controversus

The Pink-gilled Milk Cap is a handsome species, similar in size to the Peppery Milk Cap. The cap is white with pinkish zones, but it can easily be distinguished among the white milk caps for its crowded, pale-pink gills, a color not found in any other milk cap. It is fairly uncommon, frequenting damp grass under poplars or alders. It's particularly acrid flavor makes it inedible.

- H: 3¼-4½ in (8-18 cm)
- Ø: 4-8 in (10-20 cm)
- White spores

The Burning Milk Cap
Lactarius pyrogalus

Alternative Latin name : *Lactarius hortensis*.

Classification : Cl. Homobasidiomycetes - O. Russulales - F. Russulaceae.

- H: 2½-4½ in (6-12 cm)
- Ø: 2-4 in (5-10 cm)
- Ocher spores

Grayish-beige-cap

Milk white turning yellowish-olive

is grayish, shaded with beige, ranging from ocher to greenish and rather viscous. It may have concentric rings.

The **gills**, are slightly decurrent and quite widely spaced. They are cream at first, then changing quite rapidly to luminous ocher-orange.

The cylindrical **stem** ends in a point at the base. It is white to grayish and has a smooth or slightly striated surface. The white **flesh** develops a fruity odor which does not persist. On the other hand, the flavor, especially of the milk, has a very peppery taste which persists for a long time; this milk is white and copious and turns yellowish-olive as it dries.

This species is obviously inedible.

■ Where and when to find it

The Burning Milk Cap forms groups of various sizes in groves of hazelnuts, and more rarely under other broad-leaved trees. It is quite common from late summer onward.

■ How to recognize it

The **cap** soon becomes funnel-shaped with a thin, sinuate, almost lobed, margin. The cuticle

The Saffron Milk Cap
Lactarius deliciosus

Classification : Cl. Homobasidiomycetes -
O. Russulales - F. Russulaceae.

- H: 1½-4 in (4-10 cm)
- Ø: 2-4½ in (5-12 cm)
- Whitish spores with pink highlights

Decurrent, orange gills, stained with green

Little orange pits

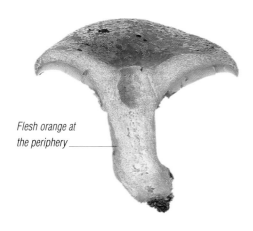

Flesh orange at the periphery

▼ **Lookalike:**
The Wooly Milk Cap
(Lactarius torminosus) (p. 56)

▐ How to recognize it

The fleshy **cap** is of average size, convex at first, then flattening and opening into a wide funnel. The cuticle has concentric rings of darker patches against the bright orange background. The margin is overhanging, but flattens out with age.

The orange **gills** are crowded and fragile, decurrent and forked at the base. They gradually show spotting and patches of green.

The **stem** is generally short and sturdy, attenuating at the base. It becomes hollow and soft quite quickly. The upper part is covered with a whitish down and at the bottom it is pitted with bright orange crevices against an orange background.

The **flesh**, ranges from white to pale orange and is firm and friable. Almost as soon as it is broken, it reveals a bright orange milk which darkens on contact with the air. It eventually turns green, which accounts for the green patches on the gills and elsewhere, especially if the mushroom is damaged.

▐ Where and when to find it

The Saffron Milk Cap grows in moss and on humus in coniferous forests, especially under pine trees. It prefers calcareous or siliceous soil. It is a common species, growing in large groups throughout the temperate zone in summer and fall, and even as late as the start of winter.

In some places, such as Catalonia, the Saffron Milk Cap is considered a great delicacy.

▐ Features and edibility

Not everyone considers this milk cap to be delicious, despite its Latin epithet. Many find its reputation to be exaggerated, and prefer the Bleeding Milk Cap. As a matter of fact, the epithet is due to an error. G. Becker relates that his mentor, the great taxonomist, Linnaeus, so named it because he had confused it with the Bleeding Milk Cap. This sort of confusion with its close relatives that favor larch woods may well explain the great variations in assessing its eating qualities.

This handsome mushroom is always sought after for its thick, friable, firm flesh when it is young. When older, it softens and the greenish appearance is not particularly appetizing. It grows in abundance and may be found in markets in some countries. Some restaurateurs appreciate its herby, spicy flavor which can be incorporated in a large range of dishes. It should not be cooked for too long; a good way to prepare it is to broil it quickly, for instance. It should be noted that eating the Saffron Milk Cap turns the urine red, but this has no negative effect and does not indicate that the mushroom is poisonous.

Lookalike

The Wooly Milk Cap (Lactarius torminosus) *(p. 56), is also orange but with a dinstinctively fleecy cap. It grows mainly under deciduous trees and has a very acrid, white milk. It is a violent purgative.*

There are several species of milk caps whose milk is red, which are closely related to the Saffron Milk Cap, whose eating qualities are very variable

THE SPRUCE MILK CAP
Lactarius deterrimus

The Spruce Milk Cap is quite commonly found in spruce undergrowth, especially in the mountains. Its beautiful orange color darkens almost completely to green with age. The stem is slightly pock-marked and ringed with white just under the gills.

The milk is orange at first but soon darkens and finally turns green. The taste is bitter and for that reason this mushroom is inedible.
- H: 2-4 in (5-10 cm)
- Ø: 2-4½ in (4-12 cm)
- Pale ocher spores

THE BLEEDING MILK CAP
Lactarius sanguifluus

This milk cap grows in southern Europe in pine forests. The cap is far less orange and darker than in the previous species, being gray-ish-ocher shaded with pur-plish-russet. It only turns slightly green, and does so in stages. The flesh is russet to vinous red and it exudes a little blood-red milk when broken. The Bleeding Milk Cap may have a deceptive appearance, since it is very good to eat and even considered to be the best milk cap, tastier than the Saffron Milk Cap. It is best broiled, then generously sprin-kled with parsley.
- H: 2-4 in (5-10 cm)
- Ø: 2-4½ in (5-12 cm)
- White spores

*Cap duller
in color with ochraceous-gray patches*

THE SALMON-COLORED MILK CAP
Lactarius salmonicolor

The Salmon-colored Milk Cap is larger than the Saffron Milk Cap and its gills are typically salmon-colored. The orange milk tinted with salmon pink, hardly changes color at all, another typical fea-ture. Despite its resinous flavor, this Milk Cap, which grows under mountain fir trees, is not

inedible and is some-times eaten.
- H: 2¾-5 in (7-13 cm)
- Ø: 3¼-6 in (8-15 cm)
- Pale ocher spores

Salmon-colored gills

	Saffron Milk Cap *Lactarius deliciosus*	Bleeding Milk Cap *Lactarius sanguifluus*	Spruce Milk Cap *Lactarius deterrimus*	Salmon-colored Milk Cap *Lactarius salmonicolor*	Wooly Milk Cap *Lactarius torminosus*
Cap	bright orange, zoned	ochraceous to purplish, patchy	orange, then green, zoned	bright orange, zoned	pink to reddish-orange, wooly
Gills	orange	dull orange	orange, then green	salmon-pink to orange	pinkish-cream
Stem	orange	ochraceous	orange	salmon-pink to orange	pinkish-cream
Milk	bright orange, then green	dark red, then greenish	orange, then green	orange, unchanging	white unchanging
Habitat	pine trees	pine trees	spruce plantations	fir trees	deciduous and coniferous trees
Edibility	good to eat	excellent eating	not worth eating	not worth eating	purgative

The Wooly Milk Cap

Lactarius torminosus

Classification : Cl. Homobasidiomycetes -
O. Russulales - F. Russulaceae.

- H: 2-4 in (5-10 cm)
- Ø: 2-4 in (5-10 cm)
- Cream or pink-tinged spores

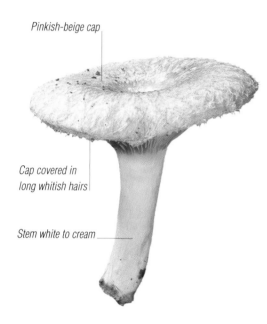

Pinkish-beige cap

Cap covered in
long whitish hairs

Stem white to cream

crowded. They are cream in color with dark red highlights. Little droplets of milk adorn their edges.

The **stem** is cylindrical, attenuate toward the base, at first full and firm but soon becoming hollow. The surface is lightly colored pinkish cream, and is covered in a fine down.

The **flesh** is white to cream, thick and friable. When broken, it exudes a white milk, which does not change color and is very acrid and bitter. The odor is slightly fruity.

▮ Where and when to find it

The Wooly Milk Cap grows mostly under-broad-leaved trees. It particularly favors well-lit birch woods and the grassy verges around them. It can also be found in mixed woods, and even under conifers in mountainous regions. It usually fruits in summer and fall.

▮ Toxicity

The bitterness and acridity of the Wooly Milk Cap make it inedible. It contains particularly acrid constituents which are very irritant and could cause serious stomach upsets. That is why the Latin epithet means the Tormenting Milk Cap.

How to recognize it

The flesh-colored Wooly Milk Cap is of average size with a thick wooly coating on the cap. The **cap** is fleshy and soon becomes depressed inthe center, while the margin which is very inrolled at the beginning, remains overhanging. The mushroom is covered with a whitish fleece. The cuticle is covered with concentric circles of darker, reddish, color on a background color ranging from carmine to orange. The decurrent **gills** are narrow, straight, and

Lookalikes

It is important to avoid confusion with the edible milk caps whose milk is red and whose odor which is generally sweet, including:

*The **Saffron Milk Cap** (Lactarius deliciosus) (p. 54), whose milk is carrot-colored, slowly turns green in contact with the air.*

*The **Bleeding Milk Cap** (Lactarius sanguifluus) (p. 55), is not as bright in color and its milk is dark red at first.*

▼ Lookalikes:

Saffron Milk Cap *(Lactarius deliciosus)* (p. 54)
The Bleeding Milk Cap *(Lactarius sanguifluus)* (p. 55)

	Wooly Milk Cap *Lactarius torminosus*	Saffron Milk Cap *Lactarius deliciosus*
Cap	pink to russet-orange, fleecy	bright orange, glabrous
Gills	pinkish cream	orange
Stem	pinkish cream	orange
Milk	white, unchanging	bright orange, drying to green
Habitat	deciduous trees, conifers	conifers
Features	poisonous	good to eat

The Curry-scented Milk Cap
Lactarius camphoratus

Classification : Cl. Homobasidiomycetes -
O. Russulales - F. Russulaceae.

- H: 4¼-3¼ in (4-8 cm)
- Ø: 1¼-2½ in (3-6 cm)
- Whitish or cream spores

*Reddish cap
darker in the center*

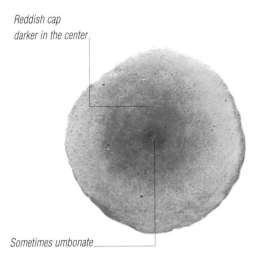

Sometimes umbonate

*Pale gills
later turning red*

▌ How to recognize it

The **cap** of this little milk cap soon becomes
hollow. Sometimes it has a central umbo. The
margin is often lightly furrowed. The matt, dry
cuticle is reddish to reddish-brown and uniform, except in the center which is darker.

The **gills** are quite crowded and slightly decurrent. At first they are pale red, later turning
reddish-brown.

The **stem** is fairly slender, soon becoming hollow. It is the same color as the cap but the base
tends to be darker.

The **flesh**, which is carmine to wine-red in
color, contains a whitish or off-white milk, and
has a sweet taste that later turns slightly bitter.
The odor is strong and distinctive. Some claim
this mushroom smells of camphor when fresh,
but some authorities claim the smell is of
woodlice. When dry, the smell changes to that
of ground chicory or of curry leaf.

At any event, the odors are not particularly
attractive and they affect the flesh, making it a
mushroom of little culinary interest.

▌ Where and when to find it

The Curry-scented Milk Cap is frequent in
summer and fall, and can be found under
deciduous trees (especially oaks and chestnuts)
or under conifers, on condition that the soil is
acidic and well-drained.

It is found growing both in the ground and on
moss-covered stumps and logs.

1 - Hygrophorus

- Thick, widely-spaced gills with the consistency of beeswax.
- Cap often humid or viscous.

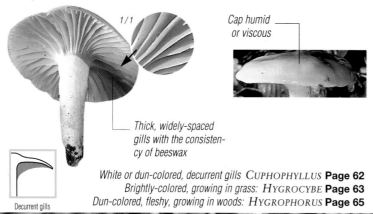

1 / 1

Cap humid or viscous

Thick, widely-spaced gills with the consistency of beeswax

Decurrent gills

White or dun-colored, decurrent gills CUPHOPHYLLUS **Page 62**
Brightly-colored, growing in grass: HYGROCYBE **Page 63**
Dun-colored, fleshy, growing in woods: HYGROPHORUS **Page 65**

2 - Pleurotacea

- Stem absent, lateral or excentric.
- Mushroom grows on wood *(except for Pleurotus eryngii)*.

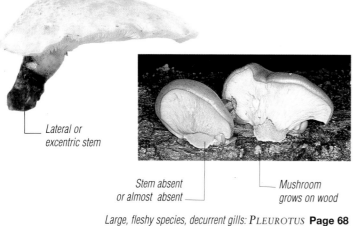

Lateral or excentric stem

Stem absent or almost absent

Mushroom grows on wood

Large, fleshy species, decurrent gills: PLEUROTUS **Page 68**
Lateral or absent stem : PANELLUS **Page 69**
Dentate gills: LENTINELLUS **Page 70**
Stem more or less central, flesh more or less leathery: LENTINUS **Page 70**

3 - Omphalia - Clitocybe: the Funnel Cap

- Species have very small, funnel-shaped caps and long, slender stems.

- Decurrent gills.

- Thin, decurrent gills.
- Species more or less fleshy, often with funnel-shaped cap.

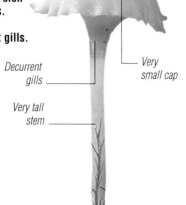

Decurrent gills

Very small cap

Very tall stem

Thin, decurrent gills

Species more or less fleshy, often with funnel-shaped cap

Decurrent gills

RICKENELLA, OMPHALINA, GERRONEMA **Page 71**

CLITOCYBE **Page 72**

FEATURES OF THE TRICHOLOMATALES

- Flesh has fibrous texture.
- Gills attached to stem (not free), decurrent, sinuate, or adnate.
- Gills white, pale, or yellow (except *Laccaria*).
- Absence of volva or ring (except *Oudemansiella*, *Armillaria* and *Tricholoma cingulatum*).
- Stem and cap not separable.

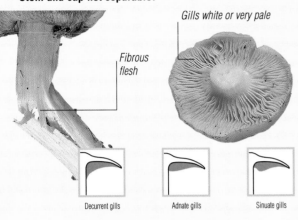

Gills white or very pale

Fibrous flesh

Decurrent gills

Adnate gills

Sinuate gills

4 - Armillaria

- Cap more or less scaly, honey-colored to brown.
- Species growing in clumps on wood or tree roots.

Cap more or less scaly, ranging from honey-colored to brown

Presence of a ring (except A. tabescens)

Species growing in clumps on wood or tree roots

ARMILLARIA **Page 76**

5 - Lepista

- Fleshy species.
- Gills sometimes separable from the flesh.

Gills sometimes separable from the flesh

LEPISTA **Page 78**

6 - Laccaria

- Gills thick and widely-spaced, protruding and wide.

Gills thick and widely-spaced

Gills protruding and wide

LACCARIA **Page 82**

7 - Tricholomopsis

- Bright yellow, denticulate gills.
- Mushrooms growing on wood.

Bright yellow, denticulate gills

Mushrooms growing on wood

TRICHOLOMOPSIS **Page 84**

8 - Tricholoma

- Fleshy species, growing on the ground.
- Sinuate gills.

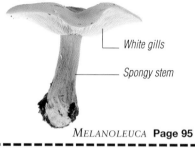

Sinuate gills

Sinuate gills

Growing on the ground

TRICHOLOMA **Page 85**

- Very white gills.
- Spongy and fibrous stem.

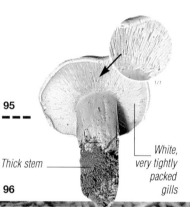

White gills

Spongy stem

MELANOLEUCA **Page 95**

- White, tightly-packed gills.
- Thick stem. Odor of flour.

CALOCYBE **Page 96**

Thick stem

White, very tightly packed gills

9 - Leucopaxillus

- Fleshy species, growing in the ground.
- Decurrent gills, detachable from the cap.

Decurrent gills, detachable from the cap

Fleshy species, growing in the ground

Decurrent gills

LEUCOPAXILLUS **Page 94**

10 - Nyctalis

- Small mushroom which grows on other dessicated or rotting mushrooms.

Small mushroom which grows on other dessicated or rotting mushrooms

NYCTALIS **Page 97**

11 - Flammulina

- Viscous, orange cap, mushroom grows on wood.
- Velvety stem, embedded in the wood.
- Brown gills.

Viscous, orange cap

Velvety stem embedded in the wood

Mushroom grows on wood

FLAMMULINA **Page 98**

12 - Cystoderma

- Armilla (ring) same color as the cap.

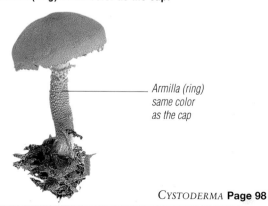

Armilla (ring) same color as the cap

CYSTODERMA **Page 98**

FEATURES OF THE TRICHOLOMATALES
(CONTINUED)

14 - Collybia

- Striated cap.
- Mycelial cords.
- Very wide gills.

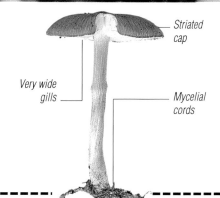

Striated cap

Very wide gills

Mycelial cords

MEGACOLLYBIA **Page 102**

- Viscous or shaggy cap.
- Rooting stem.

Viscous or shaggy cap

Rooting stem

OUDEMANSIELLA **Page 102**

- Cartilaginous or elastic flesh.
- Cap flattened and smooth, flesh thin.
- Tightly packed, adnate gills.

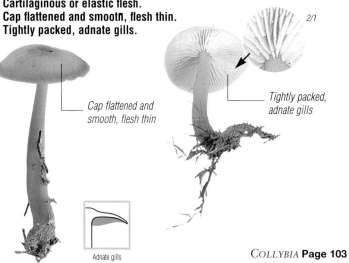

2/1

Cap flattened and smooth, flesh thin

Tightly packed, adnate gills

Adnate gills

COLLYBIA **Page 103**

13 - Marasmius

- Small or medium-sized species which are not fleshy and which do not rot.
- Stem thin but coriaceous.

Them thin but coriaceous

MARASMIUS **Page 99**

- Species growing on conifer cones.

Growing on conifer cones

BAEOSPORA - STROBILURUS **Page 100**

- Very small mushrooms with long-lasting flesh, growing on branches or twigs.

Growing on branches or twigs

MARASMIELLUS **Page 101**

15 - Mycena

- Small mushroom.
- Cap striated, hemispherical, conical, or bell-shaped.
- Stem narrow, tubular, and friable.

Cap striated, hemispherical conical, or bell-shaped

Striated cap

Stem, narrow, tubular and friable

MYCENA **Page 107**

The Meadow Wax Cap

Cuphophyllus pratensis

Latin synonyms: *Hygrophorus pratensis,*
Camarophyllus pratensis.

Classification : Cl. Homobasidiomycetes -
O. Tricholomatales - F. Hygrophoraceae.

- H: 1½-3¼ in (4-8 cm)
- Ø: 1½-3¼ in (4-8 cm)
- White spores

*Gills widely spaced
and decurrent*

*Stem short,
tapering toward
the base*

▮ How to recognize it

The Meadow Wax Cap is small to medium in
size with a **cap** which is rounded or conical at
first, but which soon expands, retaining a clear
central umbo. The thickening in the center
gives it the shape of a spinning top. ,The cuticle is dry. fawn to pale russet, tending toward
yellow or orange. The thin, toothed margin
becomes wavy with age.

The **gills** are bow-shaped at first and widely-
spaced. They are wide, thick and decurrent.
The spaces between them are filled with tiny
gill-shaped excrescences of the same color,
cream when young, ochraceous yellow when
the mushroom matures.

The **stem** is generally quite short, though sometimes tall, cylindrical, curved and tapering at
the base. It is full and firm, whitish in color,
and streaked with fine long fibrils shaded the
same color as the cap.

The **flesh** is thick and firm, friable and with a
pleasant flavor and odor.

▮ Where and when to find it

The Meadow Wax Cap grows in grassland,
pasture, along paths and even in well-lit
woods, where it is often hard to find due to its
small size. It can be found throughout the temperate zone of the northern hemisphere, especially on mountains, such as the Alps.

Although it has a wide growing range, it is not
always very common because suitable habitats
are very localized. The mushroom appears
quite late in the season, like most of the wax
caps, preferring the cool rains of the fall to the
heat of late summer.

▮ Features and edibility

The Meadow Wax Cap is a delicious mushroom with aromatic, mild-flavored, delicate
flesh. It is one of the best-tasting wax caps, all
the more so because the cap is in no way slimy
or sticky. Unfortunately, it does not grow in
abundance.

Related species

THE SNOW-WHITE WAX CAP
Cuphophyllus niveus

This is another edible wax cap
which favors grassland. It is
white all over, sometimes slightly
tinted with ocher.

- H: 1½-3¼ in (4-8 cm)
- Ø: ½-1½ in (1-4 cm)
- White spores

Crimson Wax Cap

Hygrocybe punicea

Latin name : *Hygrophorus puniceus.*

Classification : Cl. Homobasidiomycetes -
O. Tricholomatales - F. Hygrophoraceae.

- H: 3¼-4½ in (8-14 cm)
- Ø: 2¾-4½ in (7-12 cm)
- White spores

red conical cap

Waxy yellow gills

Stem yellow
to orange

▮ How to recognize it

The **cap** of the Crimson Wax Cap is conical but flat-topped at first, later expanding into an irregular shape with a slightly umbonate top. The cuticle is viscous and shiny in wet weather and is a brilliant red in color, varying from scarlet to crimson lake.

The color fades in dry weather or with age and becomes orange, then yellow. The thin, fragile margin tears and soon splits the cap.

The **gills** are widely spaced, thick, and swollen alternating with short gill-like excrescences, and they have the typical waxy consistency. The color varies from pale yellow to orange, sometimes tinged with crimson.

The **stem** may be sturdy, almost swollen, or slender, curving or twisted, and it is often fibrillose. It soon becomes hollow and it is then very fragile. It is a similar red or yellow color to the cap but not as bright, except at the base, which always remains white.

The **flesh**, is white or red-tinted and not very thick, almost inconsistent, very fragile and almost odorless and insipid.

▮ Where and when to find it

The Crimson Wax Cap grows exclusively in grassland and pastures, especially at high altitudes.

It is found throughout the European mountain ranges, sometimes growing in little colonies. It appears in the fall.

▮ Features and edibility

The Crimson Wax Cap has a high reputation as an edible mushroom which is rather exaggerated since it has neither a particularly interesting odor nor flavor. It tastes best when smothered with chopped parsley which will help to bring out the flavor.

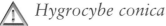
Several brightly-colored species of wax cap, all of them quite small in size, are related to the Crimson Wax Cap. All of them inhabit grassland and meadows and appear in summer and fall.

THE CONICAL WAX CAP
⚠ *Hygrocybe conica*

The Conical Wax Cap has a typical cap in the shape of a Chinese coolie hat. It is fragile with thin flesh, and is orange-yellow in color, blackening in large patches with age. The striated margin is often split, sometimes into deep lobes. The gills are thick and widely-spaced, white at first then yellowing. They also tend to blacken in old specimens. The stem is striped and soon becomes hollow. It is lemon yellow. It peels into strips and turns black like the flesh, though it is whitish at first. This wax cap is considered to be suspect.
- H: 1¼-2¾ in (3-7 cm)
- Ø: 1¼-2 in (3-5 cm)
- White spores

LEMON HYGROCYBE
Hygrocybe chlorophana

The Lemon Hygrocybe is not worth eating, as it is a small mushroom with a slimy cap. The cap is convex at first then flattened and even depressed. The color ranges from golden to lemon yellow. The whitish gills, are tinged with yellow. The tall, slender stem is also viscous and has similar coloring to the cap. The flesh which is whitish to pale yellow, is very fragile.
- H: 1½-2¾ in (4-7 cm)
- Ø: 1¼-2½ in (3-6 cm)
- White spores

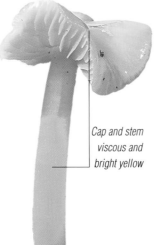

Cap and stem viscous and bright yellow

THE PARROT WAX CAP
Hygrocybe psittacina

This attractive little species is of no culinary interest but its brilliant colors are reminiscent of the plumage of a gaudy parrot.
The cap is campanulate, then extended and umbonate. At first it is slimy, shiny and bright green. It later adds patches of yellow and red. The gills are greenish-yellow in color. The tall thin stem is very fragile and, like the flesh, it has the same colors as the cap.
- H: 2-2¾ in (5-7 cm)
- Ø: ¾ -1¼ in (2-4 cm)
- white spores

Two other mushrooms are also bright, turning paler or yellowing with age, and it is hard to distinguish between them.

THE SCARLET WAX CAP
Hygrocybe coccinea

Bright red all over, except for the base of the stem where it is yellow, fading to yellow with age. It grows in clusters in upland pastures.
- H: 2-3¼ in (5-8 cm)
- Ø: ¾-2½ in (2-6 cm)
- White spores

Red cap

Stem yellow to red

THE VERMILLION WAX CAP
Hygrocybe miniata

The Vermillion Wax Cap is smaller than the other three wax caps on this page. The cap is covered in fine scales with flesh of a deeper orange color.
- H: ¾-2 in (2-5 cm)
- Ø: ½-1¼ in (1-3 cm)
- White spores

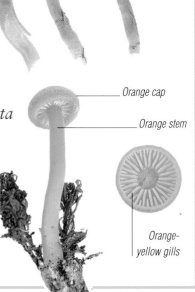

Orange cap

Orange stem

Orange-yellow gills

The March Wax Cap

Hygrophorus marzuolus

Classification : Cl. Homobasidiomycetes -
O. Tricholomatales - F. Hygrophoraceae.

● H: 1½-3¼ in (4-8 cm)
● Ø: 2½-6 in (6-15 cm)
● White spores

ick,
ay, irregular cap

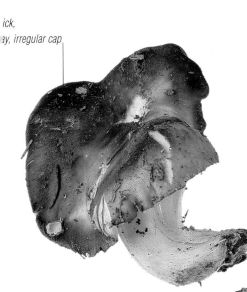

Sturdy white stem, turning gray

Gills white, turning gray

▌ How to recognize it

The **cap** of this large mushroom is thick and fleshy. It is convex at first, but soon extends and becomes irregular in shape with an uneven surface, slightly umbonate, but eventually depressed. The cuticle is smooth and matt, and may be damp or dry but is never slimy or sticky. Young specimens may be entirely white, but soon become splashed with gray, and the color gradually intensifies until it darkens to the color of slate or anthracite, and finally almost becomes black. The margin is lighter, inrolled in young specimens but flattening and even raised, finally taking on quite an unusual irregular shape .
The **gills** of the March Wax Cap are white, becoming tinted gray or slate-colored. They are typically thick, crowded at first and slightly curved, then spaced out, but never very decurrent.
The white **stem**, is short and thick at first but later elongates. It turns grayish from the base upward as the mushroom ages.
It is often curved toward the bottom, and is full and firm, striped with lengthwise fibrils and downy on the upper part.
The white **flesh** of the March Wax Cap is tender and compact, graying lightly under cuticle, firmer and more fibrous in the stem. The odor is faint but pleasant and the flavor is mild.

▌ Where and when to find it

The March Wax Cap prefers to live under fir trees, growing on mountains in siliceous soil. It can also be found in pine forests and growing among Norway spruce and mixed forests of fir and beech. As its name indicates, the March Wax Cap appears very early in groups, sometimes emerging just after the last snows have melted. It should thus be looked for after the first thaw marking the end of winter or early in the spring.
Although it is common in certain locations and of quite a respectable size, the March Wax Cap is not always easy to find.
That is because it develops under a carpet of moss or in thick leaf litter under which it may remain buried and it may not emerge until it is fully mature. For this reason it is not as well known as it deserves to be.

▌ Features and edibility

The March Wax Cap is considered to make very good eating. It is even sold in some markets, especially in Switzerland, where it is highly esteemed. However, certain mycologists consider its reputation to be exaggerated as the flesh is rather insipid in flavor. Its detractors even claim that it is merely the early appearance of this mushroom that makes it an attractive proposition as a food. Whatever the truth, the March Wax Cap certainly deserves to be tasted.

The Scented Wax Cap
Hygrophorus agathosmus

Classification : Cl. Homobasidiomycetes -
O. Tricholomatales - F. Hygrophoraceae.

- H: 2½-4¼ in (6-11 cm)
- Ø: 2-4 in (5-10 cm)
- White spores

Viscous gray cap

Stem farinaceous at the top

Gills white, thick and widely spaced

▌ How to recognize it

The **cap**, which is convex at first and very regular, later flattens, retaining an umbo which
may or may not be obvious. It is covered with
a thick slime. The whitish-gray or ashen cuticle
is darker in the center, is covered in viscous
papilla. The margin, which is slightly upturned
in young specimens, flattens out later.
The **gills** are thick, white and widely spaced.
They are quite sharply curved and are decurrent down the stem.
The **stem** is quite tall and often sinuate is
surprisingly firm and dry. It is white, and is
mealy in the upper part. The mealy flecks
darken with age.
The **flesh** is white and thick, graying under
the cuticle. The flavor is mild but the most
distinctive feature this mushroom is its
strong odor of bitter almonds or amaretto.

▌ Where and when to find it

The Scented Wax Cap is found frequently in coniferous woods, especially at high
altitudes under larch, often along pathways, growing from moss or needle litter.
It grows in clusters in late summer but it
more often found in the fall, often quite
late in the year. Its thick coating of slime
helps protect it from the first night
frosts.

▌ Features and edibility

Thanks to its strong smell of bitter
almonds, this wax cap can only be used
as a flavoring. It helps bring out the flavor of other mushrooms or of white
meats. But under no circumstances could
it be eaten on its own.

Related species

THE RUSSULA WAX CAP
Hygrophorus russula

**The genus Hygrophorus
consists of numerous
species, some of which,
are quite highly-prized
edible mushrooms.**

This fleshy edible wax cap is
soon stained with patches of dark
crimson. It differs from the others by
virtue of its crowded gills. It is found on
calcareous soils under deciduous trees.

- H: 2-4½ in (5-12 cm)
- Ø: 3¼-6 in (8-15 cm)
- White spores

IVORY WAX CAP
Hygrophorus eburneus

This all-white species whose stem and cap are viscous is inedible. The smooth stem is speckled with tiny flakes under the gills. It grows in deciduous woods and has a pleasant fruity odor.

- H: 2½-4½ in (6-12 cm)
- Ø: 1½-4 in (4-10 cm) ● White spores

WAX CAP OF THE WOODS

Hygrophorus nemoreus

This species has an ocher or fawn cap covered with radial fibrils. Despite the mealy odor, it is good to eat. It is found in calcareous soils in broad-leaved woods.

- H: 1½ -3¼ in (4-8 cm)
- Ø: 2½ -6 in (6-15 cm)
- White spores

STINKING WAX CAP
Hygrophorus cossus

Similar to the Ivory Wax Cap, and sharing the same habitat, this mushroom is recognizable by its unpleasant odor which is said to smell like boiling shellfish.

- H: 2-4 in (5-10 cm)
- Ø: 1¼-3¼ in (3-8 cm)
- White spores

YELLOW-GILLED WAX CAP
Hygrophorus hypothejus

This wax cap has a white annular zone at the top of the stem, and the gills are orange-yellow. It is commonly found under conifers, and only fruits after the first frosts.

- H: 2½-4 in (6-10 cm)
- Ø: 1¼ -2¾ in (3-7 cm)
- White spores

OLIVE WAX CAP
Hygrophorus olivaceoalbus

This wax cap has an olive brown umbonate cap and a stem covered in yellow-brown striations, except at the top which is white.

It is fairly common under larches.

- H: 3¼-6 in (8-15 cm)
- Ø: 1¼-2¾ (3-7 cm) ● White spores

FAWN WAX CAP

Hygrophorus penarius

This is another large, fleshy species with a white or pale beige cap. Neither cap nor stem are slimy. It is very good to eat. It can be found on calcareous soils in deciduous woods.

- H: 2¾-4 in (7-10 cm)
- Ø: 2½-4½ in (6-12 cm)
- White spores

The Oyster Mushroom

Pleurotus ostreatus

Classification : Cl. Homobasidiomycetes -
O. Tricholomatales - F. Pleurotaceae.

- H: ¾-4 in (2-10 cm)
- Ø: 1½-6 in (4-15 cm) (sometimes more)
- Very pale, lilac gray, almost white spores

Grows in a compact clump

Smooth cap

Sinuate margin

Crowded, ivory gills

Stem very short or absent

How to recognize it

The **cap** is generally quite large, and is indicated by the variability of its colors. It may be black or white, violet-gray or yellowish. It is fairly fleshy, convex at first, but rapidly flattening and eventually adopting its definitive, shell-like shape. The cuticle is smooth and shiny. The sinuous margin remains inrolled for a long time.

The **gills** are swollen, decurrent, and are a typical ivory color.

The lateral **stem** is rudimentary or absent. When present, it is a thick, firm appendage, covered in white hairs.

The thick, white **flesh**, is tender at first and becomes elastic as the mushroom matures. It has a mild flavor and delicate fragrance which disappears with age or becomes unpleasant.

Where and when to find it

The Oyster Mushroom grows on wood and should be sought in coppices and damp woods. It grows in large, compact tufts, on tree stumps and logs, and on various broad-leaved fallen trees. The Oyster Mushroom grows all over the world and is fairly common, usually from fall to late winter. However, it can also be found at other times of the year in its favored habitat, in climates where the mushroom season does not occur in the fall.

Features and edibility

If harvested when young, the Oyster Mushroom is very good to eat and is popular throughout the world, especially in China, for its tender texture and delicate flavor. Older examples should be ignored or discarded. The flesh will be too tough and the flavor and odor will be slightly acrid.

The Branded Oyster Mushroom and the Eryngo Pleurotus are also highly prized and the same criteria apply to them, as regards age. Furthermore, older specimens are likely to be worm-eaten. The tough, leathery stem should always be trimmed away before cooking.

Cultivation

The Oyster Mushroom has been cultivated since the 1970s on an artificial substrate consisting of vegetable debris of various kinds such as straw from cereal crops, wood shavings, sawdust, etc. The mushroom is cultivated all over the world. In France, for instance, after a period of strong growth, production seems to have stagnated at 3,000 tons a year. This is because, despite its early promise, the oyster mushroom does not appear to have the important place in the kitchen as, say, the store mushroom or the Portobello mushroom in the United States, both cultivated varieties of the Field Mushroom.

Members of the Pleurotus genus have an excentric or lateral stem and decurrent gills. The Oyster Mushroom, the Eryngo Pleurotus, and the Branded Oyster Mushroom are all delicious, edible mushrooms.

BRANCHED OYSTER MUSHROOM
Pleurotus cornucopiae

Very pale cap

Deeply decurrent gills, anastomosed at the base

The Branched Oyster mushroom has a cape of average size which is cone-shaped or funnel-shaped and typically pale in color, ranging from whitish to pinkish-beige. The cuticle is downy at first, then smooth and becomes shiny in damp weather. The gills are thin and skin-colored and taper into an anastomosed reticulation which persists to the base of the stem. The flesh is white and tender when young, but later becomes fibrous, especially in the stem. The odor is complex, predominantly mealy, and rather unpleasant in old speci-mens. The Branched Oyster Mushroom is fairly common, growing in large, tightly-packed tufts welded together at the base of the dead trunks of deciduous trees in spring and summer. It may also appear on damaged, living trees.

- H: ¾-4 in (2-10 cm)
- Ø: 1½-4½ in (4-12 cm)
- Pale lilac spores

ERYNGO PLEUROTUS
Pleurotus eryngii

This mushroom appears to be terrestrial but is in fact growing in association with the roots of umbelliferous plants, especially Eryngo and the maritime cardoon, near the sea. It can be found on sparse grassland from spring through fall.

- H: 1¼-3¼ in (3-8 cm)
- Ø: 1½-4½ in (4-12 cm)
- Whitish spores

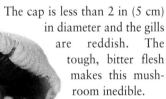

STYPTIC MUSHROOM
Panellus stipticus

The cap is less than 2 in (5 cm) in diameter and the gills are reddish. The tough, bitter flesh makes this mushroom inedible.

- H: ½-1½ in (1-4 cm)
- Ø: ½-1½ in (1-4 cm)
- whitish spores

VEILED OYSTER MUSHROOM
Pleurotus dryinus

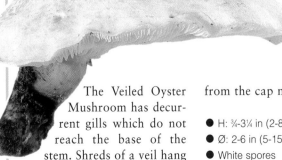

The Veiled Oyster Mushroom has decurrent gills which do not reach the base of the stem. Shreds of a veil hang from the cap margin.

- H: ¾-3¼ in (2-8 cm)
- Ø: 2-6 in (5-15 cm)
- White spores

THE WINTER PANELLUS
Panellus serotinus

The Winter Panellus is larger than the Styptic Mushroom and greenish or yellow-green in color. The tightly-packed gills are whitish and the short, thick stem is scaly.

- H: ¾-2 in (2-5 cm)
- Ø: 1¼-4½ in (3-12 cm)
- White spores

The Spiral Lentinus
Lentinellus cochleatus

Classification : Cl. Homobasidiomycetes -
O. Tricholomatales - F. Pleurotaceae.

- H: 1¼-4 in (4-10 cm)
- Ø: ¾-3¼ in (3-8 cm)
- White spores

Cone-shaped cap

Very decurrent,
saw-edged or ragged gills

▮ How to recognize it

The **cap** of this average-sized mushroom may be cone-shaped, spatulate or funnel-shaped. The cuticle, which is almost smooth, is fawn to brown in color, with flesh-colored shading. The margin is deeply lobed and typically upturned.

The **gills** are swollen and often split and irregular in shape. They are paler than the cap and washed with a reddish tint. They are strongly decurrent, running a long way down the stem. The **stem** is excentric to lateral and is deeply ridged lengthwise. It is often distorted or twisted in on itself in a spiral..

The **flesh** of the Spiral Lentinus is reddish-white and soon becomes tough with age. The mushroom has a strong and penetrating odor of aniseed which is characteristic, although a variety exists called *inolens* which is completely devoid of odor.

▮ Where and when to find it

The Spiral Lentinus grows in the high season for mushrooms, in summer through fall. It is quite common on the stumps of various broad-leaved trees, especially beeches, but it it occasionally found on conifers. It forms dense tufts, consisting of a number of specimens whose caps are often imbricated and the stems welded together at the base.

▮ Features and edibility

The Spiral Lentinus is edible when young. At this stage, the flesh is tender, but it becomes tough and leathery as the mushroom ages. The aniseed odor makes it usable in small quantities to flavor a sauce or a dish which contains other varieties of mushroom.

Related species

STRIPED LENTINUS
Lentinus tigrinus

The Striped Lentinus has a rather small cap which it is flat to convex when young and later spreads out and even becomes funnel-shaped with age. The cuticle is typically striped with small reddish-brown downy scales against a whitish to yellowish background. The margin tears as the cap expands and is

characteristically split, sometimes almost to the center of the cap. The whitish gills are saw-toothed at the edge and decurrent. The curved stem tapers toward the base which is also finely striped. The white flesh is elastic at first, but toughens as the mushroom ages. The Striped Lentinus grows in small groups on logs or fallen trunks of willows and poplars, so it is to be found beside rivers,

canals, and lakes, from spring through fall. The Striped Lentinus is only edible when young.
- H: 11/2-31/4 in (4-8 cm)
- Ø: 11/2-4 in (4-10 cm)
- White spores

The Orange Nail Fungus
Rickenella fibula

Latin name : *Omphalina fibula.*

Classification : Cl. Homobasidiomycetes - O. Tricholomatales - F. Tricholomataceae.

- H:¾-2¾ in (3-7 cm)
- Ø: ⅛-¼ in (0.5-1 cm)
- White spores

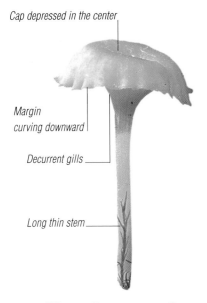

Cap depressed in the center

Margin curving downward

Decurrent gills

Long thin stem

▌How to recognize it

This tiny mushroom looks very much like a stickpin or a nail.

The **cap** is no bigger than ¼ in (1 cm) in diameter and has an unusual shape largely overhanging the gills like a frill and deeply depressed in the center.

The smooth **cuticle** is orange-yellow and transparent, so that the gills are visible through it. The **gills** are widely spaced, curved, very decurrent, and cream or pale yellow in color.

The **stem** is the same color as the cap, long and very thin; it is covered with a fine down which can only be seen under the magnifying glass. The **flesh** is pale and odorless and obviously very thin, so that the mushroom is entirely unsuitable for eating.

▌How to recognize it

The Orange Nail Fungus grows in moss in damp grassland, marshes, and forests. It is common sight from late spring through fall.

Related species

There are several species of mushroom with funnel-shaped caps and decurrent gills. They look like members of the Mycena family but they have often posed classification problems which explains why their Latin names have been changed so often. They are generally thicker in shape than the Orange Nail Fungus.

THE PIXIE FUNNEL CAP
Omphalina pyxidata

The Pixie Funnel Cap has a larger, reddish-brown or ocher-gray cap, which is more clearly striped. It also grows on lawns, and sometimes on bare soil.

- H: ¾-2 in (2-5 cm)
- Ø: ½-1¼ in (1-3 cm)
- White spores

THE MOSS OMPHALIA
Gerronema ericetorum

The cap of this mushroom is beige to pale ocher in color and the stem is very short, mostly of the same color, but darker at the top. It prefers damp, cold, and acid environments colonized by mosses and sphagnum moss.

- H:¾-2 in (2-5 cm)
- Ø: ½-¾ in (1-2 cm)
- White spores

The Clouded Agaric
Clitocybe nebularis

Classification : Cl. Homobasidiomycetes -
O. Tricholomatales - F. Tricholomataceae.

- H: 2¾-6 in (7-15 cm)
- Ø: 3¼-8 in (8-20 cm)
- Very pale yellow spores

Very crowded gills

Swollen base

Gray cap with mealy
surface

■ How to recognize it

The **cap** of the Clouded Agaric may grow to as much as 8 in (20 cm) in diameter. It is rounded at first, with a strongly inrolled margin, which later flattens out, retaining a slight umbo, though this may eventually disappear completely. The mouse-gray surface looks as if it had been sprinkled with white flour, giving it the clouded appearance of its name.

The **gills** are whitish to cream in color, very fine and crowded. They are bow-shaped at first, later becoming slightly decurrent.

The grayish, finely striped **stem** is covered with a cottony white down. The stem is thick and sturdy when young, later extending and thinning, though the base remains swollen. The stem gradually becomes hollow and may collapse when old, since it is often worm-eaten.

The **flesh** is firm and white when young but rather soft in the mature specimen. It emits the smell characteristic of the genus, a strongly cyanic odor.

■ Where and when to find it

The Clouded Agaric grows in coniferous and deciduous woods, appearing in circles and clusters. It is common throughout the temperate zone of the northern hemisphere where it grows at all altitudes. The mushroom fruits quite late in the season, appearing in October and sometimes lasting through December, persisting even after the first frosts.

■ Features and edibility

The Clouded Agaric is the subject of some controversy. Although generally considered good to eat, some people cannot digest it and suffer from stomach upsets if they eat it. Furthermore, some people are deterred from trying it due to its rather strange smell, though others do not find the smell unpleasant.

In any case, only young specimens are worth eating. Since they can be dried, they can easily be preserved for flavoring winter dishes.

Lookalike

The Livid Entoloma (Entoloma lividum) *(p. 116) is an imposing mushroom which displays itself in open spaces in deciduous woods. However, if eaten, it causes serious stomach upsets which are bad enough to require hospital treatment.*

The Livid Entoloma is distinguishable by its mealy odor and emarginate gills which are yellow, never white, then pink when mature .

▼ Lookalike:
The Livid Entoloma *(Entoloma lividum)* (p. 116)

	Clouded Agaric *Clitocybe nebularis*	The Livid Entoloma *Entoloma lividum*
Cap	gray, mealy	grayish-white, fibrillose
Gills	slightly decurrent, whitish	emarginate, yellow, turning pink
Stem	gray, swollen	white, swollen
Odor	complex, cyanic	mealy
Habitat	broad-leaved trees, conifers	broad-leaved trees
Features	good to eat	poisonous

Monk's Head

Clitocybe geotropa

Classification : Cl. Homobasidiomycetes -
O. Tricholomatales - F. Tricholomataceae.

- H: 4-10 in (10-25 cm)
- Ø: 3¼-8 in (8-20 cm)
- White spores

Cap becomes deeply funnel-shaped in older specimens

Gills decurrent

Cap smooth, yellow, and ochraceous

Massive, club-shaped stem

How to recognize it

The Monk's Head is a handsome mushroom, smooth and glabrous, which looks slightly waxy, ochraceous yellow to flesh-color. The **cap** bears some resemblance to a monk's tonsure, hence the name. As it grows older, it becomes funnel-shaped while retaining a central umbo. The margin is inrolled at first and slightly downy but later turns upward, becoming undulating and lobed.

The **gills** are whitish to cream, uneven and crowded, and are typical of the Clitocybe genus in that they are deeply decurrent.

The long, strong, full **stem** turns spongy with age. It is cylindrical in shape, thickening right up to the base which is enveloped in a downy mycelial mass. It is similar in color to the cap. The firm, white **flesh** has a pleasant but complex odor which is typical of the Clitocybes.

Where and when to find it

This imposing mushroom is easy to spot in pastures and forest clearings where it grows in fairy rings. It is quite common in summer and fall, but may also fruit quite late in the season.

Features and edibility

The pleasant odor and large size make the Monk's Head a mushroom that is sought after for the table. However, it should be picked when young and the fibrous stem should be discarded. When mature, the flesh becomes spongy; older specimens are too leathery and tough to be palatable.

Related species

CLUB-FOOT FUNNEL CAP
Clitocybe clavipes

The stem of this mushroom is very swollen at the base. The cuticle is smooth. The pale color of the gills contrasts with the gray-brown coloring of the rest of the mushroom. The thick gills run decurrently down the stem. The flesh is soft, with an odor that is reminiscent of orange blossom. However, its consistency, which has been described as being like "wet cotton" makes it unpalatable .

- H: 2½-4 in (6-10 cm)
- Ø: 1½-3¼ in (4-8 cm) ● White spores

Aniseed Mushroom
Clitocybe odora

English synonym: Blue-green Funnel Cap

Classification : Cl. Homobasidiomycetes -
O. Tricholomatales - F. Tricholomataceae.

- H: 2-4 in (5-10 cm)
- Ø: 2½-2¾ in (4-8 cm)
- Pinkish white spores

Smooth, gray-green or blue-green cap

Slightly decurrent gills

▮ How to recognize it

The Aniseed Mushroom has a typical gray-green or blue-green **cap** which fades with age. The shape varies from convex to conical or gently rounded at first, flattening and sinking in the center, until almost funnel-shaped, though it still retains a central umbo. The margin is inrolled at first and often lobed. It later turns upward, finally becoming sinuate. The **gills** are thin and straight, rather crowded and pale in color, being whitish or grayish and shaded the same color as the cap. They are adnate or slightly decurrent, and thus atypical of the genus Clitocybe.

The **stem** is generally short and cylindrical, slightly thickened at the base, fibrillose and paler than the cap. It is sometimes tinged with pink. It is fleshy and fibrous at first but soon becomes hollow and frail but remains upright. The **flesh** is firm then elastic, white with a green tint, and has the typical delicate yet penetrating odor of aniseed.

▮ Where and when to find it

The Aniseed Mushroom grows in leaf or pine needle litter in shady undergrowth in coniferous or deciduous woods. It generally fruits in circles or small groups, especially in beech and Norway spruce woods in summer through fall.

▮ Features and edibility

The strong scent of aniseeds means that this mushroom is generally used in small quantities. One or two specimens will suffice to flavor a dish of other mushrooms whose taste may be slightly insipid. The tough stem should always be discarded before cooking.

The Ivory Mushroom
Clitocybe dealbata

English synonym : The Sweating Mushroom

Classification : Cl. Homobasidiomycetes -
O. Tricholomatales - F. Tricholomataceae.

- H: 1¼-2½ in (3-6 cm)
- Ø: ¾-2 in (2-5 cm)
- White spores

▼ Lookalikes:
The Snow-white Wax Cap
(Cuphophyllus niveus) (p. 62)
The White Funnel Cap
(Lepista luscina) (p. 79)
The Fairy Ring Champignon
(Marasmius oreades) (p. 99)
Miller or The Sweetbread Mushroom
(Clitopilus prunulus) (p. 114)

▮ How to recognize it

The **cap** of this small mushroom is typical by its flat top and the satiny, glazed, white color of the cuticle. With age or in wet weather, the cuticle may become tinted with cream or even turn reddish in places, at which time this mushroom can easily become confused with a range of edible species. The margin is thin and remains upturned for a long time. The center of the cap is more fleshy and slightly umbonate.

The **gills** are whitish to grayish and fairly crowded. They are adnate to slightly decurrent. The short, white **stem**, lengthens with age, soon becoming fibrillose. The surface is silky and fibrillose and gradually turns gray or russet from the base upward.

The white **flesh** is tender to fibrous and has a strong and complex mealy odor which is characteristic of numerous species of Clytocybe.

▮ Where and when to find it

The Ivory Mushroom is quite common, and is found growing in clumps or circles in grassland. It is encountered in the same habitats as the Fairy Ring Champignon in meadows or on garden lawns in summer and fall.

The Ivory Mushroom

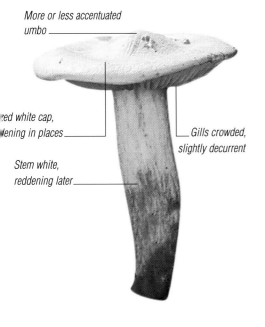

More or less accentuated umbo

~~red~~ white cap, ~~red~~dening in places

Stem white, reddening later

Gills crowded, slightly decurrent

▌Toxicity

The Ivory Mushroom and the related species of small white Clitocybes of the woods and fields are all poisonous. Like the Panther Cap and members of the genus *Inocybe*, they contain significant amount of muscarine. This toxin causes a type of poisoning associated with profuse sweating, diarrhea, vomiting, a slowing of the heart, and lowering of the blood pressure. There is a risk of fatal collapse. It is the ability to cause profuse sweating if eaten which gives this innocuous-looking mushroom its alternative English name of The Sweating Mushroom.

Lookalikes

As a general rule, beware of all-white mushrooms! These little white species of Cltocybe are very common and are found in every type of habitat. They can easily be confused with a number of mushrooms including some that are perfectly edible and even sought after.

In grassland, beware of confusion with **The Snow-White Wax Cap** *(Cuphophyllus niveus) (p. 62), whose gills are decurrent and widely-spaced and which smell of grass or hay.*

Species of Ivory Mushroom which redden could be confused with white species of Lepista (see p. 79), though their gills are colored beige to pink.

The **Fairy Ring Champignon** *(Marasmius oreades) (p. 99) has a yellowish-brown cap and stem, widely spaced, free gills and an odor of bitter almonds, but it grows in the same sort of rings as the Ivory Mushroom.*

The most similar edible species is **Miller** *(Clitopilus prunulus) (p. 114) so-called for its strong mealy odor. Its gills turn pink when mature.*

	Poisonous white Clitocybes — Clitocybe dealbata and C. phyllophila	The Snow-white Wax Cap — Cuphophyllus niveus	The Cloudy Lepiota — Lepista panaeola.	The FAiry Ring Champignon — Marasmius oreades	Miller — Clitopilus prunulus
Cap	white (to russet)	white	gray-russet	yellowish-fawn	white ty grayish
Gills	crowded,whitish, slightly decurrents	widely-spaced, white, decurrent	crowded, beige to pink, slightly decurrent	widely-spaced, beige, free	crowded, white, then pink, decurrent
Stem	white (reddening), fleshy, fibrous	white, spongy	beige, fleshy, fibrous	beige, very persistent	white, fleshy
Odor	complex, mealy	grass or hay	mealy	bitter almonds	mealy
Habitat	fields, woods	fields	fields	fields	woods
Features	poisonous	very good to eat	good to eat	excellent	excellent

The Honey Fungus

Armillaria mellea

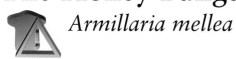

English synonym: The Bootlace Fungus

Classification : Cl. Homobasidiomycetes -
O. Tricholomatales - F. Tricholomataceae.

- H: 3½-8 in (9-20 cm)
- Ø: ¾-4 in (3-10 cm)
- White spores

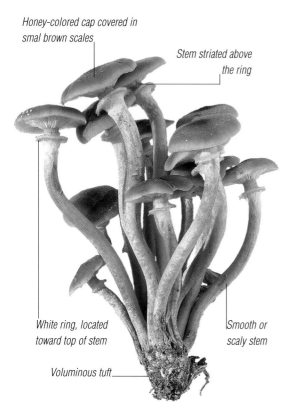

Honey-colored cap covered in
smal brown scales

Stem striated above
the ring

White ring, located
toward top of stem

Smooth or
scaly stem

Voluminous tuft

▍How to recognize it

The **cap** of this mushroom is generally of average size, globose when young but becoming convex, then flattened, and sometimes depressed.. The cuticle montre is every shade of honey, from yellow to brown, tinted with red or olive. It is covered in fine brown scales, which are denser in the center. The thin margin is very undulating in older examples.

The decurrent **gills** are white at first, then yellow, staining dark red when old.

The **stem** is tall and cylindrical, thickening at the base, especially in young specimens. It has a membranous, white ring very high up it, just under the cap. The white upper part is regularly striped. The lower part is paler than the cap and smooth or speckled.

The **flesh**, is firm and white in the cap, but very fibrous and even leathery in the stem.

▍How to recognize it

The Honey Fungus can be a dangerous parasite but also grows on stemps and living trunks of fallen trees, both broad-leaved and coniferous. When encountered in isolation and apparently growing in the ground, it is actually attached to a tree root. It can be found throughout the temperate zone in fall. The Honey Fugnus is considered a disease by foresters, thanks to its

parasitic habits. The black "bootlaces" formed by this mushroom, which are called rhizomorphs, find their way under the bark of trees and attack their vital functions. By the fruiting bodies appearit is too late to save the tree which will die of white rot or decay.

▍Features and edibility

The young Honey Fungus caps are edible, though their culinary interest is a matter of dispute. The very abundance of this mushroom makes it of culinary interest and it is suitable for pickling or preserving. However, precautions should be taken. Old specimens or those whose stems are too tough must be discarded. Furthermore, the cooking should be prolonged so as to ensure that the slight bitterness in the flesh disappears. If these rules are not observed, there may be some adverse reactions. Certain people who have eaten the Honey Fungus have found that it disagrees with them.

Lookalikes

In the fall, lots of mushrooms can be found growing in tufts on tree stumps or at the base of tree trunks. There are two species of Pholiota which look very much like the Honey Fungus:

*The **Shaggy Pholiota** or **Shaggy Pholiota** (Pholiota squarrosa) (p. 146) can be distinguished by its lemon yellow cap, and larger, reddish scales. The gills are*

▼ **Lookalikes:**
The Shaggy Pholiota or Scaly Pholiota
(Pholiota squarrosa) (p. 146)
The Two-toned Pholiota
(Kuehneromyces mutabilis) (p. 144)

paler but darken as the mushroom ages. The stem is very scaly, tough, sinuous and tapering, though it also has a ring placed very high up, just below the cap. This species is too tough to be edible and in any case, the flavor is unpleasant.

The **Two-toned Pholiota** also known as the **Brown Stew Fungus** (Kuehneromyces mutabilis) (p. 144), inhabits deciduous woods exclusively. The cap is smooth, furrowed and is colored two distinct shades, cinnamon brown in the center then yellowing brown toward the margin. It is very good to eat if the long, tough stem is discarded.

	The Honey Fungus *Armillaria mellea*	The Shaggy Pholiota *Pholiota squarrosa*	The Two-toned Pholiota *Kuehneromyces mutabilis*
Cap	honey color, brown scales	yellow, reddish scales	yellow to cinnamon, smooth
Gills	white, young splashed with rust	yellow, then rust	yellow, then rust
Stem	pale, smooth or spotted	brunissant, ecailleux	brun-roux, mechuleux
Ring	white	brown	turning brown
Habitat	broad-leaves, conifers	conifes, broad-leaves	broad-leaves, conifers
Features	good to eat	inedbile	good to eat

Related species

THE NORTHERN AGARIC
Armillaria borealis

This is an uncommon mushroom which lives in at high altitudes in warmer climates and in colder regions of the northern hemisphere. It grows in clumps on deciduous trees or conifers. The cap is brown and striated at the margin, which is paler than the rest of the ocher or yellow-brown cap. The central umbo is hidden under a number of dense scales which tend to brown with age. The stem has a fragile, white ring.

- H: 4-6 in (10-15 cm)
- Ø: 2¼-4 in (6-10 cm)
- White spores

THE DARKENING ARMILLARIA
Armillaria ostoyae

This has darker scales on a reddish-brown cap, and a fluffy ring edged with brown.

- H: 2¾-6 in (7-15 cm)
- Ø: 2¾-4¾ in (7-12 cm)
- White spores

THE RINGLESS ARMILLARIA
 ### *Armillaria tabescens*

This mushroom is more fragile and has no ring. It grows in tuftswhich are smaller but just as dense as those of the Honey Fungus. It prefers oak stumps or roots. The species is edible but much rarer than its close relative.

- H: 3¼-5¼ in (8-13 cm)
- Ø: ¾-2½ in (3-6 cm)
- White spores

The Inside Out Agaric
Lepista inversa

Latin name : *Clitocybe inversa.*

Classification : Cl. Homobasidiomycetes -
O. Tricholomatales - F. Tricholomataceae.

- H: 2-4 in (5-10 cm)
- Ø: 1½-4 in (4-10 cm)
- White spores

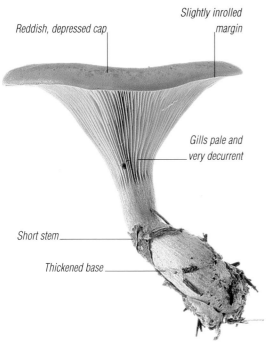

Reddish, depressed cap

Slightly inrolled margin

Gills pale and very decurrent

Short stem

Thickened base

■ How to recognize it

The cap of this small to medium-sized mushroom is slightly convex at first, then flattening and eventually becoming depressed. It is quite fleshy in the center, thinning toward the margin. The cross-section of this unusually shaped mushroom is what gives it its name. The cuticle is a russet color of varying intensity, or it may be yellow ocher. It is very smooth and shiny, but may split into shreds in dry weather..

The **gills** and thin and very crowded; they are deeply decurrent. The mushroom is creamy white at first, reddening with age.

The **stem** is short and tough, similar in color to the gills. The slightly thickened base is covered with a cottony fluff of mycelium.

The whitish **flesh** is friable under the cap and almost odorless. Some consider that the taste is slightly bitter.

■ Where and when to find it

The Inside Out Agaric grows commonly in tightly-packed clumps or occasionally in circles on needle litter in coniferous forests, in shady places under spruce. It appears in the mushroom season, though it is sometimes a late arrival.

■ Features and edibility

The Inside Out Agaric is considered good to eat by some people, but others do not like it. They find the flesh is too tough and find that the flavor is bitter and unpalatable.

Related species

Other Clitocybes in this group have an orange or brick-red cap.

THE FLACID AGARIC
Lepista flaccida

This species is similar to the Inside Out Agaric. It is cone-shaped with a more sinuous margin and lives under deciduous trees.

- H: 2-4 in (5-10 cm)
- Ø: 1½-4 in (4-10 cm)
- White spores

THE FUNNEL CAP
Clitocybe gibba

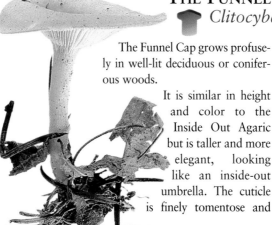

The Funnel Cap grows profusely in well-lit deciduous or coniferous woods.

It is similar in height and color to the Inside Out Agaric but is taller and more elegant, looking like an inside-out umbrella. The cuticle is finely tomentose and the gills are much paler. The stem, is longer and more slender. The thin, fragile cap contrasts with the fairly solid and thick outline of the Inside Out Agaric. The flesh has a complex cyanic odor typical of the Clitocybes; it is good to eat.

- H: 2-4 in (5-10 cm)
- Ø: 1½-4 in (4-10 cm)
- White spores

The Cloudy Tricholoma

Lepista panaeolus

Alternative Latin names:
Rhodopaxillus panaeolus, Lepista luscina.

Classification : Cl. Homobasidiomycetes -
O. Tricholomatales - F. Tricholomataceae.

- H: 1½-2¾ in (4-7 cm)
- Ø:1¼-4 in (3-10 cm)
- Pale pink spores

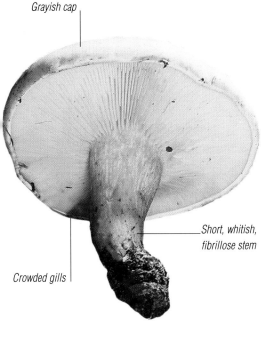

Grayish cap

Short, whitish, fibrillose stem

Crowded gills

How to recognize it

The **cap** of the Cloudy Tricholoma is quite small and fleshy, convex then flattened and often irregular and undulating along the margin. Darker concentric circles decorate the grayish cap which may be gray-brown or reddish-gray. This is the reason why this member of the Tricholoma family has the epithet "cloudy", but the feature is not always very apparent. This fact makes The Cloudy Tricholoma hard to identify positively.

The crowded **gills** are thin and white in young speciments, shading to gray tinged with pink when the spores mature. They are sinuate at first but tend to become decurrent in old specimens of this fairly small mushroom.

The **stem** is quite short, full and fleshy, then fibrous and may break when the mushroom is picked. The fibrillose surface is almost concolorous with the cap, though slightly paler.

The thick, tender **flesh** is grayish-white and has a pleasant mealy odor and flavor

Where and when to find it

The Cloudy Tricholoma is quite a common sight in the fall in the grass of fields and meadows. It grows in groups of several individual specimens, and occasionally in circles that are so packed that the mushrooms are piled on top of each other.

Features and edibility

The Cloudy Tricholoma is found abundantly in its habitat which means that it can be used to produce several delicious dishes. It has the reputation of being a delicacy with its odor of fresh flour which becomes spicy during cooking, a little like the Blewit.

However, it would seem to be a good idea to eat it in moderation and to use only young specimens in good condition. In fact, a few cases of indigestibility have been reported, but these may be due ingestion of a similar looking species which had been confused with the Cloudy Tricholoma.

Lookalike

*Beginners should be very careful not to confuse this mushroom with any of the small white Clitocybes such as **The Ivory Mushroom** (Clitocybe dealbata) (p. 74) which also grows in grassland. These mushooms are very poisonous but some may even have concentric patches on the cap, just like the Cloudy Tricholoma, so confusion is easy.*

Lookalike:
The Ivory Mushroom Mushroom
(Clitocybe dealbata) (p. 74)

	The Cloudy Agaric *Lepista panaeolus*	The Ivory Mushroom *Clitocybe dealbata*
Cap	rather small, reddish-gray	petit, blanc à roux
Gills	sinuate to slightly decurrent, whitish to pinkish-gray	slightly decurrent, whitish
Stem	beige	white, reddening
Odeur	mealy	complex, floury odor
Habitat	fields	fields
Features	very good to eat	poisonous

Wood Blewit

Lepista nuda

English synonyms: Blue Stalks, Blue Foot
Alternative Latin name : *Rhodopaxillus nudus*.

Classification : Cl. Homobasidiomycetes -
O. Tricholomatales - F. Tricholomataceae.

- H: 2½-4½ in (6-12 cm)
- Ø: 2-6 in (5-15 cm)
- Pale lilac gray spores

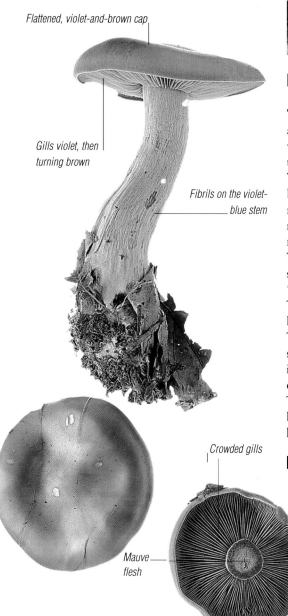

Flattened, violet-and-brown cap

Gills violet, then turning brown

Fibrils on the violet-blue stem

Mauve flesh

Crowded gills

Lookalike:
The Purplish Cortinarius
(*Cortinarius purpurascens*) (p. 130)

▌ How to recognize it

This handsome mushroom, which is large or average in size, is often an intense mauve or violet color when young. As it ages, the color tends to become dull and faded.

The fleshy, convex **cap** is tinted with pale brown, especially in the center, and sometimes right up to the margin, making identification more difficult. However, the stem always retains at least some of the original violet color. The cuticle, which is perfectly smooth and shiny, is responsible for the Latin epithet "nudum."

The crowded, sinuate **gills**, are violet, shading to brown when mature.

The **stem** is fleshy and slightly fibrous, quite sturdy and thickening at the base. The surface is covered with whitish to silver velvety fibrils on a violet-blue background.

The **flesh** is tender and impregnated with lilac but whitens in mature specimens. The odor is hard to define but slightly spicy.

▌ Where and when to find it

The Wood Blewit is usually to be found in the leaf and needle litter of deciduous and coniferous woods, where it often forms fairly rings. Magnificent displays of this beautiful mushroom have been observed, but unfortunately many have been in remote plantantions of Norway spruce! Sometimes it grows alongside the Fairy Ring Mushroom in meadows close to trees. The species is fairly common and grows throughout the world, appearing in temperate zones as early as spring, but it is most prolific in the fall, from October through November.

▌ Features and edibility

The Wood Blewit is a delicious edible mushroom with tender flesh and a delightful spicy flavor and fragrance. However, some people find that for them, the taste is too strong or rather acrid. If you find the flavor too intense, you can blanch the mushroom first but only the soft flesh will survive this treatment intact. At any event, it is unwise to eat any but young specimens which are still fleshy and whole, untouched by slugs and maggots. The tough stem, which soon becomes fibrous, should be discarded. elimine. The Wood Blewit can be cooked with related edible species such as the Field Blewit or the Lesser Blue Foot.

▌ Cultivation

The Wood Blewit was is sold in mushroom markets and is cultivated on compost based on horse manure , where it grows well under cool, damp conditions. The cultivated specimens are grown from wild mycelium, yet they look slightly different from the mushrooms that grow in nature. The cap is often more undulating, less fleshy and a stem that is club-shaped or swollen at the base.

Lookalike

A few of the violet Cortinarius species may bear a superficial resemblance to the Wood Blewit.
*The **Purplish Cortinarius** (Cortinarius purpurascens) (p. 130) and related species are recognizable by the fibriollose aspect of the cap and the residues of a cortina or veil on the stem, which, like the gills, turn rust-colored when mature, due to the color of the spores. These species of Cortinarius are not poisonous but are not good to eat.*

There is a species which is related to the Wood Blewit and just as good to eat,
so it deserves the attention of the mushroom-hunter.

THE LESSER BLUE-FOOT

Lepista sordida

The Lesser Blue-foot looks like a miniature version of the Wood Blewit, as it is half the size. It is often more brightly colored, but the mauve color also fades with age. It can be found in grassy clearings or verges, especially on cultivated and fertile soil.

- H: 1½-2½ in (4-6 cm)
- Ø: 1¼-2¾ in (3-7 cm)
- Pale lilac-gray spores

Field Blewit

Lepista saeva

English synonym: Blue Leg.
Alternative Latin name : *Rhodopaxillus saevus*, *Lepista personata*.

Classification : Cl. Homobasidiomycetes - O. Tricholomatales - F. Tricholomataceae.

- H: 2-4 in (5-10 cm)
- Ø: 3¼-6 in (8-15 cm)
- Pale pink spores

Fleshy cap

Thick stem

violet in young imens

Violet fibers

▌How to recognize it

The **cap** of the Field Blewit or Blue Leg is of a respectable size, and can grow up to 6 in (15 cm) in diameter. It is globose at first, then convex and fleshy and looks very solid. The uniformly smooth and shiny cuticle changes from beige to gray-brown and is eventually dun-colored. The slightly frilly margin only flattens out in mature specimens, becoming sinuous.

The **gills** are thin and unequal, emarginate, and slightly paler in color than the cap.

The thick, solid **stem** is lightly streaked and velvety. It is a beautiful amethyst color in young specimens though it loses its magnificent coloration quite early on, and is positively dun-colored when old.

The thick, tender, compact **flesh**, when fresh has a pleasant fungal odor and a mild but subtle flavor.

Where and when to find it

The Field Blewit or Blue Leg grows in impressive fairy rings in fields and meadows. It may even be found growing in isolation, hidden in tall grass.

It is sometimes very common and like many other species of Tricholoma, it emerges late in the season, in late fall or even winter. ,

▌Features and edibility

The texture of the flesh of this mushroom is unequalled It is often considered better than that of the Wood Blewit which is itself excellent, simply because it is thicker.

It is all the better as an edible mushroom since there is very little else that is edible in the fungal world that grows in late winter, when it tends to fruit. It is often displayed on market stalls in continental Europe.

The Amethyst Deceiver
Laccaria amethystea

Alternative Latin name : *Clitocybe amethystina.*

Classification : Cl. Homobasidiomycetes - O. Tricholomatales - F. Tricholomataceae.

- H: 2-4½ in (5-12 cm)
- Ø: ¾- 2¾ in (2-7 cm)
- White-to-lilac spores

Amethyst-colored cap, gills and stem

Inrolled margin

Very spaced gills

White felting

Lookalikes:
The Pure Mycena (*Mycena pura*) (p. 107)
The Common White Inocybe (*Inocybe geophylla*) (p. 137)

▮ How to recognize it

This little mushroom is violet-colored all over and has a thinnish **cap** which is convex at first, gradually spreading and with a circular central furrow or umbilicus. The matt, dry cuticle, is granulose then scaly and brightly colored in young specimens, darkeing and turning gray with age or in wet weather. The very inrolled margin then becomes upturned but is finally undulating and streaky.

The **gills** are thick, swollen, and widely spaced. They are uneven, adnate, or decurrent. Upon maturity the violet color disappears under the white dust of the spores.

The **stem** is long, slender, and sinuous with a fragile appearance. It soon becomes fibrous and is very persistent. It is deeply furrowed, and covered with a very apparent down on the lower part.

The **flesh** of the cap is quite tender but very thin. It is also impregnated with violet. It emits a slightly fruity odor.

▮ Where and when to find it

This little mushroom appear in carpets of moss or on the leaf mold and carpet of needles in all types of woods. It prefers very damp places and may even emerge in marshes and bogs, growing among sphagnum moss. It is very common and grows in profusion in the mushroom season.

▮ Features and edibility

The Amethytst Deceiver, despite the thinness of the flesh and the fibrose stem which is inedible is nevertheless excellent eating and well deserves to be tasted. It is strongly flavored and lends itself to being an accompaniment to meats and makes a delicious ingredient in an omelet. It is found in abundance because it is not often picked by mushroom eaters. In fact, some people assume that a mushroom that is violet in color cannot be edible.

The Deceiver is just as good to eat, though slightly less good than the closely related Amethyst Deceiver.

Lookalikes

*The **Pure Mycena** (Mycena pura) (p. 107), which is found in the same habitats as the Amethyst Deceiver, is violet or pink. It is slightly larger than the latter, from which it can be distinguished mainly by its watery consistency and by its pronounced odor of radish. Furthermore, the cap is umbonate and the gills are more crowded and much paler than the cap and the stem. Eating the Pure Mycena has resulted in poisonings that required hospitalization.*

*The **Common White Inocybe** (Inocybe geophylla) (p. 137), a little mushroom whose color varies considerably between white, red and lilac, is poisonous. It is distinguishable from the Amethyst Deceiver by its conical cap. Several suspect small varieties of Cortinarius such as the reddish **Cortinarius gentilis** also grow in mossy undergrowth.*

THE DECEIVER

Laccaria laccata

The Amethyst Deceiver was once considered a mere variety of The Deceiver, which is almost identical to it except for its color which is pinkish-orange. There are some minor differences, however. The cap of The Deceiver has a slightly clearer umbilicus and the stem is a little more fibrous.

The Deceiver is an extremely common mushroom, living in the same type of undergrowth as The Amethyst Deceiver and it can often be gathered and used in a mixed mushroom dish in the fall season.
- H: 2-4 in (5-10 cm)
- Ø: ½-1½ in (1-4 cm)
- White spores

THE TWO-TONE DECEIVER
Laccaria bicolor

The Two-tone Deceiver has a cap that is similar to that of The Deceiver but the stem and gills are the color of The Amethyst Deceiver.
- H: 2-3½ (5-8 cm)
- Ø: ¾-1½ in (2-4 cm)
- White spores

THE CLOSE DECEIVER
Laccaria proxima

This mushroom occurs later and likes wetter places than the lother Deceivers. It is also less fragile. The cap is covered with very fine scales which reveal themselvesin dry weather.
- H: 2-4½ in (5-12 cm)
- Ø: 1¼-2¾ in (3-7 cm)
- White spores

	The Amethyst Deceiver *Laccaria amethystea*	Pure Mycena *Mycena pura*	The Mauve-capped Inocybe *Inocybe geophylla var. lilacina*
Cap	bright purple, paling, umbilicate, finely granulose	pink or lilac, more or less umbonate, smooth	lilac, umbo often ocher, pointed or umbonate, smooth
Gills	widely-spaced, violet	fairly widely spaced, white or pink	crowded gray then brown
Stem	fibrous, persistent, violet	fragile, pink or violet	long, slender, lilac
Odor	slightly fruity	of radishs	unpleasant
Features	edible	poisonous	poisonous

Plums and Custard
Tricholomopsis rutilans

Alternative Latin name : *Tricholoma rutilans.*

Classification : Cl. Homobasidiomycetes -
O. Tricholomatales - F. Tricholomataceae.

- H: 2½-4½ in (6-12 cm)
- Ø: 2-6 in (5-15 cm)
- White spores

Brick red to wine red, scales or patches against a yellow background

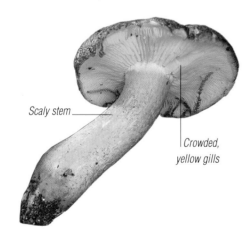

Scaly stem

Crowded, yellow gills

How to recognize it

The **cap** of this beautiful, brightly-colored mushroom is convex at first, almost hemispherical, flattening out considerably when older. The surface is uneven, but it retains a central umbo. The cuticle ranges in color from brick-red to the rich purple of plums. which is particulary spectacular in young specimens. It has a uniformly velvety appearance. With age, the cap splits and large patches of scales are formed which stand out against the pale yellow background. Eventually, all that is left of the bright yellow color is a dull, dirty greenish color which may not even show any red at all. The paler margin stay inrolled for a long time and only flattens at a later stage, when it becomes slightly furrowed.

The **gills** are bright yellow in young specimens, but darken on maturity. They are very crowded and flocculose at the edges. They appear to be adnate and are almost free on the stem.

The central **stem** is often curved, cylindrical to bulbous and is similar in color to the cap, with bright yellow in the upper part and scaly and splashed with brick-red to plum color below.

Where and when to find it

Plums and Custard is a distinctive species which immediately attracts the mushroom-hunter. It prefers clearings in coniferous woods. It is commonly to be found growing on stumps, but it may also appear on decaying,

partly buried branches of pine, spruce, or fir trees. Sometimes it grows in isolation but more often in clumps and can be found in summer through fall.

Features and edibility

Despite its delicious appearance, Plums and Custard is merely a description of the aspect of the mushroom and is not an indication of the flavor or even edibility. It is generally not considered to be of culinary interest due to its unpleasant smell. However, it is sometimes served in a mixture with other species, and is sold in markets in central Europe.

ELEGANT TRICHOLOMA
Tricholomopsis decora

This mushroom is much smaller and golden yellow all over, with fine spots on the cap which are darker in the center. The Elegant Tricholoma adorns the dark undergrowth of coniferous woods. It is not very common, however, and can be found mainly on rotten, moss-covered spruce stumps in mountainous regions. It is not good to eat.

- H: 2-3¼ in (5-8 cm)
- Ø: 2-3¼ in (5-8 cm)
- White spores

The Dove-like Tricholoma

Tricholoma columbetta

Classification : Cl. Homobasidiomycetes -
O. Tricholomotales - F. Tricholomataceae.

- H: 3¼-5 in (8-13 cm)
- Ø: 2-4 in (5-10 cm)
- White spores

Undulating cap

Completely white

*Cap soyeux,
parseme de debris du sol*

Stem fibrilleux

Lookalike:
The Livid Entoloma *(Entoloma lividum)*
(p. 116)

▮ How to recognize it

This mushroom has a silky or satiny texture, of a brilliant white, like that of a white dove. The **cap** is of average size and covered with fine radial fibrils which give it its typical satiny look. It is quite fleshy but fragile, always irregular, convex-umbonate to flat. It is often flecked with pink or violet patches. When the margin unrolls it tends to split in mature specimens. The **gills** are pure white and emarginate.
The sinuous **stem** is fleshy and slightly fibrous. It tears easily when picked. It's silky white surface is often stained pink, blue, green, or violet at the base. Although the presence of this characteristic is a determining factor, it is not systematically present. Furthermore, the earth needs to be scraped away from the stem in order for the staining to be revealed. The **flesh** is also white and is quite thick and tender. It is often odorless but may also have a faint but pleasant fragance

▮ Where and when to find it

The Dove-like Tricholoma displays its whiteness in the undergrowth of beech or birch woods, and is found more rarely under conifers, especially in siliceous soil. It appears in little clumps of isolated individuals, which are generally half-buried in moss or hidden under leaves. It is found throughout the temperate zones of the northern hemisphere. This mushroom fruits in September through October.

▮ Features and edibility

This beautiful white mushroom is edible. It is fleshy and the aroma and consistency are pleasant. Furthermore, it is rarely attached by insects and slugs. Its only disadvantage is its rarity, since it is only found in certain habitats and tends to grow only in small groups .

Lookalike

*The **Livid Entoloma** (Entoloma lividum) (p. 116), is very poisonous and not as white as the Dove-like Tricholoma and the cap is heavily fibrillose. The pale yellow gills become pink upon maturity. Care must be taken, as specimens which are unusually pale might well be mistaken for Dove-like Tricholomas.*

	The Dove-like Tricholoma *Tricholoma columbetta*	The Livid Entoloma *Entoloma lividum*
Cap	white, satiny	grayish white, fibrillose
Gills	pure white	yellow, then pink
Stem	white, satiny	white, thinly furrowed
Odor	faint, pleasant	strongly mealy
Habitat	deciduous trees, conifers	broad-leaved trees
Features	excellent	poisonous

The Fawn Tricholoma
Tricholoma fulvum

Classification : Cl. Homobasidiomycetes -
O. Tricholomatales - F. Tricholomataceae.

- H: 3¼-5 in (8-13 cm)
- Ø: 2-4 in (5-10 cm)
- White spores

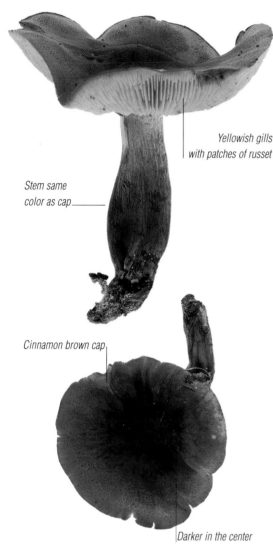

Yellowish gills
with patches of russet

Stem same
color as cap

Cinnamon brown cap

Darker in the center

▮ How to recognize it

The **cap** is convex at first, and sometimes displays a large, prominent umbo. The margin appears fairly clearly furrowed, at least at first. The cuticle is smooth and dry but may become viscous in the rain. It is warm brown in color and is slightly yellower at the edge of the cap. The **gills** are crowded, sinuate, and saw-edged as in all the Tricholomas. The pale yellow color of the gills tend to stain with rust color with age. The **stem** is long and rather thin and gives this mushroom a slender outline. Viscous in the young specimen, it is yellowish-brown in color and is striated with russet fibrils which darken slightly with age. The **flesh** is one of the easiest ways of recognizing this mushroom because it is the only reddish Tricholoma whose flesh is lemon yellow in the stem. In the cap, however, it is white. The mealy odor is quite strong and it has a slightly bitter taste.

This Tricholoma is not edible.

▮ Where and when to find it

The Fawn Tricholoma prefers the company of birch trees which, like it, prefer damp, acid soil, though it can be found under other broadleaved trees. It is a fairly common species in late summer, and grows in small clumps in lowland areas as well as in the mountains.

Related species

The Fawn Tricholoma belongs to the group of brown Tricholomas with russet or reddish-brown caps which are more or less viscous.

THE POPLAR TRICHOLOMA
Tricholoma populinum

This mushroom, which resembles The Bitter Tricholoma, is not good to eat. The cap is brownish-pink. The strong smell of cucumber and its poplar habitat help to identify it.

- H: 2¾-3½ in (7-9 cm)
- Ø: 4-6 in (10-15 cm)
- White spores

THE SHINY TRICHOLOMA
Tricholoma pseudonictitans

The shiny cap of this Tricholoma is reddish-brown and the margin is not furrowed. It grows mainly in coniferous woods.

- H: 2¾-4 in (7-10 cm)
- Ø: 2½-4 in (6-10 cm)
- White spores

THE TAWNY TRICHOLOMA
Tricholoma ustaloides

Unlike the Bitter Tricholoma, there is a clear line of separation between the white and russet sections of the stem. The color of the cap is less easy to distinguish, and is a brighter red. The flesh is very bitter-tasting and the mushroom has a strong odor of meal or cucumber; it is thus inedible. It is also found in deciduous woods.

- H: 3¼-4¼ in (8-11 cm)
- Ø: 2½-4¼ in (6-11 cm)
- White spores

THE BRINDLE TRICHOLOMA
Tricholoma vaccinum

The Brindle Tricholoma is often under conifers. The cap is covered with clearly marked, fluffy scales especially on the margin which looks wooly. The flesh turns visibly pink, especially in the stem and gills, and the mushroom exudes a faintly mealy odor.

- H: 2½-4 in (6-10 cm)
- Ø: 1½-3¼ in (4-8 cm)
- White spores

THE BITTER TRICHOLOMA
Tricholoma ustale

This Tricholoma lives mainly in beechwoods on calcareous soil. The reddish base of stem gradually fades to white at the top.

This mushroom is not edible.

- H: 2-4 in (5-10 cm)
- Ø: 1½-3¼ in (4-8 cm)
- white spores

THE PINE TRICHOLOMA
Tricholoma fracticum

Like The Tawny Tricholoma, The Pine Tricholoma has a two-colored stem, the colors separated by a clearly marked annular zone (a circle). It is found mainly under conifers (especially pines) in warm climates, and prefers calcareous soil. The bitter flesh makes it inedible.

- H: 3¼-4 in (8-10 cm)
- Ø: 4-6 in (10-15 cm)
- White spores

The Pretentious Tricholoma
Tricholoma portentosum

Classification : Cl. Homobasidiomycetes -
O. Tricholomatales - F. Tricholomataceae.

- H: 2½-4½ in (6-12 cm)
- Ø: 2-4½ in (5-12 cm)
- White spores

mouse-gray cap, very fibrillose

Stipe whitish yellow

Stem sometimes rooting

Whitish-yellow gills

Loolkalikes:

The Striped Tricholoma
(*Tricholoma pardinum*) (p. 89)
The Acrid Tricholoma
(*Tricholoma virgatum*) (p. 93)

▮ How to recognize it

The **cap** is generally of medium size, campanulate to conical at first, and retains a more or less prominent umbo well into maturity. The cuticle is slightly viscous in damp weather and is typically streaked with very obvious, blackish, hairy fibrils. They are so prominent that the slate-gray background has yellow-green reflections. The margin is undulating then lobed and tears easily. The **gills** are wide and quite thick and widely spaced. They are whitish or washed with yellow.

The **stem** is robust and slightly bulbous. It soon becomes fibrous, then slender and rooting. It is white and fibrillose, and may be washed with yellow or violet-gray.

The white **flesh** is firm yet friable. When fresh it emits a slightly mealy odor and has a flavor of oysters which becomes stronger in the mouth.

▮ Where and when to find it

The Pretentious Tricholoma "swells with importance" in coniferous woods (pine and spruce), especially in hilly country. It is occasionally found under beeches. It grows profusely in its favorite habitats in the temperate zone of the northern hemisphere where it will be found in October through December.

▮ Features and edibility

The Pretentious Tricholoma is an excellent food, with a pleasant aroma and flavor but it needs to be eaten young, before it is attacked by slugs. As usual, the stem should be discarded before cooking. It grows abundantly and is often harvested in large quantities, finding its way into the wild mushroom markets. It is also pickled and preserved.

Lookalikes

Two species of gray-capped Tricholoma are to be avoided for eating purposes:

The Striped Tricholoma (Tricholoma pardinum) *(p. 89), which is very poisonous. Its large cap is covered in gray scales which produce a striped effect.*

The Acrid Tricholoma (Tricholoma virgatum), *(p. 93) the metallic gray cap is fibrillose, but can be distinguished by its pointed umbo and gray gills tinted flesh color.*

Related species

EMARGINATE TRICHOLOMA
Tricholoma sejunctum

This species is much more likely to be found under deciduous trees. The cap looks like a cockade, the upturned margin forming a circle around the umbo in the center. The cap is yellow shading to olive in the center where the cuticle is darker and covered in brownish fibrils. The gills are white, often tinted yellow at the edge, hence its Latin epithet. The flesh is white as is the stem, and smells of rancid meal. The bad odor and bitter flavor make this mushroom inedible.

- H: 2½-4½ in (6-10 cm)
- Ø: 2-4 in (5-10 cm)
- White spores

The Striped Tricholoma

Tricholoma pardinum

Latin name : *Tricholoma tigrinum*.

Classification : Cl. Homobasidiomycetes -
O. Tricholomatales - F. Tricholomataceae.

- H: 2¾-6 in (7-15 cm)
- Ø: 2-6 in (5-15 cm)
- White spores

Cap striped with concentric scales

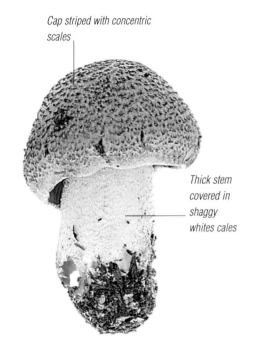

Thick stem covered in shaggy whites cales

▌How to recognize it

The **cap** of this handsome species which is average to large, is typically covered in fine gray scales which range from brownish-bister to ashen in color. They are arranged in concentric circles and stand out against the paler gray background, giving the impression of tiger stripes. The cap is very thick, fleshy, and compact, convex at first, but developing an umbo as it expands. The **gills** are fairly crowded, wide and thick, free or sinuate, and are creamy white or grayish in color.

The white **stem** is extremely thick, often distorted, and bulbous at the base. It lengthens with age. It is thickly flocculose at the top and covered in ochraceous to brownish scales toward the base.

The white **flesh** is firm and compact and it has a mild flavor. It emits a noticeable odor of meal.

▌Where and when to find it

The Striped Tricholoma grows among beech and fir trees in mountainous areas, preferring calcareous soil. It is abundant in some localities, but may be totally absent from others which appear just as suitable. It grows in clusters and sometimes in circles in the mushroom season.

▌Toxicity

The Striped Tricholoma has caused serious cases of gastro-enteritis in the populations of the mountain ranges, such as the Jura in France, where it grows abundantly. It is all the more dangerous for its attractiveness. and the fact that its firm white flesh has a pleasant mealy odor and mild flavor.

Lookalikes

It is a large, imposing mushroom whose cap is covered with distinctive concentric gray scales, so it is easy to recognize. However, care must be taken not to confuse it with the best edible mushrooms.
The Dirty Tricholoma *(Tricholoma terreum) (p. 92), is much more slender and the cap is smaller, conical and covered with gray scales. The gills are white at first but soon become earth-colored. The slender stem is whitish like the flesh, thin, almost odorless and fairly insipid. It is good to eat, however, and grows mainly under conifers, although its close relation, The* **The Coppice Tricholoma** *(Tricholoma argyraceum) grows under deciduous trees.*
The Pretentious Tricholoma *(Tricholoma portentosum) (p. 88) has a fibrillose cap. It would be hard to confuse The Striped Tricholoma with this species, as the Pretentious Tricholoma has a smooth gray cap which no one would describe as striped.*

▼ **Loolkalikes:**

The Dirty Tricholoma
(Tricholoma terreum) (p. 92)
The Pretentious Tricholoma
(Tricholoma portentosum) (p. 88)

	The Striped Tricholoma *Tricholoma pardinum*	The Dirty Tricholoma *Tricholoma terreum*	The Pretentious Tricholoma *Tricholoma portentosum*
Cap	scaly, flattened, gray	scaly, conical, gray	fibrillose, flattened, yellow,-gray
Gills	whitish through grayish	white,then gray	white to yellowish
Stem	very thick, white to brownish	slender, white to grayish	thick,white to yellowish
Odor	mealy	none	of fresh meal
Habitat	conifers, deciduous trees	conifers	conifers, deciduous trees
Features	poisonous	good to eat	excellent

The Saddle-shaped Tricholoma

Tricholoma equestre

Alternative Latin name : *Tricholoma flavovirens*.

Classification : Cl. Homobasidiomycetes -
O. Tricholomatales - F. Tricholomataceae.

- H: 2¾-4 in (7-10 cm)
- Ø: 2-4 in (5-10 cm)
- White spores

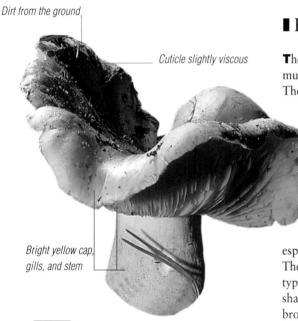

Dirt from the ground

Cuticle slightly viscous

Bright yellow cap, gills, and stem

▼ Lookalikes:

The Death Cap *(Amanita phalloides)*
(p. 176)
The Splendid Cortinarius
(Cortinarius splendens)

▮ How to recognize it

The Saddle-shaped Tricholoma is a handsome mushroom of a uniform bright yellow color.
The medium-sized **cap** is campanulate at first then convex, becoming umbonate and finally flattening in the center, forming the characteristic saddle shape. The flesh is thick and firm, and it is especially fleshy in the center. The cap is slightly sticky, so that sand, dirt, and vegetation cling to it. The bright lemon yellow coloring is spotted with tiny reddish, brownish, or olive flecks, especially in the center.
The crowded **gills** are swollen, unequal, and typically emarginate. The lemon yellow color, shaded with sulfur or chrome yellow, may turn brown with age or in dry weather.
The **stem** is usually cylindrical. It swells up considerably in species growing in sandy pine woods by the sea, but becomes slender and extraordinarily long when the mushroom grows in carpets of moss in mountain forests. The surface is fibrillose, and of a similar color to the gills.
The white **flesh** is fairly thick and firm and is tinted yellow under the cuticle and in the stem. The Saddle-shaped Tricholoma is almost odorless and the flavor is mild.

▮ Where and when to find it

The Saddle-shaped Tricholoma can be found in the undergrowth of broad-leaved woods, especially oak, but it also grows under confers. It is fairly common, and can be found at any altitude from sea level upward. It appears late, and may be encountered after the first snows.

▮ Features and edibility

This mushroom grows abundantly in certain locations where it is easily recognizable due to its shape and yellow color. The flesh is quite firm, almost odorless, and with a very pleasant flavor, so it is very good to eat.
It is said that in the Middle Ages, French knights reserved pride of place at their table for this imposing mushroom, leaving the worthless Bovine Bolete for the peasants! If The Saddle-shaped Tricholoma is picked in sandy soils, it is wise to cut it out of the soil by slicing it with a sharp knife immediately below the gills—provided it has been positively identified. This will prevent grains of sand getting between the crowded gills, which will make the mushroom impossible to clean. The Saddle-shaped Tricholoma is sold in European markets and preserved in various ways.

Lookalikes

Any unpleasant effects caused by confusing this mushroom with the Sulfur Tricholoma are minor compared to the danger of mistaking it for one of the following two species, both of which are deadly poisonous. That is why it is not always wise to trim the cap away from the stem while the mushroom is still in the ground.

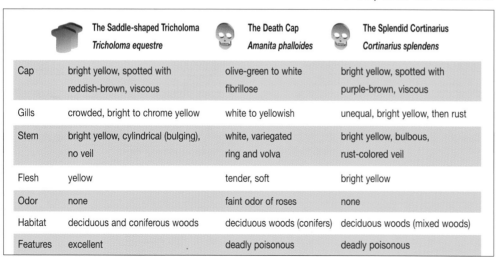

	The Saddle-shaped Tricholoma *Tricholoma equestre*	The Death Cap *Amanita phalloides*	The Splendid Cortinarius *Cortinarius splendens*
Cap	bright yellow, spotted with reddish-brown, viscous	olive-green to white fibrillose	bright yellow, spotted with purple-brown, viscous
Gills	crowded, bright to chrome yellow	white to yellowish	unequal, bright yellow, then rust
Stem	bright yellow, cylindrical (bulging), no veil	white, variegated ring and volva	bright yellow, bulbous, rust-colored veil
Flesh	yellow	tender, soft	bright yellow
Odor	none	faint odor of roses	none
Habitat	deciduous and coniferous woods	deciduous woods (conifers)	deciduous woods (mixed woods)
Features	excellent	deadly poisonous	deadly poisonous

The **Death Cap** (Amanita phalloides) *(p. 176) is easily recognizable by its white gills and softer consistency of the flesh. Always look for the ring and volva on the stem, both of which are also white.*
The **Splendid Cortinarius** (Cortinarius splendens), *which grows under deciduous trees was long considered to be edible but caused a death in 1979. If the stem, which has the remains of the veil and is clearly bulbous at the base, is absent, the main distinctive criteria are constituted by the rusting gills and bright yellow flesh.*

THE GOLDEN TRICHOLOMA
Tricholoma auratum

This species was once considered a variety of the Tricholoma described above. It is thicker and larger and the cap is more ocher than yellow in color. The stem is pale yellow and the flesh is yellow to white. It grows in sandy pine woods in late fall.

ocher cap

- H: 2¾-4 in (7-10 cm)
- Ø: 2½-6 in (6-15 cm)
- White spores

Pale yellow stem

THE SULFUR TRICHOLOMA
Tricholoma sulfureum

This is a paler version of the Saddle-Shaped Tricholoma, but with an unpleasant gaseous odor. Other distinctive features are the widely spaced gills and dry cuticle.

- H: 2½-4½ in (6-12 cm)
- Ø: 1¼-4 in (3-10 cm)
- White spores

The Soapy Tricholoma
Tricholoma saponaceum

Classification : Cl. Basidiomycetes -
O. Tricholomatales - F. Tricholomataceae.

- H: 3¼-6 in (8-15 cm) ● Ø: 2½-5 in (6-13 cm)
- White spores

Gills wide and spaced

Gray, brownish-green cap

Irregular margin

▮ How to recognize it

The **cap** of this mushroom which is of average size is convex or campanulate at first, then extended, and even depressed, although the fleshy center remains umbonate. The cuticle presents very variable coloration against a gray background which may vary in color from greenish, to olive, to brownish, to yellowish, or whitish. It may also become rust-tinted, especially with age. It is often smooth and moist with a few grayish hairs, and in dry weather it may crack, revealing the red flesh.

The **gills** are widely spaced for a Tricholoma, and are wide, irregular, and typically emarginate. They are generally whitish with brown or olive tints, and are typically covered in bister or rust-colored patches.

The cylindrical **stem** is full and firm; the base may vary in shape from swollen, bowed, pointed, and sometimes straight. It is whitish to grayish but paler than the cap, and may also be spotted with rust color. It may appear smooth, fibrillose, or even squamose.

The **flesh** is white, turning red at the base of the stem, and the flavor is slightly bitter. It releases a strong and typical odor of soap.

▮ Where and when to find it

The Soapy Tricholoma is common in low-lying deciduous woods, especially under oak. It can also be found growing under spruce in the mountains. It can be found in large groups, growing on leaf litter in summer and fall.

The Dirty Tricholoma

Tricholoma terreum

Classification : Cl. Homobasidiomycetes -
O. Tricholomatales - F. Tricholomataceae.

- H: ¼-4 in (3-10 cm)
- Ø: 1½-3¼ in (4-8 cm)
- White spores

Gray cap, covered in fine hairs

White stem

Gills white,
turning gray

▮ How to recognize it

The **cap** of this rather small mushroom is conical like a coolie hat. It is covered with silky
gray squamules that are imbricated and of uniform size. The cap is thin and fragile and tears
easily especially at the margin which is eventually upturned.

The **gills** are quite widely spaced and unequal
in size. They are white at first but eventually
turn a dirty brown, the color of the soil, hence
the name of the mushroom.

The **stem** is tall and thin and gives this mushroom an elongated appearance. It is smooth
and silky, whitish washed with gray especially
toward the bottom.

The white **flesh** turns gray in places and is thin
and fragile. It has no particular odor or flavor.

▮ Where and when to find it

The Dirty Tricholoma hides exclusively under
conifers, especially pine and spruce. It can be
found growing in the grass in parks close to
these conifers.

It is quite common at all altitudes throughout
the temperate zone of the northern hemisphere
and appears in small colonies or in circles in

late summer, lasting until the first winter frosts.
Like several other species of Tricholoma it may
even be found growing under early snows.

▮ Features and edibility

The Dirty Tricholoma is good to eat, despite its
name. It has the same features as most edible
Tricholomas but unfortunately the flesh is thin.
Choose young, undamaged specimens and pick
them with great care as they are fragile.

The Dirty Tricholoma is sold in mushroom
markets, often alongside the Clouded Agaric
and the Pretentious Tricholoma.

Lookalikes

*There are two other gray-capped Tricholomas, one
of them inedible, the other poisonous.*

*The **Acrid Tricholoma** (Tricholoma virgatum) (p. 93),
has a gray, pointed cap which is fibrillose but not
squamose.*

*The large **Striped Tricholoma** (Tricholoma pardinum)
(p. 89), is dangerously toxic. It is easily recognizable,
however, due to its size and its massive stem, which is
frequently deformed. The cap is particularly characteristic, because of its covering of circular patches of
tiny, dark gray hairs which give it its characteristic
tiger stripes.*

▼ Lookalikes:
The Acrid Tricholoma
(*Tricholoma virgatum*) (p. 93)
The Striped Tricholoma
(*Tricholoma pardinum*) (p. 89)

	The Dirty Tricholoma *Tricholoma terreum*	The Acrid Tricholoma *Tricholoma virgatum*	The Striped Tricholoma *Tricholoma pardinum*
Cap	conical, scaly	conical, fibrillose	obtuse-angled, scaly
Gills	white, turning gray	white, turning gray	whitish to grayish
Stem	average	average	large
Odor	none	slight, fruity	mealy
Habitat	conifers	conifers, deciduous trees	conifers, deciduous trees
Features	good to eat	inedible	poisonous

This group of Tricholomas with non-viscous, gray scaly or hairy caps contains several species which are closely related to the Dirty Tricholoma

THE MOUSY TRICHOLOMA
Tricholoma myomyces

Very similar to the Dirty Tricholoma. The cap is more woolly and the gills remain white.

- H: 2-3¼ in (5-8 cm)
- Ø: 1½-3¼ in (4-8 cm)
- White spores

THE YELLOWING TRICHOLOMA
Tricholoma scalpturatum

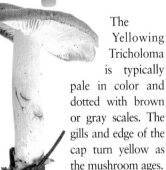

The Yellowing Tricholoma is typically pale in color and dotted with brown or gray scales. The gills and edge of the cap turn yellow as the mushroom ages.

- H: 1½-3¼in (4-8cm)
- Ø: 1½-2¾ in (3-7 cm)
- White spores

THE GRAY TRICHOLOMA
Tricholoma scioides

This mushroom is umbonate and its grayish pink gills have black spots on their edges.

- H: 2-4 in (5-10 cm)
- Ø: 1¾-2¾ in (4-7 cm)
- White spores

THE ACRID TRICHOLOMA
Tricholoma virgatum

The Acrid Tricholoma grows under beech and fir trees and has a pointed, metallic gray cap, which is fibrillose but not squamose (scaly.) Although the flesh smells fruity, the flavor is very acrid, making it inedible.

- H: 2½-4 in (6-10 cm)
- Ø: 2-2¾ in (5-7 cm)
- White spores

THE BELTED TRICHOLOMA
Tricholoma cingulatum

A small Tricholoma whose stem has a ring, and which appears under willow trees.

- H: 2-3¼ in (5-8 cm)
- Ø: 1½-2½ in (4-6 cm)
- White spores

Ring

THE COPPICE TRICHOLOMA
Tricholoma argyraceum

This is the Dirty Tricholoma's opposite number which grows under broad-leaved trees. It is also good to eat.

- H: 2-3¼ in (5-8 cm)
- Ø: 1½-2½ in (4-6 cm)
- White spores

THE BLUSHING TRICHOLOMA
Tricholoma orirubens

This Tricholoma is characterized by its yellow mycelium visible at the base of the stem and reddening flesh and gills. Its typical mealy odor develops when it is cut. It grows under beech and fir.

- H: 2½-4¼ in (6-11 cm)
- Ø: 6-10 cm
- White spores

THE BLACK-SCALED TRICHOLOMA
Tricholoma atrosquamosum

This Tricholoma is recognizable by its peppery odor, very dark, almost scaly cuticle and black-fringed gills. It is good to eat and appears under conifers, on calcareous soil.

- H: 2½-4 in (6-10 cm)
- Ø: 1½-3¼ in (4-8 cm)
- White spores

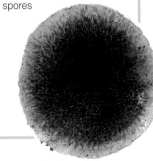

The Giant Funnel Cap

Leucopaxillus giganteus

Alternative Latin name : *Clitocybe gigantea.*

Classification : Cl. Homobasidiomycetes -
O. Tricholomatales - F. Tricholomataceae.

- H: 4-6 in (10-15 cm)
- Ø: 6-12 in (15-30 cm)
- Cream spores

▮ How to recognize it

This handsome mushroom has a very large, fleshy **cap** normally measuring 4-8 in (10–20 cm) in diameter, 16 in (40 cm) at the maximum. It is milk-white in color, which may occasionally be tinted with brownish-yellow, especially in the center in wet weather. The cap is flat at first, becoming irregularly depressed. The margin is inrolled at first, then upturned and it becomes typically furrowed with age, when it appears to be undulate or lobed.
The **gills** are crowded, white through cream and more or less clearly decurrent.
The **stem** is thick and firm when young but it soon becomes spongy. The surface appears to be covered with a velvety white down.
The **flesh** is white and compact and has a complex cyanic odor which is very penetrating and reminiscent of bitter almonds.

▮ Where and when to find it

The Giant Funnel Cap forms long lines or large circles in open grassland. It would be hard to miss it, growing in the short grass of meadows and pastures, or at the edge of pine forests to which it appears to be linked in some way. It is quite common throughout Europe, especially in the mountains, and is found growing in large numbers in September through October.

▮ Features and edibility

The Giant Funnel Cap is much sought after for its firm, fragrant flesh. Thanks to its size, a few specimens will fill a basket and are enough for a large dish. The best specimens for the table are young and are picked at altitude. Shortly after World War II, a closely related species, Clitocybe candida, looked as though it could be used to cure tuberculosis. French scientists

extracted the clitocybin, a substance which clearly inhibited the growth of Koch's bacillus. However, this research, which in any case was controversial, was abandoned as soon as streptomycin was discovered.

Lookalikes

*Large, white species of **Lactarius** or **Russula** which tend to grow in undergrowth may emerge on to verges and grassland. However, both these species have granular flesh, not the fibrous structure of the Clitocybes and this feature is very obvious when the mushroom is broken to reveal the flesh. The acrid, peppery flavor of the flesh of such species also shows that it is not a Giant Funnel Cap, and in the case of Lactarius, the presence or absence of milk is a strong indication.*

Related species

BITTER FUNNEL CAP
Leucopaxillus gentianeus

This rather unusual mushroom has a pinkish-brown or reddish-brown cap and the margin is striated or slightly furrowed. It grows mainly under conifers.

- H: 3¼-4½ in (8-12 cm)
- Ø: 21/2-6 in (6-15 cm)
- White spores

The Stripe-stemmed Tricholoma
Melanoleuca grammopodia

Classification : Cl. Homobasidiomycetes -
O. Tricholomatales - F. Tricholomataceae.

- H: 4½-7 in (12-18 cm)
- Ø: 4-6 in (10-15 cm)
- Whitish spores

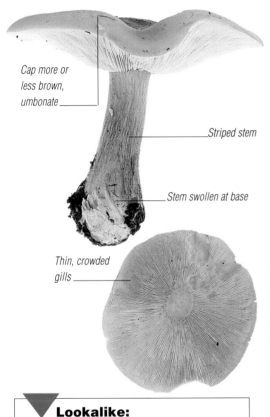

Cap more or
less brown,
umbonate

Striped stem

Stem swollen at base

Thin, crowded
gills

▼ **Lookalike:**
The Monk's Head Agaric *(Clitocybe geotropa)*
(p. 73)

▮ How to recognize it

The **cap** of the Stripe-stemmed Tricholoma is average to large in size. It is quite fleshy at first and slightly convex in young specimens. It later expands and eventually becomes slightly funnel-shaped with a rounded central umbo. The cuticle is perfectly smooth and is brownish to grayish, turning pale in dry wether, darkening when the weather is damp. The margin is incurving and thin and becomes strongly sinuous with age.

The thin **gills** are very crowded, usually white but sometimes cream-colored. They are sinuate when young, becoming slightly decurrent.

The **stem** is very typical of the species, being striated with fibrils which are the same color as the cap. It is quite thick but tall, cylindrical in shape but swelling to club-shaped at the base. The white **flesh** is tender in the cap; in the stem, it is more fibrous at first, but turns spongy in old specimens. Despite its mild flavor, this mushroom often has a rather unpleasant odor of mice or of mold and decay. Although classed as a Melanoleuca, there is not much contrast in color between cap and stem.

▮ Where and when to find it

It is often encountered in open spaces: meadows, pastures, grass verges, or forest clearings, mainly in the mountains, from summer through fall. In open grassland it may form circles, but more often is found in groups.

▮ Features and edibility

The Stripe-stemmed Tricholoma is of limited culinary interest. For one thing, the fibrous or spongy stem should always be discarded. As for the flesh of the cap, it is not very palatable when fresh due to the unpleasant odor. However, it is said to smell of gingerbread when cooked, and some people find it tasty.

Lookalikes

*Large specimens of The Stripe-Stemmed Tricholoma might be confused with **The Monk's Head Agaric** (Clitocybe geotropa) (p. 73) which has the same habitat. It has a yellowish to orange cap and is generally thicker. The gills are decurrent and it has the pleasant, complex odor which is typical of the genus Clitocybe, the funnel caps.*

Related species

The genus Melanoleuca, a sub-genus of the Tricholoma family, is characterized by the pale gills which contrast with the darker color of the cap and stem. The word "Melanoleuca" means "black and white" in Greek. The species are very difficult to distinguish from each other without microscopic examination.

THE BLACK-AND-WHITE AGARIC
Melanoleuca melaleuca

This mushroom is smaller. The cap is more regular and more funnel-shaped with age. The stem is grayish, fibrillose, and short. It grows in open spaces, but may invade coppices or shelter under various broad-leaved trees. Not worth eating.

- H: 2½-4 in (6-10 cm)
- Ø: 2-4 in (5-10 cm)
- White spores

St. George's Mushroom

Calocybe gambosa

Latin name : *Tricholoma georgii.*

Classification : Cl. Homobasidiomycetes -
O. Tricholomatales - F. Tricholomataceae.

- H: 2-4 in (5-10 cm)
- Ø: 2-4½ in (5-12 cm)
- Creamy spores

Very crowded gills

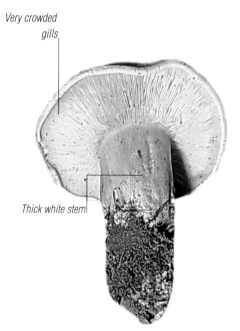

Thick white stem

Thick, white, swollen stem

■ How to recognize it

The St. George's Mushroom is a handsome white mushroom. whose fleshy **cap** is remarkably thick in the center. It is hemispherical then convex and may grow as large as 6 in (15 cm) in diameter. The matt cuticle is creamy white, with occasional yellowish or grayish patches.
It is particularly smooth and very soft to the touch. The margin is paler but thick and clearly inrolled.
The **gills** are white to cream, emarginate, thin and crowded. They seem disproportionately small in relation to the very thick cap.
The **stem** is robust, fleshy, and mealy at the top, fibrillose and striped below, and is the color as the cap.
The thick, white, compact **flesh** has a pleasant but penetrating odor of fresh meal.

■ Where and when to find it

The St. George's mushroom grows in grass in woodland, along forest paths, in glades, and meadows. It is fairly common throughout the temperate zones of the northern hemisphere, growing in clusters or circles in the spring. The reason for the name is that it usually emerges around St. George's Day (April 23), though it fruits more commonly in May and June. It may be found rarely in summer or fall.

■ Features and edibility

There are few edible species in the spring, making the St. George's Mushroom of particular interest. It is very sought after and sold in the markets and tastes truly delicious. There are those who consider it to be the best of all the mushrooms. However, a few people dislike the taste and the penetrating odor of fresh meal. It may occasionally be found "heavy" to digest so it should be eaten sparingly. It has certain hypoglycemic properties but could never be used as a substitute for insulin.

Related species

THE GRAY-CAP LYOPHYLLUM
Lyophyllum decastes

It grows in large clumps in mixed woods The cap is gray or grayish-brown. It is edible.
- H: 2¾-5¼ in (7-13 cm)
- Ø: 2-6 in (5-15 cm)
- White spores

	St. George's Mushroom *Calocybe gambosa*	The Livid Entoloma *Entoloma lividum*	Red-staining Inocybe *Inocybe patouillardii*
Cap	convex, thick, white, smooth	umbonate, white, gray fibrillose	conical, white to straw-colored reddening, fibrillose
Gills	white to cream	yellow, then pink	white, then reddish-brown
Stem	thick, white	thick, white	slender to thick, white, reddening
Odor	mealy	mealy	fruity
Habitat	hedges, grass verges	well-lit woods	parks, well-lit woods
Features	excellent	very poisonous	very poisonous

▼ Lookalikes:
The Livid Entoloma *(Entoloma lividum)* (p. 116)
Red-staining Inocybe
(Inocybe patouillardii) (p. 134)

Lookalikes

Although there is little resemblance, pickers sometimes confuse the St. George's mushroom with the species of Entoloma that grow in the spring, since these mushrooms also have a mealy odor. Confusion with the following two species could have extremely serious consequences.

The Livid Entoloma (Entoloma lividum) (p. 116), is large, grayish-white, and has yellow gills which turn pink. It is often found at the edge of woods. It grows exclusively in the fall, so it is unlikely to be confused with the St. George's Mushroom.
The Red-staining Inocybe (Inocybe patouillardii) (p. 134) on the other hand, is a poisonous species

which is one of the rare spring mushrooms. It is smaller with a conical. fibrillose cap which is white to straw-colored. As it ages, the margin often splits and reveals the flesh which stains red in places.
This mushroom is fairly common in clearings, parks and grassy spaces, especially in northern Europe. It is very poisonous, due to its high muscarine content.

The Star-bearing Nyctalis
Nyctalis asterophora

Latin name : *Asterophora lycoperdoides.*

Classification : Cl. Homobasidiomycetes - O. Tricholomatales - F. Tricholomataceae.

- H: ½-1¼ in (1-3 cm)
- Ø: ½-1½ in (1-4 cm)
- White spores

Hemispherical cap

Café latte color

Growing here on a decayed and dessicated russula

▌How to recognize it

The genus Nyctalis contains small mushrooms which grow only on other mushrooms. They may be saprophitic or parasitic.
The **cap** is globose to hemispherical, white at first, but soon becoming covered with a thick layer of dust which is the color of café latte. These are the spores produced by the cap.
The **gills** are rudimentary, reduced to a few folds, or non-existent, and whitish to grayish in color.
The **stem** is curved, only ⅛-¾ in (1-2 cm) long, and whitish.
The thick, white or gray **flesh** has an unpleasantly rancid odor.

▌Where and when to find it

The species of Nyctalis are not easy to see due to their small size. The easiest way is to find a decayed, blackened species of mushroom. Only subsequently will the cap or gills display small, round, paler protuberances. The Star-bearing Nyctalis often colonizes old specimens of The Blackening Russula *(Russula nigricans)* which persist for many weeks, drying out without actually rotting away.

It may also be found on species of Milk Cap (*Lactarius*), such as The Velvet Milk Cap (*Lactarius vellereus*) or The Peppery Milk Cap (*Lactarius piperatus*). This species of Nyctalis appears in summer, after heavy rains and storms, as well as in the fall.

▌Features and edibility

This genus is of no culinary interest whatsoever. In any case, the habitat and odor of the Nyctalis species are most offputting to anyone who is looking for edible mushrooms.

─ *Related species* ─

THE PARASITIC NYCTALIS
Nyctalis parasitica

This is a rarer species of Nyctalis, growing on old specimens of Russula or Lactarius. The cap is conical at first, before extending and becoming umbonate. It is fibrillose or silky, and stays white or pale gray. The gills are well-developed, grayish, very thick and widely spaced. The stem is thinner and grows to 2 in (5 cm) in length.

- H: ¾-1½ in (2-4 cm)
- Ø: ½-1¼ in (1-3 cm)
- White spores

Velvet Shank

Flammulina velutipes

English synonym: Velvet Foot
Alternative Latin name : *Collybia velutipes*.

Classification : Cl. Homobasidiomycetes -
O. Tricholomatales - F. Dermolomataceae.

- H: 1½-4 in (4-10 cm)
- Ø: 1¼-4 in (3-10 cm)
- White spores

Reddish-orange, viscous cap

Stem blackish -brown,
velvety, leathery

How to recognize it

The brightly colored **cap** of this species, which is compared to that of a little flame, hence the Latin name of the genus *Flammulina*.

The mushroom is small and the **cap** is not thick but quite fleshy. It is convex in young specimens but soon flattens and becomes irregularly umbonate when old. The cuticle is yellow-orange to fawn-orange, and darker in the center. The texture is typically waxy, becoming sticky in damp weather.

The **gills** are thin but swollen, adnate to emarginate, sand separated by smaller incomplete gills growing from the margin. They are paler than the cap, cream at first but tending to redden when mature.

The **stem** is cylindrical, slender and elongated and toward the bottom the texture is characteristically brown and velvety, contrasting sharply with the palor of the gills and upper part of the stem.

The **flesh** is soft and quite elastic in the cap but fibrous and tenacious in the stem. The flavor is mild and the mushroom has a pleasant, delicately fruity odor.

Where and when to find it

The Velvet Shank grows in small clumps on the stumps or dead trunks of various deciduous trees, especially elms or at the base of broom bushes, in clearings. It is common, persisting until late fall and sometimes until the spring. The waxy coating on the cap is efficient at protecting it from the frost.

Features and edibility

In Europe, the Velvet Shank is not adequately appreciated for its eating qualities, even if the leathery stem is discarded. Yet this is a pleasant winter mushroom whose elastic consistency seems to be very suitable for oriental cooking, and particularly for dishes based on rice, just like Jew's Ear (*Hirneola auricula-judae*) and Shiitake (*Lentinellus edodes*).

The Saffron Parasol

Cystoderma amianthinum

Classification : Cl. Homobasidiomycetes -
O. Tricholomatales - F. Dermolomataceae.

- H: 1¼-2¾ in (3-7 cm) ● Ø: ¾-2 in (2-5 cm) ● Whitish spores

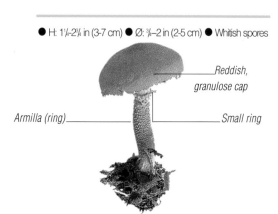

Reddish,
granulose cap

Armilla (ring)

Small ring

How to recognize it

The **cap** is easily detachable from the stem is at first campanulate, then convex or flat with a ragged, saw-edged margin. The surface is wrinkled or veined in the center. The cuticle is bright yellow-orange to reddish-fawn and is granulose or sometimes covered with a powdery deposit.

The **gills** are white or cream.

The **stem** is the same color as the cap and is covered in coarse, reddish flakes on the upper two-thirds of its length, which is separated from the smooth top by an annular zone. The **flesh** has an earthy smell. The species is inedible.

Where and when to find it

The Saffron Parasol is common in summer and fall, living in damp deciduous or coniferous woods, particularly on acid soil.

The Fairy Ring Champignon

Marasmius oreades

Classification : Cl. Homobasidiomycetes -
O. Tricholomatales - F. Marasmiaceae.

- H: 1½-3¼ in (4-8 cm)
- Ø: ¾-2½ in (2-6 cm)
- White spores

Persistent umbo

Beige to fawn
depending on
the humidity in
the atmosphere

Thin, very leathery stem

Very widely spaced gills, beige turning
reddish-fawn

Lookalikes:
Hill Marasmius
(Marasmius collinus)
The Ivory Mushroom
(Clitocybe dealbata) (p. 74)

How to recognize it

The **cap** of this little mushroom, which is conical to obtuse when young, extends with age. It retains a large central umbo while the margin become undulating, and sometimes irregular. In dry weather, the cuticle is a pale fawn to yellow-brown, but when the weather is damp or the mushroom is old, it becomes darker and reddening in patches specially in the center but sometimes around the edge as well.

The **gills** are swollen and free on the stem. They are beige, typically pale, not very numerous, and widely spaced.

The long, slender **stem** appears fragile, but in fact, it is tough and persistent like a reed. Thanks to its elasticity, and the fact that it is sometimes twisted or spiral, it "bends but does not break". Surprisingly for such a small mushroom, the **flesh** is relatively thick in the center of the cap. It is white and firm, and emits a pleasant, characteristic smell of almonds.

Where and when to find it

The Fairy Ring Champignon grows in open grassland, where it inevitably forms large rings as the name implies. These rings may attain several hundred yards in diameter! Some enormous rings have formed in airfields and are visible from the air, even at high altitude. The mushroom grows almost year-round, from spring through fall, and even in the winter when the climatic conditions are right, in uplands and lowlands.

Features and edibility

The Fairy Ring Champignon is known throughout the world. Its pleasant odor and flavor combine well with meat dishes or as an ingredient for an omelet.

It would seem preferable not to eat it in too large a quantity, as it may prove indigestible. It is very delicious however, and very sought after, as long as the fibrous stem is eliminated. It is sold fresh in markets, and dried or pickled in gourmet stores, even in the United States, where it fetches a high price. It can thus be used all year round. It is particularly suitable for drying, because when it is soaked in warm water, it quickly recovers its original shape and all the flavor is restored.

Lookalikes

There are, in fact, very few mushrooms that look like the Fairy Ring Champignon, though several other species of Marasmius and other small brown mushrooms, such as the Deceiver, might be mistaken for it. The habitat of the Fairy Ring Champignon, the only mushroom given the French name of Champignon in English, is as important as its other characteristics. Remember that it is only to be found in grassland.

Hill Marasmius *(Marasmius collinus) has crowded gills and a more fragile stem and smells of onions. It is a lookalike which can cause stomach upsets if eaten. It is much rarer than the Fairy Ring Champignon.*

The Ivory Mushroom *(Clitocybe dealbata) (p. 74) is poisonous. A beginner might possibly confuse it with the Fairy Ring Champignon with serious consequences. It is about the same size but is grayish white, reddening with age. The real danger is that it sometimes grows in grass near circles of the Fairy Ring Champignon and sometimes right in amongst it. A careless picker might well put both mushrooms in his or her basket. If they both cooked, a mistake like this might involve hospitalization.*

The Mousetail Collybia

Baeospora myosura

Latin name : *Collybia conigena.*

Classification : Cl. Homobasidiomycetes - O. Tricholomatales - F. Marasmiaceae.

- H: ¾-1½ in (2-4 cm)
- Ø: ½-1¼ in (1-3 cm)
- White spores

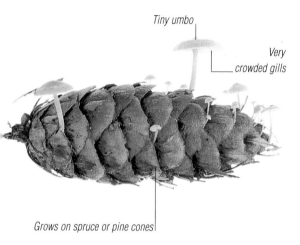

Tiny umbo

Very crowded gills

Grows on spruce or pine cones

▌How to recognize it

This tiny mushroom is found on fallen pine and spruce cones.

The **cap** is convex before it flattens, and is sometimes slightly umbonate. The cuticle is smooth and dry. The color is ocher or pale date-brown, lighter at the margin.

The **gills** are very crowded and white, or possibly pale gray.

The **stem** is similar in color to the cap or paler and covered with a white, powdery deposit. The base extends into a sort of "root" covered in white hairs which is buried in the substrate.

The **flesh** is pale brown and very thin, and is not of any interest. It has no particular flavor or odor, and the species is too small to be of any culinary interest.

▌Where and when to find it

The Mousetail Collybia grows on fallen pine or spruce cones, or even on individual scales that have become detached from the body of the cone. If the cone is buried under needles or moss, the mushroom appears to be growing in the soil. It is a common species in fall and right up into early winter and grows in woodlands, plantations and in parkland, wherever there are conifers.

Related species

A few other species of mushroom grow on pine cones and it is not always easy to distinguish between them.
The species of Strobilurus shown below fruit at different seasons to the Mouse-tail Collybia, in late winter and in spring.

THE EDIBLE COLLYBIA
Strobilurus esculentus

This species grows only on spruce cones. The gills are fairly crowded. Despite the name, the Edible Collybia is not particularly edible, because it is so small and the stem is certainly inedible due to its tough consistency.

- H: ¾-2 in (2-5 cm)
- Ø: ¼-2¼ in (0.5-3 cm)
- Whitish spores

THE TENACIOUS COLLYBIA
Strobilurus tenacellus

This is a less common species which looks very much like the Mouse-tail Collybia, but the stem is not powdery and it has a bitter flavor. It is found on pine cones.

- H: ¾-2½ in (2-6 cm)
- Ø: ½-1¼ in (1-3 cm)
- White spores

The Branch-gilled Mushroom
Marasmiellus ramealis

Latin name : *Marasmius ramealis.*

Classification : Cl. Homobasidiomycetes - O. Tricholomatales - F. Marasmiaceae.

- H: ¼-1¼ in (0.5-3 cm)
- Ø: ⅛-⅝ in (0.4-1.5 cm)
- White spores

White coloration at top of stem

Gills widely-spaced

Stem reddish brown with white scales

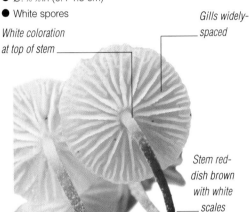

How to recognize it

This tiny mushroom colonizes fallen branches. The **cap** is obtuse at first, but soon becomes cream-colored or beige, sometimes tinged with pink. It is darker in the center, and slightly wrinkled, especially in dry weather.
The **gills** are widely spaced and cream-colored. The **stem** is short and incurving, darker at the base which is dotted with white scales. It is not worth eating.

Where and when to find it

The Branch-gilled Mushroom is very common in the fall, where it grows all along fallen, dead branches and twigs. Although wet weather helps it to penetrate the woody substrate, once it has taken hold it can cope very well with long dry spells.

Related species

Other very small species of Marasmius grow on dead branches or on the stems of dessicated plants None are edible.

THE STINKING MARASMIUS
Micromphale fœtidum

The cap is striated, brown, and darker in the center. The stem is black and velvety. It grows on rotten wood and has a bad smell.
- H: ½-1½ in (1-4 cm
- Ø: ¼-1¼ in (0.5-3 cm)
- Whitish spores

THE WHEEL MUSHROOM
Marasmius rotula

The cap looks like a parachute, with deep furrows emanating from a central umbilicus. The gills are very widely spaced and linked near the stem in a sort of collar *(collarium)*. The blackish-brown stem is whitish at the very top.
- H: ¾-1½ in (2-4 cm)
- Ø: ¼-¾ in (0.5-2 cm)
- Whitish spores

THE HORSEHAIR MUSHROOM
Marasmius androsaceus

This tiny mushroom resembles the Wheel Mushroom but the gills do not form a *collarium*. The stem is very long and thin, rigid and completely black. It grows on pine needles, leaves, or twigs.
- H: 1-2 in (2.5-5 cm)
- Ø: ⅛-½ in (0.3-1 cm)
- White spores

The Shredded Collybia
Megacollybia platyphylla

Alternative Latin name: *Collybia platyphylla, Oudemansiella platyphylla*.

Classification : Cl. Homobasidiomycetes - O. Tricholomatales - F. Marasmiaceae.

- H: 2¾-5 in (7-13 cm) ● Ø: 2½-4½ in (6-12 cm)
- Light cream spores

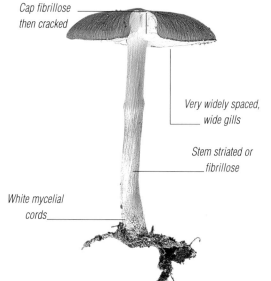

Cap fibrillose then cracked

Very widely spaced, wide gills

Stem striated or fibrillose

White mycelial cords

How to recognize it

The **cap** is of average size not very fleshy and convex at first, soon becoming completely flat to slightly depressed.The gray-brown to dark brown cuticle is typically striated with darker gray fibrils which close together at first, then spaced out. The cap may split more rapidly in dry weather and radiating cracks will then appear, starting from the margin.

The white **gills** are washed with bister or pale brown and sinuate near the stem. They are widely spaced and are particularly large, justifying the Latin epithet.

The **stem** is whitish with shading of the same color as the cap. It is fibrillose and covered with long striations. At the base there is a typical network of thick mycelial filaments which are known as rhizomorphs. These spread to nearby leaves, moss, and humus in order to propagate the mushroom. They are white and cottony and very friable.

The **flesh** is thin and whitish and breaks easily.

Where and when to find it

The Shredded Collybia is commonly found in broad-leaved woods or along the paths in copses. It prefers rotten logs—especially of oak—or leaf litter. It fruits almost throughout the year, from spring through to fall.

Features and edibility

Although the flesh is mild, The Shredded Collybia is not particularly worth eating. It is unfortunate that such a common mushroom should have such a poor consistency and be so flavorless.

Related species

PORCELAIN MUSHROOM
Oudemansiella mucida

Three similar species of a related genus (Oudemansiella), all of them not worth eating, deserve to be described.

This species has a brilliant, pure white cap, at most lightly tinted with greenish-gray in the center. It looks translucent thanks to its slimy coating. The margin is often wrinkled or furrowed. The large, widely-spaced gills are white. The stem curves in order to ensure that the cap remains parallel to the ground, and has a thick, membranous ring.

The Porcelain Mushroom grows on stumps or on the branches of dead or dying beech trees.
- H: 1¼-3¼ in (3-8 cm)
- Ø: 1¼-4 in (3-10 cm)
- Pale cream spores

THE TALL COLLYBIA
O. longipes

This mushroom is similar to the Porcelain Mushroom, but has a brownish-fawn cap which is not viscous. It is less common but has a similar habitat, particularly beech and oak,and has a rooting stem to help it burrow into wood.
- H: 4-6 in (10- 15 cm)
- Ø: 1½-4 in (4-10 cm)
- Pale cream spores

ROOTING-SHANK
O. radicata

This mushroom has a typical tall, straight stem which roots deep into the soil thanks to its pivoting action. The little cap is typically viscous and wrinkled or furrowed. The yellow-brown color shaded with bister is the same as on the stem, but darker. The gills are quite crowded and white. It is frequently found growing in association with rotten branches, especially of beech.
- H: 4-8 in (10-20 cm)
- Ø: 1½-6 in (4-15 cm)
- Pale cream spores

The Wood Woolly Foot
Collybia peronata

Latin synonyms: *Marasmius peronatus, Marasmius urens.*

Classification : Cl. Homobasidiomycetes - O. Tricholomatales - F. Marasmiaceae.

- H: 2-3¼ in (5-8 cm)
- Ø: 1¼-2½ in (3-6 cm)
- Whitish or light cream spores

Gills free

Stem slender and leathery

Yellowish, woolly hairs at the base of the stem

How to recognize it

The small, thin **cap** of the Wood Woolly Foot, is convex at first, then flattened, with a slight central umbo. It has an elastic consistency, and is reddish-ocher in damp weather, becoming leathery, rough-textured, and pale when the weather is dry. The very thin margin is upturned at first and becomes fringed as the mushroom ages.

The **gills** are quite large and widely spaced, sinuous and free. They are attached to a membrane, the *collarium*, which is separate from the stem. They are cream to yellow-colored, and eventually become stained with dark red. The **stem** is paler than the cap and gills and is encased in a sleeve of yellow, woolly hairs. It is often curved at base. Although slender, it is fibrous and leathery.

The thin, persistent, yellowish **flesh** starts to burn the mouth if chewed for a few seconds.

Where and when to find it

The Wood Woolly Foot usually grows in clusters, some of the very large, in beech woods among the dead leaves. It is more rarely to be found in the needle litter beneath conifers.

Related species

CLUSTERED TOUGH SHANK
Collybia confluens

The Clustered Tough Shank is the same size, but with a longer stem. The stem may also be hairy, but much less so than the Wood Woolly Foot. The Latin and English epithets evoke its habit of growing in tufts or tight clumps. It is also easy to recognize by its very crowded gills and the cap which is off-white to beige in color.

- H: 2-4 in (5-10 cm)
- Ø: 1¼-1½ in (3-4 cm)
- Whitish or pale cream gills

The Russet Tough-shank
Collybia dryophila

Classification : Cl. Homobasidiomycetes -
O. Tricholomatales - F. Marasmiaceae.

- H: 1½-2¾ in (4-7 cm)
- Ø: 1¼-2 in (3-5 cm)
- Cream spores

Smooth, Hygrophanous
pale fawn to reddish cap

Sturdy stem
concolorous with cap

Creamy-white gills

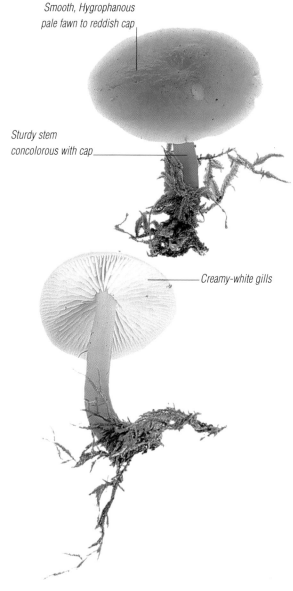

▌How to recognize it

The **cap**, is quite small and thin. It soon spreads out and even becomes depressed. It is very smooth and has a very variable color, especially as the cuticle is Hygrophanous. It is generally yellowish-fawn to reddish but may pale to whitish, especially in dry weather.

The narrow **gills** are crowded. They are white or off-white, sometimes yellow. They are emarginate.

The tall, slender **stem** is cylindrical but remarkably persistent as in the genus Marasmius. It gives this mushroom its tall, elegant appearance. It is similar in color and texture to the cap.

The thin, white **flesh** of the Russet Tough-shank has a pleasant fungal odor, but it is worthless for culinary purposes.

▌Where and when to find it

This species grows very commonly in oak woods. It can also be found less frequently under other species. It emerges in large colonies in late spring and lasts until the fall.

Related species

RED-STEMMED COLLYBIA
Collybia kuehneriana

The Red-stemmed Collybia is similar to the Russet Tough-shank though less common. The stem is dark red, except at the very top where it is yellow. It grows on stumps decomposition.

- H: 1½-2¾ in (4-7 cm)
- Ø: ¾-2 in (2-5 cm)
- Whitish or light cream spores

Buttery Tough-shank
Collybia butyracea

English synonym : Butter Cap

Classification : Cl. Homobasidiomycetes - O. Tricholomatales - F. Marasmiaceae.

- H: 2-4 in (5-10 cm)
- Ø: 1½-3¼ in (4-8 cm)
- Whitish spores

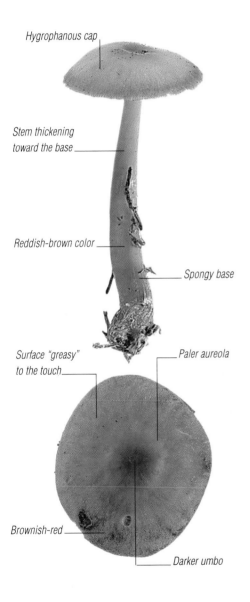

Hygrophanous cap

Stem thickening toward the base

Reddish-brown color

Spongy base

Surface "greasy" to the touch

Paler aureola

Brownish-red

Darker umbo

How to recognize it

The **cap is** convex at first, then extended, retaining a slight umbo in the center. The margin appears to be slightly striated when damp. The cuticle is smooth and greasy to the touch, as if it had been "buttered." The cap is very Hygrophanous, drying out from the center. It has a paler aureola around the umbo which is always darker than the rest of the cap. The cuticle may be reddish-brown or grayish, paling to cream in dry conditions. The **gills** are sinuate, crowded, and white.

The **stem** thickens gradually toward the bottom. It is fibrous and hollow, spongy at the base and almost the same color as the cap, ocher at the top, brown to dark red below. Vegetable debris adheres easily to it, as can be seen when the mushroom is plucked from the soil.

The **flesh** of the Buttery Tough-shank is pale and odorless, and has no particular features. Due to its unpleasantly greasy consistency, this mushroom is not edible.

Where and when to find it

The Buttery Tough-shank is a very common species, especially on fairly high ground and in acid soil. It may grow alone or in groups scattered over the leaf litter of various deciduous trees, and it is occasionally found under conifers. It can be found throughout the fall, and it is not uncommon to find it as late as December, in the right habitat.

Related species

ASEMA BUTTER CAP
Collybia butyracea
var. *asema*

This is a variety of the Buttery Tough-shank which is at least as common, and is sometimes elevated to the rank of a separate species. It is paler in color, without a trace of reddish-brown, and prefers pine-needle litter to leaf litter.

- H: 2-4 in (5-10 cm)
- Ø: 1½-2¾ in (4-8 cm)
- Whitish spores

Spindle Shank

Collybia fusipes

Classification : Cl. Homobasidiomycetes - O. Tricholomatales - F. Marasmiaceae.

- H: 2¾-7 in (7-18 cm)
- Ø: 1½-3¼ in (4-8 cm)
- White spores

Rusty brown cap

More or less umbonate

Gills white shading to rust color

Stem spindle-shaped, white, then spotted with rust

Rooting base

∎ How to recognize it

The Spindle Shank is easy to recognize due to its twisted, ridged, pointed stem which is shaped like a spindle on a spinning wheel. The **cap** of this medium-sized mushroom is fleshy and convex, extending late but remaining umbonate. It is white at first but soon becomes rust-colored, like the rest of the mushroom.

The **gills** retain their white coloring for a long time, but become spotted with rusty brown, and are eventually completely rust-colored.

The **stem** which is so typical of this species owes its appearance to its deep longitudinal furrows and its shape which is swollen in the center and slender at the two extremities. It produces a sort of perennial root-like structure which ensures that the mushroom survives for several years at a time.

The **flesh** is almost odorless and has a mild flavor. It is tender at first but soon becomes leathery, especially in the stem.

∎ Where and when to find it

The Spindle Shank is a common sight in broad-leaved woods in summer through fall. It grows in large clumps, especially on oak stumps.

∎ Toxicity

Although considered edible when young and tender, The Spindle Shank can prove to be an extremely indigestible mushroom.

Related species

DISTORTED TOUGH SHANK
Collybia distorta

This inedible mushroom has crowded gills. The stem is no wider than ⅛ in (1 cm) in diameter but has unusual, spiral furrows which give it its "distorted" look. It lives under conifers.

- H: 2½-4½ in (6-12 cm)
- Ø: 1½-4 (4-10 cm)
- Whitish spores

SPOTTED TOUGH SHANK
Collybia maculata

The cap is pure white at first, like the stem, but soon becomes spotted with characteristic rust-brown patches. The gills are as crowded as in the Spindle Shank, but the spores are paler in color. It lives in deciduous and coniferous woods, preferring the latter.

- H: 2¾-5½ in (7-14 cm)
- Ø: 2-4½ in (5-12 cm)
- Pinkish-orange spores

The Pure Mycena

Mycena pura

Classification : Cl. Homobasidiomycetes -
O. Tricholomatales - F. Marasmiaceae.

- H: 1¼-3½ in (3-9 cm)
- Ø: 1¼-1½ in (3-4 cm)
- White spores

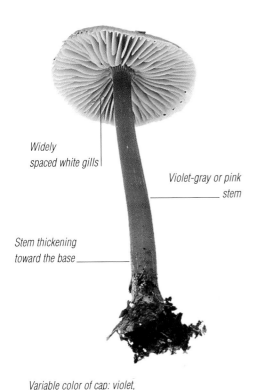

Widely
spaced white gills

Violet-gray or pink
stem

Stem thickening
toward the base

Variable color of cap: violet,
gray, bluish, etc.

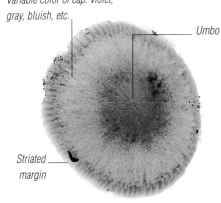

Umbo

Striated
margin

Lookalikes:
The Amethyst Deceiver
(Laccaria amethystina) (p. 82)
Deceiver *(Laccaria laccata)* (p. 83)

■ How to recognize it

The rather thin **cap** is conical to campanulate, then convex and finally expanded with a central umbo. It grows to about 2 in (5 cm) in diameter The smooth cuticle varies considerably in color. It is generally lilac, violet or pink but may also be grayish, bluish, and even whitish. The thin margin is deeply furrowed where the gills are attached below the cap.
The **gills** are quite widely spaced to sinuate, are swollen. They are off-white, tinted with pink or lilac.
The **stem** is concolorous with the cap or slightly paler. It is long and slender, thickening slightly toward the base. It is lightly furrowed and rigid at first, soon becoming frag-

ile and hollow. The thin **flesh** is watery, a feature typical of the genus Mycena. It is white or tinged with pink or violet and has the strong odor of radish, another typical feature.

■ Where and when to find it

The Pure Mycena grows in clusters in the dense undergrowth of broad-leaved or coniferous woods. lIt is very common in summer through fall.

■ Toxicity

For a long time it was believed that no purple or violet mushroom was poisonous, and the Pure Mycena, although of little culinary interest, featured on the list of edible mushrooms. However, poisonings have been reported involving violent stomach upsets followed by serious nerve damage and even halucinatory effects have been reported. On the other hand, some people have eaten this mushroom without experiencing the slightest problem. It may be that only one form of the Pure Mycena is poisonous. Whatever the truth, the Pure Mycena is best avoided and considered to be a poisonous species.

Lookalikes

Due to its suspect status, the Pure Mycena must not be confused with other violet or lilac-colored mushrooms which are very good to eat, such as:
*The **Amethyst Deceiver** (Laccaria amethystina) (p. 82) which has the same habitat and grows in the same season, in summer through fall. It differs in its granulose cap which has no umbo but is umbilical, its widely spaced, violet gills, its persistent stem and fruity odor.*
*The **Deceiver** (Laccaria laccata) (p. 83) is very closely related to the Amethyst Deceiver, which was once considered just a variety of the Deceiver, but is pinkish-orange in color.*

	The Pure Mycena *Mycena pura*	The Amethyst Deceiver *Laccaria amethystina*	Deceiver *Laccaria laccata*
Cap	pink or violet, umbonate, smooth	violet, umbilical, granulose	pink, umbilical, granulose
Gills	quite crowded, white to pinkish	widely-spaced, violet	widely spaced, pink
Stem	hollow, fragile, pink or violet	plein, tenace, violet	full, persistent, pink
Odor	of radish	slightly fruity	slightly fruity
Features	poisonous	very good to eat	very good to eat

Various forms of the Pure Mycena have been described, due to the very variable coloration of this species. The Pure Mycena has a number of close relations, all of them inedible or toxic. Here are a few of them.

THE PINK MYCENA
⚠ *Mycena rosea*

The Pink Mycena is encountered mainly under beech trees and is similar to the Pure Mycena, although it is slightly larger, as such it is sometimes considered a variety of the latter. It differs in the pinkish color of the entire mushroom, which is paler on the gills and stem. It is also considered poisonous.

- H: 2-4 in (5-10 cm)
- Ø: ¾-2½ in (2-6 cm)
- White spores

Violet-rose cap

pale pink gills and stem

THE FERN MYCENA
Mycena epipterygia

The yellow or ocher cap is covered with a detachable viscous film. The upper part of the stem is bright yellow. It is tough and viscous.

- H: 1½-3¼ in (4-8 cm)
- Ø: ½-¾ in (1-2 cm)
- Cream spores

Edge of gills olive green

OLIVE-MARGINED MYCENA
Mycena olivaceomarginata

This species grows on lawns and pastures. The cap is straw-colored and the stem is brownish-yellow. It has typically whitish gills edged with olive.

- H: 1¼-2½ in (3-6 cm)
- Ø: ½-1¼ in (1-3 cm)
- White spores

TWO-TONED MYCENA
⚠ *Mycena pelianthina*

This Mycena lives in beech woods on calcareous soil and resembles the Pure Mycena. The cap is grayish-violet or brownish, shading to violet in places, but the gills are brown and edged in a darker brown, almost black. It also smells of radish.

- H: 1½-3¼ in (4-8 cm)
- Ø: 1¼-2½ in (3-6 cm)
- White spores

THE ROSE MYCENA
Mycena rosella

This tiny mushroom grows on conifers and is uniformly pink in color. The pink is slightly darker on the edge of the gills, this being its most noticeable feature.

- H: 1¼-2 in (3-5 cm)
- Ø: ½ in (1 cm)
- Off-white spores

The Iodine-scented Mycena
Mycena filopes

Alternative Latin names:
Mycena amygdalina, Mycena iodolens.

Classification : Cl. Homobasidiomycetes -
O. Tricholomatales - F. Marasmiaceae.

- H: 2-4 in (5-10 cm)
- Ø: ½-¾ in 1-2 cm)
- White spores

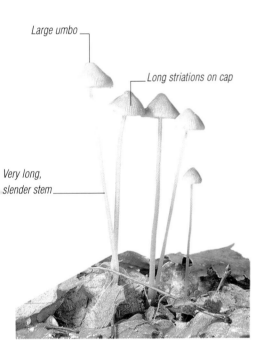

Large umbo

Long striations on cap

Very long,
slender stem

How to recognize it

The Iodine-scented Mycena is one of those Mycenas which is hard to identify with certainty unless it is examined microscopically.
The **cap** is convex at first, with a large umbo. The cuticle is dry and gray in color, with a paler, downy, striated margin.
The **gills** are fairly crowded, almost free, and off-white to white.
The **stem** is long, slender, and fragile, the same color as the cap, but darker toward the base.
The **flesh** is very thin; it smells of iodine, the smell becoming stronger when the mushroom dries out, hence the name. The Iodine-scented Mycena is inedible.

Where and when to find it

The Iodine-scented Mycena is a fairly common sight in the fall, preferring well-fertilized soils. It grows in moss, humus, and on leaf litter or bark, in both broad-leaved and coniferous woods and forests.

Related species

Several species of mycena have this odor of iodine, which is stronger when the mushroom is dry or dessicated. They have long, thin stems and grow on the ground, on moss or leaf litter, or on worm-eaten tree stumps and logs.

BLEACH-SCENTED MYCENA
Mycena alcalina

This Mycena has a dark, gray-brown cap which pales at the margin and which is striated in damp weather. The gills are pale gray. The stem is also gray and smooth. It smell strongly of ammonia or bleach. This inedible mushroom occurs frequent growing in tufts on old logs or the dead branches of conifers.

- H: 1¼-3¼ in (3-8 cm
- Ø: ¾-1½ in (2-4 cm)
- White spores

OLIVE-COLORED MYCENA
Mycena arcangeliana

This species is less common than the previous two Mycenas. It is yellowish-green or olive in color.

- H: 1¼-23/4 in (3-7 cm)
- Ø: 1/2-¾ in (1-2 cm)
- White spores

The Bonnet Mycena
Mycena galericulata

Classification : Cl. Homobasidiomycetes -
O. Tricholomatales - F. Marasmiaceae.

- H: 3¼-4½ in (8-12 cm)   ● Ø: 1¼-2¾ in (3-7 cm)
- Whitish spores

Umbo

Gray beige

Long striations

Stem same
color as cap

On rotting wood

▮ How to recognize it

This Mycena is one of the largest in this genus of tiny mushrooms. The **cap** is bell-shaped at first, then more extended, striated and even wrinkled up to the wide central umbo. The cuticle grayish-beige through brown.
The **gills** are whitish at first, tending to become stained with pink patches.
The **stem** is smooth and hollow but very tough and is concolorous with the cap, though paler at the top. The base is deeply embedded in worm-eaten wood.

The **flesh** is very thin and whitish. It has a mealy odor and flavor, which sometimes tastes and smells rancid. It is of no culinary interest.

▮ Where and when to find it

The Bonnet Mycena is a very common mushroom in summer through fall. It grows in groups and even in clusters on the dead branches and old stumps of various broad-leaved trees, thought it seems to prefer oak, and can sometimes be found on the rotten branches of coniferous woods.

Related species

STRIPE-STEMMED MYCENA
Mycena polygramma

This is quite a large Mycena and is recognizable immediately due to the deep striations along the length of the stem, which may be as long as 8 in (20 cm). It is silver-gray in color. The cap is grayish-brown and striated or furrowed to the base of the umbo. The species grows in clumps on half-buried, dead wood, on stumps, or at the base of broad-leaved trees.

- H: 2-6 in
  (5-15 cm)
- Ø: ¾-2½ in
  (2-6 cm)
- White spores

STINKING MYCENA
Mycena inclinata

This species is very common on rotten stumps of oak or other deciduous trees, on which it grows in large tufts. The gray-brown cap, which may be splashed with red, has a striated and finely dentate margin. The stem is typically dull red at the base, paling to white or yellow at the top. The flesh has an unpleasant odor of rancid fat, making it completely inedible and giving it its well-deserved English name.

- H: 3¼-4½ in (8-12 cm)
- Ø: ¾ -2 in (2-5 cm)
- White spores

THIN-CAPPED MYCENA
Mycena leptocephala

This Mycena never grows in tufts, even though it is often found in colonies. It also grows only on the ground, mainly in grassland, such as lawns and verges, showing a preference for coniferous woods. The stem is thread-like and the flesh smells of bleach.

- H: 1¼-2¾ in (3-7 cm)
- Ø: ½-¾ in (1-2 cm)
- White spores

The Milk-drop Mycena
Mycena galopus

Latin name : *Mycena galopoda*.

Classification : Cl. Homobasidiomycetes -
O. Tricholomatales - F. Marasmiaceae.

- H: 1½-3¼ in (4-8 cm)
- Ø: ½-1¼ in (1-3 cm)
- Whitish spores

Cap white to grayish-black

Stem containing a white milk

Very thin stem

down when young, which becomes smooth later. The cap is furrowed with radial lines where the gills are attached to it. It varies in color depending on its numerous varieties which some taxonomists have classified as separate species. The cap may vary in color from white to gray-black.

The **gills** are quite widely spaced for a Mycena and are white, broad, and adnate.

The **stem** is smooth and slender, barely ¹⁄₁₆ in (2 mm) in diameter, and the same color as the cap. The stem contains the only feature which serves to identify the mushroom with certainty: when broken it exudes a pure white milk.

The **flesh** is so thin as to be almost non-existent, but smells of radish. It is flavorless. For all the above reasons, the Milk-drop Mycena is completely inedible.

▮ How to recognize it

The **cap** is conical at first, then opens out into a bell-shape. The cuticle is covered in a fine

▮ Where and when to find it

The Milk-drop Mycena is very common, growing from summer right up to the onset of winter. It will grow under any type of tree and does not mind dense undergrowth, though it prefers grassy clearings, grass verges, and even open grassland and lawns.

Related species

Several other species of Mycena produce a red or orange milk when the stem is broken. None of them are edible.

THE BLEEDING MYCENA
Mycena haematopus

The red-stemmed Mycena grows in small tufts on old logs or the dead tree-trunks of deciduous trees. The cap and stem are pinkish-red and covered with a pink powder. When the stem is broken it exudes a blood-red milk.

- H: 1½-4 in (4-10 cm)
- Ø: ¾-1¼ in (2-3 cm)
- White spores

pink cap

Pinkish-red stem

THE BLOOD-RED MYCENA
Mycena sanguinolenta

Like the Bleeding Mycena, this Mycena contains a red milk. It grows on the ground rather than on wood. The stem is barely ⅛ in (1 mm) thick.

- H: 2-3¼ in (5-8 cm)
- Ø: ½ in (1 cm)
- White spores

ORANGE-MILK MYCENA
Mycena crocata

The milk of this Mycena is bright orange. That is why the gills and cap may become spotted with this color, especially when the mushroom is handled. The tip of the sis covered in white hairs. It is found mainly under beech trees.

- H: 2-4½ in (5-12 cm)
- Ø: ½-1¼ in (1-3 cm)
- Whitish spores

Cap macule d'orange

White hairs

1 - Clitopilus

- **Cap and stem not separable.**

Decurrent gills

Decurrent gills

CLITOPILUS **Page 114**

2 - Entoloma

- **Cap and stem not separable.**
- **Non-decurrent gills (unlike species of Clitopilus).**

Non-decurrent gills

Cap and stem not separable.

ENTOLOMA **Page 115**

FEATURES OF THE PLUTEALES

- Fibrous texture of the flesh.
- Pink gills in the adult mushroom.
- Absence of a ring.

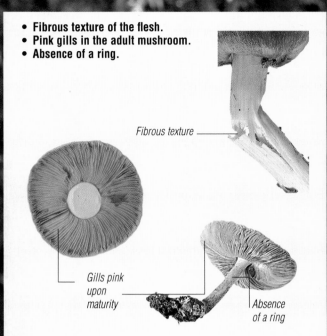

Fibrous texture

Gills pink upon maturity

Absence of a ring

3 - Pluteus

- Grows on wood.
- Absence of volva.
- Cap and stem separable.

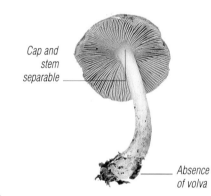

Cap and stem separable

Absence of volva

Grows on wood

PLUTEUS **Page 119**

4 - Volvaria

- Large volva.
- Cap and stem separable.

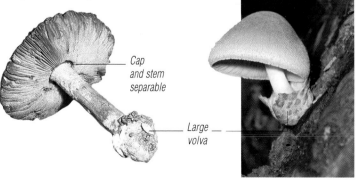

Cap and stem separable

Large volva

VOLVARIELLA **Page 121**

The Miller

Clitopilus prunulus

English synonym: The Sweetbread Mushroom

Classification : Cl. Homobasidiomycetes -
O. Pluteales - F. Entolomataceae.

- H: 1½-3¼ in (4-8 cm)
- Ø: 1½-4½ in (4-12 cm)
- Pinkish spores

Cap white downy, irregular

Decurrent gills

Short stem

Gills white, turning pink

Lookalikes:
The Leaf-mold Agaric
(Clitocybe phyllophila) (p. 75)
The Ivory Mushroom
(Clitocybe dealbata) (p. 74)
The Livid Entoloma
(Entoloma lividum) (p. 116)

∎ How to recognize it

The fleshy **cap** of this average-sized to small mushroom is convex at first, but soon flattens. The surface subsequently becomes irregular, covered in lumps and depressions, occasionally funnel-shaped in older specimens. The cuticle has the characteristic texture of a kid glove, and is sometimes shaded gray. It is covered with fine down that turns sticky in damp weather. The margin remains inrolled for a long time, eventually flattening and thinning and becoming undulating in old specimens.

The **gills** are off-white when young, turning pink when the spores mature. They are strongly decurrent.

The **stem** is short and fleshy, often excentric and curved at the base. The downy surface is similar to that of the cap and may appear to be slightly striated. The base is covered in a light, cottony fluff.

The tender, fragile, white **flesh** has a pleasant, mealy odor, hence its English name. The flavor is generally pleasantly mild.

∎ Where and when to find it

The Miller is fairly common in woods, under both broad-leaved trees and conifers. It is often found in grassy places, growing among heather or in blueberry patches, along forest paths or in neighboring pastures. It grows in small groups, and can be found in summer through fall.

∎ Features and edibility

The Miller, also known simply as Miller, is an excellent edible mushroom with tender, tasty flesh. When fresh it can be lightly sautéed in butter, either alone or mixed with species whose flesh is not as tasty. It can also be served in a Béchamel sauce. At any event, it does not require prolonged cooking. When dried, The Miller becomes stronger in flavor and makes an excellent condiment. This mushroom also has the advantage of never becoming worm-eaten. Care must be taken when picking it, as the flesh is fragile and friable.

Lookalikes

The Leaf-mold Agaric (Clitocybe phyllophila) *(p. 75) and* **The Ivory Mushroom** (Clitocybe dealbata) *(p. 74) whose gills remain white and are only slightly decurrent.*

The Livid Entoloma (Entoloma lividum) *(p. 116) has gills which are yellow, then pink and are not decurrent. The cap is covered in silver fibrils and the flesh is firm.*

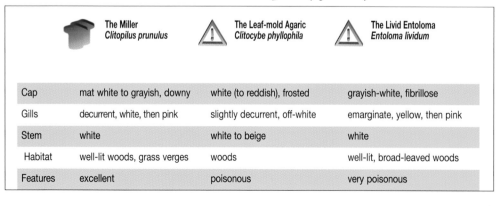

	The Miller *Clitopilus prunulus*	The Leaf-mold Agaric *Clitocybe phyllophila*	The Livid Entoloma *Entoloma lividum*
Cap	mat white to grayish, downy	white (to reddish), frosted	grayish-white, fibrillose
Gills	decurrent, white, then pink	slightly decurrent, off-white	emarginate, yellow, then pink
Stem	white	white to beige	white
Habitat	well-lit woods, grass verges	woods	well-lit, broad-leaved woods
Features	excellent	poisonous	very poisonous

The Silky Entoloma

Entoloma sericeum

Classification : Cl. Homobasidiomycetes -
O. Pluteales - F. Entolomataceae.

- H: 1½-4 in (4-10 cm)
- Ø: 1¼-2½ in (3-6 cm)
- Pinkish spores

Gills pink when mature

Sinuate gills

Then, striated stem

Smooth surface turning very dark when damp

How to recognize it

The **cap** is convex at first, pointed or umbonate, but extends very rapidly, while retaining an inrolled margin. The margin has striations which are more easily visible in damp conditions. The cuticle is smooth and silky, gray-brown when dry but darkening to sepia, almost to black, when the cap becomes moist again.
The emarginate **gills** are white to grayish at first, turning dirty pink when mature.
The **stem** is thin and striated and becomes hollow. It is the same color as the cap but paler. The gray **flesh** smells strongly of meal.

Where and when to find it

The Silky Entoloma grows in small groups on lawns or in open grassland, where it is commonly found in late summer through fall.

Toxicity

With the exception of a few species that emerge in spring, the Entolomas are mostly inedible. They should never be picked once spring is over, since many of them are poisonous or, like The Silky Entoloma, suspected of being so.

Related species

THE STAR-SPORED ENTOLOMA
Entoloma conferendum

This Entoloma is very similar to the Silky Entoloma but the stem is more clearly covered in silvery fibrils against a brown background. It is found on open grassland as well as in damp woods. It is also poisonous.
- H: 1¼-2¾ in (3-7 cm)
- Ø: ¾-1½ in (2-4 cm)
- Pinkish spores

THE OCELOT ENTOLOMA
Entoloma cetratum

The Ocelot Entoloma is suspected of being poisonous and has a cap which is more ochraceous or honey-colored than the Silky Entoloma. It lives in damp coniferous woods, growing on moss and sphagnum moss.
- H: 2-3¼ in (5-8 cm)
- Ø: ⅝-1½ in (1.5-4 cm)
- Pinkish spores

The Livid Entoloma

Entoloma lividum

English synonym: The False Miller.
Alternative Latin names: *Entoloma sinuatum -
Rhodophyllus lividus.*

Classification : Cl. Homobasidiomycetes -
O. Pluteales - F. Entolomataceae.

- H: 4½-8 in (12-20 cm)
- Ø: 3¼-7 in (8-18 cm)
- Pinkish spores

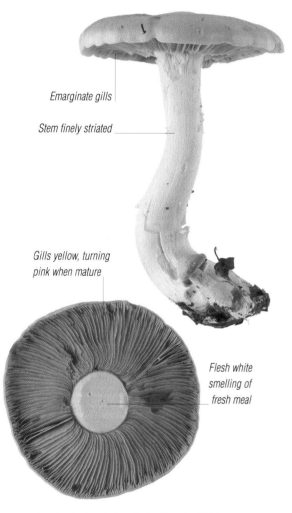

Emarginate gills

Stem finely striated

Gills yellow, turning
pink when mature

Flesh white
smelling of
fresh meal

▌ How to recognize it

The **cap** of this large, medium to tall mushroom
may be as large as 8 in (20 cm) in diameter. It is
campanulate at first, then convex, and finally
extended and with an irregular surface. It is
very thick and fleshy. The cuticle is livid in
color, ranging from off-white to yellowish or
grayish. The typically silky look is due to its
fine coating of silvery fibrils. The margin is
irregularly sinuate or torn.

The **gills** are emarginate, yellow at first then
turning pink when mature.

The long, sturdy **stem** is full, firm, and swollen
at the base. It is white, then turns yellow, showing fine striation which make it look fibrillose.
It is slightly spotted beneath the gills.

> **▼ Lookalikes:**
>
> The Miller *(Clitopilus prunulus)* (p. 114)
> The Clouded Agaric *(Clitocybe nebularis)* (p. 72)
> The Dove-like Tricholoma
> *(Tricholoma columbetta)* (p. 85)
> St. George's Mushroom *(Calocybe gambosa)* (p. 96)

The firm white **flesh** emits a strong odor of
fresh meal.

▌ Where and when to find it

The Livid Entoloma is to be found in summer
through fall in deciduous woods, especially
under oak and chestnut trees, or along forest
paths and verges. It may be abundant locally,
especially on clay soil. It is quite common.

▌ Toxicity

The Livid Entoloma is also called the False
Miller because it is frequently confused with
that edible mushroom, especially in France. Its
handsome appearance makes it look good to eat
but it causes serious gastro-enteritis, leaving the
victim very weakened, and what is worse, it
causes liver damage. The French mycologist,
A. Quelet, who suffered Entoloma poisoning
termed it "The Miller's Purge." Ingestion of the
Livid Entoloma often requires a hospital stay,
though it is rarely fatal. The mushroom is
responsible for eighty percent of fungal poisonings in France.

	The Livid Entoloma *Entoloma lividum*	The Miller *Clitopilus prunulus*	Clouded Agaric *Clitocybe nebularis*	The Dove-like Tricholoma *Tricholoma columbetta*
Cap	grayish white, fibrillose	grayish-white, downy	grayish, mealy	white, satiny
Gills	yellow, then pink	whitish, then pink	whitish	white
Stem	white, finely striated	white, downy	gray, finely striated	white, satiny
Odor	mealy	mealy	complex, cyanic	faint, pleasant
Habitat	broad-leaved trees	broad-leaved trees, conifers	broad-leaved trees, conifers	broad-leaved trees, conifers
Features	poisonous	excellent	good to eat (with reservations)	excellent

Lookalikes

In the fall, in woods or on grass verges, **The Livid Entoloma** may be mistaken for a Tricholoma and can create confusion with perfectly edible species. **The Miller** (Clitopilus prunulus) *(p. 114)*, also smells of meal and its strongly decurrent gills turn pink when mature, as do those of The Livid Entoloma. However, it has a much more slender appearance the flesh is not as firm.
The Clouded Agaric (Clitocybe nebularis) *(p. 72)* has an aromatic smell that is not in the least mealy. The stem becomes hollow very rapidly.

The Dove-like Tricholoma (Tricholoma columbetta) *(p. 85)* is almost odorless and its gills are pure white. **St. George's Mushroom** (Calocybe gambosa) *(p. 96)* with which it is least likely to be confused is all-white and rarely grows in the fall, being a spring-fruiting mushroom.

The Silky-stem Entoloma

Entoloma rhodopolium

Classification : Cl. Homobasidiomycetes - O. Pluteales - F. Entolomataceae.

- H: 2¾-6 in (7-15 cm)
- Ø: 1½-4½ in (4-12 cm)
- Pinkish spores

Umbonate cap

Gills pink when mature

Silky white stem

∎ How to recognize it

The **cap** is not very fleshy, and soon becomes flattened and undulating. It is umbonate and striated on the margin. The ocher-gray or grayish-brown color of the cuticle is paler in dry weather and darker in damp weather.
The **gills** are cream at first, turning pink in the mature specimen, as the spores mature.
The fragile **stem** is off-white and silky.
The **flesh** is odorless but the *nidorosum* variety, sometimes considered as a separate species, has an unpleasant nitrous odor.

∎ Where and when to find it

The Silky-stem Entoloma is quite common in deciduous woods, especially beech, in summer and fall. It grows mainly at high altitudes.

∎ Toxicity

This Entoloma has been responsible for poisonings which appear to be due to simple intolerance or indigestibility. It is closely related to the large species of Entoloma which appear in spring, which are edible, and which smell strongly of fresh meal. Special care must be taken to avoid confusion if apparently edible Entolomas are found in early summer.

Related species

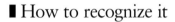

THE STINKING ENTOLOMA

Entoloma rhodopolium var. *nidorosum*

This Entoloma was once considered to be a separate species but is now believed to be a variety of *Entoloma rhodopolium* by some authorities. It is taller and paler in color, but differs principally in its unpleasant nitrous odor. It is poisonous and has caused numerous incidents of gastro-intestinal disorders, though these are less serious than those attributed to the Livid Entoloma.

- H: 2¾-6 in (7-15 cm)
- Ø: 1½-4½ in (4-12 cm)
- Pinkish spores

The Shield-shaped Entoloma
Entoloma clypeatum

Alternative Latin name: *Rhodophyllus clypeatus*.

Classification: Cl. Homobasidiomycetes -
O. Pluteales - F. Entolomataceae.

- H: 4-6 in (10-15 cm)
- Ø: 2½-4 in (6-10 cm)
- Pink spores

Denticulate gills, turning pink

Stem fibrillose

Umbo

■ How to recognize it

The **cap** of the Shield-shaped Entoloma is of average size and very firm. It is campanulate at first, but soon flattens out. It always retains a marked umbo in the center. The cuticle varies in color from bister to ochraceous brown. It is slightly viscous in wet weather and tends to turn pale in dry weather. It is covered in fine radial fibrils. The margin is inrolled at first and overhangs the gills for a long time, eventually flattening, and becoming irregularly sinuous and lobed.

The swollen **gills** are saw-edged, and turn pink as the spores mature, as in all the Entolomas. The cylindrical **stem** is full and firm at first and it is tall and slender. It is covered in brownish longitudinal fibrils which stand out against the white background color.

The **flesh** is white, but tends to turn brown in wet weather. It is firm and compact in the cap, but fibrous in the stem. It has a pleasant, characteristic odor of fresh meal.

■ Where and when to find it

The Shield-shaped Entoloma emerges early in the year, from April through to June, shortly after the flowering of the trees and bushes under which it grows in large numbers. It favors hedges of sloe and hawthorn as well as apple and plum orchards. It is found throughout the temperate zone of the northern hemisphere and is fairly common.

■ Features and edibility

The Shield-shaped Entoloma is one of the few edible species in this genus. The mealy odor is similar to that of the St. Georges Mushroom which grows during the same season, but it is not nearly as delicious as the latter. Nevertheless, it is sufficiently appreciated to find its way into several mushroom markets and as long as care is taken not to confuse it with the poisonous species which it resembles, it is worth the effort of hunting and harvesting.

▼ **Lookalikes:**
The Stinking Entoloma *(Entoloma rhodopolium),* (p. 117)
The Livid Entoloma *(Entoloma lividum)* (p. 116)
Red-staining Inocybe *(Inocybe patouillardii)* (p. 134)

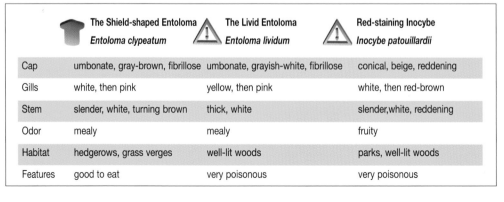

	The Shield-shaped Entoloma *Entoloma clypeatum*	The Livid Entoloma *Entoloma lividum*	Red-staining Inocybe *Inocybe patouillardii*
Cap	umbonate, gray-brown, fibrillose	umbonate, grayish-white, fibrillose	conical, beige, reddening
Gills	white, then pink	yellow, then pink	white, then red-brown
Stem	slender, white, turning brown	thick, white	slender, white, reddening
Odor	mealy	mealy	fruity
Habitat	hedgerows, grass verges	well-lit woods	parks, well-lit woods
Features	good to eat	very poisonous	very poisonous

The Shield-shaped Entoloma belongs to a group of spring Entolomas, which are closely related, edible, and smell of meal.

Lookalikes

The Silky-stem Entoloma (Entoloma rhodopolium), *(p. 117) resembles the Shield-shaped Entoloma but grows later in the year and is poisonous.*

The Livid Entoloma (Entoloma lividum) *(p. 116), is poisonous and generally grows in the fall but could be found at the edge of woods at a time when the Shield-shaped Entoloma is still around. It can be distinguished by its much sturdier appearance.*

Red-staining Inocybe (Inocybe patouillardii) *(p. 134) is a particularly dangerous spring species because its gills redden like those of the Entolomas and its cuticle is straw-colored. The conical cap, is often deeply split, showing the reddening flesh and it has quite a strong odor which is not mealy.*

THE APRIL ENTOLOMA

Entoloma aprilis

This small, fragile Entoloma grows under elms and hornbeam, and in hedgerows. It is recognizable by its brownish cap which is greasy when wet, and its silvery stem, striped with brown fibrils.

- H: 2-3¼ in (5-8 cm)
- Ø: 1¼-2½ in (3-6 cm)
- Pinkish spores

THE BLACKTHORN ENTOLOMA
Entoloma sepium

Another close relative that lives under blackthorn. It is fleshier, paler, and with a satiny sheen. The flesh turns red when broken.

- H: 3-5 in (5-13 cm)
- Ø: 1½-4½ in (4-12 cm)
- Pinkish spores

The Fawn Mushroom

Pluteus cervinus

Latin name : *Pluteus atricapillus.*

Classification : Cl. Homobasidiomycetes - O. Pluteales - F. Pluteaceae.

- H: 4-6 in (10-15 cm) ● Ø: 2-6 in (5-15 cm)
- Pink spores

Fawn-colored cap

Stem gradually thickening toward the base

Gills emarginate

▌How to recognize it

The **cap** is of medium size, convex at first then flattening and retaining a small central umbo. In color and texture it is reminiscent of the coat of a fawn or fallow deer.

The brown cuticle appears to be covered in a multitude of fine fibrils like the coat of an animal. It may split with age, or in dry weather and then becomes scaly.

The **gills** are typically emarginate. They are white at first, turning pink upon maturing and eventually becoming brown.

The **stem** has no ring or volva, and thickens slightly toward the base. It is striped with longitudinal fibrils which are white at first but later turn brown.

The thin, white **flesh** is quite soft in the cap and fibrous in the stem, when fresh it smells faintly of radish.

Fawn Mushroom

▮ Where and when to find it

The Fawn Mushroom normally grows as a saprophyte on tree stumps, branches, or pieces of wood in an advanced state of decomposition. It is often found, usually growing alone, from spring onward, often in May, but specimens will be found until the fall.

▮ Features and edibility

The species is edible, but of little culinary interest.

The genus Pluteus is easy to distinguish from the genus Volvaria, as it lacks a volva.

THE LION PLUTEUS
Pluteus leoninus

This is the commonest Pluteus. Despite its small size, its golden-yellow cap makes it stand out from afar against the fall carpet of leaves. It grows on partially buried rotting wood . It is of no culinary interest.
- H: 2-3¼ in (5-8 cm)
- Ø: ¾-2 in (2-5 cm)
- Pinkish spores

THE YELLOW PLUTEUS
Pluteus chrysophaeus

This species resembles the Veined Pluteus, but the cap is less wrinkled and yellowish. The stem is also pale yellow.
- H: 1¼-3¼ in (3-8 cm)
- Ø: ¾-2 in (2-5 cm)
- Pinkish spores

THE VEINED PLUTEUS
Pluteus phlebophorus

The brown cap is very wrinkled and veined, especially in the center; the margin is paler and slightly striated. This inedible mushroom lives on leaf litter in deciduous woods through summer and early fall.
- H: 1¼-3¼ in (3-8 cm)
- Ø: ¾ 2 in (2-5 cm)
- Pinkish spores

The Fawn Mushroom does not always live up to its name. The color can vary quite considerably as the above photos prove. It is hard to believe that all these are the same species!

The Pink-spored Grisette
Volvariella speciosa

Classification : Cl. Homobasidiomycetes -
O. Pluteales - F. Pluteaceae.

- H: 5½-8 in (14-20 cm)
- Ø: 2¾-6 in (7-15 cm)
- Pinkish spores

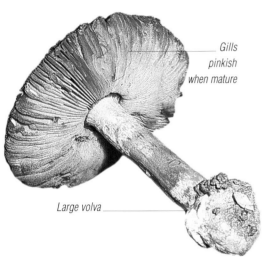

Gills
pinkish
when mature

Large volva

▼ **Lookalike:**
The Death Cap (*Amanita phalloides*)
(p. 176)

■ How to recognize it

The **cap** is of average size, almost ovoid at first, flattening later, and retaining a large central umbo. It is pure white at first, turning brown later, and the cuticle is very slimy, especially in damp weather, so that particles of dirt adhere to the cap, especially in young specimens. The membranous margin is furrowed at the edge and sometimes irregularly lobed.
The **gills** are regular and crowded, white at first and turning pink as the spores mature.
The **stem** is cylindrical and concolorous with the cap. It has no ring. If the mushroom is unearthed whole, the base can be seen to be sheathed in a thick, white, membranous volva, which tears into wide lobes.
The soft, white **flesh** is of a similar consistency to that of the Amanitas. When fresh, it smells faintly of radish.

■ Where and when to find it

The Pink-Spored Grisette fruits sporadically from spring through fall in cultivated fields, gardens, on dung-heaps, compost, rotting straw, and similar substrates.

■ Features and edibility

This mushrooms once had the reputation of being fatal, due to its being confused with the whites species of Amanita. In fact, The Pink-spored Grisette is edible.

Lookalike
*The white varieties of Amanita and the **Death Cap** (Amanita phalloides) (p. 176) bear some resemblance in the color of the cap to the gloiocephala variety, but the latter has no ring on the stem and the gills of the Amanitas always remain white.*

Related species

GREEN-CAPPED GRISETTE
Volvariella speciosa, var. *gloiocephala*

This form of the Pink-spored Grisette has a cap which is glaucous green in color. The other features are similar.

- H: 4-8 in (10-20 cm)
- Ø: 3¾-4½ in (8-12 cm)
- Pinkish spores

*Couleur plus
ou moins
verdatre*

Pink,
emarginate gills

SILKY AGARIC
Volvariella bombycina

This Agaric has a large silky cap and grows on wood. It is very good to eat.

- H: 3¾-7 in (8-18 cm)
- Ø: 4-7 in (10-18 cm)
- Pinkish spores

1 - Cortinarius

- Presence of a cortina (veil).
- Gills tinged with rust-color upon maturity.

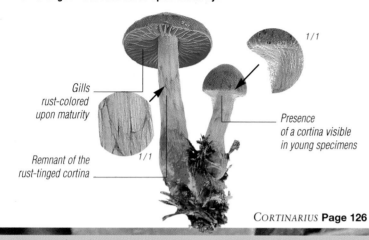

1/1

Gills
rust-colored
upon maturity

Remnant of the
rust-tinged cortina

1/1

Presence
of a cortina visible
in young specimens

CORTINARIUS **Page 126**

2 - Hebeloma

- Dun-colored cap.
- Coffee-colored, sinuate gills.

Dun-colored
cap

Coffee-colored
sinuate gills

Sinuate gills

HEBELOMA **Page 132**

3 - Inocybe

- Split or fibrillose cap, sometimes silky.
- Gills tobacco-brown color upon maturity.

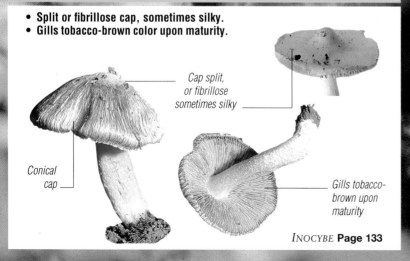

Cap split,
or fibrillose
sometimes silky

Conical
cap

Gills tobacco-
brown upon
maturity

INOCYBE **Page 133**

4 - Rozites

- Wrinkled cap.
- Ring.
- Rusty ocher gills.

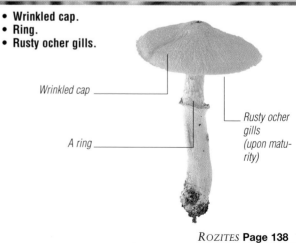

Wrinkled cap

A ring

Rusty ocher
gills
(upon matu-
rity)

ROZITES **Page 138**

FEATURES OF CORTINARIALES

- Flesh fibrous in texture.
- Stem and cap not separable.
- Gills adhering to stem (not free), but not decurrent.
- Color of gills upon maturity: rust, brown, purple-brown, brownish black.

Stem and cap not separable

Fibrous flesh

Gills attached to stem (not free), not decurrent

Gills brown in color

Gills purple-brown in color

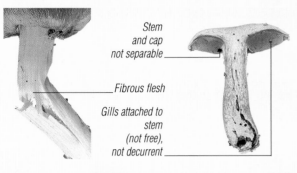

Rust-colored gills

Brownish-black gills

5 - Gymnopilus

- Grows on wood.
- Ocher-rust gills.

Reddish-ocher gills (upon maturity)

Ring or cortina

Grows on wood

GYMNOPILUS **Page 138**

6 - Crepidotus

- Small round or kidney-shaped mushroom, growing on wood.
- Non-existent stem.

Small round or kidney-shaped mushroom

Growing on wood

Non-existent stem

CREPIDOTUS **Page 139**

7 - Galera

- Ocher-rust gills.
- Small mushroom.
- Convex or bell-shaped cap.

Convex or bell-shaped cap

Ocher-rust gills

Thin stem

GALERINA **Page 140**

8 - Stropharia

- Violet-brown gills, darker upon maturity.
- Presence of a ring or scales on the stem.

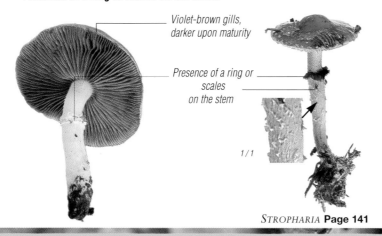

Violet-brown gills, darker upon maturity

Presence of a ring or scales on the stem

1 / 1

STROPHARIA **Page 141**

9 - Hypholoma

- Gills violet-brown upon maturity.
- No ring or floccules on the stem.

Violet-brown gills upon maturity

Stem without a ring and not floccose

HYPHOLOMA **Page 143**

10 - Pholiota

- Smooth and hygrophanous cap.
- Presence of a ring.

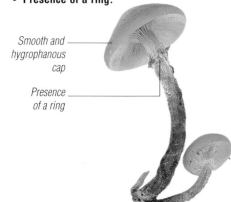

Smooth and hygrophanous cap

Presence of a ring

KUEHNEROMYCES **Page 144**

- Scaly or viscous cap and stem.
- Rusty or rusty-brown gills upon maturity.

Scaly or viscous cap and stem

Rusty or rusty-brown gills upon maturity

PHOLIOTA **Page 146**

FEATURES OF THE CORTINARIALES
(CONTINUED)

12 - Panaeolus

- **Brownish-black gills upon maturity.**
- **Hemispherical or concave cap.**
- **Long, thin stem.**

Cap hemispherical or concave

Blackish-brown gills upon maturity with paler edges.

Long, thin stem

PANAEOLUS **Page 149**

13 - Agrocybe

- **Wrinkled cap.**
- **Gills tobacco brown upon maturity.**
- **Presence of a ring.**

Tobacco brown gills upon maturity

Wrinkled cap

Presence of a ring

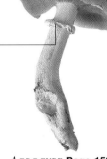

AGROCYBE **Page 150**

11 - Psilocybe

- **Hemispherical or pointed cap.**
- **Long, thin stem.**
- **Purplish-brown gills.**

Hemispherical or pointed cap

Purplish-brown gills

Long, thin stem

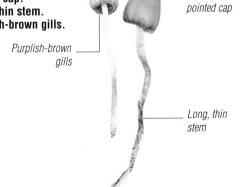

PSILOCYBE **Page 148**

14 - Bolbitius

- **Very fragile, yellow mushroom.**
- **Striated, viscous cap.**

Very fragile, yellow mushroom

Striated viscous cap

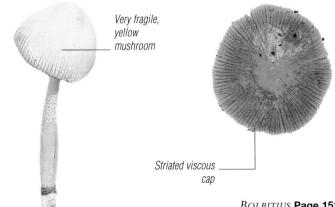

BOLBITIUS **Page 151**

The Annatto-colored Cortinarius

Cortinarius orellanus

Classification : Cl. Homobasidiomycetes -
O. Cortinariales - F. Cortinariaceae.

- H: 2½-4½ in (6-12 cm)
- Ø: 1¼-3¼ in (3-8 cm)
- Rust-brown spores

Reddish-orange, fibrillose, silky cap

Widely spaced, yellow-orange, then rusty gills

Yellowish-red, fibrillose stem

Lookalike:
The Tubular Chanterelle *(Cantharellus tubaeformis)* (p. 204)

How to recognize it

The Annatto-colored Cortinarius is quite small but is distinctive thanks to its brilliant coloring, similar to that of annatto or even of fire. The **cap** is campanulate to convex at first, but it soon extends, though generally retains the central umbo. It is not very fleshy but is quite firm, dry, silky and fibrillose on the cuticle. The thin, slightly hairy margin is regular at first, then sinuous, and it splits in dry weather.

The **gills** are widely spaced and swollen; they are slightly adnate. Their handsome orange-yellow color changes to bright rust-red as the spores ripen.

The tall, cylindrical **stem**, is usually curved, full, and firm. The surface is covered in darker, fawn fibrils. The whitish cortina (veil) is fugaceous.

The firm **flesh** is a paler version of the color of the cap. It smells strongly of radish and has an acid flavor.

Where and when to find it

The Annatto-colored Cortinarius develops in the fall under deciduous trees, especially birches, but also under oaks and chestnut trees, more rarely under conifers. It grows throughout southern Europe, especially in mountainous areas and in some years it fruits in large colonies. It is also found in lowland. It used to be called the Mountain Cortinarius in French but this name is wrong and is the result of a mistranslation of the Latin epithet. *Orellanus*

does not derive from the Greek word *oros*, which means "mountain", but from the scientific name for the annatto tree, *Bixa orellana*, the tropical, South American tree whose seeds are used to make annatto, the edible coloring rich in a reddish-orange pigment called bixine.

Toxicity

Until 1952, it was believed that all the species of Cortinarius were harmless. However, under its flamboyant exterior, the Annatto-colored Cortinarius conceals a deadly poison. It was found in large quantities in Poland, in that year, and caused serious poisoning in 102 people, of whom eleven died. The relationship of cause and effect was only established five years later, because the poison is particularly pernicious and accumulates very slowly in the body. The incubation period varies, in fact, from three to seventeen days!

The delayed onset of the symptom presents certain analogies with the type of poisoning caused by The Death Cap. The first symptoms are those of a stomach upset, involving diarrhea and vomiting, both of which are painful and weakening. But the poison slowly works on the kidneys where the real damage is done. Acute nephritis ensues; it may be incurable and lead to death. Survivors may be so badly damaged as to experience permanent kidney failure. Their only remedy is kidney dialysis or a kidney transplant.

The Annatto-colored Cortinarius may thus be admired, but should never be eaten.

Lookalike

There is a slight possibility of confusion with mushrooms of similar size and coloration but a completely different shape, such as The Tubular Chanterelle.

However, it must be remembered that **The Tubular Chanterelle** (Cantharellus tubaeformis) *(p. 204)*, has forked folds instead of gills, and the cap is deeply funnel-shaped. At any event, none of the tall, slender species of Cortinarius should be consumed, but it is worthwhile trying to recognize them to avoid unpleasant surprises!

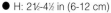

Related species

THE SUSPECT CORTINARIUS
Cortinarius speciosissimus

The Suspect Cortinarius is just as dangerous but not as frequent. It can be found under conifers, growing on very damp, acid soil, even on marshy ground. The orange-yellow cap has a fairly acute umbo. The stem has several paler annular zones.

- H: 2½-4½ in (6-12 cm)
- Ø: 1½31/4 in (4-8 cm)
- Rust-brown spores

THE RED-BROWN CORTINARIUS
Cortinarius bolaris

This Cortinarius is suspected of being poisonous. The cap and stem are covered with rusty scales on a yellow background. The orange-red mycelium is sometimes visible at the base of the stem. It grows on acid soil in deciduous or mixed woods.

- H: 2-4 in (5-10 cm)
- Ø: 1¼-2½ in (3-6 cm)
- Cinnamon-rust spores

The Red-banded Cortinarius

Cortinarius armillatus

Classification: Cl. Homobasidiomycetes - O. Cortinariales - F. Cortinariaceae.

- H: 4-6½ in (10-17 cm)
- Ø: 2½-4 in (6-10 cm)
- Rust-brown spores

Rust-colored bands or variegations

Gills beige at first

Bulb

The **stem** is firm and full, cylindrical except at the base when it swells into a bulb. It is decorated with reddish-orange filamentous bands which are sometimes oblique and occasionally reduced to faint zigzags. The white cortina is thick but fugaceous.

The **flesh** is pale brown, reddish under the cuticle. It has a fairly noticeable smell of radish. The flavor may be mild or bitter.

It is wise to consider the species as poisonous.

▋ How to recognize it

The fleshy **cap** is bell-shaped at first, then extended. The thin margin is eventually upturned and may bear the remains of the veil in the form of little membranous fragments. The cuticle is fawn and is covered in a fine reddish down.

The beige **gills** soon turn rust-colored. They are uneven in length and there are many short gills interleaved with long ones.

▋ Where and when to find it

The Red-banded Cortinarius, which appears from late summer, grows at all altitudes. It hides under birch trees on very wet, siliceous ground, and among sphagnum moss.

The Semi-sanguine Cortinarius

⚠ Cortinarius semisanguineus

Classification : Cl. Homobasidiomycetes -
O. Cortinariales - F. Cortinariaceae.

- H: 2-4 in (5-10 cm)
- Ø: 1¼-2¾ in (3-7 cm)
- Fawn-rust spores

Blood red gills

Cinnamon-colored cap

*Long, sinuous, yellow stem,
rust-colored cortina*

▋ How to recognize it

The **cap** is campanulate at first and until it extends it has a small umbo surrounded by a small circular depression. The cuticle is shiny but not damp and is cinnamon or yellowish-brown in color.
The **gills** are of varying lengths and are a magnificent blood-red in color at first, then turning rusty due to the ripening of the spores.
The long, sinuous **stem** is hollow. It is chrome yellow or ocher, sometimes partially covered by red fibrils. The cortina is thin, yellowish, and fugaceous. The golden-yellow **flesh** tastes and smells of radish, a common property in species of Cortinarius.

▋ Where and when to find it

The Semi-sanguine Cortinarius grows in highland and lowlands. It fruits in the fall on moss in the damp undergrowth of coniferous woods, sometimes in marshes and bogs.

▋ Toxicity

Like all the other species of Cortinarius described in this section, it is poisonous. All the brightly colored Cortinarius must be considered poisonous, or at best, suspect.

Related species

The following species of Cortinarius have dry caps and are brightly-colored (especially the gills).

BLOOD-RED CORTINARIUS
⚠ *Cortinarius sanguineus*

This handsome species is blood-red all over, including the flesh. It appears in damp woods of fir and spruce, and sometimes in mixed woods.
- H: 1½-2¾ in (4-7 cm)
- Ø: ¾-2 in (2-5 cm)
- Rust-brown spores

PHOENICIAN CORTINARIUS
⚠ *Cortinarius phœniceus*

This Cortinarius resembles the Annatto-colored Cortinarius in its appearance and reddish-fawn cap. The gills rare blood-red, then rust-tinged, like the Semi-sanguine Cortinarius. The lower part of the stem is covered with a fiery red down. It is a rare variety which mostly grows under birch trees in warmer latitudes.
- H: 2-3½ in (5-9 cm)
- Ø: 1½-4 in (4-10 cm)
- Fawn-rust spores

CINNAMON CORTINARIUS
⚠ *Cortinarius cinnamomeus*

The cap is yellow or cinnamon-colored and the gills and stem are saffron to olive. It grows in marshes and damp undergrowth.
- H: 2-4 in (5-10 cm)
- Ø: 1¼-2½ in (3-6 cm) ● Rust-colored spores

The Mauve-tinted Cortinarius
Cortinarius alboviolaceus

Classification : Cl. Homobasidiomycetes -
O. Cortinariales - F. Cortinariaceae.

- H: 2¾-5½ in (7-14 cm)
- Ø: 2-3¼ in (5-8 cm)
- Rust-brown spores

Bluish white cap

Cap with wide umbo

Bluish white cortina , turning rusty due to ripening spores

Stem swollen at the base

How to recognize it

The **cap** which is campanulate in young specimens, has a very large umbo in the mature mushroom which may become flattened in older ones. The cuticle is covered with a bluish-white vei,l which at first is fibrillose and silky. It is very pale violet in color and may be yellow in the center. The **gills** are quite crowded, sinuate, lilac-gray then rust-colored.

The **stem** is swollen and club-shaped at the base. It is fibrillose and silky, and the same color as the cap, but the thick cortina is soon stained with the rust color of the spores. The **flesh** is thick under the umbo, but very thin around it. It is lilac-colored or bluish especially at the top of the stem. It is odorless and mild in flavor. The species is edible but not recommended as it is not particularly tasty.

Where and when to find it

The Mauve-tinted Cortinarius is common in late summer through fall, often growing in groups on acid soil under broad-leaved trees, and sometimes under conifers.

Related species

THE STINKING CORTINARIUS
Cortinarius traganus

The repellent odor of this mushroom distinguishes it from all the related species. The widely spaced gills are ocher or saffron in young specimens, and the flesh is brighter in the base of the stem. The stem is large and club-shaped.

- H: 3¼-4½ in (8-12 cm)
- Ø: 2-4½ in (5-12 cm)
- Fawn-rust spores

THE SILKY CORTINARIUS
Cortinarius pholideus

The cap of the Silky Cortinarius is covered in tiny, tight brown, pointed hairs. The gills are bluish-violet in very young specimens. The stem is covered in bands of hairy striations up to the annular zone, above which the stem is fibrillose and pale violet. The flesh is also tinted violet at the top of the stem.

- H: 2¾-4½ in (7-12 cm)
- Ø: 1½-3½ in (4-9 cm)
- Rust-colored spores

The Purplish Cortinarius
Cortinarius purpurascens

Classification : Cl. Homobasidiomycetes - O. Cortinariales - F. Cortinariaceae.

- H: 2½-4½ in (6-12 cm)
- Ø: 2½-4½ in (6-12 cm)
- Rust-colored spores

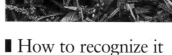

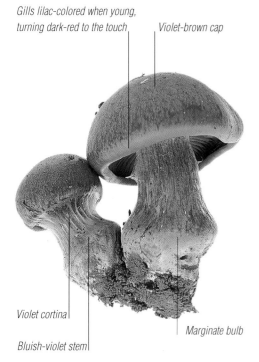

Gills lilac-colored when young, turning dark-red to the touch

Violet-brown cap

Violet cortina

Bluish-violet stem

Marginate bulb

touched. It is covered with shreds of the cortina which becomes rust-colored from the spores.

The violet **flesh** smells faintly of cocoa powder.

▮ Where and when to find it

The Purplish Cortinarius is a fairly common species which grows under broad-leaved and coniferous trees. It appears in little groups in the high season for mushroom, from September through November.

▮ Features and edibility

This mushroom is edible and is often mistaken for the Blewit. Some authors, such as the Frenchman A. Maublanc, consider it to be good, others find it insipid, and the consensus is that this species is of no great culinary merit.

Lookalikes

*All the violet species of Cortinarius have a cortina and gills which turn rust-colored upon maturity. Although they are edible, they do not make the best eating and it is a good idea to be able to distinguish between them and the tastier species. The **Field Blewit** (Lepista saeva) (p. 81) has a uniformly beige, smooth cap. The gills are brown, and the stem is violet and velvety and there is no trace of a cortina or of any rust coloring. It grows in grassland.*

▮ How to recognize it

This handsome mushroom has a fleshy **cap** which is convex at first then umbonate with an overhanging margin which becomes upturned in mature specimens. The viscous cuticle is chestnut brown to violet and typically covered in darker fibrils.

The **gills** are typical of the species, since they turn deep purple when rubbed. When mature, they are splashed with rust-color due to the ripening of the spores, but still retain some violet coloring. They are adnate to free on the stem.

The cylindrical **stem** ends in a ridged bulb which is known as marginate. It is also bluish-violet, and also darkens when

Related species

There are numerous violet species of Cortinarius, many of which are common and some are quite spectacular. It is hard to identify them due to their variability, and only experienced mycologists are able to do so. The amateur ought to be content with learning to recognize a few species which have the most easily recognizable characteristics.

THE WIDE CORTINARIUS
Cortinarius largus

Despite its viscous cap, it resembles the Blewit even more closely due to its shape and color. It possesses the distinct features of the Cortinarius: a rust-colored cortina and spores, and a stem with a bulb at the base. It is edible and grows under deciduous trees on sandy soil.

- H: 4-6 in (10-15 cm)
- Ø: 3¼ -4½ in (8-12 cm)
- Rusty spores

Lookalikes:
Field Blewit *(Lepista saeva)* (p. 81)
Wood Blewit *(Lepista nuda)* (p. 80)

The **Wood Blewit** (Lepista nuda) *(p. 80)* has a cap that is smooth and not slimy, violet to brown in color, with lilac gills that may turn slightly brown and a bluish-violet stem. It has a delicate fruity or spicy. odor.

The Purplish Cortinarius

	The Purplish Cortinarius *Cortinarius purpurascens*	Wood Blewit *Lepista nuda*	Field Blewit *Lepista saeva*
Cap	viscous, violet-brown, fibrillose	fleshy, violet to brown, smooth	thick, beige, smooth
Gills	violet, then rust-colored	lilac, turning brown	brownish
Stipe	fibrillose, blue-violet, rust-colored cortina	fibrillose-floccose, blue-violet, no cortina	velvety, violet, no cortina
Odor	faint smell of cocoa	fruity to spicy	fungal
Habitat	woods	woods (fields)	fields
Features	not very tasty	excellent	excellent

The Wrinkled Cortinarius
Cortinarius elatior

Classification : Cl. Homobasidiomycetes - O. Cortinariales - F. Cortinariaceae.

- H: 4-8 in (10-20 cm)
- Ø: 2-4½ in (5-12 cm)
- Cinnamon-brown spores

Wide umbo

Viscous surface

Wrinkled margin

Stem robust, viscous, swelling toward the base

Several annular rings

Pointed stem

The **gills,** are wide and sinuate, widely spaced and joined by veins. They are ochraceous, tinted with lilac when young, and turning rusty brown when mature.

The **stem** is long, sturdy, and cylindrical, slightly swollen toward the base and ending in a point. It is whitish at first washed with violet, then turns pale, while the cortina forms violet filaments which may disappear with age. They are covered with a thick mucous in dry weather.

The whitish **flesh** is rather soft, almost odorless, and mild in flavor.

∎ Where and when to find it

The Wrinkled Cortinarius grows in leaf litter, especially in beech woods on siliceous soil. It is quite common from summer through fall.

∎ How to recognize it

Although it is less imposing than the Purplish Cortinarius, The Wrinkled Cortinarius has a thin **cap** which is campanulate at first, then convex and eventually flattened, with a large central umbo. It is straw-colored to yellowish-brown and darker in the center. The cuticle is smooth and very slimy, so that it is shiny in damp weather. The cap is covered in long wrinkles near the margin.

∎ Features and edibility

Despite its tall and imposing appearance, The Wrinkled Cortinarius is of little culinary interest or importance.

Poison Pie

Hebeloma crustuliniforme

Classification : Cl. Homobasidiomycetes -
O. Cortinariales - F. Cortinariaceae.

- H: 2-4 in (5-10 cm)
- Ø: 2-4 in (5-10 cm)
- Light brown spores

Smooth, golden fawn cap

Gills pale ocher, turning brown

White flakes at the top of the stem

How to recognize it

The **cap** is quite small but relatively fleshy, especially in the center. It is convex at first, then spreading, but it often retains a large umbo. The smooth cuticle becomes shiny and sticky in damp weather. It darkens in the center, varying from ochraceous to russet in color. The paler margin is inrolled at first, then spreading and it becomes sinuate with age.

The **gills** are quite crowded; they are denticulate at the edge and sinuate on the stem. They are pale at first, turning ocher and then brown when the spores are ripe.

The cylindrical **stem** is solid and firm, and may be straight or curved near the slightly bulbous base. It is whitish, becoming tinted reddish from the base upward. It is characteristically dotted with fine white flakes at the top.

The white **flesh** is quite thick and emits a strong smell of radish, especially when it is cut. The flavor is bitter.

Where and when to find it

Poison Pie grows in large groups in the woods. It may form circles under deciduous trees, but also grows under conifers or in neighboring heathland. It is common, fruiting in summer through fall.

Toxicity

Poison Pie is not as bad as its name suggests, being merely indigestible by people with delicate stomachs. It is thus wise to avoid it because it can cause serious stomach upsets. In any event, it is not particularly good to eat, and looks very like The Peppery Hebeloma which is definitely poisonous.

Features

The Hebelomas are of great importance in forestry because they form mycorrhizal associations with tree roots and thus actively help in

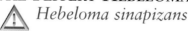

Related species

THE PEPPERY HEBELOMA

Hebeloma sinapizans

This is a much larger mushroom than Poison Pie but it is often hard to distinguish between the two species solely on the basis of this criterion. The bitter, burning flavor, like that of undiluted English mustard powder, and a bunch of hairs hanging down inside the stem, like the epiglottis inside the throat, are the best indicators. The Peppery Hebeloma is common under conifers and deciduous trees. Despite the flavor it has been eaten and has caused serious disorders.

- H: 4-8 in (10-20 cm) ● Ø: 2¾-6 in (7-15 cm) ● Tobacco-brown spores

promoting the growth of those species of tree with which they are symbiotically linked. The cultivation of species of Hebeloma is thus very beneficial for promoting the growth of woodland. In France, two species of Hebeloma are currently being studied for use in forestry, *Hebeloma mesophaeum* and especially *Hebeloma cylindrosporum*.

Lookalike

The poisonous Hebelomas bear a superficial resemblance in their appearance to the paler-colored edible Tricholomas. The odor of radish and the fact that the gills turn brown are indications that these are species to be rejected for culinary purposes.

THE TWO-TONE HEBELOMA
⚠️ *Hebeloma mesophaeum*

The two-colored cap, which is often umbonate, is reddish-brown in the center and much paler at the margin. The whitish stem, which is paler at the top, has a sort of underdeveloped fibrillose ring on it. It grows almost anywhere - in mixed woods, on lawns, or in parks. It is normally found in late summer through fall. The Two-tone Hebeloma is not edible and may well be poisonous.

- H: 2-4 in (5-10 cm)
- Ø: 1¼-2¾ in (3-7 cm)
- Tobacco-brown spores

THE ROOTING HEBELOMA
Hebeloma radicosum

This Hebeloma has a long rooting stem which burrows into rotting wood. The scaly base of the stem and cap and the presence of a ring high up on the stem, caused this mushroom to be classified previously as a Pholiota. It is rarer than the Burning Hebeloma and grows in isolation in deciduous woods. Although it is harmless, it smells strongly of bitter almonds and is inedible.

- H: 2¾-8 in (7-20 cm)
- Ø: 2-4½ in (5-12 cm)
- Tobacco-brown spores

The Bittersweet Inocybe
Inocybe dulcamara

Classification : Cl. Homobasidiomycetes - O. Cortinariales - F. Cortinariaceae.

- H:1¼-2 in (3-5 cm)
- Ø: ¾-2 in (2-5 cm)
- Tobacco-brown spores

Ocher gills

Short stem

Cap
ocher to fawn

Fibrillose
or hairy surface

The **gills** are slightly bowed, and are ochraceous yellow at first.

The short, cylindrical **stem** is the same color as the cap. It has a fugaceous cortina and sometimes a cottony ring which is not always visible.

The **flesh** presents no special characteristics. The faint smell is supposedly reminiscent of honey and the flavor may be bitter or even sweet.

This species is not edible.

■ How to recognize it

The convex **cap** is not very fleshy, and flattens extensively with age. The ocher-to-brown cuticle is fibrillose or hairy. It is covered at first with a white cortina.

■ Where and when to find it

The Bittersweet Inocybe is frequent in summer and early fall. It prefers sparsely wooded areas, open grassland, heaths, lawns, grass verges, and forest leaf litter.

The Silken-haired Inocybe

Inocybe rimosa

Alternative Latin name : *Inocybe fastigiata.*

Classification : Cl. Homobasidiomycetes -
O. Cortinariales - F. Cortinariaceae.

- H: 2¾-4½ in (7-12 cm)
- Ø: 1¼-3¼ in (3-8 cm)
- Tobacco-brown spores

Fibrillose, fissured cuticle

White stem

Gills turning brown

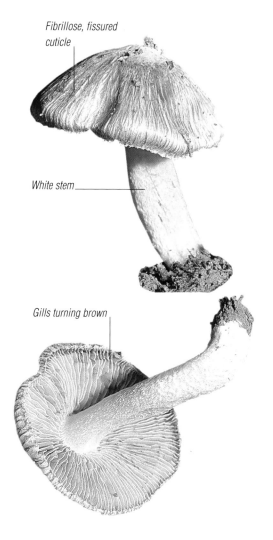

▌ How to recognize it

The **cap** is conical at first, then the edges extend though a pointed umbo remains. The margin eventually cracks with age, sometimes right up to the umbo. The cuticle varies in color from pale yellow to ocher, through golden. The most striking feature of the cap is its striation with very noticeable fibrils.

The **gills** are grayish-yellow, with green highlights. They turn brown in older specimens.

The **stem** is cylindrical or expanded at the base (but it does not form a bulb.) It is slightly scaly at the top, and is white or tinted with the color of the cap.

The white **flesh** does not change color and has an unpleasant odor. Although the flavor is mild at first, it has a bitter aftertaste.

▌ Where and when to find it

The Silken-haired Inocybe is fairly common on forest paths and grassland beside broad-leaved trees, and is found less commonly under conifers. It forms little groups from summer through fall on non-acid soils.

▌ Toxicity

The poisonous species of Inocybe, like the poisonous species of Clitocybe, produce symptoms which include profuse sweating. The early signs of a stomach upset are accompanied by other heavy secretions. Apart from the general weakening of the system, the greatest danger is that this can slow the heart rate and cause death from a heart attack. The risk is greatest with The Red-Staining Inocybe which has already caused serious, and even fatal, poisonings.

Related species

Inocybe species with a conical cap which is torn or split are mostly poisonous.
This one has a very bad reputation.

RED-STAINING INOCYBE
Inocybe patouillardii

This species is recognizable by the reddening of all parts that occurs when the mushroom is touched or when it is old. The white flesh turns pink with age mainly in the stem. It is only common in particular locations and fruits early, from May through July. It occurs in open spaces such as parks, especially under lime (linden) trees. However, it may also grow under other broad-leaved trees. It is dangerously poisonous.

- H: 2-3½ in (5-9 cm)
- Ø: 1¼-3¼ in (3-8 cm)
- Tobacco-brown spores

The Star-spored Inocybe

Inocybe asterospora

Classification : Cl. Homobasidiomycetes -
O. Cortinariales - F. Cortinariaceae.

- H: 2½-4 in (6-10 cm)
- Ø: 1¼-2½ in (3-6 cm)
- Tobacco-brown spores

White cracks between the
reddish-brown fibrils

Umbonate cap

Stem reddish or
orange-brown

Flattened white bulb

▌ How to recognize it

This mushroom is named for an anatomical feature that is only visible under the microscope, namely that the spores of this Inocybe are covered in projections that make them look star-shaped.

The **cap** is conical at first and flattens but remains umbonate to the end. It is covered in reddish-brown radial fibrils in between which there are cracks revealing the white flesh.

The slightly swollen **gills**, are dirty beige, then cinnamon in color.

The full, firm **stem** is cylindrical, ending in a large whitish bulb which is flattened and turnip-shaped. The color of the stem is reddish-brown and it is covered in a fine down. The **flesh** is white in the cap, and rosier in the stem. It has an unpleasant odor.

▌ Where and when to find it

The Star-spored Inocybe may well be frequent but it is difficult to identify with certainty. It grows in summer through fall under broad-leaved trees such as beech and in hazelnut orchards.

▌ Toxicity

Due to their high muscarine content, many species of the genus Inocybe are poisonous, and this also holds true for the Star-spored Inocybe. Even where members of this genus are supposedly "harmless", they are worthless from a gastronomic point of view. It is unlikely, however, that any confusion will arise, since they bear little resemblance to any of the edible wild mushrooms.

Related specie

THE SCALY-BROWN INOCYBE
Inocybe lanuginosa

This brown Inocybe is fairly easy to recognize due to the little brown scales that are erect on the cap, with the exception of the top of the stem which is also paler in color. It grows on sandy, acid soil on damp heathland, marshland or under pines and in mixed woods. Although it is not poisonous, this mushroom is not edible.

- H: 2-3¼ in (5-8 cm)
- Ø: ½-2½ in (1-6 cm)
- Brown spores

The Deceiving Inocybe

Inocybe fraudans

Latin name : *Inocybe piriodora*.

Classification : Cl. Homobasidiomycetes - O. Cortinariales - F. Cortinariaceae.

- H: 1½-4 in (4-10 cm)
- Ø: 1¼-3¼ (3-8 cm)
- Tobacco-brown spores

Cap straw-colored at first _____

Stem reddening _____

Gills reddish-brown when mature _____

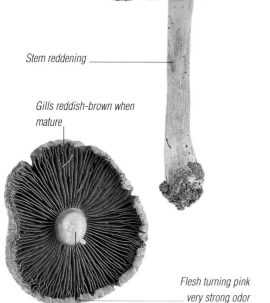

Flesh turning pink very strong odor

■ How to recognize it

The umbonate, fibrillose or hairy **cap** often cracks at the margin. The cuticle is straw-colored to golden-yellow, becoming reddish-ocher with age.
The **gills** remain pale for quite a long time before turning reddish-brown.
The **stem**, which is all-white at first, eventually reddens at the base.
The white or pinkish **flesh** has a mild flavor but is distinctive because it has a peculiarly strong, even heady, and unique odor, which has almost defied description. Some people say that it smells of jasmine, of fruit liqueur, of pears, etc.

■ Where and when to find it

This Inocybe grows in the fall under broad-leaved trees and conifers, particularly on clay and calcareous soils.

■ Toxicity

Although its toxicity has not been clearly established, it is wise to consider this mushroom as poisonous, like all the other species of Inocybe described on this page.

Related species

GREEN-CAPPED INOCYBE
Inocybe corydalina

This common species also has a straw-colored cap but the central umbo is bright emerald green, hence the name. It has a strong but pleasant odor. It is extremely poisonous and grows in the fall beneath deciduous trees.

- H: 3¼-5 in (8-13 cm)
- Ø: 1½-2¾ in (4-7 cm)
- Tobacco-brown spores

TORN-CAPPED INOCYBE
Inocybe lacera

The reddish-brown cap of this small mushroom has a cracked, inrolled margin. The cap is fibrillose or downy and the rusty gills are edged with white. The stem blackens at the base. This fall mushroom grows on heaths and on grass under conifers. It is suspect.

- H: 1¼-2 in (3-5 cm)
- Ø: ¾-1½ in (2-4 cm)
- Tobacco-brown spores

MAUVE-STEMMED INOCYBE
Inocybe griseolilacina

This small, poisonous, species has an ocher or brown cap and reddish scales. The margin is pale violet and the stem is the same color with fine hairs at the top.

- H: 1½-2¾ in (4-7 cm)
- Ø: ¾-1¼ in (2-3 cm)
- Tobacco-brown spores

The Common White Inocybe

Inocybe geophylla

Classification : Cl. Homobasidiomycetes - O. Cortinariales - F. Cortinariaceae.

- H: 1¼-1½ in (3-6 cm)
- Ø: ½-1½ in (1-4 cm)
- Tobacco-brown spores

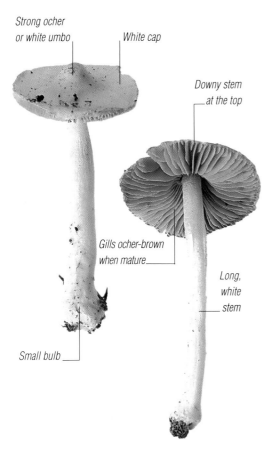

Strong ocher or white umbo

White cap

Downy stem at the top

Gills ocher-brown when mature

Long, white stem

Small bulb

▼ **Lookalike:**
The Amethyst Deceiver
(Laccaria amethystina) (p. 82)

■ How to recognize it

This small, fragile mushroom is highly poisonous. There are several sub-species of it, whose color is not white as in the main variety. The **cap** is conical at first, then expands while retaining a prominent umbo. Unlike in most of the other members of this species, the cuticle is smooth and silky, but sometimes sticky in young specimens. It is white, except for the umbo which may be ocher.

The crowded, swollen **gills** are cream or pale gray at first, but turn ocher-brown or earth-colored in mature specimens.

The **stem** is long and thin, and swollen at the base into a small bulb. It has a thick cortina in young specimens, which leaves downy shreds at the top of the older mushroom.

The white or cream **flesh** is unchanging and has an unpleasant odor and a mild or slightly acrid flavor.

■ Where and when to find it

Although it often passes unnoticed due to its small size, The Common White Inocybe is a very common species in summer and fall, especially in shady undergrowth where it sometimes grows in large colonies.

■ Toxicity

The Common White Inocybe is one of the most poisonous of the Inocybes. The poison in question is muscarine which can act very fast, sometimes in just a few minutes. When absorbed, it manifests itself in enhanced secretions, such as heavy sweating. Appropriate treatment often helps to avoid complications of a more serious nature.

Lookalike

*The mauve-capped variety of this Inocybe bears some resemblance to **The Amethyst Deceiver** (Laccaria amethystina) (p. 82). Although both mushrooms are about the same size, The Amethyst Deceiver is never umbonate and its widely-spaced gills are the same bright violet as the cap.*

Related species

THE MAUVE-CAPPED INOCYBE

Inocybe geophylla var. *lilacina*

There are numerous varieties of the Common White Inocybe, the Mauve-capped variety being the commonest. The umbo, however remains ocher-yellow. The stem may also be colored. This variety is just as poisonous as the main species.

- H: 1¼-1½ in (3-6 cm)
- Ø: ½-1½ in (1-4 cm)
- brown spores

	The Mauve-capped Inocybe *Inocybe geophylla* var. *lilacina*	The Amethyst Deceiver *Laccaria amethystina*
Cap	lilac with an umbo that is often ocher, pointed or umbonate, smooth	bright violet, paling, umbilical, finely granulose
Gills	crowded, gray then pale brown	widely spaced, bright violet
Stem	long, slender, lilac-colored	fibrous, tenacious, violet
Odor	unpleasant	slightly fruity
Features	poisonous	good to eat

The Wrinkled Rozites

Rozites caperata

Classification : Cl. Homobasidiomycetes -
O. Cortinariales - F. Cortinariaceae.

- H: 3¼-6 in (8-15 cm)
- Ø: 2½-4½ in (6-12 cm)
- Ocher-brown spores

Wrinkled yellowish to pale brown cap

Ring creamy white

∎ How to recognize it

The Wrinkled Rozites has a **cap** of average size which is wrinkled or furrowed. It is globose at first, then convex, remaining umbonate even when it expands, and eventually becoming depressed. It is fleshy, especially in the center. The cuticle is covered in radiating, irregular, sinuous and prominent wrinkles or furrows. In young species the cap is sprinkled with a white down When this disappears it reveals the straw-colored or yellowish-brown coloration. The **gills** are crowded or adnate, and denticulate on the edge. They are pale yellow at first, and turn ochraceous yellow, then brown, when mature. The tall, sturdy **stem** is cylindrical, full, and fibrous. It has a persistent, membranous ring which is striated on the underside. It is whitish or cream when young, turning ocher with age. The tender, fragile **flesh** is thin except under the umbo. It is cream to whitish, shaded violet immediately under the cuticle. It has a faint but pleasant odor and a mild flavor.

∎ Where and when to find it

The Wrinkled Rozites grows in broad-leaved woods, especially under beech and under conifers, especially spruce. It prefers siliceous soil where it may appear in large numbers in summer and fall. This is a mushroom which prefers the cool climate of northern Europe, particularly Scandinavia.

∎ Features and edibility

The Wrinkled Rozites is an excellent edible mushroom with tender flesh, a mild flavor, and delicate odor. However, it must be harvested young, before it is attacked by larvae. The fibrous stem should be discarded.
This species has not received the attention it deserves and is not often sought by mushroom-hunters. Yet it is excellent and has the advantage of being suitable for drying.

The Penetrating Agaric

Gymnopilus penetrans

Latin name : *Flammula penetrans.*

Classification : Cl. Homobasidiomycetes -
O. Cortinariales - F. Crepidotaceae.

- H: 2¾-4 in (7-10 cm) ● Ø: 1¼-2½ in (3-6 cm)
- Rust-ocher spores

Cap orange-yellow or reddish

Bright yellow then rust-colored

Rust-colored Ring

Reddish fibrils

White down

On coniferous wood

∎ How to recognize it

The convex or expanded **cap** is not umbonate and is bright orange-yellow to russet. The cuticle is smooth or slightly fibrillose. The crowded **gills** are sulfur-yellow at first, later staining with rust color, as the rust-red spores ripen.

The white or yellowish **stem** thickens toward the base. It is covered in darker fibrils. The base is covered with a fine down. The whitish cortina is fugaceous but sometimes persists in the form of a little ring. The white or pale yellow **flesh** is odorless and very bitter. This species is poisonous.

∎ Where and when to find it

This mushroom is extremely common in summer and fall, appearing on rotting twigs or branches, which are sometimes buried in the soil, mainly in coniferous woods, more rarely under broad-leaved trees. It grows in isolation or in clumps consisting of several specimens.

The Fiery Agaric

Gymnopilus spectabilis

Alternative Latin name : *Pholiota spectabilis.*

Classification : Cl. Homobasidiomycetes -
O. Cortinariales - F. Crepidotaceae.

- H: 4⅘-8 in (12-20 cm)
- Ø: 2-6 in (5-15 cm)
- Rust-brown spores

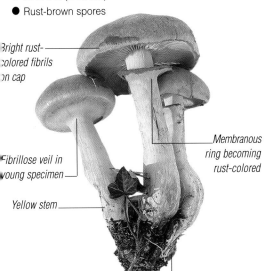

Bright rust-colored fibrils on cap

Fibrillose veil in young specimen

Yellow stem

Membranous ring becoming rust-colored

Grows in tufts

How to recognize it

The Fiery Agaric is certainly a spectacular sight due to its bright coloration.

The very thick **cap** is convex and sometimes very umbonate. The silky, fibrous cuticle is a magnificent reddish or orange-fawn color.

The **gills** are sinuate where they meet the stem. Their bright rust-red changes to brownish-red when touched.

The fibrous, yellow **stem** is swollen or club-shaped. It has a large, membranous ring which is the same fiery color as the rest of the mushroom.

The thick, firm **flesh** is yellow in color. It has a faint odor but a bitter flavor.

The Fiery Agaric probably has halucinogenic properties. It is suspected of being responsible for some quite serious poisonings.

Where and when to find it

The Fiery Agaric is a fairly common sight in summer through fall, growing on stumps, branches, or at the base of tree-trunks, usually at ground level, especially on oak. Although sometimes found in isolation, it generally grows in small clumps.

The Variable Crepidotus

Crepidotus variabilis

Classification : Cl. Homobasidiomycetes -
O. Cortinariales - F. Crepidotaceae.

- Ø: ¼-1¼ in (0.5-3 cm) ● Tobacco-brown spores

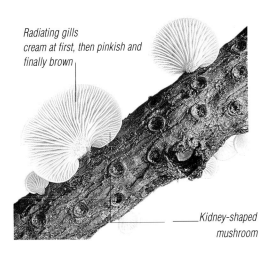

Radiating gills cream at first, then pinkish and finally brown

Kidney-shaped mushroom

How to recognize it

The kidney-shaped **cap** is a pure matt white. It is often attached at the back, revealing the small gills interspersed with the larger ones. The **gills** radiate in a fan-shape from the point at which

the cap is attached to a piece of wood. they are cream at first, becoming rose-colored before finally turning cinnamon brown thanks to the ripening of the spores.

The **stem** is absent. The **flesh** is thin, white, and odorless. This species is not edible, due mainly to its small size.

Where and when to find it

The Variable Crepidotus grows along branches and twigs of broad-leaved trees, often in piles of branches or brushwood in damp woods. It is common in summer and fall, but may occasionally fruit all year round.

The Marginate Galera

Galerina marginata

Latin name : *Galera marginata*.

Classification: Cl. Homobasidiomycetes -
O. Cortinariales - F. Crepidotaceae.

- H: 1½-3¼ in (4-8 cm)
- Ø: ¾-2¾ in (2-7 cm)
- Ocher spores

Reddish convex cap

More or less
visible ring

Yellow
or pale brown gills

Silvery fibrils

▼ **Lookalike:**
The Brown Stew Mushroom
(Kuehneromyces mutabilis) (p. 144)

▌ How to recognize it

The small **cap** is barely 2 in (5 cm) in diameter.
It is conico-campanulate, remaining convex for
a long time and more or less umbonate, and
later expanding.
The smooth, matt cuticle is hygrophanous,
being fawn in wet weather and turning honey-
colored in dry weather. The margin is so thin
that the gills show through it.
The adnate, straight **gills** are yellowish or light
brown.
The long **stem**, is cylindrical, quite thin and
often sinuous, thickening slightly toward the
base. Toward the top it has a vestigial, membranous, fragile ring which often disappears
with age.
The yellowish surface, is striated along its
length with silvery fibrils, which stain brown at
the base.
The fragile **flesh** is thin, except at the center of
the cap; it is yellowish in the cap, but brown in
the stem. It smells strongly of meal.

▌ Where and when to find it

The Marginate Galera is gregarious, growing in
tight clumps on decaying coniferous wood, such
as stumps, fallen or dead branches, on which it
lives as a saprophyte. It normally appears in
summer through fall, mainly in the mountains.

▌ Toxicity

In 1954, The Marginate Galera caused fatal
poisonings in North America. Since then a few
poisonings have been reported in Europe. A
mycologist who merely tasted a specimen to
check whether it had a mealy flavor ended up
in hospital, just because he ingested a fragment
of the mushroom he was dealing with. The
Marginate Galera also caused the death of a
little girl who swallowed a specimen while
playing with her friends.
The Marginate Galera contains large amounts
of amanitine, a substance which is found in an
even greater concentration in The Death Cap.
Consumption of a raw specimen makes the poison more powerful, but The Marginate Galera
may contain even more toxic substances than
amanitine. The poisoning syndrome is of the
paraphalloidian type, like that produced by the
deadly, small brown Lepiotas and the treatment is identical.

Lookalike

*The **Brown Stew Mushroom** or **Changing Pholiota**
(Kuehneromyces mutabilis) (p. 144), which is an
excellent edible mushroom and forms very dense
clumps – not colonies – on the trunks of broad-
leaved and coniferous trees. The base of the stem is
scaly and it has a fruity odor.*

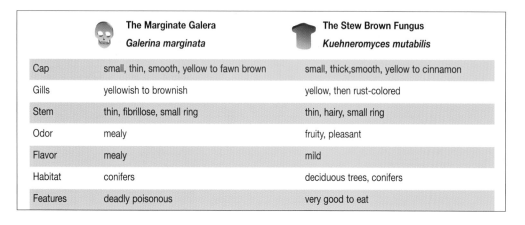

	The Marginate Galera *Galerina marginata*	The Stew Brown Fungus *Kuehneromyces mutabilis*
Cap	small, thin, smooth, yellow to fawn brown	small, thick,smooth, yellow to cinnamon
Gills	yellowish to brownish	yellow, then rust-colored
Stem	thin, fibrillose, small ring	thin, hairy, small ring
Odor	mealy	fruity, pleasant
Flavor	mealy	mild
Habitat	conifers	deciduous trees, conifers
Features	deadly poisonous	very good to eat

Most of the Galeras are very thin, delicate species. It is often difficult to differentiate between them with the naked eye.

THE MOSS GALERA
Galerina hypnorum

The entirely ochraceous yellow, The Moss Galera grows in damp moss in woods, heathland, and swamps, from spring through fall. It is too small and fragile to be of culinary interest.

- H: 1¼-2 in (3-5 cm)
- Ø: ¼-⅝ in (0.5-1.5 cm)
- Ocher spores

THE AUTUMN GALERA
 ### *Galerina autumnalis*

This species is also deadly poisonous. It differs mainly from The Marginate Galera in that its cap is viscous. It is an uncommon species, appearing in late summer through fall on the dead branches of broad-leaved or coniferous trees.

- H: ¼-3½ in (3-9 cm)
- Ø: ¾-2½ in (2-6 cm)
- Rusty-ocher spores

The Verdigris Agaric

 ## *Stropharia aeruginosa*

Classification : Cl. Homobasidiomycetes - O. Cortinariales - F. Strophariaceae.

- H: 2½-4 in (6-10 cm)
- Ø: 1¼-3¾ in (3-8 cm) ● Dark red spores

White flakes

Very slimy, blue-green cap

Brownish-purple gills

Violet-brown gills

Viscous stem covered with white flakes

Whitish veil *Young* *Mature*

flakes which themselves are coated in the slime at the edge of the cap. The cap turns yellow later, starting from the center.

The adnate **gills** are whitish at first, changing to purplish-brown, but their edges remain white.

The **stem** is also slimy but has a fluffy texture thanks to the small white flakes with which it is covered. The top is whitish and the base is blue-green. It has a fragile membranous ring, which remains tinted brownish-violet by the spores. The base is extended by means of white strings of mycelium.

The bluish-white **flesh** has a nauseating odor. Although once considered edible, the species is now believed to be poisonous.

▌ How to recognize it

The Verdigris Agaric is striking due to its unusual coloring and slimy coating.
In young specimens, the very slimy **cap** is a magnificent blue-green color, covered in white

▌ Where and when to find it

The Verdigris Agaric is frequently encountered in summer through fall growing in compost or leaf litter in deciduous or conifers woods, in undergrowth, and in grassland.

The Crowned Roundhead
Stropharia coronilla

Alternative Latin name : *Geophilla coronilla*.

Classification : Cl. Homobasidiomycetes - O. Cortinariales - F. Strophariaceae.

- H: 1¼-2 in (3-5 cm)
- Ø: 1¼-2½ in (3-6 cm)
- Crimson-brown spores

Smooth yellow cap

Striated ring darkened by spores on the upper part

Violet-brown gills upon maturity

White ring and stem

▌How to recognize it

The **cap** of this small mushroom is hemispherical, then convex, very regular, firm, and fleshy. The cuticle is slightly viscous when wet and has a typically yellow coloration, varying from matt ocher to bright lemon yellow. The paler margin is covered in white flakes.

The **gills** are also regular and look like the spokes of a little wheel mounted on an axis represented by the stem. They are yellowish-gray at first, turning violet then purplish-brown as the spores mature.

The cylindrical white **stem** is rather short and fleshy. It has a white ring which is strongly furrowed in the upper part, later becoming colored by the spores. The thick **flesh** is firm and white. The odor is faint and the flavor is quite mild.

▌Where and when to find it

The Crowned Roundhead is often found in the grassland of meadows, pastures, and fields, up to the edge of woods. It sometimes grows in isolation, but more often in small groups, from spring through fall, as soon as the conditions of humidity and temperature are favorable.

▌Features and edibility

The Crowned Roundhead is not good to eat. The flesh is insipid and the mushroom is small and never grows in large numbers. It is said to be suspect, simply because this is the case for other species of Stropharia, but it is probably not true.

On the other hand, its close, cultivated relative, The Rough-ringed Agaric should indeed be tasted.

Related species

Members of the genus **Stropharia** have a ring which looks like a collar or bracelet, adnate gills, purplish-brown spores and a cap that is slimy, especially when wet.

THE DUNG ROUNDHEAD
Stropharia semiglobata

The stem is long and thin and has a median fugaceous ring. This inedible Stropharia grows on cattle dung, especially cow-pats, in meadows. The mushroom is common from late spring through fall.

- H: 1½-4 in (4-10 cm)
- Ø: ¾-2 in (2-5 cm)
- Dark purplish-brown spores

THE ROUGH-RINGED AGARIC
Stropharia rugosoannulata

The Rough-ringed Agaric is a large mushroom that grows on dung, but is rare in nature and is currently cultivated on damp straw in parts of Europe. It bears some resemblance to the cep and has been called the "straw cep." But it does not have the same fragrance and some people even claim is smell strongly and has an unpleasant taste. France produces about 2,000 tons of it annually.

- H: 2½-8 in (6-20 cm)
- Ø: 3¼-6 in (8-15 cm)
- Purplish-brown spores

Sulfur Tuft

Hypholoma fasciculare

Classification : Cl. Homobasidiomycetes -
O. Cortinariales - F. Strophariaceae.

- H: 1½-5 in (6-13 cm)
- Ø: ¾-2¾ in (2-7 cm)
- Crimson-brown spores

Tightly-packed gills olive-colored when mature, then turning brown

Sulfur to reddish-ocher cap

Stem yellow turning red at the base

In tufts

▎How to recognize it

As its name indicates, Sulfur Tuft forms handsome, bright greenish-yellow tufts of multiple tall specimens.

The **cap** is globose at first but soon expands and may retain an umbo which eventually flattens completely. It is thin and not very fleshy. The sulfur yellow to ochraceous cuticle reddens with age, especially in the center. The very narrow margin displays the remains of the fugaceous cortina.

The adnate **gills** are thin and very crowded, and have a sulfur-yellow coloration which is characteristic. When mature, it tends to turn olive, then greenish-brown.

The thin, sinuous **stem** stretches out into a point at the base. It is sulfur-yellow but tinged with red at the base. The upper part bears a few traces of a whitish cortina, forming a faint annular zone which becomes stained purplish-brown by the spores.

The thin **flesh** is fibrous, especially in the stem, and has a tenacious consistency. It is washed with sulfur yellow at the base of the stem. The flesh has an unpleasant smell of iodine and tastes extremely bitter.

▎Where and when to find it

The Sulfur Tuft is a very common mushroom, forming huge tufts of specimens joined at the base of the stem. Its sulfur-yellow caps are often seen cover the fallen trunks and stumps of conifers and broad-leaved trees.

This common species fruits almost year round, but particularly during the mushroom season.

▎Toxicity

The Sulfur Tuft is very bitter and has an unpleasant smell like iodine, so it would appear to be inedible. Nevertheless, it does not seem to have repelled everyone and several cases of poisoning have been attributed to it. It causes gastro-enteritis and more serious symptoms, and these have been observed in the Far East, when it has been eaten.

THE GRAY-GILLED TUFT AGARIC
Hypholoma capnoïdes

This species is not as slender as Sulfur Tuft but is often confused with it. It is less common and is confined to conifer logs on which it forms very thick clumps.

It differs from the sulfur tuft mainly in the absence of any green or sulfur color. The cap is ochraceous yellow to fawn in the center. Shreds of the veil often hang from the margin. The gills, which are typically smoky, are pale at first, and ash-colored but turn violet-gray upon maturity. The long, yellow stem is darker at the base and covered with whitish fibrils. Its whitish flesh has a mild odor and is edible but worthless.

- H: 1½-5 in (6-13 cm)
- Ø: 1¼-1½ in (3-6 cm)
- Dark brown spores

BRICK CAP

Hypholoma sublateritium

This specimen is larger with a typically brick-red cap which soon becomes dull. It can be distinguished from the Sulfur Tuft by observing the paler margin, especially in young specimens, the flaky shreds which are the remains of the veil, and the color of the gills, which are pale yellow then olive, eventually turning blackish-violet. The stem is long and slender and tinted with the same color as the cap. The cortina is thicker and less fugaceous. The flesh of the Brick Cap is very bitter and is not edible. It is quite common all year round growing on the fallen logs of any species of tree.

- H: 1½-8 in (6-20 cm)
- Ø: 2-4 in (5-10 cm)
- Crimson-brown spores

The Brown Stew Mushroom

Kuehneromyces mutabilis

English synonym: Two-toned Pholiota
Classification : Cl. Homobasidiomycetes -
O. Cortinariales - F. Strophariaceae.

- H: 1½-4 in (4-12 cm) ● Ø: 1¼-3¼ in (3-8 cm)
- Ocher spores

▼ Lookalikes:
Sulfur Tuft *(Hypholoma fasciculare)* (p. 143)
The Marginate Galera
(Galerina marginata) (p. 140)
The Honey Fungus (Armillaria mellea)
(p. 76)

▌How to recognize it

The Brown Stew Mushroom is a small species whose color changes depending on the amount of humidity in the air. The **cap** is convex at first, then expanded and is fleshy, especially in the center, which remains umbonate. It is yellowish, rather dull and it cracks in dry weather. When the weather is damp, the cuticle turns cinnamon brown and becomes shiny. The cap looks like a rosette with a center which is either darker or lighter than the edge. Shreds of the veil sometimes adhere to the margin which appears to be finely striated since the gills can be seen through it.

The **gills** are pale yellow at first, turning rusty-brown upon maturity.

The **stem** is elongated and sinuous, thin but tenacious. It has a dark ring at the top which is fairly fugaceous. The upper part, which is yellow, is clearly striated, while the lower part is covered in darker, reddish-brown scales.

The whitish **flesh** which is darker at the base of the stem, is quite soft in the cap and fibrous in the stem. It has a mild flavor and pleasant fruity odor.

Brown Stew Fungus

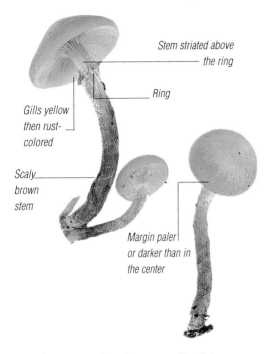

Stem striated above the ring

Ring

Gills yellow then rust-colored

Scaly brown stem

Margin paler or darker than in the center

▌ Where and when to find it

The Brown Stew Mushroom covers various broad-leaved trees in dense tufts, seeming to prefer beech, but also growing on conifers, especially spruce. It is quite common throughout the temperate zone, appearing in spring and persisting until the first frosts.

▌ Features and edibility

The Brown Stew Mushroom has a soft consistency and is thus a suitable addition to soups and sauces to which it imparts its fruity odor and flavor.

For various reasons, it is considered to be good eating. However, in order to appreciate its finer points, only young specimens should be chosen and the leathery stems should be discarded.

Lookalikes

Sulfur Tuft (Hypholoma fasciculare) *(p. 143) is very bitter and would appear to be inedible and may even be poisonous. The sulfur color and yellow-green gills are distinctive. It fruits under the same conditions as the Brown Stew Mushroom.*

The Marginate Galera *(Galerina marginata) (p. 140) is also lignicolous and grows in groups on conifer logs. It is deadly poisonous. It has a strong mealy odor which is one way of recognizing it. Fortunately, it is quite rare.*

The Honey Fungus (Armillaria mellea) *(p. 76) is larger than the Brown Stew Mushroom. Unlike the latter it has a white ring and a cap which is normally scaly. The Honey Fungus is edible. It may be saprophitic but also parasitic and it lives on coniferous and deciduous wood. It has been known to be seriously indigestible.*

	The Brown Stew Fungus *Kuehneromyces mutabilis*	Sulfur Tuft *Hypholoma fasciculare*	The Marginate Galera *Galerina marginata*	The Honey Fungus *Armillaria mellea*
Cap	small, quite thick, smooth, yellow to cinnamon	small, thin, smooth, bright yellow	small, thin, smooth, yellow to fawn	average, thick, spotted, honey-colored
Gills	yellow, then rust-colored	yellow-green to brown	yellowish to brownish	white, yellow, then rust-spotted
Stem	fine, scaly, small ring	thin, smooth, fugaceous cortina	thin, fibrillose, small ring	thick, smooth to spotted, large ring
Odor	fruity, pleasant	unpleasant, like iodine	mealy	faint
Flavor	mild	very bitter	mealy	mild to bitter
Habitat	broad-leaved, conifers	broad-leaved, conifers	conifers	broad-leaved trees, conifers
Features	very good to eat	poisonous	deadly poison	good to eat when young

The Slimy Pholiota
Pholiota lenta

Classification : Cl. Homobasidiomycetes -
O. Cortinariales - F. Strophariaceae.

● H: 1½-4½ in (6-12 cm) ● Ø: 1½-3¼ in (4-8 cm)
● Brown spores

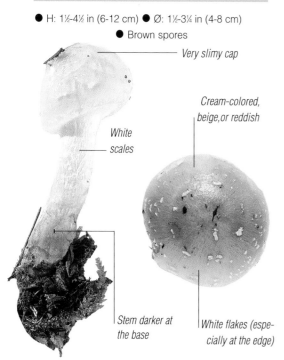

Very slimy cap

White scales

Cream-colored, beige, or reddish

Stem darker at the base

White flakes (especially at the edge)

▌ How to recognize it

The **cap** is regular in shape but soon flattens, and has a very viscous surface, especially in rainy weather. The cuticle is quite variable in color, creamy-white to beige, sometimes yellow or russet. A few thick white scales may remain on the edge.

The **gills** are quite crowded. They are whitish-yellow at first with olive highlights, and turn rust-brown as the spores mature.

The white **stem** darkens toward the base, where it is often swollen. It is thickly covered with white scales which become sparser with age.

The **flesh** is white, but rust colored in the base of the stem. The odor is mild. This mushroom is edible but not good.

▌ Where and when to find it

The Slimy Pholiota is fairly common, fruiting late, and only in groups of two or three specimens, on branches or twigs buried in humus. It can be found in broad-leaved woods (especially beech) as well as in coniferous woods.

The Shaggy Pholiota
Pholiota squarrosa

Classification : Cl. Homobasidiomycetes -
O. Cortinariales - F. Strophariaceae.

● H: 4½-8 in (12-20 cm)
● Ø: 2-4 in (5-10 cm) ● Rust-brown spores

Lemon-yellow then rusty gills

Ring membranous very high up the stem

Cap and Stem scaly, yellow-brown

▼ **Lookalike:**
The Honey Fungus (*Armillarea mellea*)
(p. 76)

▌ How to recognize it

The fleshy **cap** is of average to large size and is globose at first, then convex or flattened and very regular. The cuticle is covered with reddish-brown scales arranged in concentric circles, which stand out against the lemon yellow background. The cap eventually fades to ochraceous fawn. Flakes of the same color as the scales slightly overhang the margin.

The thin, crowded **gills** are adnate or decurrent by one tooth. They may be pale to bright yellow, become spotted with rust color as the spores mature.

The **stem** is full, firm and long. It is sinuous and is pointed at the base. It has a membranous ring, situated very high up it, just under the gills. It is concolorous with the cap and reddens then turns brown from the scaly base, in the same way as the cap.

The **flesh** is firm, yellowish, and thick in the cap becomes leathery and brown in the stem. It has a strong, unpleasant smell and tastes of radish.

■ Where and when to find it

Tufts of The Shaggy Pholiota which are often dense and voluminous invade stumps and the base of trunks of broad-leaved trees and conifers. Although the species is parasitic on living trees it does not appear to do them much harm. Spruces, for example, may host its clumps of fruiting bodies for many years. Thanks to its habitat, the Shaggy Pholiota is quite common, generally appearing in the fall.

■ Features and edibility

The mushroom soon becomes tough and leathery and its has an unpleasant odor, so it is certainly not worth eating. It is also indigestible, even when picked young.

Lookalike

The Honey Fungus *(Armillaria mellea) (p. 76) has a similar appearance and habitat to the Shaggy Pholiota and is good to eat (though sometimes indigestible). It differs from the latter by the white color of the ring and gills which stain yellow or russet with age. The scales are much less abundant and prominent and the stem is generally smooth or spotted.*

Related species

Many species of Pholiota have a cap and stem that is scaly or slimy, and are yellow or reddish in color. The stem has a ring or scales.

THE POPLAR PHOLIOTA
Hemipholiota populnea

The Poplar Pholiota is a thick, sturdy mushroom which grows on the trunks of felled poplar trees, using a very tough, blade-like mycorrhiza, which is an extension of the stem.
- H: 4½-6 in (8-15 cm) ● Ø: 4-8 in (10-20 cm) ● Tobacco-brown spores

THE FLAMBOYANT PHOLIOTA
Pholiota flammans

The stem and cap and covered in white scales, but underneath they are a beautiful sulfur-yellow-to-orange color. This magnificent mushroom grows on spruce stumps. It is harmless but not good to eat.
- H: 1½-4 in (6-10 cm) ● Ø: 2-2¾ in (5-7 cm) ● Rust-colored spores

THE CHARCOAL PHOLIOTA
Pholiota highlandensis

This inedible species can be encountered in late winter on bare soil on which a fire has been built. The cap is reddish-brown in the center and yellow at the margin.
- H: 1½-3¼ in (4-8 cm)
- Ø: 1¼-2½ in (3-6 cm)
- Brown spores

THE ALDER PHOLIOTA
Pholiota alnicola

The slimy, bright yellow cap becomes splashed with red in the center. The fibrillose stem is yellow, but reddens noticeably from the base. This mushroom has a bitter taste but smells very fruity. It grows in dense clumps on alder branches, more rarely on other trees in damp places.
- H: 4½-6 in (8-15 cm)
- Ø: 1½-4 in (4-10 cm)
- Rust-brown spores

THE GILDED PHOLIOTA
Pholiota cerifera

This inedible mushroom has a viscous, golden-yellow cuticle, sprinkled with large reddish or brown scales which tend to thin out on the margin. The stem is the same color and covered in pointed, brown scales. The Gilded Pholiota forms tufts on wounds of living branches of deciduous trees, especially beech. It often grows high up.
- H: 4-7 in (10-18 cm)
- Ø: 3¼-6 in (8-15 cm)
- Brown spores

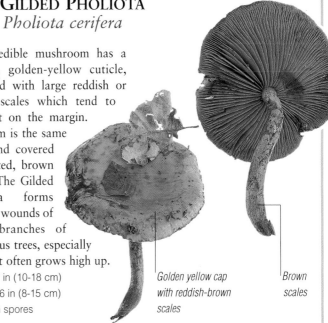

Golden yellow cap with reddish-brown scales

Brown scales

The Liberty Cap

Psilocybe semilanceata

Classification : Cl. Homobasidiomycetes -
O. Cortinariales - F. Strophariaceae.

- H: 2½-4½ in (6-12 cm)
- Ø: ¼-¾ in (0.5-2 cm)
- Dark purplish brown spores

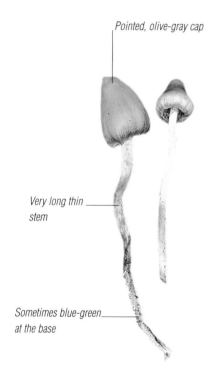

Pointed, olive-gray cap

Very long thin
stem

Sometimes blue-green
at the base

∎ How to recognize it

The **cap** is conical, with a very pointed umbo, a wrinkled, finely striated margin. The cuticle is smooth, covered with a detachable slimy film. In view of the hygrophanous nature of the cap, the olive-gray cuticle or brownish pales to cream when dry. It is sometimes blue-green on the margin.

The gray to olive **gills** turn dark violet-brown when mature, retaining a white edge.
The **stem** which is very thin and long, is smooth or slightly fibrillose, the same color as the cap, sometimes shaded with blue-green in the lower part.

∎ Where and when to find it

The Liberty Cap may be common in one location and rare in another. It grows in late summer through late fall in groups in meadowland, pastures, heaths, or on grass verges in fairly acid soil.

∎ Toxicity

The Liberty Cap is the most hallucinogenic mushroom of the temperate zone. When eaten, it produces a state of euphoria in most people, with delirium and brightly-colored visions. Perceptions of time and space are modified. Most species of Psilocybe that are hallucinogenic grow in the tropics. In southern Mexico, for instance, indigenous peoples use certain species of Psilocybe in their religious rituals.
The active principles of these hallucinogenic mushroom are well known. There are two of them, psilocin and especially psilocybin. Their use in the treatment of certain mental disorders has been studied and research continues along these lines.

Related species

HAIRY-STEMMED PSILOCYBE
Psilocybe crobula

The brown cap is not umbonate and flattens with age. At first it has a few small scales some of which persist on the margin. The stem is covered in whitish scales and the gills turn rust-red upon maturity. This hallucinogenic mushroom may be common in fall growing on leaf litter or twigs.

- H: ¾-2 in (2-5 cm)
- Ø: ¼-¾ in (0.5-2 cm)
- Red-brown spores

THE DARK RED PSILOCYBE
Psilocybe montana

Like other species of Psilocybe, the Dark Red Psilocybe has a thin viscous film on the cap which can be detached from it. The cap itself is dark brown when wet, turning pale in cream patches when dry. The gills are slightly decurrent and turn brownish-purple when mature. It grows on mossy lawns and should be treated as poisonous.

- H: ¾-1½ in (2-4 cm)
- Ø: ¼-⅝ in (0.5-1.5 cm)
- Dark crimson spores

Brown Hay Cap

Panaeolus foenisecii

Classification : Cl. Homobasidiomycetes -
O. Cortinariales - F. Bolbitiaceae.

- H: 1½-2¾ in (4-7 cm)
- Ø: ¾-1¼ in (2-3 cm) ● Dark brown spores

*Reddish-brown cap
turning pale when dry*

*Stem pruinose
at the top*

Long, thin stem

▌How to recognize it

The **cap** is convex at first but soon flattens, with a finely striate margin. The cuticle is smooth or slightly granulose and reddish-brown in damp weather, fading to pinky-beige when dry, although the margin tends to remain darker.

The **gills** are thick, often widely spaced, and swollen. They are pale brown at first, marbling with purplish-brown as the spores mature.

The **stem** is hollow and paler than the cap but reddish-brown toward the base and scaly at the top.

The pale-brown **flesh** has no particular odor. This poisonous mushroom is probably hallucinogenic.

▌Where and when to find it

The Brown Hay Cap gets its name from the fact that it appears in the hay-making season. It is common in summer on fertile grassland, from lawns to pastures.

Related species

Unlike the Brown Hay Cap, the other species of Panaeolus have black spores and gills which blacken when mature.
All are poisonous and some are hallucinogenic.

DUNG MUSHROOM

Panaeolus semiovatus

The cap always retains its campanulate or ogival shape. It is whitish to grayish cream, and is shiny and viscous in damp weather. The stem is very long and thin. It has a small ring which blackens at the same time as the gills. It appears from spring through summer on horse manure and old cow-pats.

- H: 2½-6 in (6-15 cm)
- Ø: 1¼-2½ in (3-6 cm)
- Black spores

HOOP PETTICOAT MUSHROOM

Panaeolus sphinctrinus

The campanulate or ogival cap, is grayish-brown, turning pale in dry weather. It is edged with tiny white shreds on the margin. The stem is very long and slender. The gray gills become flecked with dark and light patches which are typical of the genus Panaeolus. The Hoop Petticoat Mushroom also grows on or near decomposing dung in meadows.

- H: 4-6 in (10-15 cm)
- Ø: ¼-1½ in (2-4 cm)
- Black spores

The Poplar Agrocybe

Agrocybe aegerita

Alternative Latin name : *Agrocybe cylindracea.*

Classification : Cl. Homobasidiomycetes -
O. Cortinariales - F. Bolbitiaceae.

- H: 3½-6 in (9-15 cm) ● Ø: 2-4½ in (5-12 cm)
- Tobacco-brown spores

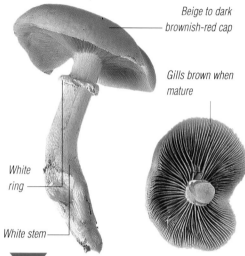

Beige to dark brownish-red cap

Gills brown when mature

White ring

White stem

Lookalike:
The Poplar Pholiota *(Hemipholiota populnea)*
(p.147)

■ How to recognize it

The fleshy **cap** is globose extending to convex and has an irregular surface which eventually becomes depressed. The smooth, dry cuticle becomes creased or wrinkled, splitting in the mature specimen. It is fawn or brown in the young mushroom, paling to creamy white at the edge. The margin is inrolled and regular at first, then becoming wavy and cracked when old.

The thin, crowded **gills** are decurrent by a thread on the stem. They are cream-colored at first, turning brown when mature.

The **stem** is firm and fibrous and typically cylindrical. High up, just below the gills, it has a drooping, white, thick, membranous ring. This ring persists in the mature specimen. The stem is white and silky but becomes spotted with dark brown when the spores are released. The white **flesh** is compact and firm, becoming tough and leathery in the stem. It has a pleasant nutty flavor and the unusual smell of a cork or barrel.

Related species

A few species which grow in the soil belong to the same genus as the Poplar Pholiota.

THE EARLY AGROCYBE
Agrocybe praecox

This is a little spring mushroom which is very common in open spaces, such as forest clearings, fields and meadows.

The cap is whitish to pale ocher and slightly hygrophanous. The gills are whitish at first then stained with rust when mature. The long, slender stem is often bulbous at the base, and is fibrous, and fibrillose on the surface. It has a white ring, which becomes stained with rust color, and which tears in young specimens leaving a few shreds on the margin. The soft, white flesh emits a pleasant, mealy odor but may be bitter in some specimens. The Early Agrocybe is harm- less but its eating qualities are unpredictable and irregular.

- H: 2½-4½ in (6-12 cm)
- Ø: 1¼-2¾ in (3-7 cm)
- Tobacco-brown spores

THE CRACKLING AGROCYBE
Agrocybe molesta

This mushroom grows in the same habitat as the Early Agrocybe but is much rarer. It differs from the latter, mainly in that its flesh is very firm, almost tough, and it has a fungal, rather than a mealy, odor. The Crackling Agrocybe is not good to eat and may even be suspect.

- H: 2¾-4¼ in (7-11 cm)
- Ø: 2½-4 in (6-10 cm)
- Tobacco brown spores

THE OCHER AGROCYBE
Agrocybe pediades

This little mushroom appears in grassland in high summer. The cap is yellow-ocher and smooth, and the gills are widely spaced, swollen, beige then brown, with a white edge to them.

- H: 1¼-2 in (3-5 cm)
- Ø: ¼-1½ in (2-4 cm)
- Tobacco brown spores

Where and when to find it

The Poplar Agrocybe, despite its name, also grows on willow trees, and sometimes on elder. where it can be found on dead stumps and on the roots.

It favors fairly southern climates, being quite common in the Paris region, southern France, and Italy, but is rarer in central Europe. It first appears in late spring if the weather conditions are right and persists until winter.

Features and edibility

In the spring, just after the Morels and St. George's Mushroom have died out, nature presents the mushroom-eater with the large pale clumps of Poplar Agrocybe. It is very sought after in its native habitat and is indeed very delicious. Furthermore, one poplar stump can yield a large harvest of this mushroom, amply filling a basket. The flesh has a delicate flavor and is slightly crunchy, making it a delight for the palate. Whether eaten alone, as a side-dish or in a cream sauce it is always much appreciated, though the tough, fibrous stems must be discarded. The Poplar Agrocybe is sold in wild mushroom markets in Mediterranean regions.

Culture

The Poplar Agrocybe is fairly easy to grow and southern Europeans, particularly the Italians, have tried to cultivate it since ancient times. Poplar logs merely have to be rubbed with the gills of young Poplar Agrocybe specimens and keep them well watered having half-buried them in the earth. The logs will then fruit in successive clumps from spring through to fall.

Lookalike

The Poplar Agrocybe has a more dangerous competitor which penetrates the cut trunks of felled poplars and causes them to rot.

The Poplar Pholiota *(Hemipholiota populnea), (p. 147) is a strong species which favors poplar and species of the willow family. The cap is thick and the stem is sturdy. The whole mushroom is beige and downy as it had been covered in a down of absorbent cotton. The mushroom has a very strong odor and a very bitter flavor, and is inedible.*

The Yellow Cow-pat Toadstool
Bolbitius vitellinus

Classification : Cl. Homobasidiomycetes - O. Cortinariales - F. Bolbitiaceae.

● H: 2½-4 in (6-10 cm)
● Ø: ¼-2 in (2-5 cm)
● Rust-brown spores

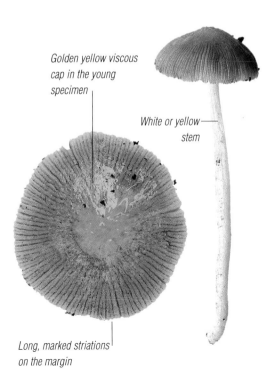

Golden yellow viscous cap in the young specimen

White or yellow stem

Long, marked striations on the margin

How to recognize it

The Yellow Cowpat Toadstool is one of the most fragile of the mushrooms and disintegrates at a touch. The **cap** is oval then conical, extending and flattening and the margin then splits right to the center. It is so thin that the flesh is almost transparent. The margin is deeply and extensively striated. The viscous cuticle is bright egg-yellow at first, but as the cap expands, it discolors to ocher or beige. The straw-colored **gills** turn rusty ocher upon maturing, thanks to the ripening of the spores.

The hollow, brittle **stem** is white, yellowing at the top, and it is slightly flocculose.
The very thin, fragile **flesh** is of no culinary interest whatsoever.

Where and when to find it

The Yellow Cow-pat Toadstool grows in midsummer but has a very short life, so it may not be encountered frequently. It can be found growing on fertile lawns, decaying straw, old compost, fertilized fields, and on grassy verges, in fact on any open grassland which has been heavily manured.

1 - Psathyrella

- Bell-shaped or flattened cap, not striated.
- Gills blackish-brown upon maturity.

Bell-shaped or flattened cap, not striated

Absence of a ring

Blackish-brown gills upon maturity

PSATHYRELLA **Page 154**

2 - Coprinus

- Cap ovoid or conical, or very flat and ribbed, or heavily striated.
- Flesh thin and fragile.
- Gills blackening upon maturity, often deliquescent.
- Stem often separable from cap.

Cap ovoid or conical or very flat and ribbed, or heavily striated.

Stem often separable from cap

Flesh thin and fragile

Gills blackening upon maturity, often deliquescent

COPRINUS **Page 156**

3 - Agaricus

- Pink gills darkening to upon maturity.
- Membranous ring.
- Stem and cap separable.

Membranous ring

Gills pink then brownish-black upon maturity

Stem and cap separable

AGARICUS **Page 160**

FEATURES OF THE AGARICALES

- Flesh of fibrous texture.
- Cap and stem more or less separable.
- Gills remaining white or turning black upon maturity (first turning pink in the case of the Agaricus genus).

Gills not attached to stem and more or less free

Fibrous flesh

Gills remaining white (Lepiota, Amanita)

Gills pink and ring present (Agaricus)

Brownish-black gills (Psathyrella, Coprinus, Agaricus)

4 - Lepiota

- Gills free, remaining white or slightly colored.
- Stem scaly or having a ring.
- Large scales on cap.

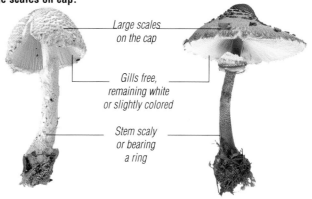

Large scales on the cap

Gills free, remaining white or slightly colored

Stem scaly or bearing a ring

Ø less than 4 in (10 cm) : LEPIOTA - LEUCOAGARICUS **Page 167,172**
Ø more than 4 in (10 cm) : MACROLEPIOTA **Page 170**

5 - Limacella

- Viscous cap.
- White gills.

Cap viscous and white

White gills

LIMACELLA **Page 173**

6 - Amanita

- Amanita with a ring on the stem. (sub-genus: AMANITA)

With a well developed volva

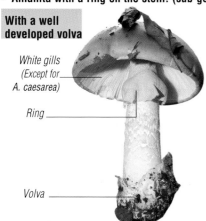

White gills (Except for A. caesarea)

Ring

Volva

BEWARE: this genus contains the Death Cap, which is responsible for 95% of mushroom poisonings.

With a poorly developed volva

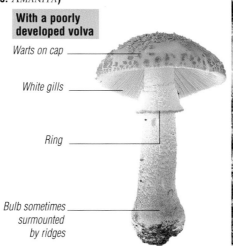

Warts on cap

White gills

Ring

Bulb sometimes surmounted by ridges

- Amanita without a ring on the stem. (sub-genus: AMANITOPSIS)

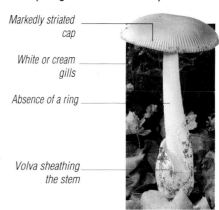

Markedly striated cap

White or cream gills

Absence of a ring

Volva sheathing the stem

AMANITA **Page 173**

Weeping Widow
Psathyrella lacrymabunda

Alternative Latin name: *Lacrymaria velutina,*
Psathyrella velutina.

Classification : Cl. Homobasidiomycetes -
O. Agaricales - F. Coprinaceae.

- H: 2½-4½ in (6-12 cm)
- Ø: 1½-4½ in (4-12 cm)
- Black spores

*Gills brown,
turning black*

White cortina

How to recognize it

The **cap** of Weeping Widow is covered in flattened scales which give it its velvety appearance. It is not very fleshy and is campanulate in the young specimen, flattening subsequently while retaining a more or less visible umbo. The surface is generally a dull dark brown fawn which is sometimes brightened with ocher patches. When the spores are matured, the cap may be covered with black patches of "soot." The **margin** is attached to the stem by means of a white veil and soon tears into characteristic pendant, wooly shreds. The **gills** weep fine, clear droplets, hence the English and Latin names for this unusual mushroom. They are brown at first with a white edge, blackening in stages as the spores mature. The **stem** is long, hollow, and fibrous and detaches easily lengthwise. The white, fibrillose surface is stained with brown, especially at the base. At the top, it retains a sort of necklace consisting of a few blackening traces of cortina. The **flesh** is tinted brown and is not very thick but is quite firm and brittle. It is almost odorless, but tastes rather bitter.

Where and when to find it

Weeping Widow prefers grassy open spaces and fruits in parks, lawns, on grass verges and beside pathways. It grows in tight clumps, in which the specimens are often attached to each other and is fairly common in the fall.

Features and edibility

Weeping Widow does not look particularly appetizing, and is often ignored as far as edibility is concerned. However, some people like the firm flesh. Like species in the genus Coprinus, it must be picked while young, before the spores have matured, and the hollow, fibrous stem should be discarded before cooking.

Related species

Other species of Psathyrella are common in lawns, clearings, grass verges,, etc., where they grow in tufts from spring through fall, like Weeping Widow. They are of no culinary interest, because they are too small and have little flesh.

THE SATIN-STEMMED AGARIC
Psathyrella piluliformis

This species has a cap that is campanulate at first, then convex, with a few white shreds of a veil attached to the margin. The cuticle is yellowish-gray in dry weather, turning brown in wet weather. The thin gills are pale lilac, but brown at maturity.

The white stem has the satiny look which gives it its English name. It is long, slender, tubular, and fragile. The flesh is thin and brittle.
- H: 2-4½ in (5-12 cm)
- Ø: ¾-2½ in (2-6 cm)
- Reddish-brown spores

THE CLUMPED AGARIC
Psathyrella multipedata

This mushroom grows on the ground in large clumps of numerous individuals. The stem is long and very slender (less than ⅛ in (0.5 cm) in diameter), fragile and white. The Clumped Agaric can be found in forest clearings and parks, and in many grassy places.

- H: 3¼-6 in (8-15 cm)
- Ø: ½-1½ in (1-4 cm)
- Blackish spores

Stem very long, slender, and white

Tuft consisting of numerous specimens

THE LILAC-GRAY AGARIC
Psathyrella melanthina

The cap is conical as in most species of the genus Psathyrella, before expanding, while retaining its central umbo. It is very fibrillose and woolly and may be various shades of brown. The pinkish-beige gills darken with age, except at the edge which remains whitish. The Lilac-gray Agaric grows in summer through fall on stumps and litter in deciduous and coniferous woods, alone or in groups. It is not edible.

- H: 1½-4 in (4-10 cm)
- Ø: 1¼-2 in (3-5 cm)
- Crimson-brown spores

CRUMBLE TUFT
Psathyrella candolleana

Crumble Tuft *(Psathyrella candolleana)* looks like a more attractive and slender version of the Satin-stemmed Agaric. The coloring is paler, however, ranging from whitish to yellowish-brown, almost rosy. The very thin gills vary in color from lilac to purplish-brown, depending on age, while the white stem is less satiny than that of the Satin-stemmed Agaric, but is taller and more fragile. Although no substitute for insulin, Crumble Tuft has some hypoglycemic properties.

- H: 1½-4 in (4-10 cm)
- Ø: 1¼-2¾ in (3-7 cm)
- Crimson-brown spores

Cap creamy white to ocher

Stem white and rather thin

Gills purplish-brown upon maturity

THE CONE-CAPPED AGARIC
Psathyrella conopilus

The cap is dark reddish-brown, but may turn pale ocher when the weather is dry. It is campanulate at first, expanding later but always remaining conical, with a finely striated margin. The stem is very long and whitish. This species lives in woodland, as well as in parks, growing in soil that contains a lot of decayed wood.

- H: 4-8 in (10-20 cm)
- Ø: 1¼-1½ in (3-6 cm)
- Black spores

The Common Ink Cap

Coprinus atramentarius

Classification : Cl. Homobasidiomycetes - O. Agaricales - F. Coprinaceae.

- H: 2-6 in (5-15 cm)
- Ø: 1½-2¾ in (4-7 cm)
- Black spores

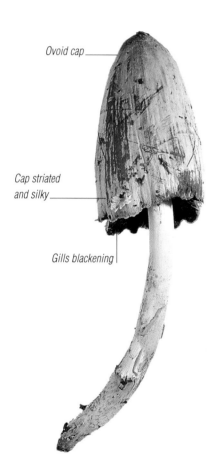

Ovoid cap

Cap striated and silky

Gills blackening

How to recognize it

The **cap** of the Ink Cap is ovoid at first, but eventually opens out like an umbrella and soon begins to weep drops of liquid like black ink, liquefying completely with age. The surface is silky, striated, and varying in color from cream to ash, while the center is covered with brown scales. Eventually, the margin becomes upturned and spreads the black coloration to the whole of the cap.

The **gills** are bow-shaped, free and grayish at first, then briefly pink, before liquefying, like the cap, into a black ink as the spores ripen.

The **stem** is short and thick at first and has a slightly swollen annual zone just below the cap. The rough-textured lower part is white, then brown, and narrower at the base. The upper part is hollow and fragile, and extends considerably with age.

The **flesh** is thin, fragile, and brittle. It is grayish at first, but soon blackens, and eventually deliquesces when the spores have ripened.

Where and when to find it

The Common Ink Cap is a familiar sight in grassland, from forest clearings and grass verges, gardens, and lawns, where it grows on humus or rotting wood. It generally appears in small clumps of tightly-packed specimens stuck together or welded at the base of the stem. It is common throughout the northern hemisphere and can be found growing almost throughout the year, from spring through fall.

Toxicity

The Common Ink Cap does not have nearly as good a flavor as The Shaggy Ink Cap and furthermore, certain precautions must be taken when eating it.

Only young specimens should be picked, in which the cap does not display the slightest sign of liquefaction. Furthermore, if alcohol of any kind is drunk when the mushroom is eaten, it causes some strange symptoms of poisoning. The face and thorax are congested, and the sufferer experiences palpitations, anxiety attacks, etc. A single glass of wine or beer will often be enough to suffuse the nose and face. Fortunately, these symptoms soon disappear and there are usually no after-effects. However, what is surprising is they do not only occur if the mushroom and alcohol are ingested simultaneously. If alcohol is drunk even a few days after eating a large portion of the these mushrooms, the same effects will be produced.

In some cases, the victim may suffer symptoms each time alcohol is consumed and this may last for many months.

The Common Ink Cap should therefore only be eaten by teetotallers or at least anyone who intends to refrain from drinking alcohol for at least several days. The toxin which produces the unpleasant effects is an amino-acid called coprine, and the symptoms it causes are very similar to those of disulfiram, the drug best known under the name of Antabuse, which used to be used for curing alcoholism.

THE DOMESTIC INK CAP
Coprinus domesticus

This Ink Cap looks very like the Glistening Ink Cap described below. The cap is beige or pale yellowish-brown, but fawn in the center (the top). The flakes sprinkled over the cap especially at the top are white or reddish. The cap becomes deeply striated, then splits as it expands. The stem thickens toward the base, which disappears into a tangle of reddish mycelium.

From spring onward, this Ink Cap can be found on all types of rotting wood.

- H: 2-6 in (5-15 cm)
- Ø: 1¼-2 in (3-5 cm)
- Dark brown spores

GLISTENING INK CAP
Coprinus micaceus

This mushroom is smaller and more fragile than the Common Ink Cap, and has shiny specks on the top of the cap, which look like flakes of mica. The thin, white, slender, silky stem is sometimes encircled with a black ring; it is hollow and fragile. It grows in tufts in woods, on rotting wood. It is not edible.

- H: 2-4 in (5-10 cm)
- Ø: 1¼-2 in (3-5 cm)
- Black spores

THE PLEATED INK CAP
Coprinus plicatilis

The Pleated Ink Cap grows in isolation on fertile grassland, on lawns or at roadsides.

It looks just like a parasol with its deeply furrowed, grayish cap and clearly defined central fawn disk.

The flesh is extremely thin and fragile and it is thus inedible.

- H: 1½-2¾ in (4-7 cm)
- Ø: ¾-1¼ in (2-3 cm)
- Black spores

FAIRIES' BONNETS
Coprinus disseminatus

Fairies' Bonnets is a common mushroom whose tiny caps cover grassy places or old tree stumps. It differs from the other species of Coprinus in that its gills are not deliquescent but remain firm after the spores have ripened.

- H: ¾-2 in (2-5 cm)
- Ø: ½-¾ in (1-2 cm)
- Black spores

Shaggy Ink Cap

Coprinus comatus

English synonym: Lawyer's Wig

Classification : Cl. Homobasidiomycetes -
O. Agaricales - F. Coprinaceae.

- H: 4-8 in (10-20 cm)
- Ø: ¾-2½ in (2-6 cm)
- Black spores

Top often ocher
and smooth

White, shaggy,
ovoid cap

Gills white turning
progressively pink,
then black, starting at the
base of the cap

Hollow stem

How to recognize it

When young, The Shaggy Ink Cap is easy to recognize by its thick fleece of white scales, which turn reddish. However, it develops very quickly and in an unusual way.

The **cap** is medium to large, ovoid or oblong, and begins to blacken from the margin which turns up and gradually begins to roll up. This makes it look like a bell. Eventually it becomes totally liquefied, and all that remains is the tiny disk at the top.

The white **gills** turn pink but quickly blacken when the spores mature.

The cylindrical **stem** has a thin, white, fugaceous ring. At first it is the same color as the cap which sheathes it completely, but it sometimes extends rapidly quite late in its life. The white, silky surface becomes stained with pink, then with black. The thin, fragile, white **flesh** turns pink, then black and deliquescent in the cap and has a cottony consistency in the stem.

Where and when to find it

The Shaggy Ink Cap generally grows in grassland, on lawns or in meadows, gardens, grass verges, and at the roadside. Despite its fragile appearance, this mushroom is capable of growing through blacktop! It is very common, and grows, sometimes in quite large clumps, throughout the temperate zone from April through December, but especially in summer through fall.

▌Features and edibility

This delicious edible mushroom is particularly tasty when young. It can even be eaten raw, dressed only with salt and pepper. If cooked, it can be added to a Béchamel Sauce or sautéed with minced parsley. Unfortunately, The Shaggy Ink Cap cannot be preserved, because it will blacken and liquefy in the space of a few hours. For the same reason, it must be eaten as soon as possible after harvesting, and only the youngest specimens in the best possible conditions should be picked. Older specimens become unreliable and can cause indigestion or stomach upsets.

▌Cultivation

A famous French chef, Monsieur Lorca, who works at the Restaurant Troisgros in Roanne, said when questioned that his three favorite mushrooms which he would like to find all year round were The Chanterelle, The Shaggy Ink Cap, and Caesar's Mushroom.

The fact that The Shaggy Ink Cap was chosen by this great chef should promote its cultivation. It has been cultivated successfully in Germany, similarly to the store mushroom. In fact, The Shaggy Ink Cap often invades insufficiently fermented manure on mushroom farms. A serious drawback to commercial cultivation is the impossibility of preserving it. However, research is proceeding and there is reason to hope that through chilling or sterilization, The Shaggy Ink Cap will be available at all the best tables, all year round in a few years' time.

Related species

Coprinus species are characterized by their deliquescence as the black spores rapidly mature. Their color turns the flesh black.
Some authors have described varieties of The Shaggy Ink Cap which differ only in the shape and appearance of the cap.

MAGPIE MUSHROOM OR MAGPIE CAP
Coprinus picaceus

This mushroom is much smaller but when young it looks very similar to The Shaggy Ink Cap. The cap is covered with a white veil which breaks as it develops. Large white patches of it persist on the cap, contrasting with the brownish-black cap, like the colors of a magpie. The tall, cylindrical stem is white, and covered with concoloro us variegations. It grows in isolation or in small clumps in copses and woods, under conifers, from spring through fall. It is insipid and has a rather unpleasant smell, so it is of no culinary interest.
- H: 4-10 in (10-25 cm)
- Ø: 1¼-2¾ in (3-7 cm)
- Black spores

THE SNOW WHITE INK CAP
Coprinus niveus

Like most of the small white species of Coprinus, the Snow White Ink Cap grows in grassland on cow-pats and rotting manure. It is inedible.
- H: 1½-3¼ in (4-8 cm)
- Ø: ½-1¼ in (1-3 cm)
- Black spores

THE HARE'S FOOT INK CAP
Coprinus lagopus

The cap is ovoid or cylindrical at first, and covered with a grayish or silvery coating of scales. As the bell opens, it reveals a surface that is striated almost to the center. The gills are white and widely spaced and the downy stem which has no ring soon turn black. The stem is thicker at the base and elongates with age.
- H: 2½-4½ in (6-12 cm)
- Ø: ¾-1½ in (2-4 cm)
- Black spores

The Horse Mushroom

Agaricus arvensis

Alternative Latin name : *Psalliota arvensis*.

Classification : Cl. Homobasidiomycetes - O. Agaricales - F. Agaricaceae.

- H: 4-7 in (10-18 cm)
- Ø: 4-6 in (10-15 cm)
- Chocolate-brown spores

Gills gray, then pink, eventually dark brown

Hemispherical white cap, yellowing with age

Very crowded gills

Thick, double ring

Stem thickening toward the base

How to recognize it

The **cap** is globose at first and then expands but the margin remains inrolled for a long time. It is large and fleshy. The surface is immaculate at first, but turns lemon yellow if rubbed.

The very thin, crowded **gills** remain grayish for a long time before turning pink. They only become purplish-brown when old.

The sturdy **stem** is deeply embedded in the soil, and thickens toward the base. It has a thick, membranous double ring, whose lower fold is toothed like a gear-wheel, and which is one of the means of identification. The surface is white but it yellows like the cap, especially at the base.

The **flesh** is thick, firm and white, yellowing then eventually turning pink. It has a delicate fragrance of aniseed, another typical sign.

Where and when to find it

The Horse Mushroom grows in fields and pastures, and sometimes in heather. It may be common in some locations but it is irregularly spread over the temperature zone of the northern hemisphere. It may be found in spring, but fruits mainly in the fall.

Features and edibility

The Horse Mushroom is a delicious mushroom very much sought after by anyone who has ever tasted its exquisite flesh. It is the largest and best of all the pink-gilled mushrooms.

Lookalike

The Yellow-staining Mushroom (Agaricus xanthoderma) *(p. 165), grows in well-lit woods and copses but may also be found in meadows. It has a rather unpleasant smell and is often slightly poisonous.*

Lookalike:
The Yellow-staining Mushroom
(*Agaricus xanthoderma*) (p. 165)

	The Horse Mushroom *Agaricus arvensis*	The Yellow-staining Mushroom *Agaricus xanthoderma*
Cap	thick and swollen	flattened, not very thick
Gills	white, pink, then purplish-brown	white,pink, then purplish-brown
Stem	short, sturdy	long, bulbous, yellowing to the touch
Ring	double, thick	single, thick
Flesh	yellowing gradually (lemon yellow)	yellowing quickly (chrome yellow)
Odor	aniseed, pleasant	sharp, unpleasant, of ink
Habitat	grassland	meadows, grass verges
Features	excellent	slightly poisonous

Related species

The Horse Mushroom is one of a group of the genus Agaricus whose flesh turns yellow when touched. It includes the following mushrooms all of them edible.

THE WOOD MUSHROOM
Agaricus silvicola

This mushroom is very similar to The Horse Mushroom but is taller and the stem is often flexible. However, since it lives exclusively in coniferous or deciduous woods there can be no confusion between the two species. In any case, the Wood Mushroom is also a delicious edible mushroom.

- H: 2³/₄-5¹/₂ in (7-14 cm)
- Ø: 2-4¹/₂ in (5-12 cm)
- Chocolate-brown spores

Cap yellowing to the touch

White cap and stem

THE LARGE-BULBED MUSHROOM
Agaricus essettei

The large-bulbed mushroom lives mainly in coniferous woods, especially spruce, and is extremely similar in appearance to The Wood Mushroom. The only difference is the base of them which has a clearly marginate and flattened base of the stem. It is even more delicious than The Wood Mushroom.

- H: 2¹/₂-4¹/₂ in (6-12 cm)
- Ø: 2-4 in (5-10 cm)
- Chocolate-brown spores

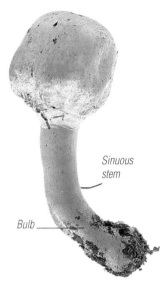

Sinuous stem

Bulb

ALBERT'S MUSHROOM
Agaricus albertii

This is a huge mushroom, whose white cap can be as large as 12 in (30 cm) in diameter. The very sturdy stem is slightly in the lower third and slightly scaly under the very downy ring.

- H: 2³/₄-7 in (7-18 cm)
- Ø: 3¹/₄-8 in (8-20 cm)
- Chocolate-brown spores

Very fleshy

Stem swollen toward the center

Downy ring

THE PRINCE
Agaricus augustus

The flesh of this species turns slightly yellow or reddish before becoming darker red. The cap has red scales, in a regular arrangement on a pale ocher-yellow background with a darker center. It smells of bitter almonds, but the thick, tender flesh makes it a delicious mushroom which is unfortunately not very common. It grows in forest clearings and at the edge of woods.

- H: 3¹/₄-6 in (8-15 cm)
- Ø: 3¹/₄-6 in (8-15 cm)
- Chocolate-brown spores

Uniform reddish scales

Thick, scaly stem

THE YELLOW-BULBED MUSHROOM
Agaricus semotus

This little agaric possesses a cap covered in small, pinkish-lilac scales, which are more brightly colored in the center. The surrounding area is much paler, yellowing at the margin. The bulbous stem is white, though it is yellow at the base. The flesh is yellow at least in the base of the stem, smells quite strongly of aniseed, sometimes mixed with bitter almonds.

This fairly rare species may be poisonous. It appears in summer through fall in grassy clearings in coniferous woods.

- H: 1¹/₄-1¹/₂ in (3-6 cm)
- Ø: 1¹/₄-2 in (3-5 cm)
- Brown spores

Field Mushroom

Agaricus campestris

Latin name : *Psalliota campestris*.

Classification : Cl. Homobasidiomycetes - O. Agaricales - F. Agaricaceae.

- H: 1½-4 in (4-10 cm)
- Ø: 1½-4 in (4-10 cm)
- Chocolate-brown spores

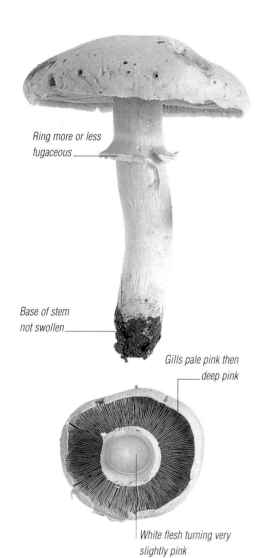

Ring more or less fugaceous

Base of stem not swollen

Gills pale pink then deep pink

White flesh turning very slightly pink

▼ **Lookalikes:**
The Yellow-staining Mushroom
(*Agaricus xanthoderma*) (p. 165)
The Red-brown Parasol
(*Lepiota brunneoincarnata*) (p. 167)

▌How to recognize it

This is the mushroom most familiar to mushroom-hunters, the one closely related to the common store mushroom and the Portobello. The **cap** is of average size and is quite thick and fleshy. It is rounded at first and thick, then it expands but remains convex for a long time. The cuticle is generally perfectly smooth and clean, though it may have a few white scales or be colored pale brown all over. The margin remains inrolled for a long time.

The free **gills** are crowded and tight. They are a delicate pale pink, the color intensifying to deep pink and that is why one of the country names for this mushroom is Pink Bottoms. They subsequently turn purplish-brown, then black, as the gills ripen.

The cylindrical **stem** is rather attenuated at the base. It is short and sturdy and has a fragile, fugaceous, white ring near the top which is single, rather than double as in related species. The **flesh**, is thick, white and firm, and it may turn a delicate pink when broken before darkening to brown. It has a delicate, fruity odor.

▌Where and when to find it

The Field Mushroom lives only in meadows, prairies, pastures, and at the edges of woods. Large numbers often emerge together in the early morning dew. It is commonly found throughout the northern hemisphere and even in Australia. Although it may occasionally be found in spring and summer, it is abundant in the fall.

▌Features and edibility

The Field Mushroom is greatly superior to the cultivated Common Store Mushroom (*Agaricus bisporus*). It has a very fine flavor, as long it is eaten young, when the gills are still pink. It subsequently becomes less tasty. It is harvested everywhere and is delicious when eaten raw, dressed in a salad, sautéed in a skillet, or eaten as a side-dish.

Lookalikes

The Yellow-staining Mushroom (Agaricus xanthoderma) *(p. 165)*, which appears in grassland (meadows, grass verges, lawns) does not turn pink, but becomes bright yellow when damaged or broken. The odor and taste are unpleasant. It is indigestible, even poisonous, for some people.
Remember that the smell is a good indicator of a Field Mushroom. All species in the genus Agaricus are edible and are mostly of excellent quality.
The Red-brown Parasol (Lepiota brunneoincarnata) *(p. 167)* and its close relatives are deadly and might be confused with the Field Mushroom, due to the fact that their flesh turns pink. However, their gills are white and there is no clear ring on the stem. They grow in grassland.

Related species

THE CULTIVATED MUSHROOM
Agaricus bisporus

The Cultivated Mushroom has gills which are not such a bright pink color.

- H: 2-3¼ in (5-8 cm)
- Ø: 1½-4 in (4-10 cm)
- Chocolate-brown spores

THE SIDEWALK MUSHROOM
Agaricus bitorquis

The ring on this Agaric is typically double. It is an excellent edible mushroom with a firm cap and very thick flesh. It grows in gardens, at the roadside, and on grass verges, but it is so strong, it has been known to lift paving stones on the sidewalk and grow through the pavement! It can be cultivated like the Field Mushroom.

- H: 2½-4½ in (6-12 cm)
- Ø: 2-4½ in (5-12 cm)
- Chocolate-brown spores

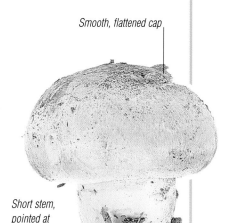

Smooth, flattened cap

Short stem, pointed at the base

The Cultivated Mushroom and its hybrids are by far the most widely grown mushroom in the world, the annual production exceeding a million tons. This is five times as much as the production of The Shiitake Mushroom (*Lentinellus edodes*) which is so popular in China and Japan but only cultivated in the Far East, of which only about 200,000 tons are produced. That is as much as the represents the commercial production of the Cultivated Mushroom in France alone.

The Cultivated Mushroom, or Common Store Mushroom and relatives such as the Portobello Mushroom are now cultivated on five continents and are an important export. There is fierce competition to export this mushroom in which wealthier countries with a temperate climate are at a disadvantage, due to their high manpower and set-up costs. In France, for example, the mushrooms must be picked by qualified manpower who sort them in order to choose only those at a certain degree of ripeness. There is no prospect of mechanization, except for "cups" or "flats" which are popular in the Netherlands and the United Kingdom, as opposed to button mushrooms which are favored elsewhere.

In temperate climates, mushrooms are cultivated below ground in cellars, vaults, or caves, as in the Paris region. (Damp limestone caves seem to be the most favorable.) In countries with a hot, damp climate, the set-up is easier and manpower costs lower. In Taiwan, for example, mushrooms are grown under simple bamboo shelters and cultivated varieties of Field Mushroom can be replaced very quickly with other species of mushroom, and even by vegetables. Thus, despite the anti-dumping measures taken by the European Union and the United States, the market is liable at any moment to be inundated with cultivated mushrooms sold at very low prices and emanating from Southeast Asia.

Mushroom cultivation in Europe dates back to the seventeenth century when gardeners in truck farms near Paris grew mushrooms in large numbers on heavily manured soil and compost heaps. This substrate is very similar to the mushroom's native habitat. It is a saprophyte which has few requirements for its development, except that it needs to grow in the soil on well-rotting vegetable matter.

	Field Mushroom *Agaricus campestris*	**The Yellow-staining Mushroom** *Agaricus xanthoderma*	**The Red-brown Parasol** *Lepiota brunneoincarnata*
Cap	swollen, not very thick	flattened, not very thick	small with brown scales
Gills	bright pink, then purplish-brown	white for a long time, pink, then purplish-brown	white, not browning
Stem	short, sturdy	long, bulbous	scaly
Ring	single, firm	single, full	very small
Flesh	turning slightly pink	clearly yellowing	turning pink
Odor	typical, pleasant	peppery, unpleasant	faint, fruity
Habitat	fields	fields, grass verges	meadows, gardens
Features	excellent	slightly poisonous	deadly

The Brown Wood Mushroom

Agaricus silvaticus

Alternative Latin name : *Psalliota silvatica*.

Classification : Cl. Homobasidiomycetes - O. Agaricales - F. Agaricaceae.

- H: 2-4½ in (5-12 cm)
- Ø: 2-4 in (5-10 cm)
- Whitish spores

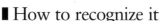

Reddish-brown, scaly cap

Ring white at first, turning brown

Gills pale at first, then pink and finally brown

Stem reddening where surface is damaged

▋ How to recognize it

The Brown Wood Mushroom is usually deeply embedded in humus, so only its cap is visible. The **cap** is of average size, convex to flattened , not thick but still fleshy. It is covered in large, brown, hairy scales which are dense in the center, and more widely spaced and larger near the margin which remains inrolled for a long time. The thin, swollen **gills** are free. They are deep pink at first, turning gray, becoming reddish-brown when the spores ripen.

The long **stem** may be thick or thin and may be cylindrical or bulbous. It is white at first, then reddening, and turning dark red when damaged. It has a single ring, which is quite thick and concolorous with the stem, but which soon disappears.

The **flesh** is white and tender, reddening when cut, especially in young specimens and when the weather is damp. It later turns brown. The odor is pleasant, a complex mixture of aniseed and resin, and the flavor is mild.

▋ Where and when to find it

The Brown Wood Mushroom appears on calcareous and siliceous soil, especially in pine needle litter, under spruce. It can also be encountered, though more rarely, under other conifers and even under deciduous trees. It is fairly common, and fruits in summer and fall.

▋ Features and edibility

Less sought after than other species of this type, perhaps because it is less common, The Brown Wood Mushroom is nevertheless very good to eat. It must be picked when young because it is then very fleshy. The stem soon becomes fibrous and must be rejected. Other Agarics can be substituted for it if necessary such as The Prince.

Lookalike

The Scaly Mushroom *(Agaricus praeclaresquamosus), (p. 166) a close relative of the Yellow-staining Mushroom, has a cap covered in fine, grayish-brown scales. The thin, sinuous stem has a noticeable bulb at the base. The obvious yellowing and the unpleasant, rather peppery, smell of the flesh are determining criteria, which are observable mainly in the base of the stem.*

This mushroom of well-lit woods and edges of forests, is suspect for the same reason as The Yellow-staining Mushroom, as it may cause stomach upsets in some people but it is not dangerous.

▼ **Lookalike:**
The Scaly Mushroom *(Agaricus praeclaresquamosus)* (p. 166)

	The Brown Wood Mushroom *Agaricus silvaticus*	The Scaly Mushroom *Agaricus praeclaresquamosus*
Cap	scaly, brownish	fine scales, brownish-gray
Gills	pinkish, turning brown	white, pink, turning brown
Stem	more or less bulbous	noticeably bulbous
Flesh	reddening	yellowing
Odor	pleasant	unpleasant
Habitat	woods (mainly conifers)	fields, grass verges, well-lit woods
Features	good to eat	suspect

BLEEDING MUSHROOM
Agaricus haemorrhoidarius

The Bleeding Mushroom differs from the Brown Wood Mushroom in that it immediately turns blood red when cut. It grows in well-lit woods and forest clearings.

- H: 4-6 in (10-15 cm)
- Ø: 3¼-5½ in (8-14 cm)
- Chocolate-brown spores

Flesh reddening strongly when cut

THE VARIEGATED MUSHROOM
Agaricus variegans

This Agaric is not very good to eat with an unpleasant odor. It grows mainly in coniferous woods, but it is not very common. The cap is spotted with gray or brown scales against a whitish background. The ring is full and the base of the stem is noticeably bulbous.

Cap spotted with scales

- H: 3¼-4½ in (8-12 cm)
- Ø: 2¾-4 in (7-10 cm)
- Chocolate-brown spores

The Yellow-staining Mushroom

Agaricus xanthoderma

Alternative Latin name : *Psalliota xanthoderma*.

Classification : Cl. Homobasidiomycetes - O. Agaricales - F. Agaricaceae.

- H: 2¾-5 in (7-13 cm)
- Ø: 2-4½ in (5-12 cm)
- Chocolate-brown spores

Cap flattened at the top

Cap more or less yellowing

White stem

Bulbous base, turning bright yellow when rubbed

▌How to recognize it

The Yellow-staining Mushroom is a handsome white mushroom with a silky look which turns yellow as soon as it is touched.

The **cap** is average to large in size and is relatively thick and typically flattened at the top, even in young specimens, so that for a long time, it looks like a round cap with overhanging edges. It eventually flattens completely and tends to turn reddish. It becomes chrome yellow as soon as it is touched.

The swollen, free **gills** remain white for a long time, becoming tinted pink and finally purplish-brown when mature. The cylindrical **stem** has a clear bulb at the base. It is full and firm at first, later extending until it is much longer and eventually becoming fragile, hollow, slender, and sinuous.

The silky, white surface becomes stained chrome yellow when rubbed, especially the bulb. The upper part has a single, white ring which turns brownish with age and can soon be slid up and down the stem.

The tender white **flesh** turns bright yellow as soon as it is scratched with a nail. It has a strong, rather peppery odor, reminiscent of phenol or iodoform.

The Yellow-staining Mushroom

▌Where and when to find it

The Yellow-staining Mushroom grows in open grassland, meadows and grass verges. But it can also hide in clumps of trees, at the edge of woods and even in clearings. It is common in specific locations throughout the temperate zone. It rarely grows in isolation and fruits in circles or large clusters from May through November.

▌Toxicity

There is a theory that it is merely the odor and unpleasant flavor that are the reason for people with delicate digestions to find this mushroom poisonous. The Yellow-staining Mushroom may prove toxic for some, causing the classic symptoms of stomach upset—diarrhea, nausea, cold sweats, sick headache, etc. However, in the majority of cases it is eaten without any ill effects. We recommend avoiding it however, preferring to consider it to be suspect at the most.

Young Yellow-staining Mushrooms have a sturdy stem. When mature, they are taller. ▶

▼ **Lookalikes:**
The Horse Mushroom *(Agaricus arvensis)* (p. 160)
Field Mushroom *(Agaricus campestris)* (p. 162)
The Off-white Parasol *(Leucoagaricus leucothites)* (p. 172)

Lookalikes

Thanks to its unpleasant flavor and supposed toxicity the Yellow-straining Mushroom must be distinguished from related edible varieties which grow in grassland, as well as from The Off-white Parasol Mushroom. Remember that The Yellow-staining Mushroom is recognizable due to the immediate and intense yellowing of the flesh immediately it is bruised, and the unpleasant smell, especially at the base of the stem.

The Horse Mushroom (Agaricus arvensis) *(p. 160) Turns lemon yellow when bruised and smells strongly of aniseed.*

The Field Mushroom (Agaricus campestris) *(p. 162) does not yellow and has a pleasant, fruity odor.*

The Off-white Parasol Mushroom *(Leucoagaricus leucothites) (p. 172), is edible. The white gills turn pinkish and there is an underdeveloped ring on the stem.*

Grayish scales on cap

Related species

There are a few varieties of this mushroom whose cap is grayish or brownish and scaly to some extent.

THE SCALY MUSHROOM
Agaricus praeclaresquamosus ⚠

The Scaly Mushroom is generally thinner than the Yellow-staining Mushroom and is easily distinguishable from it by its scaly cap which is clearly tinted with grayish-brown on a white background. This suspect species grows in the same habitat as the Yellow-staining Mushroom, and appears at some locations in large clumps on laws, for example. It has a similar, rather unpleasant odor especially at the base of the stem.

● H: 2³⁄₄-5 in (7-13 cm)
● Ø: 2¹⁄₂-6 in (6-15 cm)
● Chocolate-brown spores

	The Yellow-staining Mushroom ⚠ *Agaricus xanthoderma*	The Horse Mushroom *Agaricus arvensis*	Field Mushroom *Agaricus campestris*	Off-white Parasol Mushroom *Leucoagaricus leucothites*
Cap	flattened, thinnish	swollen, thick	convex, not very thick	white or off-white
Gills	gray, pink,then purplish-brown	white, pink, then purplish-brown	bright pink, then purplish-brown	white to pinkish
Stem	long, bulbous	short and sturdy	short and thick	white, yellows to the touch
Ring	single, full	double, thick	single, firm	visible, thin, membranous
Flesh	yellowing (chrome yellow)	yellowing (lemon yellow)	turning faintly pink	white, slightly yellowing
Odor	peppery, unpleasant	of aniseed, pleasant	typically pleasant	faint
Habitat	meadows, grass verges	grassland	grassland	grassland
Features	slightly poisonous	excellent	excellent	good to eat

The Red-brown Parasol Mushroom

Lepiota brunneoincarnata

Classification : Cl. Homobasidiomycetes -
O. Agaricales - F. Agaricaceae.

- H: 1¼-2¾ in (3-7 cm)
- Ø: 1¼-2¾ in (3-7 cm)
- White spores

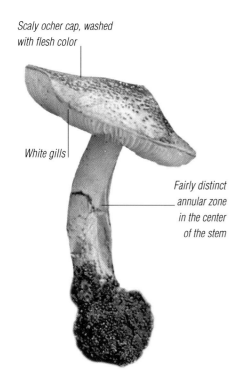

Scaly ocher cap, washed with flesh color

White gills

Fairly distinct annular zone in the center of the stem

How to recognize it

The small, thin **cap**, is barely 2 in (5 cm) in diameter. It is campanulate to convex at first, later expanding and retaining a fairly prominent central umbo.

The dry, suede-like cuticle, is ochraceous-brown to fawn in color, and tears into fine, downy scales, except at the center which looks darker. It becomes typically spotted with reddish coloring.

The **gills** are fairly crowded, swollen and free. They are white, then cream.

The cylindrical **stem** which may be quite thick or rather slender has no bulb at the base. In the middle it has a dark annular zone in the shape of a slightly raised membranous fold but there is no clear ring. The surface is white above the fold, darker below it. It is also downy and it turns pink and eventually dark red when the spores mature.

The white **flesh** turns slightly pink when cut. It has a fruity odor though sometimes this is hard to detect.

Where and when to find it

The Red-brown Parasol Mushroom is quite an uncommon species of Lepiota, and like most members of the genus, it inhabits open grassland. It may grow in isolation or in small groups of several specimens.

It can be found growing on lawns in gardens and parks, and may even invade sparse, well-lit, grassy woodland. It fruits in summer through fall.

Lookalikes:
The Frilly Parasol (*Macrolepiota excoriata*) (p. 171)
Field Mushroom (*Agaricus campestris*) (p. 162)

	The Red-brown Parasol *Lepiota brunneoincarnata*	The Frilly Parasol *Macrolepiota excoriata*	Field Mushroom *Agaricus campestris*
Cap	small, scaly	average size, scaly	average,smooth or scaly
Gills	white	white	bright pink, then purplish-brown
Stem	fairly short, cylindrical	long, bulbous	shortish,sturdy, cylindrical
Ring	dark, not marked, raised band	white, visible, loose	white, visible, membranous
Flesh	white, turning pink	white	white, turning pink
Habitat	pastures, clearings	pastures	pastures
Features	deadly poisonous	very good to eat	excellent

The Red-brown Parasol Mushroom

▇ Toxicity

In the last ten years, several small, brown-capped species of Lepiota have caused death when ingested. These include the The Brown Parasol Mushroom (*Lepiota helveola*) and its taller form, the Red-brown Parasol (*Lepiota brunneoincarnata*). Accidents are due mainly to individuals cultivating edible mushrooms in their own gardens. Any mushroom that emerges ends up in the pot, regardless of species. Unfortunately, it is not always the expected species which emerges from the ground. A poisonous variety may have found the substrate just as favorable. It should be remembered that the small brown species of Lepiota often grow in yards and gardens! Furthermore, the late-fruiting Lilac-Brown Parasol Mushroom (*Lepiota brunneolilacina*) caused the death of a little boy in Brest, France in 1986.

These species contain considerable amounts of the alkaloid amanitine which produces symptoms similar to those of the Death Cap (*Amanita phalloides.*) The first signs of poisoning do not manifest for four to six hours, minimum, after ingestion and, sometimes even later. The usual symptoms of stomach upset are followed by liver damage and hemolytic jaundice. This means that the kidneys are severely damaged. Treatment should be the same as for poisonings due to the Death Cap.

Lookalikes

When they grow in grassland, the small brown species of Lepiota may easily fruit alongside edible mushrooms, such as the large species of Lepiota as well as The Fairy Ring Champignon (Marasmius oreades), The Field Mushroom (Agaricus campestris), and similar sought-after species.

The Frilly Parasol (Macrolepiota excoriata) (p. 171) has a visible, loose, sliding ring. The stem is bulbous at the base.

The Field Mushroom (Agaricus campestris) (p. 162) has a stem which also has a clearly visible ring. It might be confused with brown species of Lepiota, due to its flesh, which turns pink when damaged. However, unlike any Lepiota, the gills are pink, darkening to purplish-brown when the spores mature.

Related species

There is a whole phalanx of small, so-called brown Parasol Mushrooms of the genus Lepiota, with scaly, whitish to brownish caps and flesh which may or may not turn pink. They are sometimes hard to separate from each other. Most of them are poisonous, and even fatal. A few of them are described below.

THE LILAC-BROWN PARASOL

Lepiota brunneolilacina

The reddish-brown scales of this Lepiota stand out against a pink background. The edge of the ring is gray-green. It is a southern species which appears late, growing in clumps in dunes and sandy soils, and on the Atlantic coast.
- H: 11/4-21/2 in (3-6 cm)
- Ø: 2-23/4 in (5-7 cm)
- White spores

THE BROWN PARASOL MUSHROOM
Lepiota helveola

This name was once used for a group of Lepiotas which have now been separated into difference species.
The true Brown Parasol Mushroom is fairly rare. The stem is stained dark red.
- H: 1½-4 in (4-10 cm)
- Ø: (2-4 in (5-10 cm)
- White spores

Not very scaly, dark red stem

The Stinking Parasol
⚠ *Lepiota cristata*

The umbo is always visible and the concentric scales of the cap are reddish-orange on a white background. The ring soon disappears. The stem is reddish-pink at the base. This is a common species which is found almost everywhere in woods, copses, and grass verges. It has an unpleasant odor. It is also known as The Crested Lepiota.
- H: 1¼-2½ in (3-6 cm)
- Ø: ¾-2 in (2-5 cm)
- White spores

The Red-stemmed Parasol
Lepiota ignivolvata

This is a fairly large species. The stem has a central ring which forms one or two oblique raised circles which are russet in color. The base of the stem turns orange with age. The cap has fixed, reddish, concentric scales. It is fairly unusual and is confined to coniferous woods on calcareous soil.
- H: 3¼-6 in (8-15 cm)
- Ø: 4-5 in (10-13 cm)
- White spores

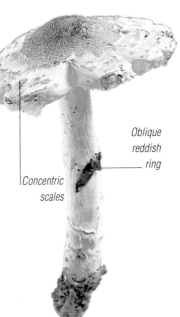

Oblique reddish ring

Concentric scales

The Cat Parasol
⚠ *Lepiota felina*

This Lepiota grows under conifers, and less frequently under broad-leaved trees. The cap has prominent, brown to brownish-black scales, on a white background. The ring and the stem below it are stained with brown. It is said to smell like geranium, though some people say the smell is of mold.
- H: 1¼-2¾ in (3-7 cm)
- Ø: ¾-1½ in (2-4 cm) ● White spores

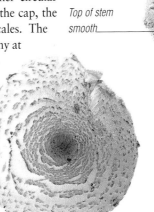

Scales brownish-ocher against a white background

Ring stained with brown

The Shield-shaped Parasol
⚠ *Lepiota clypeolaria*

There is a reddish-ocher circular patch in the center of the cap, the same color as the scales. The stem is white and downy at the top. This species grows under deciduous trees.
- H: 2½-5 in (6-13 cm)
- Ø: 1½-3¼ in (4-8 cm)
- White spores

Top of stem smooth

Downy stem

The Spruce Parasol
⚠ *Lepiota ventriosospora*

This parasol mushroom looks like the Shield-shaped Parasol , but the downy fluff on the stem is bright yellow and it grows mainly under spruce.
- H: 3¼-5 in (8-13 cm)
- Ø: 2-3¼ in (5-8 cm)
- White spores

The Parasol Mushroom

Macrolepiota procera

Alternative Latin name : *Lepiota procera*.

Classification : Cl. Homobasidiomycetes - O. Agaricales - F. Agaricaceae.

- H: 16-12 in (5-30 cm)
- Ø: 4-12 in (10-30 cm)
- White spores

Thick brown scales

Umbo

Double ring

Swollen white gills

Scaly brown stem

Basal bulb

How to recognize it

The Parasol Mushroom is the largest of the edible mushrooms.

In young specimens, the **cap** which is ovoid at first, tops a tall stem, so that the whole mushrooms looks like a large, brown drumstick. It then expands considerably and may attain 16 in (40 cm) in diameter. The central umbo is always retained. The surface is covered with concentric, grayish-brown scales, which stand out against a pale background. Shreds hang from the margin.

The swollen **gills** are free or widely spaced and are white at first, then turning gray or darkening brown with age. The tall, stiff, almost cylindrical **stem** is visibly swollen at the base and is deeply embedded in the soil. It is typically covered in brown tiger stripes and has a double ring, which is loose and sliding.

The **flesh** is tender in the cap, fibrous in the stem. It is white at first, then turns pinkish. It has a pleasant odor and a nutty flavor.

Where and when to find it

The Parasol Mushroom is easily recognizable and spreads it parasol close to woods but mainly in the grass, especially well-manured grass, but it can also be found on heaths, growing among heather or ferns in siliceous soil. Nor is it rare to find the Parasol Mushroom growing on an antheap. The ants thus help to disseminate the spores and ensure the survival of the mushroom.

The Parasol Mushroom grows throughout the world. It is commonly found in the northern hemisphere from summer through fall, from July through October.

Features and edibility

The immature Parasol Mushroom is known as The Drumstick, and is highly sought after. This mushroom, which is so distinctive, is excellent to eat, thanks to its size and abundance, though it tends to grow in small clumps or singly, not in rings.

Only young specimens should be picked for the table, preferably Drumsticks. The characteristically nutty flavor may disappear in older specimens. The stems are easily separated from the cap and should be rejected because they are always too fibrous, whatever the age of the mushroom. However, they should not be discarded to quickly because their tiger stripes help to identify the mushroom.

Parasol Mushroom caps can be broiled with a little butter, or coated in egg and breadcrumbs and shallow-fried like the Wiener Schnitzel whose flavor they are said to resemble, according to some writers.

THE GRACEFUL PARASOL
Macrolepiota rickenii

This is a tall species. The fairly thin stem is pinkish and smooth or may have thin stripes.

- H: 4-8 in (10-20 cm)
- Ø: 2-4 in (5-10 cm)
- White spores

THE FRILLY PARASOL
Macrolepiota excoriata

The cream or whitish cap has scales which are almost the same color as the background.

- H: 3¼-4½ in (8-12 cm)
- Ø: 2-6 in (5-15 cm)
- White spores

Pale platelets

Whitish cap

THE UMBONATE PARASOL
Macrolepiota mastoidea

The pale cap has a pronounced umbo which is reddish like the scales. The bulbous stem is thin and covered in dark red spots. It is found in well-lit broad-leaved woods, on grass verges, and beside hedges. It grows in summer through fall. and is sometimes picked in mistake for the Parasol Mushroom although the flesh is thinner. It is edible.

- H: 4-7 in (10-18 cm)
- Ø: 3¼-4½ in (8-12 cm)
- White spores

THE SHAGGY PARASOL MUSHROOM
Macrolepiota rhacodes

Unlike the other parasol mushrooms in this section, the Shaggy Parasol Mushroom is a woodland species and lives in forest clearings, mainly in coniferous woods. It is also very distinctive. It gets its name from the large widely spaced brown scales and small upturned clumps of fiber which cover the cap. The gills redden when bruised. The stem has a very large bulb at the base. The flesh gradually reddens when it is damaged or cut.

The Shaggy Parasol has been blamed for some minor stomach upsets. However, these may be due to a variety of the species (var. *Bohemica*), or to a very similar species which has only recently been described, and named *Macrolepiota venenata*. Both these mushrooms favor nitrate-rich, open grassland, such as gardens, garbage dumps, etc. Consequently, when what looks like a Shaggy Parasol is encountered in this sort of environment, it is best to avoid eating it.

- H: 4½-8 in (12-20 cm)
- Ø: 2-6 in (5-15 cm)
- White spores

The Off-white Parasol

Leucoagaricus leucothites

Alternative Latin names: *Lepiota subalba, Lepiota naucina.*

Classification : Cl. Homobasidiomycetes - O. Agaricales - F. Agaricaceae.

- H: 2-4 in (5-10 cm)
- Ø: 2-4½ in (5-12 cm)
- White spores

Gills white then slightly pink

Pure white cap

Fugaceous ring

Tall stem

Stem swollen at the base

▼ **Lookalikes:**
The Yellow-staining Mushroom
(Agaricus xanthoderma) (p. 165)
The white Amanitas
(Amanita virosa, Amanita verna)
(p. 173-174)
The Death Cap *(Amanita phalloides)*
(p. 176)

■ How to recognize it

The **cap** is of average size and is quite fleshy in the center. It is ovoid at first and satiny, then spreading and may eventually even become depressed. The cuticle is pure white at first but splits later and becomes tinged with red, ocher, or brown, especially in the center. The very thin margin is delicately fringed.

The thin, crowded, white **gills** are free and wide. They turn faintly rose pink when the spores mature.

The long, slender, cylindrical **stem**, is swollen at the base and on its upper third it has a thin, fragile membranous ring, which is often fugaceous. The silky surface is pure white, but stains yellow when bruised.

The thick, tender **flesh** is white or faintly yellowing. The faint odor and the flavor are pleasant. The Off-white Parasol is edible.

■ Where and when to find it

The Off-white Lepiota grows in groups, sometimes quite large ones, in fields, meadows, fallow land, gardens and above all on grass verges. It is distributed irregularly but is abundant in some locations. It fruits in summer through fall.

■ Features and edibility

This deliciously edible mushroom has thick, tender flesh. The Off-white Lepiota has a very pleasant flavor and odor. However, the mycologist G. Fourré relates that a few rare cases of intolerance have been observed. In any case, this species is often rejected due to its resemblance to the white species of Amanita which are deadly poisonous.

Lookalikes

Extreme care must be taken when picking white mushrooms, because the most deadly poisonous varieties are white or almost white.

The Yellow-staining Mushroom (Agaricus xanthoderma) *(p. 165), responsible for stomach upsets, turns bright yellow when bruised, and has an unpleasant odor and flavor.*

The white Amanitas (Amanita virosa, Amanita verna) *(p. 173-174) and the pale forms of* **The Death Cap** (Amanita phalloides) *(p. 176) may stray into grass at the edge of a wood. They differ little in appearance from the Off-white Lepiota, except for the fact that they have a volva at the base of the stem. It is always most important, when picking white mushrooms, to ensure that the whole stem is removed from the ground, so that it can be checked to see if there is a volva at the base.*

	The Off-white Parasol *Leucoagaricus leucothites*	The Yellow-staining Mushroom *Agaricus xanthoderma*	White species of Amanita *Amanita virosa, A. verna, A. phalloides var. alba*
Cap	white or faintly colored	white, turning reddish	white or faintly colored
Gills	white to pink	white, pinkish, then purplish-brown	white, unchanging
Stem	white yellowing to the touch	white, yellowing when bruised	white, unchanging
Ring	visible, thin	visible, thick	visible, thick or reduced
Base of the stem	swollen	visibly bulbous	volva
Flesh	white, turning faintly yellow	white, turning visibly yellow	white, unchanging
Habitat	grassland	grassland, copses	woods
Features	good to eat	suspect	deadly

The Lensed Lepiota

Limacella guttata

Alternative Latin names : *Limacella lenticularis, Lepiota lenticularis.*

Classification : Cl. Homobasidiomycetes - O. Agaricales - F. Amanitaceae.

- H: 3¼-5 in (8-13 cm) ● Ø: 2½-6 in (6-15 cm)
- White spores

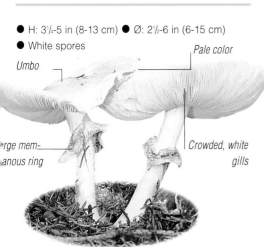

Umbo

Pale color

rge mem- anous ring

Crowded, white gills

▮ How to recognize it

The **cap** is campanulate at first, then extended, with a very regular, central umbo which looks a little like a contact lens, hence the mushroom's name. The pale beige cuticle is often darker in the center and is viscous and shiny in damp weather. In dry weather, the margin tends to crack.

The white **gills** are crowded and free.

The white **stem** is long and sturdy with a fibrillose surface and it is swollen at the base. When the mushroom is removed from the ground, it can be seen to have a bulbous stem which can occasionally be peeled like an onion. There is a thick ring, floppy, membranous, ring on the upper part of the stem. Between the gills and the ring, especially in young specimens, there are a few bister colored droplets which are very typical and distinctive. The thick, white **flesh** is yellow in the stem. It is tender and brittle and emits a pleasantly mealy odor.

▮ Where and when to find it

The Lensed Lepiota grows quite commonly in spruce plantations on mountainsides. It is more rarely found in beechwoods at lower altitudes. It fruits throughout the mushroom season, from summer through fall.

▮ Features and edibility

The Lensed Lepiota is an attractive mushroom, and has tender, well-flavored flesh. It deserves to be eaten more often, but it is not as well-known as other parasol mushrooms.

The Destroying Angel

Amanita virosa

Classification : Cl. Homobasidiomycetes - O. Agaricales - F. Amanitaceae.

- H: 4-7 in (10-18 cm)
- Ø: 2-4 in (5-10 cm)
- White spores

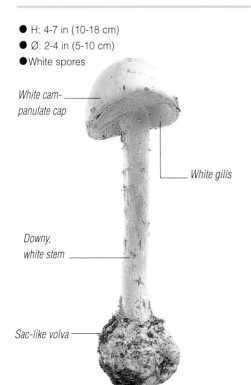

White cam- panulate cap

White gills

Downy, white stem

Sac-like volva

▮ How to recognize it

The Destroying Angel is the archetypal deadly poisonous white Amanita.

The **cap** is of average size and slightly fleshy. It is ovoid or campanulate at first, generally retaining a central umbo as it expands. The smooth, white cuticle is satiny in dry weather, becoming viscous when it is damp.

The straight, crowded, white **gills** are free.

The tall **stem** may be straight or curved; it is full at first, then hollow. Its white surface is typically covered with fibrils. It has a fragile, membranous ring, which is often lopsided and disappears in later specimens. The bulb at the base of the stem is sheathed in a white, membranous volva.

The soft, white **flesh** has a rather sickly, unpleasant odor. The flavor is also unpleasant.

▮ Where and when to find it

The Destroying Angel is commoner in cooler parts of the northern hemisphere and is common in the United States. It prefers siliceous

Destroying Angel

▼ Lookalikes:

The Wood Mushroom *(Agaricus silvicola)* (p. 161)

The Off-white Parasol *(Leucoagaricus leucothites)* (p. 172)

The Fleecy Amanita *(Amanita strobiliformis)*

The Ovoid Amanita *(Amanita ovoidea)* (p. 180)

The White Grisette *(Amanita vaginata* var. *alba)* (p. 186)

soil and lives in undergrowth where it may grow in large colonies. It seems to be commoner in beechwoods or spruce forests at high altitude. Its distribution is irregular. It sometimes fruits in spring, but is found mainly in summer through fall.

■ Toxicity

The Destroying Angel is just as dangerously poisonous as The Death Cap. It contains amanitines as well as other toxins, including virosine.

Lookalikes

It cannot be repeated often enough, the harvesting of all-white mushrooms, especially in the woods requires the most careful attention. Always check the stem of any white mushroom picked. If there is a volva, the mushroom is an Amanita.

The Wood Mushroom *(Agaricus silvicola) (p. 161) which is delicious, has a strong smell of aniseed and its yellowing flesh may turn bright yellow. The stem is embedded in the soil and has no volva, but may be bulbous at the base.*

The Off-white Parasol *(Leucoagaricus leucothites) (p. 172) also has no volva at the base of the stem.*

The Solitary Amanita *(Amanita strobiliformis) and* ***The Ovoid Amanita*** *(Amanita ovoidea) (p. 180), are both white but they are larger than than the deadly species of Amanita.*

The white form of ***The White Grisette*** *(Amanita vaginata var. alba) (p. 186), has a striated margin and no ring.*

Related species

THE SPRING AMANITA

Amanita verna

The Spring Amanita is rarer than the Destroying Angel and grows in warmer climes, in calcareous undergrowth. It is found from June onward but is still common in the fall. The cap is more regular than in its close relative and is satiny and white or cream. The ring is fairly persistent and slightly striated. The stem is smooth and the volva is globose.

The Spring Amanita is one of the trio of deadly Amanitas, the other two being The Destroying Angel and The Death Cap. It causes the same type of poisoning and its toxins are similar in composition.

● H: 2¾-4¼ in (7-11 cm)
● Ø: 1½-4 in (4 à 10 cm)
● White spores

		Destroying Angel *Amanita virosa*	The Wood Mushroom *Agaricus silvicola*	The Off-white Parasol *Leucoagaricus leucothites*	The Spring Amanita *Amanita verna*
Cap		white, satiny to viscous	white, yellowing, silky	white	white to cream, satiny
Gills		white, unchanging	grayish, pink, then brown	white, turning pinkish	white, unchanging
Stem		white, downy	yellowing, smooth	white, smooth	white, smooth
Ring		fugaceous, membranous	very full, flocculose	very small	reduced, slightly striated
Volva		white, enveloping	absent	absent	white, globose
Odor		faint, sickly	strong, of aniseed	slight	faint, sickly
Habitat		woods (siliceous soil)	woods	meadows	woods, copses (calcareous soil)
Features		deadly	excellent	good to eat	deadly

The False Death Cap

Amanita citrina

Classification : Cl. Homobasidiomycetes -
O. Agaricales - F. Amanitaceae.

- H: 3¹/₄-6 in (8-15 cm)
- Ø: 2-4¹/₂ in (5-12 cm)
- White spores

Stem striated
above the ring

Large,
striated ring

Large bulb

Citron yellow cap
covered in flat
scales

covered in large, whitish or ocher membranous plaque-like scales. The **gills** are free, crowded, and white.

The firm, pale yellow **stem** is striated above the ring. The '**ring** is well-developed, persistent, floppy, and furrowed. It is also tinged with yellow. The stem is swollen at the base into a large white bulb which is noticeably marginate, and which is sometimes covered with yellowish fragments of the volva.

The white **flesh** is firm and tender, with a flavor that is mild at first, then bitter. It smells strongly of celery or raw potato, another distinctive characteristic.

The flavor is unpleasant and the species is of no culinary interest, but it is harmless, although it was long considered deadly due to its resemblance to The Death Cap.

▌ How to recognize it

The **cap** is of average size, hemispherical at first, then flattening.

The lemon yellow or greenish-yellow cuticle is

▌ Where and when to find it

The False Death Cap is very common in late summer through fall. It grows under deciduous and coniferous trees, mainly oaks, as long as the soil is acid and well drained.

Related species

THE WHITE FALSE DEATH CAP
Amanita citrina var. *alba*

This species is completely white or at best pale yellow. Individual specimens are taller, with a bulb that is less marginate and fewer scales on the cap than The False Death Cap.
- H: 2³/₄-6 in (7-15 cm)
- Ø: 2-3¹/₄ in (5-8 cm)
- White spores

THE BROWN-CAPPED AMANITA
Amanita porphyria

This rare, inedible species is slightly smaller. The brownish cap is tinged with lilac. The ring is fragile and eventually flattens itself against the stem which turns grayish-brown.
- H: 3¹/₄-5 in (8-13 cm) ● Ø: 1¹/₂-31/4 in (4-8 cm) ● White spores

The Death Cap

Amanita phalloides

Classification : Cl. Homobasidiomycetes - O. Agaricales - F. Amanitaceae.

- H: 4-7 in (10-18 cm)
- Ø: 2-6 in (5-15 cm)
- White spores

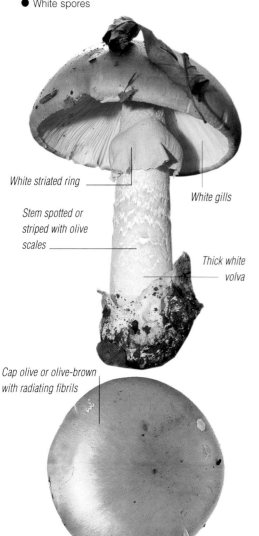

White striated ring

White gills

Stem spotted or striped with olive scales

Thick white volva

Cap olive or olive-brown with radiating fibrils

■ How to recognize it

The Death Cap is quite an attractive species which makes it all the more dangerous.

The fleshy **cap** is ovoid when it emerges from the egg. It then becomes convex, and eventually flattened. The cuticle has no warts or flakes on it, and is edged with radiating fibrils which are very characteristic. It is shiny in dry weather and slightly sticky when it is damp. The color is normally olive green but it is inconsistent and it may vary through to shades of pale green to yellow. Some forms of The Death Cap are very pale, even pure white. The smooth margin is inrolled at first, then sinuous.

The swollen **gills**, are uneven, free, and white. They are fairly crowded.

The **stem** grows up out of an egg-shaped volva, as in the case of the Stinkhorn (*Phallus impudicus*) (p.190.) The slender appearance gives the mushroom a certain elegance. The white surface is finely striped with scales which are concolorous with the cap. There is a white, striated ring and the stem is encased in a large, white, persistent volva.

The white **flesh** is thick and tender. It smells faintly of rose petals, an odor which becomes stronger with age or dessication.

■ Where and when to find it

The Death Cap normally grows under broad-leaved trees, especially in oak woods, but it is not unknown in coniferous woods.

It is common throughout the temperate zone of the northern hemisphere. In wet years it can fruit in such numbers that if often appears to be the only mushroom in the undergrowth.

It fruits in summer though mainly in the fall and can be found from July through November.

■ Toxicity

The Death Cap is Public Enemy Number One of the mushroom kingdom. It has been responsible for ninety percent of fatal mushroom poisonings. Its attractiveness and the abundance with which it fruits always leads a certain number of incautious mushroom-hunters to put it in their baskets. All the more reason why children should be taught from an early age in school to recognize it.

An odd correlation has been established in France between years when The Death Cap appears in great numbers and the quality of the grape harvest. In fact, in rainy years, The Death Cap grows abundantly at the very moment the grapes are being picked, so it is no coincidence that it is associated with a bad harvest and poor vintages.

Poisonings have increased in recent years, and in 1984 fourteen were recorded in France as being due to The Death Cap.

In some years, oak woods are carpeted with the two most poisonous varieties, The Death Cap and The Livid Entoloma. A strange association! Some sellers in the wild mushroom markets were severely reprimanded by the inspectors who check the species being sold

	The Death Cap *Amanita phalloides*	Pink Spored Grisette *Volvariella speciosa*	The Saddle-shaped Tricholoma *Tricholoma equestre*	The Pretentious Tricholoma *Tricholoma portentosum*
Cap	olive-green to fibrillose	white to grayish, viscous	bright yellow, more or less viscous	grayish-yellow, fibrillose
Gills	white to yellowish	white, then pink	bright yellow	white to yellowish
Stem	white, pitted, ring and volva	smooth white, with volva	bright yellow, smooth, no volva	white to yellowish,smooth, no volva
Flesh	tender, soft	soft	firm	firm, brittle
Odor	faint, of roses	faint, of radish	none	faint, mealy
Habitat	deciduous (conifers)	clearings, conifers (deciduous trees)	deciduous	conifers (deciduous)
Features	deadly	good to eat	excellent	excellent

over the counter. The sellers were innocently bringing in poisonous mushrooms by the basketful. Yet a single specimen of The Death Cap would be enough to cause death! The hideous symptoms of the so-called delayed phalloidian type begin with classic signs of a stomach upset with diarrhea, nausea, vomiting, and cold sweats, but these do not begin until twenty-four hours after ingestion. The vomiting becomes greater and more and more uncontrollable, and there is a danger of dehydration. The victim becomes so weak that death can ensue quite rapidly due to the strain on the heart. If this does not happen, the outward symptoms may abate while the poison is still at work on the internal organs. The victim remains lucid almost to the end, but his liver and kidneys are irreparably damaged.

Great strides have been made in treatment in the last few years, enabling a large number of the victims to survive. As soon as the diagnosis is confirmed, a doctor called out in an emergency will advise immediate hospitalization. Complete collaboration between physicians and expert mycologists is advisable in all cases. The treatment is designed to eliminate the poison from the system and help the affected organs. However, there is no real antidote. The treatment used by the French physician, Dr. Bastien, combines yeasts and an antiseptic, and is designed to restore the balance of the intestinal flora while administering therapeutic doses of vitamins B and C. It may help to the extent that the toxins are more easily eliminated and even partially destroyed by vitamin C.

Where there is serious liver damage, hepatic protectors are advisable. Cortisone and anti-enzymes are often combined with silymarin, which is extracted from a plant of the cardoon family. In the most serious cases, blood transfusions, kidney dialysis for damaged kidneys, and even liver and kidney transplants are indicated, and these have saved lives.

Lookalikes

A number of excellent edible mushrooms are unfortunately too often confused with the dangerous Death Cap.

If in doubt, always ignore or discard any mushroom with white gills and a greenish cap verging on the white or yellow and white stem with a ring and a large volva.

The Pink Spored Grisette *(Volvariella speciosa) (p. 121) has long been considered as fatal, like the False Death Cap, but it has now been rehabilitated.*

It is actually very good to eat and does not grow in woods, preferring fields or gardens. It is grayish off-white in color turning brown with age. It can be distinguished from The Death Cap by the absence of a ring, gills which turn pink, and a faint smell of radish. Species of the genus Tricholoma, whose stem has neither ring nor volva, are sometimes mixed in with The Death Cap in the basket of a careless collector who finds them in a conifer forest. It is easy to mix them up if the mushroom is removed from the ground by cutting it across with a knife just under the cap, because it means that the volva and ring of a Death Cap would be left behind. These crucial identifiers may even have been eaten by slugs, and thus partially or totally absent. In this case:

The Saddle-shaped Tricholoma *(Tricholoma flavovirens) (p. 90) differs mainly in its yellow gills.*

The Pretentious Tricholoma *(Tricholoma portentosum) (p. 88) can only be recognized by its firm flesh, a rather subjective criterion, especially for inexperienced pickers. Furthermore, the distinctive color of the cap is not always a sure sign.*

Some poisoinings have been the result of the most obvious mistakes. For instance, The Death Cap is sometimes mistaken for The Parasol Mushroom presented as a "Green Lepiota" by the untutored. It has even been mistaken for a cep and mixed with other ceps! The white form of the Death Cap strongly resembles the following edible mushrooms:

*– **The Off-white Parasol** (Leucoagaricus leucothites) (p. 172) which has a rather underdeveloped ring and a stem which swells into a little bulb at the base, but it has no volva.*

*– **The Wood Mushroom** (Agaricus silvicola) (p. 161) has no volva and its gills, which are pinkish-gray at first, eventually turning brown. Furthermore, it smells strongly of aniseed.*

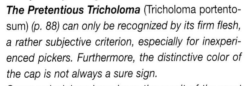

The color of the cap of The Death Cap is not a determining factor for identification purposes. Opposite is a Death Cap which is pure white all over.

Lookalikes:
Pink Spored Grisette *(Volvariella speciosa)* (p. 121)
The Saddle-shaped Tricholoma *(Tricholoma equestre)* (p. 90)
The Ominous Tricholoma *(Tricholoma portentosum)* (p. 88)
The Off-white Parasol *(Leucoagaricus leucothites)* (p. 172)
The Wood Mushroom *(Agaricus silvicola)* (p. 161)

The Blusher
Amanita rubescens

Classification: Cl. Homobasidiomycetes - O. Agaricales - F. Amanitaceae.

- H: 2³/₄-7 in (7-18 cm)
- Ø: 2¹/₂-6 in (6-15 cm)
- White spores

Grayish warts

Reddish-brown cap

White, striated ring

White gills

Reddening stem

Bulb at the base

Flesh pinkish where eaten by slugs

Flesh spotted pink where worm-eaten

How to recognize it

The fleshy **cap** is average to large in size. It is hemispherical at first, soon becoming convex, and finally extended and flattened. The cuticle varies from whitish to brownish, stained red in patches and sometimes all over.

The surface is sprinkled with irregular platelets or warts, the remnants of the cortina or veil. These are typically grayish but may tend toward yellow and be stained maroon. They may be tightly packed over the whole cap or they may be sparsely dotted over it. The margin is smooth.

The crowded, uneven **gills** are free and turn red if bruised or damaged.

The sturdy **stem** soon becomes hollow and is swollen at the base into a bulb shaped like an inverted cone. The stem is whitish to brownish, reddening with age, especially at the base. It has a large, striated white or pinkish ring.

The tender, white **flesh** is tinted with maroon where damaged. It is almost odorless, but when cooked has a pleasant, mild flavor.

Where and when to find it

The Blusher grows under both broad-leaved trees and conifers and sometimes in open spaces in the vicinity of trees.

It is very common throughout the temperate zone of the northern hemisphere, fruiting in spring and persisting throughout the year until late fall.

	The Blusher *Amanita rubescens*	The False Death Cap *Amanita spissa*	The Panther Cap *Amanita pantherina*
Cap	brownish (reddening)	gray-brown	gray-brown to yellowish
Gills	white (washed with pink)	white	white
Stem	white to browning, reddening	white, with brown scales	white (pink), striated
Ring	white (pink), striated	white, striated	white, not striated
Bulb	like inverted cone, reddening	turnip-shaped, white to brown	marginate, white
Flesh	white, reddening	white, unchanging	white, unchanging
Odor	none	of radish	none
Features	very good to eat	not good to eat	very poisonous

Lookalikes:
The False Panther Cap *(Amanita spissa)* (p. 179)
The Panther Cap *(Amanita pantherina)* (p. 181)

■ Features and edibility

Some wild mushroom gourmets consider The Blusher to be as delicious as Caesar's Mushroom. But not everyone agrees, especially as it is said to emit an unpleasant odor when cooked, which does not justify its reputation. Furthermore, it is extremely important to cook The Blusher before eating it. A quick broil or sauté is not enough, because this mushroom contains hemolysins which are capable of causing anemia by destroying the red corpuscles of the blood. Fortunately, these substances are destroyed at temperatures above 140°F (60°C.)

This means that the cooking process must be lengthy enough to ensure that the heat has time to penetrate the flesh of the mushroom. If this condition is completely fulfilled, there is no risk at all.

In this respect, it should be remembered that some other excellent edible mushrooms, such as the Morels, also contain hemolysins and that their consumption is subject to the same rules as those governing The Blusher.

Lookalikes

The Blusher varies considerably in shape and color and is not always easy to identify. No brown Amanita species which does not turn red when bruised or damaged should ever be eaten.

The False Panther Cap *(Amanita spissa) (p. 179) is not good to eat and it ought to be avoided because the danger of confusion with The Panther Cap is great and the consequences are serious (see above.)*

The Panther Cap *(Amanita pantherina) (p. 181) is very poisonous and is also variable. It is recognizable precisely because the flesh does not turn red, the margin is striated, and above all, the bulb is very distinctive, with its marked separation from the stem.*

Related species

The other brown Amanitas with unchanging, white flesh do not have blush when bruised.

THE FALSE PANTHER CAP
Amanita spissa

This imposing mushroom bears some resemblance to The Blusher. It has a grayish-brown cap covered in fugaceous, grayish warts and a smooth margin. The noticeable striation of the ring and stem above it is characteristic. The thickened, turnip-shaped base is covered in darker scales on a white background. The firm, thick flesh is white and unchanging. The odor and flavor of radish make this species uninteresting from a culinary point of view, and in any case the risks of confusing it with The Panther Cap are too great.

● H: 3¼-7 in (8-18 cm)
● Ø: 2¾-6 in (7-15 cm)
● White spores

Ring and top of stem clearly striated

Grayish warts

Ochraceous downy scales

Bulbous stem

THE TALL AMANITA
Amanita excelsa

This Amanita may merely be a variety of The False Panther Cap. It differs from the latter in its taller, narrower shape and the paler cap which is covered in thicker warty scales.

● H: 3¼-6 in (8-15 cm)
● Ø: 2½-4 in (6-10 cm)
● White spores

The Ovoid Amanita
Amanita ovoidea

Classification: Cl. Homobasidiomycetes - O. Agaricales - F. Agaricaceae.

- H: 6-10 in (15-25 cm)
- Ø: 6-10 in (15-25 cm)
- White spores

Satiny white cap

Thick, flocculose stem

Large, cream to ocher volva

How to recognize it

The Ovoid Amanita is one of the largest mushrooms in existence. Specimens have been known to reach 16 in (40 cm) in diameter! The **cap** is ovoid at first, then it expands until it is almost flat. The margin may have shreds of veil hanging from it. The cap is remarkably thick. The cuticle is smooth, satiny white, eventually turning ocher. The **gills** later darken from white to cream. They are edged with flaky scales.

The **stem** is concolorous with the cap and very massive. It is covered in downy scales and the ring, itself flocculose and fugaceous, sometimes disappears among the scales of the stem.

A large, cream-colored, thick volva, which eventually turns ocher with age, envelops the base of the stem.

The thick, white **flesh** smells of the sea, especially when the mushroom is older.

This species is edible but not very good. It is eaten more for its size than for its flavor. Care must be taken not to confuse it with The Close Amanita (*Amanita proxima*) (see below).

Where and when to find it

The Ovoid Amanita shows a marked preference for limestone soils in southern Europe, though it can also be found further north in some years.

It prefers well-lit forests, copses, clearings, and clumps of trees at the edge of fields, and grows under oaks, conifers, and boxwood. It is quite common in its preferred habitats.

Related species

Like the previous species, the following species grow in southern climates and favor calcareous soil.

THE CLOSE AMANITA
Amanita proxima

The Close Amanita so closely resembles the Ovoid Amanita that it is sometimes considered to be a variety of the latter. However, it is taller and thinner, and, above all, it has a distinct, striated, membranous ring. The volva is more noticeably reddish.

It is quite rare and it is important to know how to recognize it because it has already caused at least one death in Europe.

- H: 4-6 in (10-15 cm)
- Ø: 2½-6 in (6-15 cm)
- White spores

THE WARTY AMANITA
Amanita echinocephala

This Amanita is probably poisonous. The cap is covered with little, pointed warts which are cream or white and which can also be seen on the extended bulb. The ring is membranous and the gills have characteristic greenish highlights.

- H: 4½-8 in (12-20 cm)
- Ø: 2½-8 in (6-20 cm)
- White spores

The Panther Cap

Amanita pantherina

Classification: Cl. Homobasidiomycetes - O. Agaricales - F. Amanitaceae.

- H: 2³/₄-6 in (7-15 cm)
- Ø: 1¹/₂-4¹/₂ in (6-12 cm)
- Whitish spores

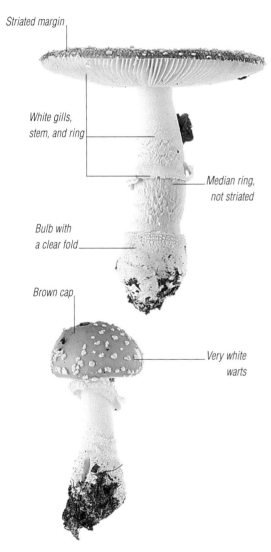

Striated margin

White gills, stem, and ring

Median ring, not striated

Bulb with a clear fold

Brown cap

Very white warts

Lookalikes:
The False Panther Cap *(Amanita spissa)* (p. 179)
The Blusher *(Amanita rubescens)* (p. 178)
Amanite engainee *(Amanita vaginata)* (p. 186)

How to recognize it

The **cap** of this species is of medium size and is not very fleshy. It is rounded at first, then flattens out noticeably. The shiny cuticle, whose color varies from grayish to ochraceous brown, is covered with small, floury warts, arranged in more or less evident concentric circles. The margin is typically furrowed.

The white **gills** are slightly swollen, crowded, and free.

The **stem** is thick in the young specimen, lengthening and thinning with age. The basal bulb has a very marked edge, surmounted by spiral raised bands. The ring is membranous and pendant and soon becomes fugaceous. It is placed half-way up the stem and is entirely white, darkening to brown underneath.

The **flesh** is white, tender and fragile and does not change color. It sometimes smells faintly of radish.

Where and when to find it

The Panther Cap is found throughout the temperate zone of the northern hemisphere under broad-leaved trees and conifers and on clay, limestone, or sandy soil. It grows from sea level to the mountains.

It is fairly common, and although it may fruit early, it is generally found in the high mushroom season from late summer through fall.

Varieties

The Panther Cap is all the more dangerous in that it is so variable. The fugaceous ring may be missing altogether and there is even a form which is remarkable for being entirely lemon yellow in color.

There is a larger variety (var. *abietum*) which lives under conifers. It has grayish, rather than white, warts and the margin becomes furrowed

only when the mushroom is mature. This variety sometimes grows in lowland in old pine forests in which some other mountain species are also found.

Toxicity

The Panther Cap is extremely poisonous containing toxic principles similar to those of The Fly Agaric (*Amanita muscaria*) (p. 182) but in different proportions. The high muscarine content causes severe poisoning, the stomach upsets being worse than those produced by The Fly Agaric. There is profuse diarrhea, uncontrollable vomiting, cold sweats, hypersalivation, etc. The symptoms appear quite quickly, one to three hours after ingestion. This makes it possible to rule out Death Cap poisoning which manifests later. However, Panther Cap poisoning is accompanied by psychotic episodes of manic or furious delirium. Hallucinations are less intense than those caused by The Fly Agaric.

Although the consumption of the Panther Cap causes physical weakness and damage to the central nervous system in victims, they do not generally die as long as they are hospitalized in time. Treatment consists of replacing lost fluids, supporting the heart, and alleviating the psychotic episodes.

Lookalikes

Due to its great variability, The Panther Cap can easily be confused with several edible species of Amanita. The abietum *variety, in particular, renders obsolete the essential recognition criterion whereby the cap is covered in white flakes and has a furrowed margin. The fact that the young specimens have grayish warts and an unstriated margin notably increases the risks of confusion with other brown species of Amanita. If in doubt, it should be recalled that The Panther Cap can be recognized by its clearly marginate bulb.*

The False Panther Cap (Amanita spissa) *(p. 179), is not good to eat, though it is harmless. The stem is extended into a turnip-shaped excrescence which is the bulb, and it has a strong smell of radish.*

The Blusher (Amanita rubescens) *(p. 182) is typified by the fact that the flesh reddens when in contact with the air. It is very good to eat as long as it is thoroughly cooked.*

The Grisette (Amanita vaginata) *(p. 186), is devoid of a ring, but may look like the Panther Cap when the latter has lost its ring. The Grisette has a volva at the base of the stem.*

Fly Agaric

Amanita muscaria

Classification: Cl. Homobasidiomycetes -
O. Agaricales - F. Amanitaceae.

- H: 4-10 in (10-25 cm)
- Ø: 3¹/₄-8 in (8-20 cm)
- White spores

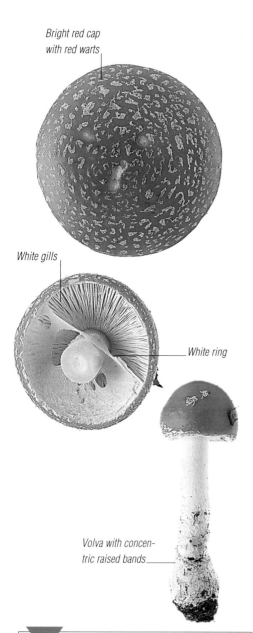

Bright red cap
with red warts

White gills

White ring

Volva with concen-
tric raised bands

▼ **Lookalike:**
Caesar's Mushroom (*Amanita caesarea*)
(p. 185)

How to recognize it

The fleshy **cap** is handsome and globulose at first, then convex, flattening later. The red cuticle varies from vermillion to orange and in the very young mushroom is almost totally covered with irregular, white or yellowish warts which later spread out in the older specimen, giving the mushroom its characteristic spotted appearance. The margin becomes finely striated with age.

The **gills** are crowded, swollen, free, and white.

The sturdy, white, cylindrical **stem** extends from a swollen base ringed with concentric raised bands. In the upper part, it is encircled by a downy, white ring. The surface is sometimes flocculose or downy, but may also be smooth.

The tender, brittle **flesh** is orange under the cuticle and white everywhere else. It is almost odorless.

Where and when to find it

The magnificent Fly Agaric brings a brilliant touch of color to the undergrowth of deciduous and coniferous trees. It seems to favor birch trees growing in acid soil, not far from heather. It can often be encountered in colonies, and grows from sea level to the treeline throughout the temperate zone from the arctic southward. It usually fruits from June through November.

Toxicity

This spectacular mushroom which is used to illustrate so many children's books is often designated as the classic poisonous mushroom. Although it is indeed dangerous, this species is nevertheless far less so than many of its relatives, such as The Panther Cap and The Death Cap. It contains far less muscarine than the Panther Cap or other poisonous mushrooms, such as the small white species of Clitocybe or members of the genus Inocybe. As in the case of the latter, if eaten it causes a type of poisoning in which a stomach upset is accompanied by excessive secretion of tears, sweat, and salivation, though this is not as serious as if any of the other mushrooms mentioned are ingested. Only one death has been attributed to The Fly Agaric in recent years. Muscarine poisoning is characterized by its psychotic effects. It leads to a condition akin to drunkenness, accompanied by hallucinations and convulsions with episodes of hilarity. There then follows a sub-comatose, depressive phase when the victim falls into a long, deep, drugged sleep. It is hard to awaken the patient and when wakened, he is in a depressed state from which it is hard for him to recover. The indigenous peoples of the Arctic region, especially the Lapps, are aware of the properties of The Fly Agaric and use it in their religious rituals.

The muscarine content and that of other toxins is very variable in Fly Agaric and although the risk of a serious poisoning remains, the fact is that in certain regions, such as northern Italy,

this species is eaten without any adverse effect. Is it free of any toxic components due to its substrate or habitat, or does the reason lie in the manner of preparation? Peeling off the cuticle in which the active principles tend to concentrate, or discarding the cooking water seem to considerably reduce the risks of poisoning. History relates, however, that Fly Agaric was a favorite poison in Ancient Rome. Did they use a concentrated extract, or is it being confused with The Death Cap?

	Fly Agaric *Amanita muscaria*	Caesar's Mushroom *Amanita caesarea*
Cap	red, white warts	orange, bare
Gills	white	yellow
Stem	white, white ring, bulb at the base	yellow, yellow ring, large volva
Flesh	white (orange under the cuticle)	white (yellow under the cuticle)
Features	poisonous	excellent

▌Features

The insecticidal properties of The Fly Agaric can be analyzed scientifically and the component responsible has been identified. It is ibotenic acid. A preparation called *Agaricus*, extracted from Fly Agaric, is used in minute doses in homeopathic medicine in order to calm nervous spasms.

Lookalike

Some forms of Fly Agaric are tinged with yellow, such as the regalis *variety found in the Nordic countries, whose cap is browner. This increases the risk of confusion with Caesar's Mushroom.*

Caesar's Mushroom (Amanita caesarea) *(p. 185) has an orange tint to the cap. It differs from Fly Agaric mainly in the voluminous volva at the base of its stem.*

Related species

There are some rarer forms of **The Fly Agaric** which differ slightly from the typical specimen described opposite.

  • The *aureola* variety has an orange cap with little or no white scabs. The stem is thinner. It is found mainly at high altitude under conifers.
• In the *formosa* variety, the warts on the cap, ring, and bulb are tinged with lemon yellow.

Yellowish-white warts

Ring edged with yellow flakes

This is the Formosa variety of Amanita muscaria

Some examples of Fly Agaric have a smooth cap completely devoid of white warts or spots, even from the very first.

The Jonquil Amanita

Amanita junquillea

Alternative Latin name: *Amanita gemmata.*

Classification : Cl. Homobasidiomycetes -
O. Agaricales - F. Amanitaceae.

- H: 2½-4½ in (6-12 cm)
- Ø: 2-4 in (5-10 cm)
- White spores

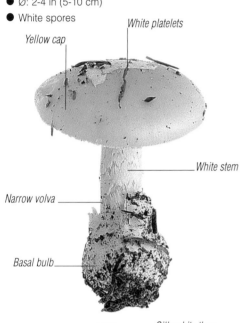

Yellow cap

White platelets

White stem

Narrow volva

Basal bulb

Gills white then beige

Lookalike:
The Tawny Grisette *(Amanita fulva)*
(p. 187)

	The Jonquil Amanita *Amanita junquillea*	The Tawny Grisette *Amanita fulva*
Cap	yellow to orange (brown), largish platelets, not very fugaceous	fawn orange, large platelets fugaceous
Gills	white to yellowish	white
Stem	white	white
Ring	fugaceous	absent
Base of stem	rounded bulb, with or without necklace	sheath-like volva
Features	poisonous	good to eat

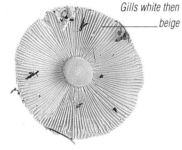

■ How to recognize it

The Jonquil Amanita has a a cap the color of the jonquil or daffodil after which it is named. The **cap** is not very fleshy and is fairly small. It is campanulate at first, spreading rapidly. The shiny cuticle is frequently decorated with white platelets which shine when wet, hence one of its French names, The Jeweled Amanita. The coloring can vary from very pale yellow to ocher, and even to orange. The thin margin is clearly striated.

The **gills** are white, almost free, and faintly tinted with ocher.

The cylindrical **stem** soon becomes hollow and fragile, and emerges from a globular basal bulb which is ringed at the top with a few shreds looking like a little necklace. The ring is located in the center of the stem; it is not well-developed and quickly becomes fugaceous. The surface of the stem is fibrillose or slightly downy and white.

The **flesh** is tender and fragile, yellow under the cuticle and white everywhere else. It has little odor.

■ Where and when to find it

The Jonquil Amanita can be found in coniferous woods (especially pinewoods) as well as under broad-leaved trees (mainly beech), from spring through to the onset of winter. It is irregularly distributed and may be common in some locations on siliceous soil, though it sometimes grows on calcareous soil. It is restricted to southern parts of the northern hemisphere.

■ Toxicity

There is a question mark as to the edibility of The Jonquil Amanita. A number of people who have tasted it consider it to have a pleasant taste, and in southern France it is eaten without any adverse effects. However, it is reported to have caused digestive troubles in other parts of the world and may even have been fatal. What could be the reason for such inconsistency? There may be some confusion with similar species, unless the toxicity is due to one of numerous sub-species of The Jonquil Amanita, which takes on diverse forms.

Lookalike

The Tawny Grisette (Amanita fulva) *(p. 187 is good to eat and is similar in shape. It has no ring but has a sheath-like volva.*

Similar specie

FRIES' AMANITA
Amanita eliae

Fries' Amanita is quite rare but probably poisonous. The stem is very tall and deeply embedded in the soil. It ends in a small bulb. The cap is ocher-yellow or beige, with some pink tones. It only grows under broad-leaved trees, favoring oak.

- H: 2¾-5 in (7-13 cm)
- Ø: 2-4 in (5-10 cm)
- Whitespores

Caesar's Mushroom

Amanita caesarea

Classification: Cl. Homobasidiomycetes - O. Agaricales - F. Amanitaceae.

- H: 4-7 in (10-18 cm)
- Ø: 3¼-8 in (8-20 cm)
- White spores

Gills, stem, and ring yellow

Very large white volva

Sometimes one or two white shreds

Striated margin

Brilliant orange cap

Lookalikes:
Fly Agaric *(Amanita muscaria)* (p. 182)
Golden Russula *(Russula aurata)*

▮ How to recognize it

The fleshy **cap**, is large and always describes a perfect circle. It is hemispherical at first, but remains convex for a long time. The cuticle is generally smooth and bare and is a brilliant orange-red, sometimes yellow. The margin is finely and regularly striated.

The **gills** are swollen and free and are a beautiful golden yellow.

The sturdy, fleshy **stem** thickens toward the base. It is golden, like the ring and full, membranous, striated, and persistent. A large, white volva covers it at the base. It represents the remains of the egg-like structure from which the young mushroom emerges.

The white **flesh** is yellow at the edge; it is thick and firm. It has a mild, nutty flavor and a faint, pleasant odor.

▮ Where and when to find it

Caesar's Mushroom is very sought after in clearings under oak and chestnut, and sometimes under conifers, especially in siliceous soil. It is important to remember that it is only found in southern parts of the northern hemisphere, and cannot withstand cold. It is hardly ever found north of the 45°N latitude and rarely grows at higher than 4000 feet. It fruits in summer, beginning in July but may be found through October in warm, wet years.

Caesar's Mushroom is found throughout the United States, though the variety found in the East is not quite as typical as the species which grow in Arizona and Mexico.

▮ Features and edibility

Caesar's Mushroom combines elegance and beauty with an incomparably delicious flavor. As far as Ancient Rome was concerned, it was the food of gods and emperors, hence the name. It is featured in mosaics and Latin poets immortalized it under the name *Boletus*. Today, if Caesar's Mushroom remains for many the ultimate edible mushroom, it is not always given its due. Any species of Amanita is likely to inspire anxiety. It is sold in the wild mushroom markets of southern France, but rarely fetches the price it deserves.

For it to retain all of its flavor, it should be eaten raw, in a salad, barely seasoned with oil, salt, and a squeeze of lemon juice. On occasions, a very few shavings of truffle, that other royal fungus, can be added, to give it more fragrance. It is also excellent when broiled, but can also be served in a sauce or used as a side-dish to accompany a meat entrée.

Lookalikes

The Fly Agaric (Amanita muscaria) *(p. 182) is poisonous and differs from Caesar's Mushroom due to its red cap, sprinkled with white warty patches, white gills, and white stem which is not encased in a volva, but which consists merely of a bulb covered in concentric raised bands.*

The Golden Russula (Russula aurata), *has an orange cap and yellowing gills and stem. It is good to eat, but nothing like as good as Caesar's Mushroom. The stem has neither ring nor volva and the flesh has the typical brittle, chalky consistency of the genus Russula.*

The Grisette

Amanita vaginata

English synonym:The Common Grisette.

Classification : Cl. Homobasidiomycetes -
O. Agaricales - F. Amanitaceae.

- H: 4-7 in (10-18 cm)
- Ø: 1½-4 in (4-10 cm)
- White spores

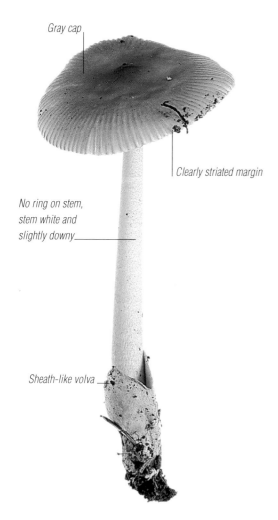

Gray cap

Clearly striated margin

No ring on stem,
stem white and
slightly downy

Sheath-like volva

The cuticle is satiny or viscous, depending on the humidity and is typically gray. The margin is clearly striated.
The uneven, free **gills** are white.
The long, slender **stem** narrows at the top and has no ring. Its white surface is covered in white or gray down. A large, white, membranous volva sheaths the base.
The white **flesh** has a soft consistency and is rather thin and fragile. The flavor is mild and there is hardly any odor.

▮ Where and when to find it

The Grisette grows in forest clearings, in mixed woods, on heaths, or meadowland, sometimes quite a long way from trees, and on all types of soil. It can be found throughout the world and is as common inside the Arctic Circle as it is in the tropics. It fruits from June through November in the temperate zone of the northern hemisphere. It is quite common in the northern United States.

▮ Features and edibility

The Grisette is an edible mushroom with a pleasant flavor, but it is not very fleshy and does not grow in large numbers. That is why its close relative which grows in the mountains, The Tawny Grisette, is often preferred.
Whatever sub-species or variety is picked, the Grisettes should never be eaten raw. Like The Blusher, they contain hemolysins, substances which can burst the red corpuscles of the blood, causing anemia by heavy reduction of the red blood cells. Fortunately, hemolysins are destroyed by heat, and are deactivated at 140-158°F (60–70°C.) Consequently, the Grisettes become perfectly safe to eat if they are properly cooked.

▮ How to recognize it

The **cap** varies in size but is more or less average, and is not very fleshy. It is campanulate at first, but soon expands and develops a small central umbo. It is covered in large white shreds of the universal veil, which are quite fugaceous and disappear in the older specimen.

▼ Lookalikes:
The Jonquil Amanita *(Amanita junquillea)* (p. 184)
The Panther Cap *(Amanita pantherina)* (p. 181)
Destroying Angel *(Amanita virosa)* (p. 173)

	The Grisette *Amanita vaginata*	The Jonquil Amanita *Amanita junquillea*	The Panther Cap *Amanita pantherina*
Cap	gray-brown, large, fugaceous platelets, marge clearly striated	yellow to orange (brown), quite large platelets, not fugaceous	brown to yellow, small warts rarely absent
Gills	white	white to yellow	white
Stem	white	white	white
Ring	absent	fugaceous	fairly fugaceous
Base of stem	sheath-like volva	bulb, with or necklace	marginate bulb, raised bands above
Features	good to eat	possibly poisonous	very poisonous

Lookalikes

The caps of the Grisettes exhibit a range of colors and can easily be mistaken for various poisonous, and even deadly, species of Amanita.

The Jonquil amanita (Amanita junquillea) *(p. 184)*, may be poisonous and has very similar characteristics to The Panther Cap. The cap is yellow.

The Panther Cap (Amanita pantherina) *(p. 181)* has a brown cap with a striated margin, and a rather fugaceous ring. It is recognizable by its stem which has a marginate bulb, surmounted by spiral raised bands. It is devoid of a volva.

The deadly white Amanitas have a ring which can be fugaceous. That is the case, in particular, with **The Destroying Angel** (Amanita virosa) *(p. 173)*. Beginners are therefore advised not to pick any white variety of what they assume to be a Grisette (see below.)

Related species

The Grisette or Common Grisette is the archetype of a group of several species, sub-species, and varieties, which vary mainly in the color of the cap but share the features of an Amanita, except that they have no ring on the stem. They must be cooked before eating.

THE WHITE GRISETTE
Amanita vaginata var. *alba*

The white form is much rarer than The Common Grisette, but is sometimes mixed in with it.

- H: 4-7 in (10-18 cm)
- Ø: 1½-4 in (4-10 cm)
- White spores

THE YELLOW-BROWN GRISETTE
Amanita battarae

The cap is yellow brown to olive with a darker zone in the center and is paler at the margin which is deeply furrowed. This is a delicious mushroom. There are separate highland and lowland forms.

- H: 4-6 in (10-15 cm)
- Ø: 1½-3¼ in (4-8 cm)
- White spores

THE SCALY GRISETTE
Amanita ceciliae

The cap varies in color from fawn to brownish. The grayish color of the volva, stem, and gills is a distinctive feature. The volva disappears prematurely. It is edible for some people, suspect for others, so it is best avoided.

- H: 4-8 in (10-20 cm)
- Ø: 3¼-6 in (8-15 cm)
- White spores

THE TAWNY GRISETTE
Amanita fulva

The Tawny Grisette has an orange to fawn cap and a volva of the same color. It is also common, and is a delicious edible species.

- H: 4-7 in (10-18 cm)
- Ø: 1½-4 in (4-10 cm)
- White spores

SAFFRON GRISETTE
Amanita crocea

This Grisette is more brightly colored than the Tawny Grisette and grows mainly in birch woods. The cap and stem are orange to saffron, but the volva is white. It is very good to eat.

- H: 4-8 in (10-20 cm)
- Ø: 23/4-6 in (7-15 cm)
- White spores

1 - Phallus

- **Tall, cylindrical fungus with a repugnant odor.**

Tall, cylindrical fungus with a repugnant odor

PHALLUS-MUTINUS **Page 190**

2 - Anthurus and Clathrus

- **Coral-colored fungus, shaped like a starfish or a rounded cage.**

CLATHRUS **Page 191**

3 - Bird's Nest Fungi

- **Fungus shaped like a miniature bird's nest or a thimble.**

CYATHUS **Page 192**

FEATURES OF THE GASTEROMYCETES

- Fungi which, when immature, are spherical and are more or less buried in the ground.
- During their development, they may remain spherical or evolve into very diverse forms without tubes or gills.

Fungus round in the immature state...

... remaining spherical in the mature stage..

... or changing into very diverse shapes.

4 - Scleroderma - Puffballs

- Fungus globular or pear-shaped, interior becoming powdery upon maturity.

Fungus globular or pear-shaped

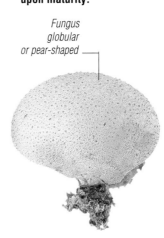

Interior becoming powdery upon maturity

SCLERODERMA - LYCOPERDON **Page 193**

5 - Earth Stars

- Gray or brown fungus shaped like a starfish.

GEASTRUM-ASTRAEUS **Page 197**

Stinkhorn
Phallus impudicus

Classification : Cl. Homobasidiomycetes -
O. Phallales - F. Phallaceae.

- H: 4-10 in (10-25 cm)
- Ø: ¾-1¼ in (2-3 cm)
- Olive-brown spore mass

Cap whitish and pitted

Finely
pitted stem

Viscous, olive-green
conical cap

Remains of
the egg

How to recognize it

The young Stinkhorn looks like a soft, rounded egg attached to branched, white, root-like mycelial cords. The embryo of the fungus can be seen when the egg is sliced in half lengthwise.

Upon maturity, the conical **cap** consists of a whitish honeycombed mass, covered in an olive green gelatinous **gleba** which disappears once the spores have been released. All that then remains is the honeycombed whitish top. The **stem** is white, elongated and hollow. The porous surface is pitted with little holes.

The **flesh** is white, brittle, and fragile. The fungus has a nauseating odor of rotting flesh.

Where and when to find it

The horrible, powerful odor makes it possible to detect the presence of this species from far away. It grows in copses, woods, or gardens from late spring through fall.

Features and edibility

Only the eggs, which have no unpleasant odor and have the peppery flavor of a radish, can be harvested. They must be eaten as soon after picking as possible because if they start to open, the persistent, repugnant odor will spread throughout the house. Homeowners have spent large sums of money on having the drains inspected, when all the time, the problem was a Stinkhorn growing in the yard!

Related species

THE DOG STINKHORN
Mutinus caninus

The Dog Stinkhorn is more slender and taller than the Stinkhorn and is also far less common. When the greenish mucous disappears the tip or cap emerges as red. The nauseating odor is also less pronounced.

- H: 3¼-6 in (8-15 cm)
- Ø:¼-⅜ in (1-1.5 cm)
- Olive-green spore mass

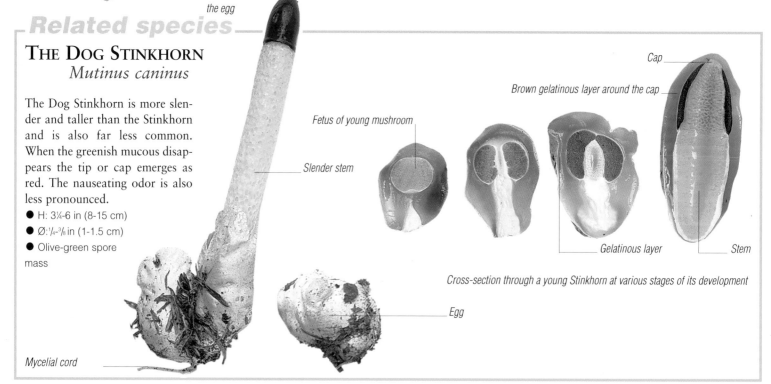

Fetus of young mushroom

Slender stem

Mycelial cord

Egg

Cap

Brown gelatinous layer around the cap

Gelatinous layer

Stem

Cross-section through a young Stinkhorn at various stages of its development

The Red Tentacle Fungus
Clathrus archeri

Alternative Latin name : *Anthurus archeri.*

Classification : Cl. Homobasidiomycetes - O. Phallales - F. Clathraceae.

- Ø: 4-7 in (10-18 cm)
- Olive-brown spore mass

Branches attached at the tip, when they emerge from the egg

Bright red branches

Remains of the egg

Patches of black gelatinous mass

▌ How to recognize it

The Red Tentacle Fungus is not very spectacular at first because it is enclosed in a grayish-white egg. But when it hatches, it is quite extraordinary. The **fruiting body** breaks into a star with four, five, or six branches of a brilliant red. The surface is spotted with black patches which are the remains of the **gleba** which tears as the spores are disseminated. The pitted, fragile **flesh** has a nauseating odor.

▌ Where and when to find it

This exotic species originally lived only in the southern hemisphere. It appeared in Europe in the 1920s. It is not known how it spread outside the Antipodes, but it is indisputably a native of New Zealand. At first, it was believed that the spores were spread by New Zealand soldiers who fought in World War I! The current theory is that the spores were attached to wool from New Zealand sheep. The Red Tentacle fungus has been found in France near woolen mills, which tends to support the theory. A related species has been introduced into North America from southeast Asia.

▌ Features and edibility

The eggs taste and smell like radish and are the only edible stage. Subsequently, the nauseating odor makes this mushroom inedible. Like all members of this family, The Red Tentacle Fungus uses a revolting smell to attract flies who eat the mucus containing the spores and thus disperse them.

Related species

THE RED CAGE FUNGUS
Clathrus cancellatus

The fruiting body of The Red Cage Fungus is spectacular, looking like a red coral cage. It also smells bad but the unopened egg which tastes like radish, can be eaten. The species grows in the south, in hedgerows and gardens.

- H: 2-4 in (5-10 cm)
- Ø: 1¹/₂-2³/₄ in (4-7 cm)
- Olive-brown spores

The Bird's Nest Fungus
Cyathus striatus

Classification : Cl. Homobasidiomycetes -
O. Nidulariales - F. Nidulariaceae.

- H: ½-⅝ in (1-1,5 cm)
- Ø: ¼-½ in (0,5-1 cm)
- White spores

Cup-shaped receptacle   Long, stiff , hairs

White peridioles   Pale gray
resembling eggs   striated interior

▌How to recognize it

This fungus is often unseen due to its small size, and looks like a miniature bird's nest. The "nest" is shaped like a deep, dark-brown cup which is entirely covered on the outside with stiff, brown hairs. At first, it is covered with a white membrane which opens to reveal a smooth, grayish interior with vertical striations. The bottom of the cup contains small white lentil-shaped "eggs" called peridioles, which turn brown when ripe and which enclose the spores. The fungus relies on raindrops to disperse the spores by falling into the "nest", detaching the periodioles and projecting them out of the next.

It is unlikely that anyone would want to eat this species, which has no culinary interest.

▌Where and when to find it

The Bird's Nest Fungus grows in colonies on twigs or branches in damp, partly-buried wood in summer through fall. It is quite a common fungus, but needs to be carefully searched for or it will escape notice.

Related species

There are several related species, of which the following is one of the commoner ones.

ORANGE BIRD'S NEST FUNGUS
Crucibulum laeve

The color is paler, ranging from ocher to brownish-yellow, outside and inside, and the external surface is not hairy. The internal surface is not striated. It grows from late spring onward.

- H: ¼-½ in (0.5-1 cm)
- Ø: ¼-½ in (0.5-1 cm) ● White spores

Common Earthball

Scleroderma citrinum

Classification : Cl. Homobasidiomycetes -
O. Sclerodermatales - F. Sclerodermataceae.

- H: 1½-3¼ in (4-8 cm)
- Ø: 1½-4½ in (4-12 cm)
- Blackish spores

Interior gray-brown
upon maturity

Mycelial cords

Cream to orange
spherical form

▌ How to recognize it

The Common Earthball is of average size. It
has a spherical **receptacle,** flattened at the top.
The outer layer or **peridium** is thick, tough,
and even leathery. The color varies from cream
to lemon yellow, and may even be orange. It is
covered in rather coarse, flattened, polygonal
warts. Upon maturity, the Earthball tears at the
top so that the spores can be disseminated.
The **gleba** is enclosed within the Earthball. It is
white at first, then turns pink and eventually
becomes violet-black, marbled with white
veins. When fully mature, it becomes powdery
and is tinged with greenish brown. It has a sickly odor. At the base of the Earthball, there is a
bunch of white, cottony, mycelial cords which
hold it in the soil.

▌ Where and when to find it

The Common Earthball lives in woods and
open spaces, copses or beside paths, mainly on
siliceous soil.
It appears commonly from summer through
fall. It is sometimes parasitized by the Parasitic
Bolete (*Xerocomus parasiticus*) (page 25.)

▌ Toxicity

The Common Earthball would not be edible
due to its leathery consistency and unpleasant
odor, but in any case it is slightly poisonous. If
eaten in quantity it can cause serious stomach
upsets, involving vomiting and diarrhea .

Related species

There are several other species
of earthball characterized
by warts that are much smaller
than those of the Common Earthball

EARTHBALL
Scleroderma verrucosum

This Earthball is brownish ocher,
or slightly reddish. It has a distinct, short, thick stem, which
ends in mycelial filaments. It
grows in groups in broad-leaved
woods in the fall.

- H: 2½-4 in (6-10 cm
- Ø: 1¼-3¼ in (3-8 cm)
- Blackish spores

Common Puffball
Lycoperdon perlatum

Alternative Latin name : *Lycoperdon gemmatum.*

Classification : Cl. Homobasidiomycetes -
O. Lycoperdales - F. Lycoperdaceae.

- H: 1½-3½ in (4-9 cm)
- Ø: 1¼-2 in (3-5 cm)
- Olive-brown spores

Round head

Conical warts

Whit stem narowing
at the base

▮ How to recognize it

The Common Puffball is of average size and
has a white **receptacle** which turns brownish-
yellow. It is club-shaped with a rounded head
on a stem from which it is hardly differentiated. Almost the whole surface is covered with
white spines or warts looking a little like rhine-
stones, hence the Latin name. Some are quite
long and can be easily pulled off, other, smaller ones remain solidly in place.

The shortened **stem** is much less spiny and
sometimes quite smooth.

The **gleba** is situated inside the fertile head and
is white at first, turning olive-yellow, then
brownish. Upon maturity, the outer layer or
peridium bursts, forming a crater in the top
which enables the spores to be blown out and
dispersed by the wind.

▮ Where and when to find it

The Common Puffball is a common sight in
woods, where it often grows in groups on
buried leaf litter and decaying wood. It can be
found almost all year round, but especially in
the fall.

▮ Features and edibility

Although edible when young, the mushroom is
not particularly tasty.

Related species

Puffballs are only edible when young, while the interior flesh is still white, but they are not very good to eat.

Stump Puffball
Lycoperdon pyriforme

This species resembles The Common Puffball, but is slightly pointed at the top. It grows on rotting wood in broad-leaved forests, to which it is anchored by white mycelial filaments which are clearly visible when the fungus is picked.

- H: 1¼-3¼ in (3-8 cm)
- Ø: ½-1¼ in (1-3 cm)
- Olive-brown spores

Color browning with age

Very short stem

Meadow Puffball
Vascellum pratense

The slightly flattened top and pointed base forming a sort of short, thick stem give this species a sturdy appearance. It is often wider than it is tall.

- H: ¾-2 in (2-5 cm)
- Ø: ¾-2 in (2-5 cm)
- Olive-brown spores

White interior in young specimens

The Leaden Puffball
Bovista plumbea

The Leaden Puffball inhabits grassland and has a smooth, white external membrane devoid of spines. It eventually breaks and splits into scales revealing another leaden gray membrane underneath.

- H: ½-1½ in (1-4 cm)
- Ø: ½-1½ in (1-4 cm)
- Olive-brown spores

Spiny Puffball
Lycoperdon echinatum

This Puffball looks like a sphere carried on a short stem and is entirely covered with tiny brown or ocher spines, giving it the hirsute aspect of a sweet chestnut case. It grows on leaf litter in deciduous forests, especially under beech.

- H: 1¼-2½ in (3-6 cm)
- Ø: 1¼-2½ in (3-6 cm)
- Olive-brown spores

Giant Puffball

Langermannia gigantea

Alternative Latin names: *Lycoperdon giganteum, Calvatia gigantea.*

Classification : Cl. Basidiomycetes - O. Lycoperdales - F. Lycoperdaceae.

- Ø: 8-16 in (20-40 cm)
- Olive-brown spores

Very large spherical shape which may not be pitted and lumpy

Satiny white surface

∎ How to recognize it

The Giant Puffball generally has the appearance and size of a balloon and can become huge, reaching a diameter of 32 in (80 cm) with an equivalent weight. The external layer or **exoperidium** is smooth and bare, looking like a cooked egg white. It is very delicate, and tinted yellow, then brown, and disappears rapidly, exposing the internal covering or **endoperidium,** which develops in exactly the same way. The **gleba,** the inner, fertile part, is compact and firm, white at first, then disintegrating and turning brown as the spores mature. Large, light brown shreds of varying sizes detach themselves and sail away on the wind, dispersing the spores into the air.

∎ Where and when to find it

An encounter with such an extraordinary natural phenomenon will leave a casual stroller reeling with astonishment. The Giant Puffball is not common but when found is an impressive sight in open grassland.

∎ Features and edibility

If picked young, when the flesh is still white and compact this species is edible. The size makes it possible to cook this edible fungus in large quantities.

Related species

PESTLE PUFFBALL
Calvatia excipuliformis

This Puffball grows in open grassland and forest clearings. It has a long, thick stem which persists in the dry state after the upper part has disappeared.
- H: 2-8 in (5-20 cm)
- Ø: 2-4 in (5-10 cm)
- Olive-brown spores

THE SADDLE-SHAPED PUFFBALL
Calvatia utriformis

This uncommon Puffball has pyramid-shaped warts which eventually turn into foam. The surface is then characteristically broken into polygonal patterns.
- H: 2-4 in (5-10 cm)
- Ø: 2¾-6 in (7-15 cm)

The Sessile Earth Star
Geastrum sessile

Alternative Latin name : *Geastrum fimbriatum.*

Classification: Cl. Homobasidiomycetes - O. Lycoperdales - F. Geastraceae.

- H: ¾-2 in (2-5 cm) ● Ø: 1¼-2 in (3-5 cm) (open)
- Chocolate-brown spores

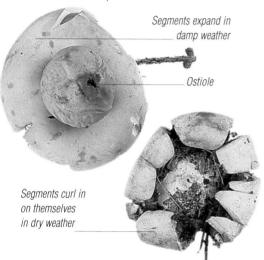

Segments expand in damp weather

Ostiole

Segments curl in on themselves in dry weather

■ How to recognize it

The Earth Stars are strange fungi which look a little like starfish. The Sessile Earth Star consists of an outer layer divided into triangular segments and a spherical central part. The outer part or **exoperidium** consists of 6-9 smooth triangular segments only a fews millimeters thick and colored cream to ocher. Depending on the weather conditions, they may extend outward on the ground (damp weather) or curve inward (dry weather). The fungus then raises itself from the ground.

The central part or **endoperidium** is spherical, sessile, and the same color as the branches or darker, gray ocher. It is of the same consistency as a wasp's nest or of thin parchment paper. There is a small ostiole or hole at the top, which is dentate and irregular in shape.

The leathery **flesh** has no particular odor. The consistency of the flesh makes the Earthstar unsuitable for eating. The interest of these species in general lies in their unusual shape and ability to react to climatic variations.

■ Where and when to find it

The Sessile Earthstar rarely grows in isolation. It generally appears in colonies on moss or pine needles in sandy forests of conifers or in mixed woods. It is quite common in summer and early fall.

Related species

Several species of Earth Star live in our forests

THE TRIPLE EARTH STAR
Geastrum triplex

This Earth Star is the largest and commonest of the genus and has very thick segments which also curve back toward the earth but are split crosswise. The central globe rests on a fleshy pad. The opening at the top is raised on a little cone around which there is a small depression.

- H: 1¼-2 in (3-5 cm)
- Ø: 2½-4½ in (6-12 cm)
- Chocolate-brown spores

REDDENING EARTH STAR
Geastrum rufescens

This Earth Star has segments ⅛ in (0.5 cm) thick. They are ocher or pinkish-cream, turning red then brown. It grows under conifers or sometimes under deciduous trees.

- H: 1½-2¾ in (4-7 cm)
- Ø: 2½-3½ in (6-9 cm)
- Chocolate-brown spores

THE HYGROMETRIC EARTH STAR
Astraeus hygrometricus

The segments have a cracked surface and spread out in damp weather, closing up when the weather is dry, like the petals of a flower.

It appears in fall and can overwinter in the dry state until the following spring. The Hygrometric Earthstar is a southern species, which likes acid, sandy soils in mixed woods.

- H: ¾-1½ in (2-4 cm)
- Ø: 2-4 in (5-10 cm)
- Chocolate-brown spores

FEATURES OF THE APHYLLOPHORALES AND PHRAGMOBASIODIOMYCETES

- Funnel-shaped caps with widely-spaced, gill-like, more-or-less marked decurrent folds under the cap.
- Fungi shaped like miniature bushes and not viscous.
- Fungi forming crusts on wood (or on the ground).
- Fungi with spines under the cap.
- Fungi with pores under the cap and growing on wood.
- Gelatinous or rubbery fungi, growing on wood.

Funnel-shaped caps with widely-spaced, gill-like, more-or-less marked decurrent folds under the cap.

Fungi not viscous, shaped like miniature bushes or club-shaped

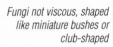

Fungi forming crusts on wood (or on the ground)

Fungi with non-gelatinous flesh, having spines under the cap

Fungi with pores under the cap

Fungi growing on wood

1/1

Gelatinous or rubbery fungi growing on wood

1/1

---

1 - Horns of Plenty - Chanterelles

- Hollow, funnel-shaped cap.
- Folds widely spaced and decurrent, more or less marked, which may resemble gills.

Hollow, funnel-shaped cap

Folds widely spaced and decurrent, more or less marked, which may resemble gills

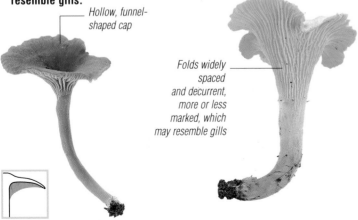

Decurrent gills

CRATERELLUS - PSEUDOCRATERELLUS - CANTHARELLUS - GOMPHUS
Page 200

---

2 - Fairy Clubs & Coral Fungi

- Shaped like a branched coral or miniature bush, or a club.

Golden Coral Fungus

Giant Fairy Club

RAMARIA - CLAVARIADELPHUS - CLAVULINOPSIS
SPARASSIS **Page 205**

5 - Polypores

- Pores under the cap.
- Presence or absence of a stem.
- Fungus growing on wood.

Pores under the cap

1/1

Presence or absence of stem. Fungus growing on wood

POLYPORUS - DENDROPOLYPORUS - GRIFOLA - MERIPILUS
LAETIPORUS - PIPTOPORUS - GANODERMA - TRAMETES - FOMES
FOMITOPSIS - DAEDALEA-FISTULINA **Page 212**

3 - Stereum

- Fungus with pores, forming a crust or platelet on wood.

STEREUM - CHONDROSTEREUM - PHLEBIA **Page 209**

6 - Jew's Ear - Jelly Fungus

- Rubbery or gelatinous fungus, growing on wood.

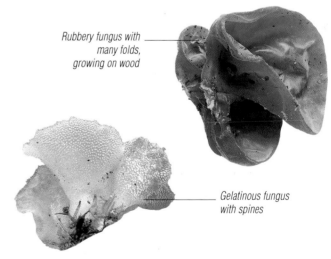

Rubbery fungus with many folds, growing on wood

Gelatinous fungus with spines

- Shapeless, gelatinous, trembling fungus.

Shapeless, gelatinous trembling fungus

4 - Hydnum

- Spines under the cap, flesh not gelatinous.

Spines under the cap

1/1

HYDNUM - PHELLODON - AURISCALPIUM - SARCODON **Page 210**

HIRNEOLA - PSEUDOHYDNUM - TREMELLA - EXIDIA **Page 220**

The Horn of Plenty

Craterellus cornucopioides

English synonym: The Trumpet of the Dead

Classification: Cl. Homobasidiomycetes - O. Cantharellales - F. Craterellaceae.

- H: 1½-4½ in (4-12 cm)
- Ø: 1¼-4 in (3-10 cm)
- White spores

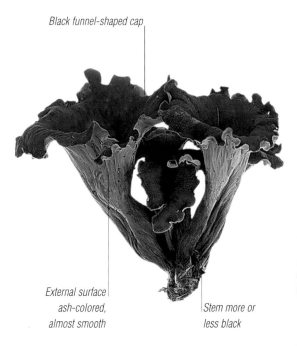

Black funnel-shaped cap

External surface ash-colored, almost smooth

Stem more or less black

▌How to recognize it

The characteristic shape of the Horn of Plenty is indeed evocative of a cornucopia. The thin, brownish-gray-to-black **cap** is fringed at the margin, which is turned back then lobed as the mushroom matures. The external **hymenium** (fertile surface) is almost smooth or at the very most slightly wrinkled. It is ash-gray, much lighter than the rest of the mushroom, due to the presence of the white spores. The blackish **stem** is hollow like the horn of a trumpet, hence its alternative name. The **flesh** is thin and black, tender at first and always slightly elastic in its consistency, especially as the mushroom matures. It has a very pleasant, fruity odor.

▌Where and when to find it

The Horn of Plenty "trumpets" its presence in broad-leaved woods in the lowlands, and in spruce forests in the highlands. From late summer through fall, dense colonies gather in the dampest spots. The mushroom only appears in large numbers in particularly rainy years and it may vary considerably in size.

The Horn of Plenty does not mind the type of soil in which it grows and is frequently encountered throughout the temperate zone of the northern hemisphere and even in southeastern Australia. It grows in the United States, but a closely related pink-spored variety, *Craterellus fallax*, is more common and equally edible.

▌Features and edibility

Despite its sinister appearance, The Horn of Plenty is a delicious mushroom with a delicate flavor and of better quality than the darker varieties of Chanterelle. It is particularly highly prized in those regions of France where cream sauces are part of the local cuisine, since the flesh, which is tender at first, but always rather elastic is best simmered in cream. It is also popular as a side-dish served with white meat which becomes deliciously impregnated with its delicate flavor. Some delicatessens in France serve "truffled" cooked meats which are actually stuffed with Horn of Plenty!

Thanks to the small size of this mushroom, it would appear that hunting The Horn of Plenty is a time-consuming task but thanks to the huge numbers in which it appears, a basket is soon filled in a good year.

Furthermore, anyone who is too lazy to go out and look for them in the woods, can always find them in wild mushroom markets and in gourmet stores. On some days, the stalls overflow with the little trumpet-shaped fungi. They also have the advantage of drying very well. However, they must be eaten quite quickly during the winter season after the harvest because if they are preserved for too long, they may turn rancid and spoil the flavor.

Lookalike

There is nothing that looks like The Horn of Plenty except The pink-spored American Craterellus fallax already mentioned, and the dark-colored Chanterelles, all of which are perfectly edible and delicious. It would be impossible to confuse this mushroom with anything else.

The caps of young Horns of Plenty are cornet-shaped. They do not become irregular and sinuous for several days.

Related species

THE BROWN FUNNEL CAP
 Pseudocraterellus cinereus

This mushroom is an uncommon sight in the woods, though it appears at the same time as The Horn of Plenty. The dark, funnel-shaped cap has an incurved margin which protects the ash-colored hymenium. The gill-like, forked folds are very straight and typical. The flesh smells of plums.

- H: 1½-2¾ in (4-7 cm)
- Ø: 1¼-2 in (3-5 cm)
- White spores

THE SINUOUS FUNNEL CAP
Pseudocraterellus sinuosus

This is another small species with a bister-brown, depressed or funnel-shaped cap and a sinuous margin, hence the name. It is easily distinguished from The Horn of Plenty by the presence of ashen, folded or swollen veins like varicose veins. The thin flesh may smell of Mirabelle plums. This unusual Funnel Cap grows in the mushroom season, in broad-leaved woods.

- H: 1½-3½ in (4-7 cm)
- Ø: 1¼-2 in (3-5 cm)
- White spores

The Chanterelle

Cantharellus cibarius

Classification : Cl. Homobasidiomycetes -
O. Cantharellales - F. Cantharellaceae.

- H: 2-4½ in (5-12 cm)
- Ø: 1¼-4 in (3-10 cm)
- Cream spores

Funnel-shaped cap

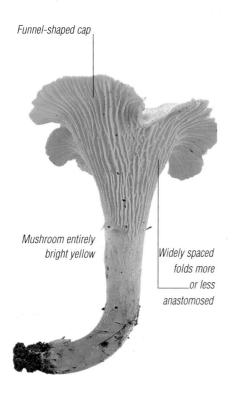

Mushroom entirely
bright yellow

Widely spaced
folds more
or less
anastomosed

Lookalikes:
Jack O'Lantern *(Omphalotus olearius)*
(p. 36)
The False Chanterelle *(Hygrophoropsis aurantiaca)* (p. 36)

▮ How to recognize it

The Chanterelle is as attractive as it is delicious and is a beautiful egg yellow in color. The thick, fleshy **cap**, soon flattens, eventually becoming depressed. The margin is inrolled at first, becoming sinuous and irregularly lobed, which makes it friable.

The **folds** which cover the hymenium are quite widely spaced. They are forked near the margin, and clearly decurrent down the stem. They sometimes look like rudimentary gills but are generally thicker. They only begin to look like veins in mature specimens.

The thick, uneven **stem** is the same color as the cap and folds.

The **flesh** is white, firm, and compact. It usually has a fruity fragrance, said to resemble that of apricots or plums.

	The Chanterelle *Cantharellus cibarius*	Jack O'Lantern *Omphalotus olearius*	The False Chanterelle *Hygrophoropsis aurantiaca*
Cap	egg yellow	yellow, orange to brown	yellow to orange
Hymenium (fertile surface)	gill-like folds, widely-spaced, non-fluorescent	thin, crowded, fluorescent gills	thick, bifurcated non fluorescent gills
Stem	unequal, not very fibrous, unchanging	thick or slender, very fibrous, unchanging	thin, elastic, turning brown
Flesh	white, compact	yellow, persistent	yellowish, soft
Habitat	soil, deciduous trees, conifers	on wood (not always obvious), deciduous trees	on the ground, conifers, deciduous trees
Features	excellent	poisonous	comestible

▌Where and when to find it

The Chanterelle is a handsome ornament to the undergrowth of broad-leaved and coniferous woods. It prefers damp places, such as ditches or hollows. Although it is a common mushroom, it is not always easy to spot, since it likes to hide under moss or leaf litter which conceal its brilliant yellow coloration.

The Chanterelle is common throughout the temperate zone. It is often found after summer storms, so it fruits early, sometimes as early as July, though the most sightings seems to be in September. However, it has been found as late in the year as Christmas Day!

Due to its popularity and the unlikelihood of mistaking it for anything else, The Chanterelle is sometimes the subject of intensive "carpet" picking. Regulations have been introduced in certain countries, in France for instance, where in the Haute-Savoie region of the Alps, picking is limited to half a kilogram (1.1 lb) per person and a kilogram (2.2 lb) per vehicle. Picking restrictions have also been introduced in Washington State, which apply to The Chanterelle and other edible mushrooms. It is important to protect prolific habitats, so care must be taken when picking Chanterelles not to use any implement which tears the moss and damages the mycelium. The Chanterelle mycelium must be allowed to fruit in subsequent years.

▌Features and edibility

The Chanterelle is universally known and recognized. It is a delicious mushroom and has been greatly esteemed since the days of Ancient Rome. It is all the more popular because the flesh, so often worm-eaten in other, older mushrooms, is generally left intact, larvae and slugs apparently being uninterested in it.

Thanks to the firm and compact consistency, The Chanterelle requires slightly longer cooking than other mushrooms. In its habitat, it grows abundantly, and so it can be cooked alone, sprinkled with parsley, in an omelet or to accompany a meat dish. Small specimens can be pickled in vinegar and make delicious condiments.

The Chanterelle has several sub-species and varieties which are also edible. However, certain people may be unable to digest them, though the consequences have not been serious. The French mycologist, A. Marchand, indicates that the consumption of large quantities of Chanterelles has a slightly laxative effect. Although The Chanterelle contains traces of amanitine, they are so minute that one would have to a whole ton of them in order to experience any toxic effect! These considerations should in no way worry the mushroom-eater. The Chanterelle remains a delicious edible mushroom.

The Chanterelle grows abundantly and does not suffer too much when transported over long distances. It is sold in all the wild mushroom markets and farmers' markets and in Europe it is preserved by canning and drying. It is an ideal candidate for cultivation. Mycorrhizal grafts have only been successful in the laboratory, however.

Lookalikes

The Chanterelle might be confused with two orange mushrooms, which were previously classified under the genus Clitocybe, but have now been transferred to the genus Paxillus:

Jack O'Lantern (Omphalotus olearius) *(p. 36) varies considerably in its appearance and could deceive the mushroom-picker by appearing to grow on the ground, if it has developed on oak or olive tree-roots that extend a long way from the tree. If in doubt, look at the flesh. It should be firm and even persistent, especially in the stem which is slightly fibrous. The yellow coloration is also an identifier. In the Chanterelle it is white and compact. Furthermore Jack O'Lantern's thin, crowded gills are fluorescent in the dark. Confusion with this species could be serious, as it causes severe gastro-enteritis.*

The False Chanterelle (Hygrophoropsis aurantiaca) *(p. 36), is smaller than The Chanterelle, it has true gills which are forked, and the flesh is not firm and elastic but soft and yielding.*

Related species

Many sub-species and varieties of The Chanterelle have been described. These related species are also relatively common. The main variations are due sometimes to a thicker shape, a smaller size, and coloration which varies from whitish to pink or flesh color.

THE PALE-ORANGE CHANTERELLE
Cantharellus friesii

This small Chanterelle is more irregular in shape. It is bright pinkish-orange in color. It is rare, growing under deciduous trees in summer through fall.

- H: 1¼-2 in (3-5 cm)
- Ø: ½-1½ in (1-4 cm)
- Cream spores

Bright pinkish-orange cap

Pinkish-orange gills

THE AMETHYST CHANTERELLE
Cantharellus cibarius var. *amethysteus*

This Chanterelle is less brightly-colored. It has purplish scales in the center of the cap, and there are sometimes purple scales on the margin. It is uncommon and grows in the summer. It is very good to eat.

- H: 2½-6 in (6-15 cm)
- Ø: 2-4½ in (5-12 cm)
- Cream spores

Small purplish scales

The Tubular Chanterelle

Cantharellus tubaeformis

Classification: Cl. Homobasidiomycetes -
O. Cantharellales - F. Cantharellaceae.

- H: 2-4½ in (5-12 cm)
- Ø: ½-2½ in (2-6 cm)
- White spores

Funnel-shaped cap
with wavy margin

Thick,
widely-spaced,
yellowish folds,
turning gray

Yellowish-
brown cap

Hollow stem yellow, then
fading to brown

Lookalikes:
The Brown Funnel Cap
(Pseudocraterellus cinereus) (p. 201)
The Cinnamon Cortinarius (Cortinarius
cinnamomeus) (p. 128)

How to recognize it

The Tubular Chanterelle is small, slender, and easy to recognize due to its tube-like shape.
The **cap** is deeply funnel-shaped. The margin is inrolled at first, then raised and wavy when mature. It is thin like the rest of the cap. The yellowish-fawn cuticle is dry and slightly downy, especially in dry weather.
The **folds** are forked at the margin; they are thick and quite widely spaced. They are a rather dull yellow in color, even when young, and turn gray when mature.
The cylindrical **stem** has an uneven or wrinkled surface and is typically hollow like a tube. The cavity is open to the exterior through a small hole in the center of the cap. It is bright orange at first, fading quickly as the mushroom ages.
The **flesh** is slightly elastic in its consistency. It develops a fairly variable odor, often one of dampness, which is not particularly pleasant.

Where and when to find it

The Tubular Chanterelle populates wet places in broad-leaved and coniferous woods. It is common throughout the northern hemisphere and grows in large colonies. Thanks to its size and color, it is well camouflaged among the leaf litter and so it is often hard to spot. It usually fruits from September through December.

Features and edibility

The Tubular Chanterelle is very good to eat Its slightly elastic consistency is still soft enough to make it an excellent omelet ingredient. The odor is quite subtle, but too faint for those who prefer the strong apricot odor of The Chanterelle. The Tubular Chanterelle is also very suitable for drying.

Lookalikes

*The only mushrooms with which The Tubular Chanterelle could possibly be confused are also good to eat. When young and still brightly colored, it looks a little like The Chanterelle though the latter is egg yellow in color, and does not turn gray with age. When it is older, it might be confused with **The Brown Funnel Cap** (Pseudocantharellus cinereus) (p. 201), which has a similar odor to The Chanterelle but is a much rarer mushroom.*
On the other hand, there are a few small, slender species of Cortinarius which might possibly lead to some confusion.
***The Cinnamon cortinarius** (Cortinarius cinnamomeus) (p. 128) and related species are poisonous, containing principles similar to those found in the deadly **Annatto-colored Cortinarius** (Cortinarius orellanus) (p. 126). These mushrooms have a long and fragile stem but the cap is never funnel-shaped and it has true gills, not thick folds on the stem. epais et fourchus.*

Related species

LUMINOUS CHANTERELLE
Cantharellus lutescens

This delicious mushroom is more brightly colored than The Tubular Chanterelle. The irregularly lobed cap is brown to bister, but the hymenium and stem are more brightly colored. The hymenium is almost smooth or slightly veined and is salmon pink, while the stem is a luminous yellow-orange. The species grows in large colonies in some coniferous woods, under spruce, mountain fir trees, or pinewoods near the seashore.

- H: 2-4½ in (5-12 cm)
- Ø: ¾-2½ in (2-6 cm)
- White spores

The Violet Chanterelle

Gomphus clavatus

Alternative Latin name: *Nevrophyllum clavatum.*

Classification: Cl. Homobasidiomycetes - O. Cantharellales - F. Gomphaceae.

- H: 2-4½ in (5-12 cm)
- Ø: 2-4 in (5-10 cm)
- Ocher spores

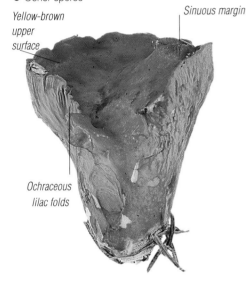

Yellow-brown upper surface

Sinuous margin

Ochraceous lilac folds

maturity when it forms decurrent, irregularly shaped and sinuous folds. They sometimes look like veins. The pinkish-lilac color fades to dirty yellow-brown.

The **stem** narrows at the base and may support several caps which are sometimes imbricated. The bright violet color disappears almost completely in older specimens.

The white **flesh** is thick and quite crunchy with a mild flavor, though older specimens may taste slightly bitter.

■ How to recognize it

The Violet Chanterelle is small to medium in size When young, looks like a thick club whose top has been broken off; later it is shaped like an ice cream cone.

The **cap** which forms the upper, truncated part of the mushroom, is a wide cup-shape at first, flattening but remaining depressed. It has a velvety texture and is lilac-colored in the young specimen, turning yellowish, then brown. The margin is raised, irregular, and sinuous, becoming ragged in older specimens. The **hymenium** is wrinkled at first, clearly differentiated at

■ Where and when to find it

This mushroom is quite common in certain locations, fruiting on carpets of moss or pine needles among spruce or mountain fir in the mushroom season.

■ Features and edibility

The Violet Chanterelle is a tasty mushroom thanks to its thick, delicate flesh. Although it softer than The Chanterelle, it does not have the delicious fragrance of the latter.

The Straight Coral Fungus

Ramaria stricta

Classification: Cl. Homobasidiomycetes - O. Clavariales - F. Ramariaceae.

- H: 1½-4 in (4-10 cm) ● Ø: 1¼-3¼ in (3-8 cm)
- Ocher-yellow spores

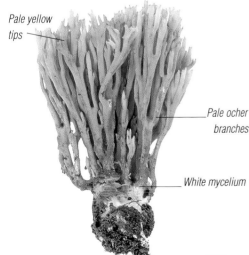

Pale yellow tips

Pale ocher branches

White mycelium

In young specimens the color of the fine pointed tips is bright yellow, and the rest of the fungus is pale ocher. The color darkens to a dirty reddish-brown with age over the whole fungus.

There appears to be no **stem**, since the lower part forms a sort of short trunk at the base of which there are fragile, white filaments of mycelium buried in the substrate.

The **flesh** is white or pale yellow, and leathery. It has a strong fungal odor and a peppery flavor. This species is not edible.

■ How to recognize it

This fungus looks like a tiny bush with tightly packed, vertical, forked branches.

■ Where and when to find it

The Straight Coral Fungus grows in small groups on rotting dead branches which are sometimes covered in moss or buried in the ground. It fruits in summer through fall.

The Golden Coral Fungus

Ramaria aurea

Alternative Latin name: *Clavaria aurea*.

Classification : Cl. Homobasidiomycetes - O. Clavariales - F. Ramariaceae.

- H: 4-8 in (10-20 cm)
- Ø: 2½-6 in (6-15 cm)
- Ocher-yellow spores

Dense golden branches

> **Lookalikes:**
> Beautiful Coral Fungus (*Ramaria formosa*)
> Pale Coral Fungus (*Ramaria pallida*)

■ How to recognize it

The **fruiting body** of The Golden Coral Fungus is quite large, and may attain 8 in (20 cm) in height and 6 in (15 cm) across.

The very numerous **branches**, are cylindrical and sinuous, vertical and very dense are divided at the top into denticulate twigs. The whole fungus is uniform in color, typically golden or egg yellow. Later, this magnificent coloration darkens to ocher as the spores are released.

The **stem** forms a massive trunk, which is thick and fleshy and is white to yellowish.

The white **flesh** is tender and brittle in the branches, slightly more elastic in the base. The flavor is mild and the odor slightly aromatic.

■ Where and when to find it

The Golden Coral Fungus produces its golden branches in the leaf litter and undergrowth of deciduous and coniferous trees on calcareous or siliceous soil. It is abundant in the dampest parts of forests, woods, or plantations. It generally fruits from summer through fall.

■ Features and edibility

In some parts of the world, The Golden Coral Fungus is picked by the truckload for the table. It must be eaten young because the flesh soon becomes leathery and even indigestible. In any case, it is best blanched and the cooking water discarded before it is cooked in other ways.

When mature and the bright color fades, this Coral Fungus might be confused with other species which include some that are notoriously toxic. This is an additional reason for only eating young, easily recognizable specimens. It is important not to take risks, even experienced mycologists have made mistaken identifications of coral fungi.

Lookalikes

It is very important not to confuse The Golden Coral Fungus and its related species with the following two species which are drastically purgative and have been responsible for some unpleasant incidents.

The Beautiful Coral Fungus (Ramaria formosa) is a slender, elegant species which is pink all over except for the tips of the branches which are yellow when young, darkening to ocher upon maturity. The bright colors disappear with age and it becomes very hard to recognize. It is poisonous.

The Pale Coral Fungus (Ramaria pallida) is pale in color, tinted lilac at the tip of the branches, turning ocher when mature. It is also poisonous.

Related species

YELLOW CORAL FUNGUS
Ramaria flava

It differs from The Golden Coral Fungus in its sulfur or lemon yellow color and stem which turns reddish-brown, especially when mature. It is common in the same locations and at the same season as The Golden Coral Fungus.

- H: 4-8 in (10-20 cm)
- L: 3½-6 in (7-15 cm)
- Yellow spores

THE CAULIFLOWER CORAL FUNGUS

Ramaria botrytis

When young, it has short, pink branches and tiny purple twigs. The thick trunk gives it its characteristic cauliflower appearance.

- H: 3½-6 in (7-15 cm)
- L: 3¼-6 in (8-15 cm)
- Ocher spores

The Squat Fairy Club
Clavariadelphus truncatus

Latin name : *Clavaria truncata.*

Classification : Cl. Homobasidiomycetes - O. Clavariales - F. Clavariadelphaceae.

- H: 3¼-6 in (8-15 cm)
- Ø: ¾-1½ in (2-4 cm)
- Yellow spores

Swollen, uneven surface

Cone-shaped, wrinkled stem

How to recognize it

This Fairy Club is of average size and is shaped like an ice cream cone or a truncated club, hence the name.

The **cap** is represented by the upper surface of the mushroom, which is swollen, uneven and very irregular, so that it often overhangs the margin. It is pale yellow at first, changing to reddish-ocher with age.

The pointed **stem**, is thick and conical, reddish on the surface and slightly wrinkled as in the chanterelles.

The white **flesh** is firm at first, but soon becomes spongy. The flavor is sweetish.

Where and when to find it

The Squat Fairy Club grows in mountain fir forests. It is not a common species but fruits in the fall.

Features and edibility

Despite its sweetish flavor, The Squat Fairy Club is not particularly good to eat.

Related species

THE GIANT FAIRY CLUB
Clavariadelphus pistillaris

The Fairy Club looks like the Squat Fairy Club, but has a rounded head. It is inedible due to its bitter flavor. It lives in beech woods.

- H: 3¼-8 in (8-20 cm)
- Ø: ¾-2½ in (2-6 cm)
- Pale yellow spores

THE HORNED FAIRY CLUB
Clavulinopsis corniculata

The branches are bright yellow, yellow-orange, or ocher. The base is covered in white down. The Horned Fairy Club is common and grows in mossy meadows.

- H: ¾-3¼ in (2-8 cm) ● White spores

Cauliflower Fungus
Sparassis crispa

English synonym: Brain Fungus

Classification : Cl. Homobasidiomycetes -
O. Clavariales - F. Sparassidiaceae.

- Ø: 4-16 in (10-40 cm)
- White spores

*Flattened cream
to ocher fronds*

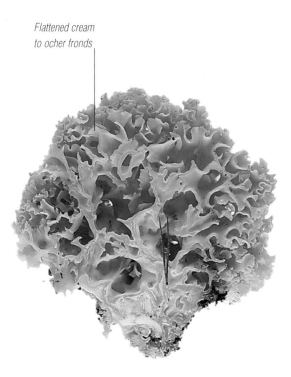

Lookalikes:
The Cauliflower Coral Fungus (*Ramaria botrytis*) (p. 206)
The Beautiful Coral Fungus (*Ramaria formosa*) (p. 206)

How to recognize it

The Cauliflower Fungus looks like a shapeless, leafless cauliflower or natural sponge. The **fruiting body** may become very voluminous, some examples reaching 12–16 in (30–40 cm) in diameter and weighing 11–13½ lb (5–6 kg.) The flattened **fronds**, are very extensive and are actually interlaced spore-bearing surfaces. They are cream at first, turning ochraceous when old. The branches at the tip are curled and frilly, giving the mushroom its characteristic look.

The **stem** forms a thick, sturdy, yellowish-white trunk from which all the fronds grow and branch. The **flesh** is white or cream and rather thin, despite the massive size of the fungus. It is tender when young but becomes elastic with age. It has an aromatic odor and a nutty flavor.

Where and when to find it

The Cauliflower Fungus lives on the roots or stumps of coniferous trees, especially pine and spruce. It generally shelters from the prevailing wind which is why it is often found facing east at the base of tree trunks. This fungus is found throughout the temperate zone of the northern hemisphere where it is commoner on high ground from September through November.

Features and edibility

The Cauliflower Fungus or Brain Fungus is sold in France under the name of Fall Morel or even just Morel, though it is not on a par with the delicious flavor of the latter. However, like the morels, it is suitable for serving with a cream sauce to which it imparts its own flavor.

The Cauliflower Fungus must always be eaten young because the flesh becomes elastic and even tough when old. There have been reports of indigestion after ingesting specimens that were too

old. The French mycologist, G. Fourré, relates that the Chinese are very fond of a related species which they call "Silver Ear" and which they cultivate. It is dried and packaged, and exported to the United States and Europe, where it is sold in oriental stores. It is considered to have medicinal properties as a stimulant, and is thus given to children and the elderly at the onset of winter.

Lookalikes

Although the unusual appearance and habitat of The Cauliflower Fungus are typical, it could be confused for two other species, one of which is a purgative.

The Cauliflower Coral Fungus (Ramaria botrytis) (p. 206) *looks even more like a cauliflower than The Cauliflower Fungus itself. It has very short cylindrical branches and twigs. They are a beautiful color, starting as pink with purple at the tips, then washed with yellow when older. This increases the risk of confusion with purgative varieties of Coral Fungus and Fairy Clubs.*

The Beautiful Coral Fungus (Ramaria formosa) (p.202) *is poisonous. It grows under broad-leaved trees, like The Cauliflower Fungus, but is more slender.*

Related species

THE SHORT-STEMMED CAULIFLOWER FUNGUS
Sparassis brevipes

This differs from the Cauliflower Fungus by its larger fronds which are almost translucent and straw-colored. It is much rarer, and grows in oak woods. It smells of bleach and soon becomes leathery so it is not recommended and is even said to be suspect.

- Ø: 8-16 in (20-40 cm)
- White spores

The Hairy Stereum
Stereum hirsutum

Latin name : *Stereum purpureum*.

Classification : Cl. Homobasidiomycetes -
O. Corticiales - F. Stereaceae.

- L: ¾-2 in (2-5 cm) but attached to each other so that they form large masses
- White spores

Mass of imbricated, superimposed caps

Downy upper surface with colored, parallel zones

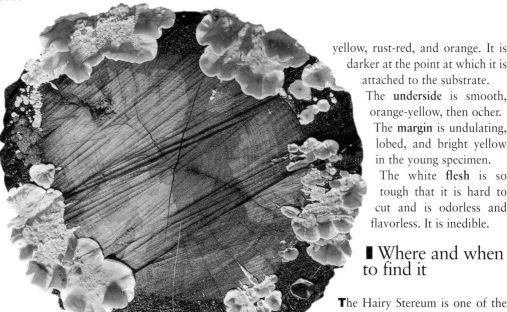

▋ How to recognize it

The Hairy Stereum has imbricated caps which are attached to each in bunches. In the early stages of development, the fungus forms a crust over wood. The edges then curl up and the fungus gathers itself into a bunch of superimposed caps which are welded to each other.

The **upper surface** is downy and is zoned in concentric circles of various colors, including yellow, rust-red, and orange. It is darker at the point at which it is attached to the substrate.

The **underside** is smooth, orange-yellow, then ocher.

The **margin** is undulating, lobed, and bright yellow in the young specimen.

The white **flesh** is so tough that it is hard to cut and is odorless and flavorless. It is inedible.

▋ Where and when to find it

The Hairy Stereum is one of the commonest fungi and grows all year round. It forms dense colonies on dead wood, from the tiniest twig to massive trunks. It often gains a foothold on felled logs, where it grows from the cut side.

Although it prefers broad-leaved trees, it can also be found on conifers such as pine and larch. It is a fungal pest which causes the destruction of the wood which as a consequence cannot be put to any useful purpose.

Related species

THE SILVER LEAF FUNGUS
Chondrostereum purpureum

This fungus looks like the Hairy Stereum but the upper surface does not have colored concentric circles. It is white or reddish and is also hairy. The underside is lilac-colored or purplish-violet, so there is no possibility of confusion. It is very common and may even attack healthy trees. It is responsible for Silver Leaf Rot in fruit trees. Like the Hairy Stereum it is inedible.

- Ø: ¾-2 in (2-5 cm)
- White spores

THE ORANGE WAX FUNGUS
Phlebia merismoides

This fungus forms a bright orange frilly, puffy crust with a central grayish-violet zone about ¹⁄₁₆ in (2–3 mm) thick. It can be found all year round growing on deciduous woods.

- Ø: 3¼-4 in (8-10 cm) ● White spores

The Hedgehog Mushroom
Hydnum repandum

English synonym: Sheep's Foot Mushroom

Classification : Cl. Homobasidiomycetes -
O. Cantharellales - F. Hydnaceae.

- H: 2-4 in (5-10 cm)
- Ø: 2-4½ in (5-12 cm)
- White spores

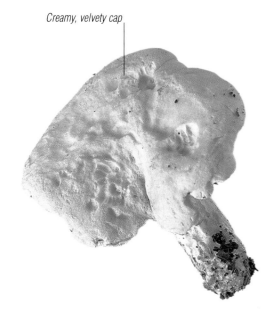

Creamy, velvety cap

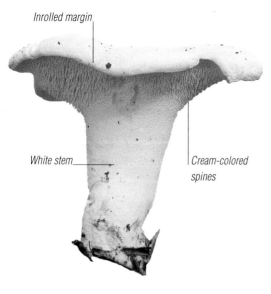

Inrolled margin

White stem

Cream-colored spines

▼ **Lookalikes:**
The Chanterelle *(Cantharellus cibarius)*
(p. 202)
The Sheep Polypore *(Albatrellus ovinus)*

■ How to recognize it

The fleshy **cap** is of medium size and is irregularly lumpy, with a matt surface. The cuticle is dry and smooth and is pale in color, varying from creamy white to yellowish-brown. The thick but fragile margin is very inrolled, becoming lobed and sinuous.

The **spines** on the hymenium are long and fragile, white at first then cream, turning brownish or reddish with age. They form a sort of beard which runs down the stem decurrently.

The whitish **stem** turns reddish in stages and is thick and fleshy, often irregular and excentric. The **flesh** is thick and firm but brittle and is white in color. It has a mild flavor but becomes slightly bitter in older specimens.

■ Where and when to find it

The Hedgehog Mushroom grows in large groups, sometimes in circles, under broad-leaved trees (especially oaks) or conifers. It can be found throughout the world, mainly at low altitudes. Its pale coloring which stands out against damp leaf litter, is instantly noticeable even by someone who is not looking for it.

It is encountered occasionally in summer, but appears mainly in the fall and even in winter, because it is capable of withstanding temperatures in the order of 41°F (– 5°C.)

■ Features and edibility

The very popular Hedgehog Mushroom, when harvested young and in good condition, is a delicious food which is all the more interesting because it often appears very late in the undergrowth, at a time when most species have disappeared. However, the quality is very often a bone of contention. Many people enjoy its firm, brittle, crunchy flesh which has a slightly fruity fragrance. Others find its worth exaggerated and dislike its lack of odor and its slightly bitter and very delicate flavor. In fact, only young examples have a good flavor. The oldest and those which have been subjected to frost have a persistent texture and develop a bitter flavor. They can be eaten but they require prolonged cooking; even then they should first be blanched and the cooking water discarded. The stems of the Hedgehog Mushroom can be sautéed and used in an omelet or to accompany a dish of meat. They also have the advantage of drying well and can be pickled in vinegar to be used as condiments. Hedgehog Mushrooms are sold in wild mushroom markets at quite a reasonable price.

Lookalikes

The Chanterelle (Cantharellus cibarius) *(p. 202) is usually egg yellow in color but occasionally it is paler and may then resemble The Hedgehog Mushroom. However, once the mushroom is turned upside down it is easy to see that it is not a Chanterelle because the latter has gill-like folds, rather than spines.*

The Sheep's Polypore (Albatrellus ovinus) *grows in coniferous woods in the mountains and looks something like the Hedgehog Mushroom. But the presence of spores instead of spines makes it instantly identifiable. This polypore is also good to eat when young, although the flesh later becomes bitter and leathery when the polypore matures.*

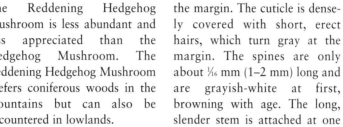

THE REDDENING HEDGEHOG MUSHROOM
Hydnum rufescens

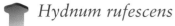

This mushroom is considered a variation on the Hedgehog Mushroom rather than a species in its own right. Although there are intermediate forms which link the two mushrooms, there are certain constant features which make it possible to distinguish between them. A typical specimen is much smaller than The Hedgehog Mushroom. The orange-red cap is irregular and darker and the spines are not decurrent on the stem and turn rusty red with age. The stem is taller and thinner.

The Reddening Hedgehog Mushroom is less abundant and less appreciated than the Hedgehog Mushroom. The Reddening Hedgehog Mushroom prefers coniferous woods in the mountains but can also be encountered in lowlands.
- H: 1½-3¼ in (4-8 cm)
- Ø: 1¼-3¼ in (3-8 cm)
- White spores

THE EAR-PICK FUNGUS
Auriscalpium vulgare

The leathery, kidney-shaped cap is brown, and slightly paler at the margin. The cuticle is densely covered with short, erect hairs, which turn gray at the margin. The spines are only about 1⁄16 mm (1–2 mm) long and are grayish-white at first, browning with age. The long, slender stem is attached at one side of the cap. It is blackish-brown and velvety.

This fungus lives on pine cones which are partially buried in the soil, on moss, or on needle litter. It appears all year round, but is inedible.
- H: 1¼-4 in (3-10 cm)
- Ø: ½-¾ in (1-2 cm)
- White spores

THE SCALY HEDGEHOG MUSHROOM
Sarcodon imbricatum

The grayish-brown cuticle is covered in large scaly platelets of a darker hue, arranged in overlapping circles. The spines are grayish at first, gradually turning brown. The Scaly Hedgehog Mushroom grows in groups in coniferous woods, mainly in the mountains. It is common in some parts of the world but unknown in others. It is not good to eat, even when young.
- H: 2½-5 in (6-13 cm)
- Ø: 4-8 in (10-20 cm)
- Brown spores

THE TOUGH HEDGEHOG FUNGUS
Phellodon tomentosus

The velvety cap is ringed with concentric bands of red and has a white margin. The spines are short, white then gray. The uneven stem is reddish-brown. Individual specimens are often welded together at the cap. The thin, tough flesh is inedible. It appears locally in the fall under conifers, on acid soil.
- H: 1¼-3½ in (3-7 cm)
- Ø: ¾-2 in (2-5 cm)
- White spores

THE BLACK HEDGEHOG FUNGUS
Phellodon niger

The cap is grayish-blue and the spines are whitish-blue. The cap blackens with age and spines turn gray. The blackish-brown stem is covered with a thick velvety down. The tough, black flesh is inedible. This unusual species appears in the fall on calcareous soil in coniferous forests.
- H: 1½-4 in (4-10 cm)
- Ø: 1½-4 in (4-10 cm)
- White spores

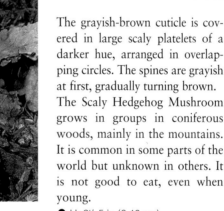

Dryad's Saddle
Polyporus squamosus

English synonym: The Scaly Polypore

Alternative Latin name: *Melanopus squamosus*.

Classification : Cl. Homobasidiomycetes -
O. Polyporales - F. Polyporaceae.

- H: 2-4 in (5-10 cm)
- Ø: 4-16 in (10-40 cm)
- White spores

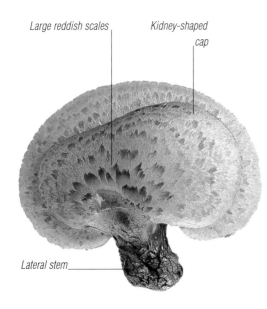

Large reddish scales Kidney-shaped cap

Lateral stem

■ How to recognize it

Dryad's Saddle is a large fungus with a typically scaly cap and a robust, lateral stem.
The **cap** is very thick and fleshy and expanded. It is circular, fan-shaped to kidney-shaped and depressed just above the stem. The large, reddish-brown scales lie flat against the pale, yellowish background.
The short, non-separable **tubes** are very decurrent. The wide, angular, whitish pores yellow with age.
The lateral **stem** is thick and sturdy. It is white at first but turns brown, then black at the base. The white **flesh** is thick and compact; it becomes tougher and more elastic and leathery as the fungus ages. When raw, it has a strong mealy odor.

■ Where and when to find it

Dryad's Saddle colonizes stumps or fallen tree-trunks of deciduous trees, particularly willow and poplar. It forms large, impressive tufts of fungi which are often imbricated. It is fairly common, and fruits from spring through fall.

■ Features and edibility

Dryad's Saddle is edible when very young, but it soon becomes tough and leathery, and is then completely inedible.

Related species

THE VARIABLE POLYPORE
Polyporus varius

Young specimens have a velvety, gray-brown cap with an inrolled margin. The underside is white, then cream, with minute pores. The stem is central and tough, and the flesh is leathery.
- H: 1½-3½ in (4-7 cm)
- Ø: 1½-4 in (4-10 cm)
- White spores

WINTER POLYPORE
Polyporus brumalis

The cap, which is often lobed, is ocher or reddish and smooth. The underside is cream, browning with age. It has a typically blackened stem at the base. It is common on dead or living wood, as well as on stumps of deciduous trees. It is inedible.
- H: 1¼-3½ in (3-7 cm)
- Ø: 2-4½ in (5-12cm)
- White spores

The Umbellate Polypore

Dendropolyporus umbellata

Alternative Latin names: *Polyporus umbellatus, Grifola umbellata.*

Classification : Cl. Homobasidiomycetes - O. Polyporales - F. Polyporaceae.

- Tufts: H: 4-12 in (10-30 cm)
- Ø: 8-16 in (20-40 cm)
- White spores

▮ How to recognize it

The Umbellate Polypore is a very large polypore that grows from a thick stump, dividing into a myriad of umbelliferous caps.

These small **caps** are depressed and umbelliferous in the center and are covered in small scales. They vary from grayish-brown to yellowish-brown in color . The thin, upturned margin is very irregular.

The short, white **tubes** end in small, angular pores and are very decurrent.

The **stem** consists of a thick white stump, which splits into numerous cylindrical branches, and these themselves divide into little twigs each of which ends in a cap.

The thin **flesh** has a soft consistency although it may be slightly fibrous. It is fragile and brittle. The flavor is mild and rather pleasant, and it has a complex, mealy odor.

▮ Where and when to find it

The Umbellate Polypore grows at the base of tree stumps or weakened tree-trunks of broad-leaved trees, mainly oak. Its distribution is irregular, but it is common in its habitat, on calcareous soil, in summer through fall.

▮ Features and edibility

The Umbellate Polypore is very good to eat, provided it is eaten young, because the flesh toughens and the smell becomes unpleasant.

Related species

HEN OF THE WOODS

Grifola frondosa

This polypore has the same habitat. It is good to eat when young, it is more compact-looking and has lateral stems which may be welded together at the base.

- Tufts : Ø: 4-12 in (20-30 cm)
- White spores

GIANT POLYPORE
Meripilus giganteus

This polypore forms large ochraceous brown masses. The pale-colored pores darken when bruised. It fruits in the fall at the base of trunks or on stumps of deciduous trees. It is edible but of no culinary interest.

- Mass: Ø: 12-28 in (30-70 cm)
- White spores

CHICKEN OF THE WOODS
Laetiporus sulphureus

This species, also known as the Sulfur Polypore, has imbricated, superimposed caps with a wavy edge. It is bright orange-yellow. The odor and flavor are spicy. In summer, it parasitizes living trees, especially fruit-trees, or woodland trees such as oak and even conifers, generally high up in the branches.

- Mass : H: 8-16 in (20-40 cm),
- Ø: 8-20 in (20-50 cm)
- White spores

The Birch Polypore
Piptoporus betulinus

English synonym: The Razor Strop Fungus
Classification : Cl. Homobasidiomycetes -
O. Polyporales - F. Polyporaceae.

- H: 1¼-3¼ in (3-8 cm)
- Ø: 4-10 in (10-25 cm)
- White spores

Kidney-shaped

Color of café latte

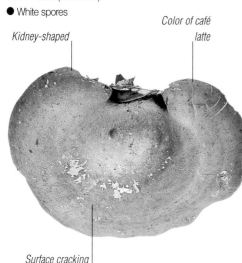

Surface cracking

Raised rim overlapping the tubes

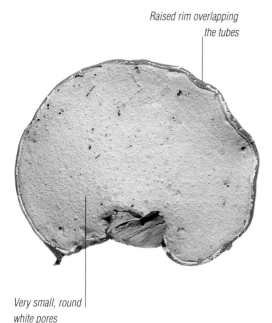

Very small, round white pores

How to recognize it

The **cap** of this average-sized polypore is globose at first, but expands rapidly. It is quite thick and is typically rounded, fan-shaped or kidney-shaped. The grayish-brown cuticle splits easily due to its thinness. The pale margin consists of a thick, whitish rim which partially covers the tubes closest to the edge.

The white **tubes** are quite short and have thick walls. They terminate in very small, round, white pores.

The lateral **stem** is not distinct. It is very short, and sometimes non-existent, in which case the cap is directly attached to the substrate.

The **flesh** is supple and tender at first, and has a pleasant fungal odor and an acidic flavor when raw. However, it soon takes on the consistency of cork.

Where and when to find it

This polypore grows exclusively on birch trees, attacking weakened specimens and causing a destructive white rot. Trees which die from it can be felled merely by pushing them over. It is not unusual to see brackets of the Birch Polypore all growing out of the same side of a tree trunk. It fruits mainly in the fall.

Features and edibility

Despite the pleasant odor and acid flavor, The Birch Polypore is not edible, due to its tough, corky consistency.

It used to be dried and cut into strips for use by barbers as a razor strop, in the days of cut-throat razors, hence its other name. In Switzerland, it has been used for polishing metal watches.

Related species

THE BURNT POLYPORE
Bjerkandera adusta

The velvety, gray-brown, upper surface contrasts with the white margin which eventually turns gray. The underside reveals tiny pores which are white, then graying. It is very common, but not edible and forms tufts of imbricated, superimposed caps on dead tree stumps and living trees, both deciduous and coniferous.

- W: 1½-4 in (4-10 cm)
- Thickness: ⅛-¼ in (0.3-0.5 cm)

The Lacquered Bracket Fungus

Ganoderma lucidum

Classification : Cl. Homobasidiomycetes - O. Ganodermatales - F. Ganodermataceae.

- H: 4-10 in (10-25 cm)
- Ø: 4-12 in (10-30 cm)
- Brown spores

Smooth, shiny, uneven, mahogany-colored surface

Lateral, irregular stem

How to recognize it

The Lacquered Bracket Fungus is completely covered in a shiny, brightly colored coating.

The **cap** when young is simply a pale projection at the top of the small reddish column which constitutes the stem. It then develops into a kidney shape or fan shape. The surface is flattened but uneven and consists of a tough crust which is elastic at first, then coriaceous. It appears to be coated with a smooth, shiny, mahogany-colored, gleaming lacquer. The margin remains pale for a long time, and is whitish to yellowish.

The **tubes** are white at first but they soon turn brown when mature, as do the pores which become gray when bruised.

The lateral, vertical **stem** is uneven and compressed and covered in the same shiny, leathery substance as the cap.

The creamy white **flesh** turns pale brown. It is spongy when young, later becoming corky.

Where and when to find it

The Lacquered Bracket Fungus colonizes the rotting stumps of various broad-leaved trees (mainly oak and chestnut). It causes a white rot of the wood, attacking the colored, tough lignin rather than the soft, white, cottony cellulose. It fruits mainly in summer and fall. Some specimens may survive until winter but generally it does not like cold weather.

Features and edibility

The Lacquered Bracket Fungus is of no culinary interest due to its consistency, but it has other attributes. It does not putrefy and retains its handsome lacquered coat for a long time. It is used to great effect in oriental flower arrangements and miniature gardens. In fact, in the Far East, it is cultivated and considered to be a symbol of happiness and long life.

In China, it is used as a medication for its tranquilizing properties and as an aid to digestion. In traditional medicine, it is said to stimulate the appetite and facilitate sleep. However, it takes a long time to prepare an infusion from The Lacquered Bracket Fungus due to its leathery consistency. It is macerated for a long time then steeped in boiling water to extract the active principles. Much research is being devoted to this fungus, especially in Japan, by pharmaceutical companies and it would appear to be of interest for relieving high blood pressure. It is therefore possible that in future it may well prolong life, substantiating the claims of traditional Chinese medicine. The Lacquered Bracket Fungus is often depicted in Chinese and Japanese art.

Related species

In the British Isles, there is a polypore related to The Lacquered Bracket which has a very large cap and reduced stem. Another fairly common species forms large, sessile brackets on the trunks or stumps of various broad-leaved trees.

THE FLATTENED POLYPORE

Ganoderma lipsiense

The large, uneven, gray-brown cap has a raised, white margin which turns brown like the pores. The fruiting-body can persist for several years.

- L: 4-20 in (10-50 cm)
- H: ¾-31/4 in (2-8 cm)
- Brown spores

The Many-zoned Polypore
Trametes versicolor

Alternative Latin name : *Coriolus versicolor.*

Classification : Cl. Homobasidiomycetes -
O. Polyporales - F. Coriolaceae.

- H: 1½-4 in (4-10 cm)
- Ø: ¹⁄₁₆-¼ in (0,1-0,5 cm)
- Creamy spores

Fan-shaped

Parallel bands of different colors

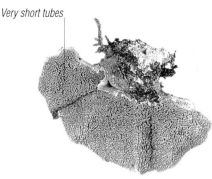

Very short tubes

Often grows in a rosette shape

▌How to recognize it

The attractive coloration of this polypore makes it an interesting addition to a floral arrangement. The colors of these bands varies considerably as does the shape, which may be circular or fan-shaped, with superimposed or imbricated caps, or it may grow in a rosette shape when growing on a flat, horizontal surface such as the top of a cut stump. It is attached to the growing medium by a thin stem. It is very thin for a polypore, and has a wavy, lobed margin.

The velvety **upper surface** is decorated with concentric, alternating bands of matt or shiny colors, ranging from gray, brown, and black, through red, violet, ocher, and sometimes enriched by green from parasitic algae. The margin is white or yellow.

The **underside** is covered in very short, white tubes, ending in pores so minute that they are barely visible to the naked eye. They are white at first, then reddish. The **flesh** is very thin and white, and leathery and is clearly inedible.

▌Where and when to find it

Although this polypore is an annual, it may persist for several years. It is one of commonest fungi, growing on every type of cultivated and wild woodland, and on all types of wood.

Related species

The Trametes have no clear separation between the flesh and the tubes,
the latter appearing to be cut out of the flesh.

THE HAIRY POLYPORE
Trametes hirsuta

As its name indicates, this pale-colored polypore is covered in long, stiff, white hairs on its upper surface. The underside is white, then turning gray and ultimately spotted by the spores. It grows all years in groups of superimposed specimens on any deciduous tree.

- Ø: 2-4½ in (5-12 cm)
- Thickness: ⅛-½ in (0.3-1 cm)
- White spores

THE GIBBOUS POLYPORE
Trametes gibbosa

The name is due to the lumpy excrescences on the surface at the point of attachment. The velvety upper surface is white but is often colored green due to the presence of microscopic algae. It grows all year round, alone, or in groups of superimposed specimens on trunks or stumps of deciduous trees such as beech and hornbeam.

- Ø: 3¼-8 in (8-20 cm)
- Thickness: ¾-2 in (2-5 cm)
- White spores

Hoof Fungus

Fomes fomentarius

English synonym: The Tinder Fungus
Alternative Latin name : *Ungulina fomentaria*.

Classification : Cl. Homobasidiomycetes -
O. Polyporales - F. Fomitopsidaceae.

- H: 4-16 in (10-40 cm)
- Ø: 1¼-8 in (3-20 cm)
- White spores

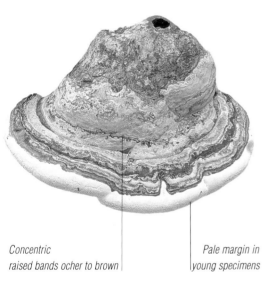

Concentric
raised bands ocher to brown

Pale margin in
young specimens

The brownish-fawn **flesh** is thin in relation to the thickness of the tubes. It is very persistent, lasting for several years at a time, and has a corky consistency.

■ Where and when to find it

The Hoof Fungus is a dangerous enemy of various broad-leaved trees, especially beech, on which it persists for several years.

Although it lives as a saprophyte on dead trunks, it is also capable of parasitizing living trees, causing a virulent white rot.

■ How to recognize it

The sessile **cap** is bracket-shaped or looks like a large wooden clog and may reach a width of 20 in (50 cm) and a thickness of 8 in (20 cm). The ash-gray surface is ringed except at the very top with concentric raised bands which are either concolorous or brownish-fawn. They form a very leathery crust. The margin is pale at first then turns brown with age. When cut in a cross-section, the rusty-brown **tubes** appear to be stratified in very thick layers. They end in very small, pale gray pores, which become stained fawn with age.

■ Features

The Hoof Fungus is inedible but its flesh once had many uses, such as a wick for tinderboxes, hence the older English name. It was also used by barbers as a styptic to staunch bleeding, thanks to its absorbent texture and high tannin content.

Related species

THE HORSESHOE POLYPORE
Fomitopsis pinicola

This polypore is yellow when young, becoming brownish red when older and appearing to be coated with a hard, shiny lacquer. The margin forms a thick orange-yellow raised band. It grows on dead conifers and deciduous trees.
- Ø: 4-16 in (10-40 cm)
- Thickness: 1¼-4 in (3-10 cm)
- White spores

MAZE-GILL
Daedalea quercina

The underside of this polypore appears to be covered in a labyrinth of thick plates which look like forked gills. The top of the cap is ocher or yellowish-gray and flat, while the underside is heavy and swollen. It grows all year round on branches, stumps, and logs of oak. It occasionally fruits on chestnut and horse-chestnut trees.
- Ø: 3¼-8 in (8-25 cm)
- Thickness: 1¼-3¼ in (3-8 cm)
- White spores

The Beefsteak Mushroom

Fistulina hepatica

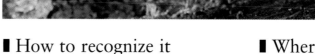

English synonym: The Jelly Tongue

Classification : Cl. Homobasidiomycetes -
O. Polyporales - F. Fistulinaceae.

- L: 4-10 in (10-25 cm)
- Thickness: ¾-2½ in (2-6 cm)
- Pale ocher spores

*Upper surface dark red
in mature specimen*

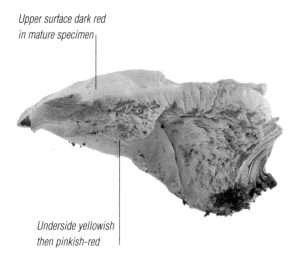

*Underside yellowish
then pinkish-red*

▌ How to recognize it

The **cap** of the Beefsteak Fungus appears at first to be a gelatinous, tuberous mass. It then grows and expands considerably into a bracket or tongue. The size, shape, and consistency are those of an ox tongue. The very slimy cuticle is very easily separable and is covered in little papillae like a tongue, and the color is that of fresh ox liver or calves' liver.

The **tubes** are yellow at first, then stained red. They are attached to each other, but not welded together so they are separable, and they end in small round pores.

The **stem** consists of a rudimentary appendage, or may be completely absent.

The **flesh** is thick and fibrous, especially in the center. It is spongy and is infused with a reddish juice which resembles blood

▌ Where and when to find it

The Beefsteak Fungus pararasitizes the trunks or stumps of oaks and chestnut trees, which it penetrates if the tree is damaged, causing a brown rot. It is common in woodland in low-lying areas, in summer through fall, especially in September.

▌ Features and edibility

When picked young, the Beefsteak Fungus has a delicious salty and slightly tart flavor. It is particularly good when eaten raw in a salad or cooked like liver. It can truly be said to be one of the best edible mushrooms.

Lookalikes

It differs from the polypores because the gills are separable, not welded together. There is no other mushroom or fungus that resembles it in the least.

Dry Rot

Serpula lacrymans

Alternative Latin names: *Gryophana lacrymans, Merulius lacrymans.*

Classification : Cl. Homobasidiomycetes -
O. Corticiales - F. Coniophoraceae.

- Ø: 4-20 in (10-50 cm)
- Olive-yellow spores

▌ How to recognize it

Dry Rot forms sterile bodies which spread over the substrate. These look like persistent, silvery strands and thick, downy, white cushions with the appearance and texture of absorbent cotton.

The **fruiting bodies** develop later on this thick, downy carpet which is formed of mycelial strands. They appear as thick, swollen, shapeless masses which are yellowish-brown in color in contrast to the wavy, whitish-violet margin. The margin remains sterile and retains it original cottony consistency.

The **tubes** and **pores** are brownish-yellow, but paler at the margin. Young specimens appear to "weep" brownish droplets from the surface, hence the Latin epithet.

The whitish, spongy or cottony **flesh** has a strong, characteristic odor which some find agreeable, but which is a sure sign that this terrible pest is present in the house.

▌ Where and when to find it

Dry Rot is the enemy of cut timber in dwellings where there is any sign of dampness and poor ventilation. It mainly attacks the resinous wood of floorboards, baseboards, and roofbeams, to such an extent that the entire fabric of a house may be infested from floor to ceiling, from attic to basement.

Wood-based packaging products, such as cardboard and paper, may also be attacked by this mushroom which lives all year round as soon as conditions are favorable for its growth and propagation. It spreads at an alarming rate.

▌Damage and Treatment

Dry Rot is remarkably well adapted to its favored environment of damp, undisturbed places and it propagates very rapidly.

The long mycelial cords which are called rhizomorphs enter the wood, which they can reach by running through soil and even through walls. They carry water in order to moisten the wood as they encroach on it and invade it. They thus ensure that Dry Rot can propagate and do its damage at a distance from the main mycelial mass. The fungus then seeks some light, and possibly warmth, in order to produce the fruiting body. This is when these shapeless masses emit huge clouds of rust-red spores which stain the floor, walls, and ceilings, to ensure that the species continues to multiply.

The damage done by Dry Rot is incalculable. It produces a deep, insidious rot which may remain invisible for a long time. The wood is reduced to inconsistent, very fragile cubes. The unexpected collapse of floorboards, staircases, and ceilings has often caused serious, sometimes fatal, accidents. Whole libraries

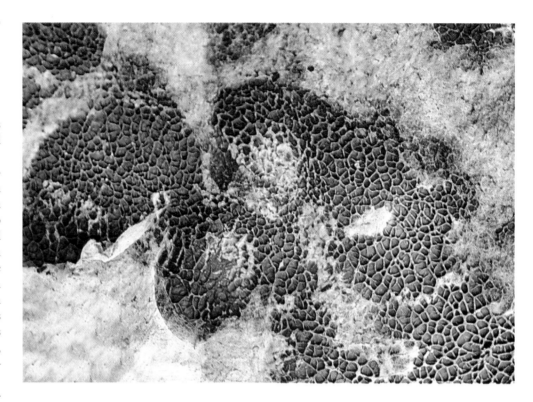

have been devastated, books and furniture alike. Only the most radical treatment can eradicate Dry Rot. The damaged wood must be burned and any which is currently under attack but is not yet destroyed must be treated with powerful fungicides such as chlorophenol and copper sulfate. But wherever possible, any wooden structure, or one containing a lot of wood, must be kept well aired, otherwise this devastating fungus will invade it.

Related species

TREMBLING ROT
Merulius tremellosus

This fungus forms gelatinous crusts or brackets on fallen tree trunks or stumps of deciduous trees and more rarely on conifers. It is thin and trembles at the slightest breeze. The upper surface is sterile and is orange-pink and rather downy, while the underside is fertile and covered in folded and anastomosed pores.

Trembling Rot is quite rare. The appearance is reminiscent of The Tripe Fungus (*Auricularia mesenterica* - page 220), whose hymenium is also folded, though the latter has no pores.

- L: 2-6 in (5-15 cm)
  (confluent fruiting bodies)
- White spores

Jew's Ear
Hirneola auricula-judae

Classification : Cl. Phragmobasidiomycetes -
O. Auriculariales - F. Auriculariaceae.

- Ø: 1½-4 in (4-10 cm)
- White spores

Smooth, folded, brownish-violet interior

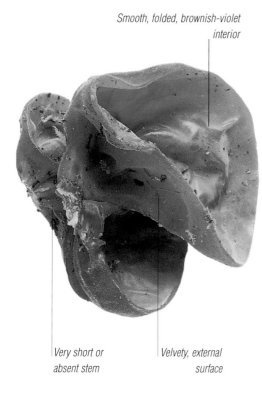

Very short or absent stem

Velvety, external surface

▊ How to recognize it

The general shape is thin, lobed and veined like an ear, this is the reason for the name of this mushroom.

The **receptacle** is of average size and is campanulate then convex, finally spreading into a large cup shape, slightly lobed and compressed. The outer surface (which is generally the upper surface) is quite variable in color, being dark red originally, then tending to reddish-brown or gray-brown, sometimes tinged with green. The typically velvety appearance is accentuated with age, when prominent veins also appear. The margin is regular at first, then thickens and becomes irregular and lobed, blackening with age.

The **hymenium** is on the inner surface and is smooth then wrinkled with anastomosed veins. It is crimson to violet-brown and whitens in places where the spores mature.

The lateral **stem** is rudimentary or absent.

The thin, translucent **flesh** has an elastic, gelatinous consistency.

▊ Where and when to find it

Jew's Ear generally grows on fallen deciduous tree trunks of many species, especially elder. It is common all year round, as soon as the climatic conditions are favorable, but it is most frequent in winter and spring. The full name is an allusion to the fact that after his betrayal of Christlidas hanged himself on an elder tree.

▊ Features and edibility

Jew's Ear must be eaten young, because it can become tough and gristly when older. It can be eaten raw in salads, and can be used like the very closely related species, *Hirneola polytricha*, known in English as Cloud Ear which is used extensively in Chinese, Vietnamese, and Japanese cuisine. It goes very well with rice dishes, flavored with various spices as an accompaniment to meat and fish. The mucilage in the mushroom which makes it viscous when damp delicately thickens sauces and gives them body. Jew's Ear is also suitable for drying and returns to its original shape and texture when merely dipped in warm water. The Cloud Ear can be found dried in oriental grocery stores under the name of Vietnamese name of *nam meo* or the Chinese name of *mu-err*. It is also used in the West in the food industry and in catering, as a soup ingredient, and has been fraudulently substituted for morels in omelets.

▊ Cultivation

The Cloud Ear is intensively cultivated in the Far East especially in China and Taiwan. More than 25,000 tons were produced in 1981, making it the sixth most cultivated mushroom, just behind The Paddy Straw Mushroom (*Volvaria volvacea*) and The Oyster Mushroom (*Pleurotus ostreatus*). In Taiwan, cultivation is facilitated by the warm, humid climate which always favors the growth of mushrooms. The Cloud Ear is grown in rudimentary shelters roofed with rice-straw on various types of organic waste which do not even need composting.

Related species

THE TRIPE FUNGUS
Auricularia mesenterica

This fungus also grows on the dead wood of various conifers. It produces fruiting bodies of average size which are flattened and expanded. The upper surface consists of concentric zones covered in gray fibrils. The grayish-violet hymenium is covered in reticulations. Since it is leathery and hairy, The Tripe Fungus is not edible.

- L: 2-6 in (5-15 cm)
- Thickness: ⅛-½ in (0.3-0.5 cm)
- White spores

Jelly Tongue
Pseudohydnum gelatinosum

Alternative Latin name: *Tremellodon gelatinosum.*

Classification : Cl. Phragmobasidiomycetes - O. Tremellales - F. Tremellaceae.

- H: 1¼-3¼ in (3-6 cm)
- Ø: 1¼-3¼ in (3-8 cm)
- White spores

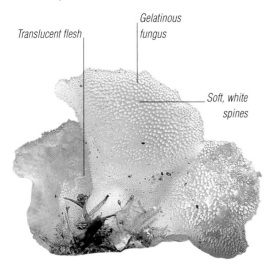

Translucent flesh

Gelatinous fungus

Soft, white spines

How to recognize it

The flattened **cap** may take various shapes. It is gelatinous and shivers when touched. The surface is downy, white at first, then becoming grayish-brown or fawn with age. The margin is quite thick and inrolled, especially at first. Thanks to its shape, consistency, and the papilla-like spines on the hymenium, the cap looks like a tongue.

The **hymenium** is covered in translucent spines which have bluish highlights. Their are soft and elastic.

The lateral **stem** varies considerably in shape and is sometimes non-existent.

The **flesh** is soft and translucent.

Where and when to find it

The Jelly Tongue is a common sight in most coniferous woods. However, it tends to favour colder climates.

It grows on rotting wood, decomposing stumps, and branches buried in pine-needle litter and sometimes appears to be growing in the soil. It is found in summer, though mostly in the fall, and even in winter, as it is protected from the winter weather by its abundant content of mucilage.

Features and edibility

Despite its unusual appearance and unappetizing consistency, The Jelly Tongue is perfectly edible. Although the flavor is always slightly resinous, perhaps as a result of its habitat, it has the advantage of being edible when raw, and can be eaten in a salad.

Related species

The Tremellaceae consists of species which generally grow on wood and whose consistency is gelatinous.
The word Tremella comes from the Latin *tremulus,* meaning "trembling" like the Aspen (*Populus tremula*), a tree whose leaves shake at the slightest breath of air. The Jelly Tongue is the only member of the species to have spines on its hymenium.

YELLOW BRAIN FUNGUS
Tremella mesenterica

The brightly colored, golden-yellow folded and lobed mass of the Yellow Brain Fungus appears on the branches or trunks of dead deciduous trees in the fall. It becomes tough and leathery, which prevents it from drying out. As soon as there is rain, thanks to its mucilage content, it easily rehydrates and the original shape is restored. It is very attractive, but is of no culinary interest.

- L: 1¼-3¼ in (3-8 cm)
- Thickness: ½-1½ in (1-4 cm)
- White spores

JELLY LEAF
Tremella foliacea

This reddish-brown fungus with flattened, undulating lobes appears from spring through fall on branches and trunks of broad-leaved trees.

- L: 1½-4 in (4-10 cm)
- Thickness : ¾-1½ in (2-4 cm)
- White spores

WITCHES BUTTER
Exidia glandulosa

This quaintly named but unprepossessing fungus appears on the dead branches of numerous broad-leaved trees, especially oak. Its black masses are very irregularly lobed or folded. It is inedible.

- Mass may grow to 6 in (15 cm)
- Thickness: ½-1¼ in (1-3 cm)
- White spores

1 - Morel - Gyromitra - Verpa

- Cap pitted with crevices, like a sponge.
- Grows only in spring.

Cap pitted with crevices like a sponge

Stem attached to base of cap

MORCHELLA **Page 224**

- Date-brown or reddish brown, globular cap covered in folds like a brain.
- Grows only in spring.

Date-brown or reddish-brown, globular cap covered in folds like a brain

Stem attached to base of cap

GYROMITRA **Page 230**

- Brown pitted or folded cap, stem long and cylindrical, hollow and white.
- Grows only in spring.

Stem attached to top of cap

Stem attached to center-top of cap

PTYCHOVERPA - VERPA **Page 227**　　MITROPHORA **Page 226**

2 - Helvella

- Very irregular cap, saddle-shaped or chalice-shaped, or shaped like a bishop's miter.
- Smooth or deeply-furrowed stem.

Very irregular cap

Saddle-shaped cap en

Smooth or deeply-furrowed stem

Chalice-shaped fungus

HELVELLA **Page 228**

3 - Elf Cups and Ear-Jack Fungus

- Thin fungus, looking like a piece of discarded orange peel.
- Grows only in spring.

Thin fungus, looking like a piece of discarded orange peel.

DISCIOTIS **Page 226**

- Cup-shaped fungi, without a stem.

Cup shape

No stem

PEZIZA **Page 231**

- Fungi shaped like a hare's ear.

Shaped like a hare's ear

OTIDEA **Page 233**

FEATURES OF THE ASCOMYCETES

- The main feature of this group can only be seen under a microscope. They may take very diverse forms like the Gasteromycetes, but never go through a spherical phase when immature (except for truffles). They may resemble a cup, a sponge, a hare's ear, a stag's antlers, etc.

Looking like tubercules in the soil

Button-shaped fungus on dead branches

Sponge-like

Cup-shaped

Like a stag's horns

4 - Spathularia

- Little yellow fungus shaped like a spatula.

SPATHULARIA **Page 234**

6 - Bulgaria and related species

- Cup-shaped or looking like pustules, growing in colonies on branches.

BULGARIA, BISPORELLA, CHLOROCIBORIA **Page 235**

8 - Xylaria

- Club-shaped or staghorn shaped fungus, black or white, growing on or at the base of tree trunks.

XYLARIA **Page 237**

5 - Leotia

- Little, nail-shaped fungus with a rubbery texture, yellow ocher or brownish-yellow in color.

LEOTIA **Page 234**

7 - Truffles

- More or less spherical fungi, growing underground.

TUBER **Page 236**

9 - Cordyceps

- Filament-like or club-shaped fungus, parasitizing various insects and subterranean fungi.

CORDYCEPS **Page 237**

The Morel

Morchella esculenta

English synonym: The Common Morel

Alternative Latin name : *Morchella vulgaris.*

Classification : Cl. Ascomycetes - O. Pezizales - F. Morchellaceae.

- H: 2-6 in (5-15 cm)
- Ø: 1¼-2¾ in (3-7 cm)
- Ocher-cream spores

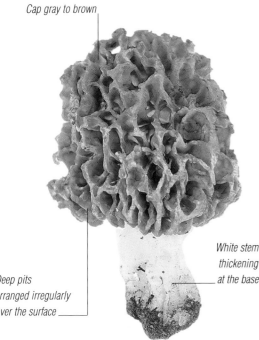

Cap gray to brown

White stem thickening at the base

Deep pits arranged irregularly over the surface

▼ Lookalikes:
The Cauliflower Fungus *(Sparassis crispa)* (p. 208)
The False Morel *(Gyromitra esculenta)* (p. 230)

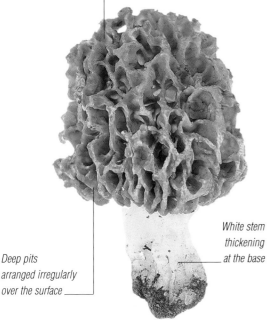

■ How to recognize it

The Morel is easily identified by its deeply pitted cap which looks like a honeycomb or a gray-brown sponge.

The **cap** is of average size and is spherical to ovoid. It is honeycombed with deep pits, which are generally vertical and the edges are usually sinuous. The color is often gray but may vary from ocher to bister or blackish; the edges of the pits are often paler and may be tinged with red. The Morel with its spongy head is often a very attractive mushroom.

The **hymenium** of the Morel is inside the pits. The hollow **stem** is attached at the base of the cap and is linked to it through the cavity. It is white and generally small, thickening noticeably at the base. The lower part is very wrinkled and furrowed and it is deeply embedded in the soil.

The **flesh** is white but then turns yellow and when fresh it has a complex odor which is both fungal and fruity, fine and penetrating but very pleasant.

■ Where and when to find it

The Morel appears in damp woods, at the edges or in unexpected places such as gardens, avenues, terraces, and garbage heaps.

It is common and may even grow abundantly in good years; it can be found throughout the temperate zone and as far south as Southern California. It is a spring-fruiting species which should be looked for from March through May. Hunting for Morels which are exclusively spring mushrooms requires patience and experience. Their favorite spots, and even the days on which they appear, need to be known. The Morel is a capricious mushroom which may suddenly appear in a sunny spot, a clearing, or on burnt ground, and never reappear in subsequent years. The date of harvesting is linked to weather conditions, especially temperature and humidity. The soil must be well drained, but one needs to wait several days after heavy rain

	The Common Morel *Morchella esculenta*	The False Morel *Gyromitra esculenta*	The Bohemian Verpa *Ptychoverpa bohemica*	The Miniature Morel *Mitrophora semilibera*
Cap	honeycombed, ocher to bister	ribbed reddish-brown	ribbed, yellow to brown	honeycombed, brown
Point of insertion of stem on the cap	at the base	at the base	at the top	in the center
Vertical Cross-section				
Stem	swollen	irregular	tall and slender	tall and slender
Features	excellent	deadly	very good to eat	good to eat

in order to ensure that there is a good crop. Furthermore, Morels are very good at blending into the background. Novice hunters will have a great deal of difficulty in locating them and can easily becomes discouraged.

■ Features and edibility

The poets of Ancient Rome immortalized the Morel under the name of *spongia*. The Common Morel is one of the most delicious edible mushrooms, especially if it grows in the mountains. It has a strong flavor and the consistency is just firm and elastic enough for it to be excellent in dishes containing cream, which it will flavor with its subtle fragrance. Anyone lucky enough to pick it in large quantities would do well to serve stuffed Morels, or cook it as a side-dish to accompany roast meats or poultry.

Morels can be bought fresh in the spring from wild mushroom markets, but it is preserved and can be purchased all year round from gourmet stores. Dried Morels are exported from central Europe and even India. There is only one slight problem which might worry the eager consumer of Morels—they contain hemolysins, substances which destroy the red blood corpuscles. They have this in common with many edible mushrooms in the order of Ascomycetes, including the Helvellas. However, they contain less hemolysin than the Helvellas and when they are thoroughly cooked the hemolysin is destroyed, so they are not dangerous.

Lookalikes

The name Morel has been applied to a dozen or so species of Ascomycete which grow in the spring and which look something like The Morel. There are Verpas, for instance, in which the stem is attached just under the top of the cap, are nothing like as taste as the Morels, but are often sold at the same price. Species of the genus Mitrophora, sometimes known as miniature Morels, in which the stem is inserted midway up the cap, are of slightly better eating quality than the Verpas but are still greatly inferior to the Morels.

*A mushroom known in France as **The Autumn Morel** or **The Pine Morel** is none other than the **Cauliflower Fungus** (Sparassis crispa) (p. 208). It is tasty but not nearly as good as a true Morel.*

*As for **The False Morel** (Gyromitra esculenta) (p. 230), it is too often mistaken for a Morel and eaten as such, though it can be dangerous and even deadly if consumed raw.*

Species of Gyromitra (False Morels) have a reddish-brown, folded and convoluted cap which is not pitted as in the Morels.

Related species

The classification of the Morchella species is very complex. However, true Morels, which can be distinguished by the fact that the stem is attached at the base of the cap, can be divided into two groups, that containing The Common Morel, which includes mushrooms with rounded heads, and a randomly honeycombed cap and that containing The Tall Morel, which contains Morels with pointed caps, rows of honeycombed pits, and more marked vertical ridges.

THE ROUND MOREL

Morchella rotunda

This mushroom differs from the Common Morel in that its cap is blonde and round, and it is slightly larger. It appears in more open spaces, often under apple trees. It fruits later in the year, in May through June, and in the mountains it may be found in July. There are several varieties of the species, all with a thick stem.
- H: 2-6 in (5-15 cm)
- Ø: 2-4½ in (5-12 cm)
  - Ocher-cream spores

THE CONICAL MOREL

Morchella conica

The Conical Morel fruits in May, especially in the mountains. The cap is smaller but much more pointed and it has a thicker, more deeply furrowed stem, which soon turns yellow or brown. There are numerous subspecies, most with thicker flesh.
- H: 2¾-5 in (7-13 cm)
- Ø: 1¼-2 in (3-5cm)
- Ocher-cream spores

THE TALL MOREL
Morchella elata

This may be the most capricious of the Morels, appearing in vast numbers in one year and inexplicably disappearing completely the next.

The flesh is very thin, but this Morel variety is very tall, and may grow to 12 in (30 cm) in height. The pointed cap is very long and intricately fashioned like a carving or a church spire. The honeycomb appears to be arranged regularly in stories, which has given it the alternative name of The Skyscraper Morel.

- H: 2½-6 in (6-15 cm)
- Ø: 1¼-2 in (3-5 cm)
- Ocher-cream spores

The Veined Elf Cup

Disciotis venosa

Classification : Cl. Ascomycetes -
O. Pezizales - F. Morchellaceae.

● Ø: 1½-4 in (4-10 cm)
● Cream spores

Cup-shaped receptacle

Whitish underside

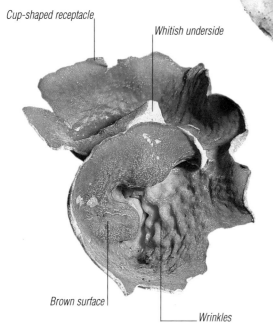

Brown surface

Wrinkles

The thick, wrinkled **stem** is whitish and appears at first sight to be absent because it is buried in the soil. It anchors the Elf Cup firmly in its place. The **flesh** is whitish like the stem. It is brittle and when fresh it smells strongly of bleach.

∎ Where and when to find it

The Veined Elf Cup is a spring species, carpeting the undergrowth of deciduous woods with its reddish cups, often growing beside water. It appears at the same time and in similar habits to The Common Morel.

∎ How to recognize it

The **receptacle** of the largest of the Elf Cups is hemispherical when young, spreading quite quickly into a brownish-form cup. The yellowish-white exterior is completely and finely granulose and wrinkled. The lobed, undulating margin is very fragile and may tear quite badly in older specimens.

The **hymenium** is inside the cup and is characterized by the presence of thick wrinkles like varicose veins, sometimes covering the cup in a dense network.

∎ Features and edibility

The unappetizing odor of The Veined Elf Cup disappears during cooking and this fungus can then produce dishes which are very acceptable both in quality and quantity. Some people claim it to be as delicious as a Morel, to which it is closely related. Harvesting The Veined Elf Cup is not particularly easy, because the flesh is very fragile and the stem embeds the fungus firmly in the soil.

The Miniature Morel

Mitrophora semilibera

Alternative Latin name : *Mitrophora hybrida*.

Classification : Cl. Ascomycetes - O. Pezizales - F. Morchellaceae.

● H: 3¼-8 in (8-20 cm) ● Ø: ⅝-1½ in (1.5-4 cm)
● Cream spores

Cap is partially detached from the stem

Vertical ridges

Long, white, wrinkled and granulose stem

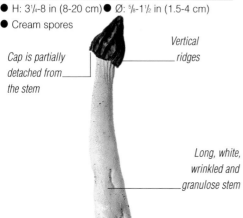

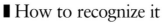

∎ How to recognize it

The **cap** is partially detached (*semilibera*) from the stem and is conical in shape. It has strong vertical ridges divided by little transverse folds forming deep and fairly regular rows of pits. The coloring is generally brown, varying frequently from bister to ocher, through olive.

The **stem** is hollow and is attached midway up the cap. It is smooth at first and whitish with a granulose surface; it extends as it ages, and turns yellow, eventually becoming lumpy and vertically ridged.

The thin **flesh** is quite tenacious. It is white, yellowing and becoming brittle with age. It has no odor at first, but older specimens have a smell described as resembling human sperm.

∎ Where and when to find it

The Miniature Morel grows in damp, grassy clearings, such as pathways, grass verges, and beside water. It is quite common in spring from April through May.

∎ Features and edibility

Although The Miniature Morel is not as prized as its larger relative, it is often eaten in mistake for a Morel. It deserves to be tasted.

The Bohemian Verpa
Ptychoverpa bohemica

Latin name : *Verpa bohemica.*

Classification : Cl. Ascomycetes - O. Pezizales - F. Morchellaceae.

- H: 3¼-8 in (8-20 cm)
- Ø: 1¼-2 in (3-5 cm)
- Yellow spores

Stem penetrating deep into the cavity of the cap attached at the top

Ridged, yellow-brown cap

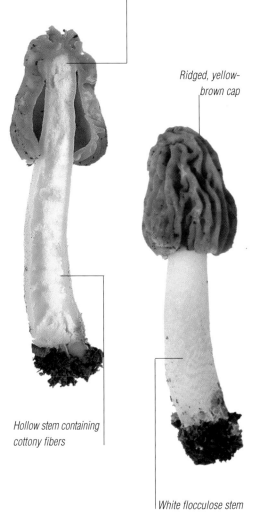

Hollow stem containing cottony fibers

White flocculose stem

▼ **Lookalike:**
The False Morel (*Gyromitra esculenta*)
(p. 230)

▍ How to recognize it

The Bohemian Verpa is of average height and sometimes taller. The campanulate **cap** to which the stem is attached only at the top of the underside, is whitish yellow inside, where it is sterile. The external **hymenium** is deeply wrinkled with thick, sinuous ridges or ribs which are generally vertical and sometimes branched. The yellow-brown to fawn ribs form the edges to furrows and shallow pits unlike the deep honeycomb pits of the Morels. The margin is free and sinuous and edged with a thin white strip.

The cylindrical **stem** is stuffed with cottony fibers at first but soon becomes hollow. It is short and thick then extends considerably, giving the mushroom a characteristically elongated appearance. The whitish-yellow surface, is covered in whitish, downy stripes.

The **flesh** is white and rather thin, fragile, and brittle. It has a fungal smell which is pleasant in young specimens; it smells of human sperm when old.

▍ Where and when to find it

The Bohemian Verpa grows mostly in the mountains, but otherwise has similar habitats to the Morels. It is a gregarious species, growing in abundance in rainy years, in clearings and under ash and elm, hazelnut trees, and in mixed woods. It should always be hunted for in the dampest places, in moss or leaf-litter, from which it only emerges when mature. In temperate zones, it fruits from March through May.

▍ Features and edibility

Once cooked, The Bohemian Verpa is very good. Even if it does not have the same quality as the Morels, it can be used in the same way, in a cream sauce for instance.

Lookalike

It is not surprising that The Bohemian Verpa is often confused with the Morels, since they have the same habitat, grow in the same season, and bear some resemblance. It is often found in wild mushroom markets under the name of Morel which it does not deserve. Remember that the main differences in spring mushrooms which are mistaken for Morels are: the point at which the stem is attached to the cap and the hymenium, which is honeycombed in the Morels, is ribbed in the Verpas and Gyromitras.

Related species

THE GLOVE-FINGER MOREL
Verpa conica

This mushroom looks very similar to the Bohemian Verpa, but differs in its smaller size, and an almost smooth cap. The cap may be lobed or slightly wrinkled but does not have vertical ridges. It grows in the same season and in the same locations. It is edible when cooked but not good, as the flesh is too thin.

- H: 2-5 in (5-13 cm)
- Ø: ⅝-1¼ in (1.5-3 cm)
- Cream or pale ocher spores

The Common Brain Fungus
Helvella crispa

Classification : Cl. Ascomycetes - O. Pezizales - F. Helvellaceae.

- H: 1½-4½ in (4-12 cm)
- White spores

Lobed, cream-colored cap

Long, white, sturdy stem

Deep furrows

▌ How to recognize it

The **cap** of The Common Brain Fungus is curved and curled with brain-like convolutions. The very irregular margin is sinuous and incurved and exposes the wrinkled, yellow ocher inner surface.

The **hymenium** is on the outer surface and is typically cream-colored. It is distorted, lumpy, and downy and has the typical look of thin ,folded calf skin.

The strong, sturdy **stem** is variable in shape, and may be thick and short or elongated and swollen at the base. The surface is covered with long, deep furrows, alternating with projecting ribs. It is white at first, but darkens to yellow at a later stage.

The **flesh** is thin in the cap and pitted in the stem. It is elastic and even slightly leathery. It has little odor and a fruity flavor.

▌ Where and when to find it

The Common Brain Fungus prefers well-lit woods, though it may escape from them to grow at their edges, on grass verges, or in near-by pastures. It is common, and sometimes appears in large colonies in the grass and in leaf-litter. It often fruits in late fall.

▌ Features and edibility

The Common Brain Fungus is edible after cooking but is far from universally acclaimed. Some find the flavor pleasant and similar to that of Morels, others consider it to be inedible due to the slightly leathery consistency. Many caseevents, it is wise to eat only young specimens whose flesh is still tender. Cooking should always be prolonged and it is advisable to blanch the mushroom first, discarding the cooking water. Like all the Helvellas, this species contains hemolysins, and must never be eaten raw or it is likely to cause serious anemia. The hemolysins are completely destroyed by the heat produced during cooking.

ELFIN SADDLE OR BLACK HELVELLA
Helvella lacunosa

This Helvellas has a darker cap which ranges from gray to black, and it is smaller in size. The stem is brighter in color and is also deeply furrowed.

Elfin Saddle or the Black Helvella is quite a common mushroom, growing under all types of tree in fall and sometimes even in winter. It is edible if thoroughly cooked.

- H: 2-4 in (5-10 cm)
- Ø: ¾-2 in (2-5 cm)
- White spores

Grayish-black cap shaped like a saddle

THE ELASTIC BRAIN FUNGUS
Helvella elastica

This fungus grows in the fall. It is inedible and is smaller than the previous species. It has a twin-lobed cap the same color as that of The Common Brain Fungus but not curled and it is often saddle-shaped. The stem is smooth.

- H: 2-4½ in (5-12 cm)
- Ø: ¾-1½ in (2-4 cm)
- White spores

THE CUP-SHAPED BRAIN FUNGUS
⚠ *Helvella acetabulum*

The Cup-shaped Brain Fungus is very different from the other Helvellas and has a short, white, wrinkled stem and a cup-shaped brownish-fawn cap. This spring Helvella is very rich in hemolysins, so it should not be eaten.

- H: 1¼-2¾ in (3-7 cm)
- Ø: 1¼-2½ in (3-6 cm)
- White spores

THE TWO-TONE BRAIN FUNGUS
⚠ *Helvella leucomelaena*

It looks like the Cup-shaped Brain Fungus but only the gray-brown upper surface grows above ground. When removed from the soil, the underside can be seen to be white at the base. It may be slightly veined and the furrows remain confined to the very short stem, not running up into the cup as they do in the Cup-shaped Brain Fungus. The gray-brown interior is smooth in young specimens and the edge of the cup is wavy. This Helvella grows in spring in tight clusters. It favors bare ground. If eaten raw it is poisonous.

- H: 1¼-2 in (3-5 cm)
- Ø: ¾-2¾ in (2-7 cm)
- White spores

The False Morel

Gyromitra esculenta

English synonym: The Turban Fungus
Classification : Cl. Ascomycetes - O. Pezizales - F. Helvellaceae.

- H: 2-4½ in (5-12 cm)
- Ø: 2-4 in (5-10 cm)
- White spores

Reddish-brown cerebriform cap

White irregular stem

▮ How to recognize it

This medium-sized mushroom has a typically convoluted cap like a brain or turban.

The **cap** is generally globular and often irregular and shapeless, with marked lobes and convolutions. The presence of swollen, twisting veins gives it the look of a human brain. The color varies from chestnut brown to mahogany and the interior is hollow.

The white **stem** which is also hollow is joined to the cavity of the cap.

The white, relatively thin **flesh** has a pleasant fruity odor when fresh. The fragrance is not always noticeable, however.

▮ Where and when to find it

The False Morel grows under pines and broad-leaved trees, especially horse-chestnut trees, and sometimes in copses and on heaths. Like the Morels, the False Morel seeks out damp places and it is often found beside running water. It is quite rare in lowlands but is common in the mountainous areas of the temperate zone of the northern hemisphere. It is particularly common in central Europe, less so in eastern Europe and the United States. It fruits from the end of winter and continues to do so through May.

▮ Toxicity

Despite the Latin epithet *esculenta*, meaning "edible" and the fact that the False Morel was long considered to be on a par with The Morels, it must be considered as poisonous, and even potentially fatal, especially when raw. However, the toxicity of The False Morel varies considerably. Some people have always eaten it, sometimes regularly and in large quantities, without the slightest ill effects. On the other hand, children appear to be particularly suscep-

tible and have died after eating it for the first time. Other fatal cases have occurred apparently at random, even when The False Morel had been eaten previously, and for many years, without a problem. The principle which is responsible is called gyromitrin and affects the liver. Furthermore, each time The False Morel is eaten it may increase the chances of poisoning. Since gyromitrin is a volatile substance, a dried specimen is much less poisonous, though never totally innocuous. The principle is also soluble in water, so that blanching the mushroom will greatly reduce the toxicity, which may still remain nevertheless. Despite numerous warnings issued by mycologists and repeated in all the recent literature about fungi, The False Morel continues to be eaten, and even sold, sometimes as a Morel.

The poison is deadly and the symptoms are just as unpleasant as those caused by The Death Cap. Twelve hours after ingestion, the symptoms of a stomach upset occur, followed by a lull. Then there are nervous disorders and the patient falls into a coma, has liver failure and severe anemia caused by destruction of the hemoglobin, all of which can end in death.

Lookalikes

Due to its toxicity, which is inconsistent but sometimes fatal, The False Morel should never be confused with other spring mushrooms which are perfectly edible once they have been cooked.

True Morels such as **The Common Morel** *(Morchella esculenta) (p. 224) look very different to the Gyromitra species (False Morels) thanks to their honeycombed caps.*

*The Bohemian Verpa *(Ptychoverpa bohemica)* (p. 227) has a ribbed cap which covers the stem like a thimble on a finger, and which is never reddish-brown in color.*

The Black Elf Cup

Peziza badia

Classification : Cl. Ascomycetes - O. Pezizales - F. Pezizaceae.

- H: ½-1¼ in (1-3 cm)
- Ø: ¾-3¼ in (2-8 cm)
- White spores

▌ How to recognize it

The **receptacle** of this mushroom is cup-shaped and it expands with age. The edge is wavy. The outer surface is very finely granulose and browning, turning reddish-brown in dry weather.

The **hymenium** inside the cup is reddish-brown, later changing to olive color.

The **stem** is absent, the cup rests on the earth. The thin, reddish-brown **flesh** contains a watery liquid.

▌ Where and when to find it

The Black Elf Cup appears in late summer and fall on bare, clay soil, or on sandy, acid soil. It tends to fruit at the roadside, in ditches and other very damp places, under birches or conifers, or even on marshy ground. It is frequent but not easy to distinguish from the many other species of Elf Cup (Peziza).

▌ Toxicity and Edibility

The Black Elf Cup is poisonous when raw. When cooked, it deserves to be eaten because it has quite a pleasant flavor.

Related species

BLADDER ELF CUP

Peziza vesiculosa

The Bladder Elf Cup is ochraceous yellow inside and out. It may contain tiny egg-like vesicles inside the cup. It is found from spring through fall, on well-manured soil, and often grows in groups. It is quite common, poisonous when raw, but edible if well cooked.

- H: ½-1½ in (1-4 cm)
- Ø: 1½-4½ in (4-12 cm)
- White spores

THE JUICY ELF CUP

Peziza succosa

It looks like the Bladder Elf Cup but the flesh is yellowish as is the milky liquid it exudes a few minutes after it is cut. It is not edible.

- H: ½-1¼ in (1-3 cm)
- Ø: ½-2 in (1-5 cm)
- White spores

The Orange Peel Fungus
Aleuria aurantia

Alternative Latin name : *Peziza aurantia.*

Classification : Cl. Ascomycetes - O. Pezizales - F. Humariaceae.

- H: ½-2 in (1-5 cm)
- Ø: ¾-4 in (2-10 cm)
- White spores

Bright orange interior

Cup shape

Outer surface paler and downy

Absence of stem

▌ How to recognize it

The Orange Peel Fungus has a cup-shaped **apothecium** which is brilliant orange in color. It is regularly concave at first, spreading and distorting into an irregular shape as it grows. The outer surface is rather pale, orange, yellow, or whitish, and downy at first, but smooth as the fungus matures.

The **hymenium** covers the whole of the inside of the cup and is bright orange, hence the name. As in all the young Elf Cups, the spores propagate in a cloud which can sometimes be seen if the fungus is merely touched.

The **stem** is almost absent, so that the cup rests directly on the soil.

The thin, fragile **flesh** is whitish to orange, and brittle. It is almost flavorless.

▌ Where and when to find it

The Orange Peel Fungus grows in glens and forest clearings or beside damp forest paths. It can fruit in large colonies consisting of small, tightly-packed clusters. It is quite common throughout the temperate zone of the northern hemisphere and fruits in the fall, sometimes quite late in the year.

▌ Features and edibility

The Orange Peel Fungus is edible even when raw, unlike the rest of its close relatives. Some other species of Elf Cup (Peziza), such as The Scarlet Elf Cup, contain hemolysins which can destroy the red blood cells. These substances are destroyed by heat during cooking.

The Orange Peel Fungus can be eaten raw in a salad or as a snack with a liqueur glass of kirsch. Even if the flavor of this fungus is not exactly ambrosial, it permits the mushroom gourmet to add a little variation to the diet.

Related species

There are numerous brightly-colored species of Peziza.

SHIELD-SHAPED ELF CUP
Scutellinia scutellata

This minute scarlet Elf Cup, edged with black hairs, is common on bare soil or rotten wood.

- Ø: ¹⁄₁₆-½ in (0.2-1 cm)
- White spores

SCARLET ELF CUP
Sarcoscypha coccinea

These little cups are lined on the inside, with a bright red, shiny hymenium that looks as if it had been painted on. The outer surface is much paler, being reddish at first then soon paling to pink or even off-white. The thin, tenacious stem is quite short and often invisible. The flesh is thin and rather leathery and it is relatively insipid.

The Scarlet Elf Cup is not worth eating but its vivid coloring brightens the hedgerows, copses and damp undergrowth. It develops on dead branches buried under moss or in humus. It is quite common, appearing mainly in winter and persisting through spring.
- H: ½-1¼ in (1-3 cm)
- Ø: ½-2 in (1-5 cm)
- White spores

THE VIOLET ELF CUP
 ### *Sarcosphaera coronaria*

This is quite a large Elf Cup and has a receptacle that is globose at first, soon opening into a star shape as the margin splits into pointed lobes. The whitish to brownish outer surface contrasts with the violet inner surface. This handsome Elf Cup grows in pine woods on calcareous soil. It is only edible if cooked. Eaten raw, it could prove fatal.
- H: 1½-4 in (4-10 cm)
- Ø: 3¼-6 in (8-15 cm)
- White spores

Ear-jack Fungus
Otidea onotica

English synonym: Hare's Ear Fungus
Classification : Cl. Ascomycetes - O. Pezizales - F. Otideaceae.

- H: ⅛-4 in (3-10 cm) ● Ø: ¾-2 in (2-5 cm)
- White spores

▌ How to recognize it

This unusually shaped fungus looks like a curved cone split at one side or the ear of an animal such as a hare, a jack-rabbit, or a mule. The tall **receptacle** is of average size and is brightly colored yellow-orange to ocher on the outside. It is very downy at first, becoming smooth when mature.

The internal **hymenium** is pinkish or orange.

The **stem** is very small and often buried, and is not apparent. However, it is recognizable by its color because it is covered in a thick white down. Tiny rootlet-like appendages branch out from the base.

The thin, beige **flesh** is fragile and brittle, despite its slightly elastic consistency.

▌ Where and when to find it

The Ear-jack Fungus fruits in the undergrowth of broad-leaved trees, especially oaks, on the ground or on moss. It is found more rarely under conifers. It often grows in clusters and is quite common from July through fall.

▌ Features and edibility

The Ear-jack Fungus has no particular odor or flavor, and its rather elastic consistency is not always appreciated. On the other hand, it makes an attractive decoration on a dish and will surprise diners due to its curious appearance.

The Spatulate Fungus
Spathularia flavida

Classification : Cl. Ascomycetes - O. Leotiales - F. Geoglossaceae.

- H: 2-3¼ in (5-8 cm)
- Ø: ½-1¼ in (1-3 cm)
- White spores

Bright yellow, fan-shaped cap

Spatulate

▮ How to recognize it

This spatulate fungus has a more or less rounded, flattened head, which is slightly lobed, wavy and swollen. It is bright yellow in color. The head covers the upper part of the stem. The stem is white or pale yellow, thick, or more or less irregular. The elastic, yellowish flesh, has no particular odor or flavor.

The species is very small, and the flesh is very thin and stringy, so it is not edible.

▮ Where and when to find it

The Spatulate Fungus is not very common. It forms circles or clusters in late summer through fall on moss or damp needles in forests of pine or spruce, especially in mountainous regions.

Related species

THE YELLOW NAIL FUNGUS
Leotia lubrica

Although most members of this family are disk- or cup-shaped, and grow on wood, The Yellow Nail Fungus looks more like a Helvella. It fruits on moss and leaf-litter in damp woods. The cap is yellow-brown, ocher, or yellowish-green, and gelatinous and flattened or depressed at the top. The stem is golden yellow. The rubbery flesh is not edible, as in the case of most members of this species.

- H: 1¼-2½ in (3-6 cm)
- Ø: ½-¾ in (1-2 cm)
- White spores

Bachelor's Button

Bulgaria inquinans

Classification : Cl. Ascomycetes - O. Leotiales - F. Leotiaceae.

- H: ½-¾ in (1-2 cm)
- Ø: ½-1½ in (1-4 cm)
- Black spores

Shiny black interior

Brown, granulose exterior

The **upper surface** is smooth, black, and shiny. When brushed with the finger, it emits a cloud of black spores so dense that covers the area around the fungus with a sooty deposit.

The **outer surface** is brown and granulose.

The firm, brown, leathery **flesh** has a rubbery consistency.

The Bachelor's Button is not edible.

■ Where and when to find it

Bachelor's Buttons are very common in fall through winter. They grow in clusters, on the recently-fallen trunks or branches of oak, beech, or horse-chestnut trees, insinuating their mycelium into cracks in the bark.

■ How to recognize it

The Bachelor's Button is **globular** when young, but it then expands into the shape of a cone or shallow bowl.

Related species

PALE BACHELOR BUTTONS
Neobulgaria pura

These Bachelor Buttons have the same habitat as the black ones, although they seem to prefer beech on which they form dense, compact clusters. The hymenium inside the cup is whitish or pale pink, the exterior is beige-pink or slightly reddish. The translucent, gelatinous flesh is inedible.

- H: ½ in (1 cm)
- Ø: ½-1¼ in (1-3 cm)
- White spores

THE YELLOW BISPORELLA
Bisporella citrina

Although this mushroom is so tiny, it is very easy to see due to the colonies which flourish on the branches of various broad-leaved trees. When seen from close up, it forms a flattened cup.

- H: ¹/₁₆-⅛ in (0.2-0.4 cm)
- Ø: ¹/₁₆-⅛ in (0.1-0.3 cm)
- White spores

THE BLUE-GREEN WOOD CUP
Chlorociboria aeruginascens

This mushroom rarely produces its fruiting bodies which are shaped like flattened cups and are blue-green. They grow on rotten oak or hazelnut branches stripped of the bark. On the other hand, the blue-green mycelium is often seen on dead wood.

- H: ¹/₁₆-⅛ in (0,2-0,4 cm)
- Ø: ¹/₁₆-⅛ in (0,1-0,3 cm)
- White spores

Black Truffle

Tuber melanosporum

English name: Perigord Truffle

Classification : Cl. Ascomycetes - O. Tuberales - F. Eutuberaceae.

- Ø: 1¼-3¼ in (3-8 cm) (sometimes more)
- Dark brown spores

Blackish-violet flesh and white veins

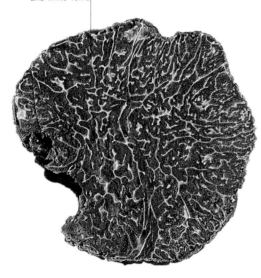

▮ How to recognize it

The Black or Perigord Truffle is instantly recognizably by its strong and incomparable fragrance and its black flesh.

The **receptacle** is a small to medium-sized black whose surface is completely covered in black warts. The size of these warts increases with the number of stones in the soil.

The interior flesh, called the **gleba** is gray at first, then reddish, but turns very black when the spores mature. It is typically marbled with thin silvery veins.

The **flesh** has the characteristic, aromatic, very pronounced flavor which makes this the most highly prized of all the edible fungi.

▮ Where and when to find it

Although The Black Truffle is famous throughout the world, its area of distribution is limited to the warmer regions of southwest Europe, especially Spain, Italy, and particularly southern France. It develops entirely underground, where it grows in relation to the roots of evergreen oaks, and more rarely with other broadleaved trees. It prefers slightly calcareous soil, which is fairly dry and well-drained.

Despite the name Perigord Truffle, The Black Truffle grows throughout southern France, in the Midi and Provence on warm, calcareous hillsides. It fruits in winter, from November through March, and the best specimens are likely to be found around Christmastime. However, unless the circumstances are exceptional, truffle-hunting is entirely a professional occupation and the amateur will never get the chance to do so. Truffle-growers guard their truffle-grounds jealously, due to the enormous sums for which these precious fungi are sold.

▮ Features and edibility

The Black Truffle is incomparable, unequalled, and unique. It has a very strong, fragrance and a flavor which many people claim is like a combination of roast meat, an omelet, and the finest delicatessen. The "black diamond of cuisine" which one rarely has the chance to find for oneself, is sold in gourmet stores for a price which it may well be worth but which is way beyond the pockets of most people.

Fraud and counterfeiting

Many tricks and frauds are perpetrated using the Black Truffle as bait. For instance, truffles are often macerated or cooked with eggs to which they impart their fragrance and flavor. The so-called truffle omelets are then sold at a price which bears no relation to their real quality. Similarly, certain dishes are sold at the delicatessen counter as being "truffled" when in fact they contain any black mushroom that comes to hand, often The Horn of Plenty, but even the (poisonous) Earthball. It also pays to read the labels. If a Perigord Truffle is supposed to be included in the ingredients, it must be listed as *Tuber melanosporum* and not some other, inferior species.

▮ Cultivation

Although the French production of The Black Truffle amounted to 1,000 to 2,000 tons a year about a century ago, it was little more than fifty tons only twenty years ago. Since then, various agricultural institutions, such as the Institut National de la Recherche Agronomique, have tried to cultivate this valuable mushroom.

It has been found that The Black Truffle can be cultivated in the right climate by transplanting young oak or hazelnut saplings whose roots have been inoculated with truffle mycelium. It takes five to ten years of patient maintenance, sometimes including irrigation, before the first truffles can be harvested.

A well-maintained truffle-ground can thus produce some 50 kg per hectare (about 45 lb per acre) annually. Harvesting is manual labor, but in order to find a fruiting body, there is often a need to resort to pigs or, more frequently, specially trained dogs who can smell the truffle growing underground, thanks to their well-developed olfactory powers.

The Candle-Snuff Fungus
Xylaria hypoxylon

Classification: Cl. Ascomycetes - O. Xylariales - F. Sphaeriaceae.

- H: 1¼-3¼ in (3-8 cm)
- Ø: ⅟₁₆-¼ in (0.2-0.5 cm)
- Black spores

Shaped like reindeer or moose horns

White tip

Black base

▮ How to recognize it

This peculiar-looking fungus looks something like a Coral Fungus or even a lichen. It is colored like the wick of an extinguished candle. It consists of small, erect **branches**, which are almost cylindrical at first and are black with a white tip. The fungus then begins to branch at the tip, so that the extremities look like the antlers of a deer, and at the same time they flatten and become covered with a white mass of spores where the branching occurs.

The **base** remains black and downy. Once the fungus is fully grown, it turns completely black and threadlike with a swollen upper part, like a match that has been extinguished. The white, leathery **flesh** is inedible.

▮ Where and When to Find It

The Candle Snuff Fungus grows all year round It is commonly found growing in colonies on the cut side of the logs of deciduous trees, especially beech wood.

Related species

DEAD MAN'S FINGERS
Xylaria polymorpha

This fungus has an irregular, cylindrical, swollen shape, very much as its sinister English name describes. It is matt black and granulose but the corky flesh is white. It is common and inedible, growing in twos and threes at the base of beech stumps or those of other broad-leaved trees.
- H: 1¼-4 in (3-10 cm)
- Ø: ½-1¼ in (1-3 cm)
- Black spores

THE CLUB-SHAPED CORDYCEPS
Cordyceps ophioglossoïdes

This fungus parasitizes other fungi which grow underground. It consists of a tall, smooth, yellow stem which terminates in a club-shaped excrescence, covered when mature with the white, powdery spores. Although it not rare, it often passes unnoticed. It grows in fall in deciduous or coniferous woods.
- H: 1½-3¼ in (4-8 cm)
- Ø: ½-1¼ in (1-3 cm)
- White spores

Index

PHOTO CREDITS

The photographs on pages 6-17, 38-39, 58-61, 112-113, 122-125, 152-153, 188-189, 198-199, 222-223 are taken from photographs which are to be found elsewhere in the book..

Anagnostidis/Nature : 187 ur, 233 ul - **Aucante/Nature** : 29 br - **A. Bidaud** : 57 hd, 120 br, 133 ul, 207 br - **R.-J. Bouteville** : 21 ur, 42 ur, 47 ur, 50 ur, 51 br, 52 ur, 71 br, 77 bl, 94 b, 97 br, 115 br, 115 bl, 133 br, 133 bl, 135 ur, 142 ur, 147 ur, 148 br, 155 bl, 161 bl, 162 ur, 180 bl, 187 ul, 197 bm, 211 bl, 213 ul, 219 u, 226 br - **Chanu/Nature** : 26 b, 43 ul, 70 b, 84 ur, 104 b, 106 br, 139 br, 144 r, 149 br, 159 ur, 196 bl, 221 ur - **Chaumeton/Nature** : 16-17, 18 br, 19 b, 21 br, 21 bl, 25 br, 25 ur, 26 ur, 32 b, 33 ur, 34 br, 34 ur, 35 b, 39 br, 39 mm, 41 bl, 41 ur, 43 ur, 45 br, 45 md, 46 br, 48 ul, 48 ur, 49 br, 50 um, 51 mg, 53 br, 53 u, 58-59, 60-61, 62 b, 65 ur, 67 bl, 69 br, 70 ur, 70 ul, 71 ur, 73 br, 74 b, 75 r, 75 l, 79 b, 79 u, 80 u, 81 b, 81 u, 81 m, 84 br, 84 l, 85 ur, 87 br, 87 bl, 88 b, 88 ur, 89 u, 91 br, 92 ur, 96 br, 96 u, 100 br, 101 bl, 102 br, 102 bm, 105 ur, 106 ur, 107 ur, 108 bl, 108 ul, 109 ur, 110 br, 111 bm, 112-113, 114 ur, 117 b, 119 ul, 126 u, 129 bl, 132 br, 136 br, 136 ur, 138 br, 139 bl, 144 l, 146 ur, 154 ur, 160 ur, 163 l, 166 l, 166 ur, 170 ur, 173 ur, 175 ur, 176 ur, 182 ur, 183 l, 188-189, 192 l, 194 br, 194 bm, 194 b, 195 bl, 197 ur, 201 u, 202 r, 205 br, 206 br, 206 ur, 206 md, 207 ur, 207 ul, 209 bl, 209 ur, 214 br, 214 ur, 215 b, 217 bl, 225 bl, 227 ur, 230 br, 234 ur, 235 ul, 236 ur - **Desvilles/Nature** : 196 ur - **M. Dupic** : 142 b, 157 br - **Grospas/Nature** : 20 br, 22 ur, 23 ur, 24 ur, 25 ul, 28 ur, 32 ur, 35 ur, 36 ur, 48 bl, 49 ur, 52 br, 56 ur, 56 ul, 63 l, 64 bl, 64 ul, 66 ur, 67 ul, 67 mg, 69 md, 71 ul, 74 ur, 77 br, 87 mg, 91 ul, 98 br, 101 bm, 101 ul, 105 b, 108 ur, 109 bl, 111 ur, 116 ur, 119 br, 120 um, 127 ur, 129 br, 136 bl, 141 ur, 143 ur, 146 br, 151 ur, 154 b, 169 br, 169 ul, 173 br, 186 ur, 192 ur, 193 br, 193 ur, 195 ul, 196 br, 197 br, 197 bl, 200 ur, 201 br, 209 ur, 210 ur, 211 br, 211 ul, 212 br, 212 ur, 213 bm, 215 ur, 217 ur, 218 u, 219 b, 220 br, 220 ur, 221 bl, 231 bl, 232 br, 234 b, 235 br, 235 ur, 237 ur - **J. Guimberteau** : 31 bl, 69 ul, 168 u - **Lamaison/Nature** : 62 ur, 62 ul, 63 r, 94 u, 98 ur, 119 ur, 121 ur, 149 bl, 150 b, 213 br, 226 ur, 233 ur - **Lamothe/Nature** : 195 br - **Y. Lanceau** : 4, 5, 18 bl, 18 ul, 19 ur, 19 ul, 19 mg, 20 bl, 20 ur, 20 ul, 21 ul, 22 br, 22 bl, 22 ul, 23 br, 23 bl, 23 ul, 24 bl, 24 ul, 25 bl, 25 m, 26 ul, 27 ur, 27 ul, 28 bl, 28 ul, 29 bl, 29 ur, 30 bl, 30 ur, 30 ul, 31 br, 31 ul, 32 ur, 33 bl, 33 ul, 34 bl, 34 ul, 35 ul, 35 mg, 36 br, 36 bl, 36 ul, 37 br, 37 bl, 37 ul, 38-39, 40 br, 40 ur, 40 ul, 40 mg, 41 ul, 42 br, 42 l, 43 bl, 44 l, 44 ur, 45 bl, 45 ur, 45 ul, 46 l, 46 ur, 47 br, 47 l, 48 br, 49 l, 50 b, 50 md, 51 ul, 52 bl, 53 bl, 54 l, 55 r, 55 ul, 57 l, 64 br, 64 ur, 64 md, 65 l, 66 b, 66 l, 67 br, 67 ur, 67 md, 68 l, 68 ur, 69 ur, 71 bl, 72 ur, 73 bl, 73 ur, 73 ul, 77 u, 78 br, 78 ul, 80 l, 82 b, 83 br, 83 bl, 85 l, 86 b, 86 l, 87 ur, 88 l, 89 b, 91 bl, 91 ul, 91 um, 92 l, 93 br, 93 ur, 93 ul, 93 mbg, 93 mhd, 93 mhg, 95 ur, 95 ul, 97 bl, 97 um, 98 br, 99 l, 100 bl, 100 ur, 100 l, 101 ur, 102 bl, 103 b, 103 ur, 104 l, 105 l, 106 bl, 106 bm, 107 br, 108 br, 108 ul, 108 m, 110 bl, 110 bm, 111 br, 111 bl, 114 l, 115 ul, 116 l, 117 ul, 119 bl, 120 bl, 120 ul, 121 bl, 126 bl, 126 ul, 127 br, 127 bl, 127 ul, 128 bl, 128 bm, 128 ur, 128 ul, 129 ur, 130 br, 130 bl, 130 ur, 130 ul, 131 bl, 132 l, 133 ur, 134 ur, 135 ul, 136 bm, 136 ul, 137 br, 137 l, 137 ur, 138 ul, 139 ur, 140 l, 141 ur, 141 bl, 141 bm, 142 l, 143 bl, 145 ur, 145 ul, 146 bl, 147 br, 147 mg, 148 bl, 150 ur, 150 ul, 152-153, 154 l, 155 br, 155 ur, 155 ul, 156 r, 157 l, 159 l, 160 l, 161 br, 161 ur, 161 ul, 161 mg, 162 l, 163 r, 164 l, 164 ur, 165 bl, 165 ur, 165 ul, 166 r, 167 r, 168 b, 169 bl, 169 ur, 169 md, 170 ul, 171 ur, 171 ul, 171 md, 172 bl, 173 bl, 173 ul, 175 l, 176 bl, 176 ul, 177 b, 177 u, 178 bl, 178 ur, 178 ul, 179 l, 180 br, 180 ur, 180 ul, 181 l, 181 ur, 182 l, 183 r, 184 l, 185 l, 185 ur, 186 l, 187 bl, 187 md, 190 br, 190 bl, 191 br, 192 br, 193 l, 196 ul, 197 ul, 200 l, 201 bl, 202 l, 203 r, 203 l, 204 l, 205 ul, 206 bl, 206 bm, 208 br, 208 ur, 208 ul, 209 ul, 210 bl, 210 ul, 211 ur, 211 md, 212 ul, 213 bl, 216 br, 216 ul, 216 mg, 217 br, 217 ul, 218 bl, 221 ul, 224 ul, 224 ul, 225 br, 225 bm, 228 l, 229 bl, 229 ur, 229 ul, 230 l, 232 l, 234 ul, 235 bl, 236 l, 237 br, 237 bl, 237 ul - **Lanceau/Nature** : 31 ul, 40 bl, 41 br, 43 br, 50 ul, 52 ul, 54 ur, 55 b, 78 bl, 78 ur, 83 ur, 86 ur, 90 b, 90 u, 93 bl, 93 mbd, 95 b, 96 l, 99 ur, 101 br, 102 ur, 104 ur, 110 ur, 111 ul, 117 ur, 118 ur, 121 br, 121 ul, 122-123, 124-125, 128 ur, 131 br, 132 ur, 134 b, 134 bl, 134 ul, 135 b, 138 ur, 141 ul, 147 ul, 157 ul, 165 br, 171 b, 172 ur, 174, 175 br, 175 bm, 179 r, 182 br, 184 br, 184 ur, 187 br, 190 ur, 191 l, 191 ur, 198-199, 204 ur, 207 bl, 213 ur, 216 ur, 221 br, 221 bm, 222-223, 226 ul, 228 ur, 231 u, 232 ur, 233 b - **Mayet/Nature** : 24 br, 82 u - **J. Montégut** : 115 ul, 118 l, 120 ur, 148 ur, 148 ul, 205 ur - **Nature** : 18 ur, 149 ur, 149 ul - **Pertin/Nature** : 6-7 - **Polese/Nature** : 76 ul, 98 ul, 129 ul, 138 bl, 139 ul, 143 ul, 190 ul, 190 um, 194 bl, 194 ul, 195 u, 195 um, 205 bl, 235 md, 6 br(3e), 39 u, 39 md, 69 bl, 72 bl, 72 ul, 74 ul, 87 ul, 103 ul, 106 ul, 107 bl, 107 ul, 110 ul, 113 ur, 113 mh, 123 unl, 131 ul, 146 ul, 146 um, 151 bl, 151 bm, 156 l, 158 bl, 158 ul, 204 br, 212 bl, 214 bl, 214 ul, 215 ul, 216 bl, 216 bm, 220 ul, 226 bl, 227 br, 227 ul, 227 um, 229 br - **J. Riousset** : 167 l - **Sauer/Nature** : 76 ul, 158 ul, 206 ul.